VISUAL PROCEEDINGS

THE ART AND INTERDISCIPLINARY PROGRAMS OF SIGGRAPH 97

COMPUTER GRAPHICS ANNUAL CONFERENCE SERIES • 1997

A PUBLICATION OF ACM SIGGRAPH

EDITED BY

Lynn Pocock Ongoings: The Fine Arts Gallery Chair

Rick Hopkins Electric Garden Chair

David Ebert Sketches Chair

Judith Crow Computer Animation Festival Chair

SIGGRAPH LOS ANGELES

VISUAL PROCEEDINGS
The Art and Interdisciplinary Programs of SIGGRAPH 97

COMPUTER GRAPHICS
Annual Conference Series, 1997

The Association for Computing Machinery, Inc.
1515 Broadway
New York, New York 10036 USA

ISBN 0-89791-921-1
ISSN 1069-5419
ACM Order No. 428971

Additional copies may be ordered pre-paid from:
ACM Order Department
P.O. Box 12114
Church Street Station
New York, New York 10257 USA

Or, for information on accepted European currencies and exchange rates, contact:
ACM European Service Center
108 Cowley Road
Oxford OX4 1JF
United Kingdom
+44.1.865.382338
+44.1.865.381338 fax
acm_europe@acm.org

Credit card orders from the U.S. and Canada:
800.342.6626

Credit card orders from the New York metropolitan area and outside the U.S.:
+1.212.626.0500

Single copy orders placed by fax:
+1.212.944.1318

Credit card orders may also be placed by mail.

Electronic mail inquiries may be directed to:
orders@acm.org

Please include your ACM member number and the ACM order number with your order.

CONTENTS

CONTENTS

Over the years, artists have pushed the boundaries of computer art. In their ongoing explorations, they have invented their own creative processes, and they have achieved unique visual languages.

Ongoings: the Fine Arts Gallery presents an in-depth look at computer-based artists and their work. The exhibition breaks from SIGGRAPH traditions by presenting a body of work for each of a few artists, as opposed to exhibiting a survey of recent works by many artists. Thus, the Ongoings Gallery showcases artists' ongoing creative visions. In conjunction with Ongoings, Sketches features an Artist Presentation Session, where the artists can discuss their processes and content.

Artworks for Ongoings were selected in a competitive, open-submission process. Artists were welcome to submit either a long-term progression of work, including current work, or they could submit their current body of work. We particularly encouraged submission of works that use the computer in a creative way. As it turned out, the majority of the submissions were print works.

The Curatorial Advisory Committee spent three long days reviewing the work and composed a list of finalists; their recommendations were presented to Geno Rodreguiz, a curator at The Alternative Museum, for final decisions. Once the list of artists was finalized, the exhibition evolved as individual works for each artist were selected. In the end, six artists were selected to exhibit a large number of works, and seven artists were selected to exhibit two or three works. Some of the artists are new to the SIGGRAPH audience, while others are long-time favorites.

In producing an exhibition of this sort, my goal was to create a place for the world to see the ongoing creative vision of artists who are dedicated to the use of technology in their art. My hope is that the audience will come away with an understanding of the passion of these artists.

Ongoings: the Fine Arts Gallery would not have been possible without the effort and support of many wonderful people to whom I give my sincere and grateful thanks. While it is not possible to individually thank everyone, I would like to express a special thanks to the following: the SIGGRAPH 97 Conference Committee, the Ongoings: the Fine Arts Gallery Committee, the Curatorial Advisory Committee, and all of the SIGGRAPH 97 Ongoings artists. Without them, this exhibition could not have been possible.

I would also like to thank recent Art Show Chairs, Jean Ippolito, Deanna Morse, and Ken O'Connell, for their advice and support. Thank you to my Pratt Institute Chair, Rick Barry, and his former assistant, Dena Slothower, for providing me with the time and assistance needed to produce this exhibition. Thank you to Lina Yamaguchi and all of the Pratt Student Volunteers for their hard work. Thank you to George Schuessler for his support when I needed it most. For all her invaluable advice and support over the years, I would like to thank Copper Giloth. On behalf of all SIGGRAPH artists and those who appreciate their work, I would like to thank Patric Prince for her ongoing dedication to the SIGGRAPH artist community. Finally, thank you to my family and friends for their unconditional love and support.

LYNN POCOCK

CHAIR, Ongoings: the Fine Arts Gallery

Curatorial Advisory Committee

Jeremy Gardiner is an artist whose paintings and multimedia projects have been shown in the US and abroad at many venues, including the Tibor de Nagy Gallery in New York, Friends of Photography in San Francisco, The Museum of Modern Art in Paris, The Institute of Contemporary Art in London and Museu de Arte Moderna de São Paolo. Gardiner is a graduate of the Royal College of Art in London and a former Harkness Fellow at the Media Lab at MIT. He has received awards from The New York Foundation for the Arts and Prix Ars Electronica. He spent seven years helping to develop the graduate computer graphics program at Pratt Institute and taught at the School of Visual Arts in New York. His book Digital Photo Illustration was published by Van Nostrand Reinhold in 1994. His most recent project is a QTVR CD-ROM for Ricco Maresca Gallery in New York.

Andrew Glassner is a Writer-Director at The Microsoft Network, where he creates new interactive entertainments. He has worked on computer graphics research since 1978, at the NYIT Computer Graphics Lab, Case Western Reserve University, the IBM TJ Watson Research Lab, the Delft University of Technology, Bell Communications Research, Xerox PARC, and Microsoft Research. He is a popular writer and speaker. His book 3D Computer Graphics: A Handbook for Artists and Designers has taught a generation of artists. Glassner created and edited the "Graphics Gems" series and the book An Introduction to Ray Tracing. His most recent text is Principles of Digital Image Synthesis, a two-volume treatise on rendering theory and practice published by Morgan-Kaufmann. He has served as Chair of the SIGGRAPH 94 Papers Committee, Founding Editor of the Journal of Graphics Tools, and Editor-in-Chief of ACM Transactions on Graphics. He directed the short film "Chicken Crossing," which premiered at the SIGGRAPH 96 Electronic Theater. Away from work, Glassner paints, plays jazz piano, writes fiction, and hikes.

Lynn Pocock is an artist and Associate Professor of Computer Graphics and Interactive Media at Pratt Institute. Her artwork has often taken the form of experimental computer animation; her recent work takes the form of digital monotypes. Pocock's art and research have been published in scholarly journals such as Leonardo and the Art Journal, and her art work has been exhibited internationally, including in the New York Film and Video Expo, the London International Film Festival, and SIGGRAPH's Electronic Theater. Her professional activities have included directing an interactive educational project for the IBM Latin American Headquarters, co-producing the SIGGRAPH 93 Small Animation Theaters and serving on the Board of Directors of NYC SIGGRAPH. She holds a Bachelor of Arts degree in Mathematics and Art from Rutgers University, a Master of Science degree in Computer Science from the University of Maryland, and a Master of Fine Arts degree in Computer Art from the University of Massachusetts. Currently, Pocock is co-authoring a book on computer animation.

Ongoings: The Fine Arts Gallery Committee

CHAIR
Lynn Pocock Pratt Institute

CURATORIAL ADVISORY COMMITTEE
Jeremy Gardiner
Andrew Glassner The Microsoft Network
Lynn Pocock Pratt Institute

PRINT COORDINATOR
Jon Cone Cone Editions Press

PUBLIC RELATIONS CO-COORDINATOR
Dena Elisabeth Eber University of Georgia

PRODUCTION ASSISTANT
Cynthia Kuebel C K Studio

PUBLIC RELATIONS CO-COORDINATOR
Karla Loring

ARTIST PRESENTATION SESSION COORDINATOR
Jacquelyn Martino Philips Research, USA

ARTIST PORTFOLIO COORDINATOR
Andrea Meyer emDASH

ADMINISTRATIVE ASSISTANT
Mary Phillipuk Pratt Institute

PUBLICITY COORDINATOR
Karen Sullivan

ARTIST PRESENTATION SESSION MODERATORS
Jeremy Gardiner
Roger Malina Executive Editor of Leonardo Journal
Director of the NASA EUVE Observatory

JOHN S. BANKS

The work is a theory of the world (not to imply a complete one).
Its purpose is to rejoice in a sense of wonder and mystery.
to see beyond the seen into the suspected,
to hint at the mystery felt during the journey.
Some experiences want altars, others visions, yet others remembrances.
These are representative of stages of a story comprised of episodic events, peak moments, and places of discovery.

John S. Banks has been working with digital images for 16 years and with photographs for 25 years. He is currently living in Chicago, where he is on an indefinite leave of absence from his own business, Rising Star Ltd., in order to concentrate on image-making. For the previous 12 years, Banks was President or Vice President of Rising Star Ltd., a computer graphics reseller in Illinois.

Utah Portal, Iris print, 20" X 15", 1994

These images are my attempt at visualizing and clarifying a sense of discovery. By discovery, I mean finding something beyond what was known or expected. I feel this discovery at places that seem to suggest a story – a story I don't really know. In these images, I am not trying to express an actual story but rather to visualize some of the various states that may be experienced on a "journey." Doorways, paths, altars, and windows are the central elements within the context of a "site," which is the spark.

The work is derived from a photograph of a site. I try to create a visually compelling environment where there are multiple places to go. I try to clarify what the image may suggest by amplifying or reducing values and textures. Then I work outward from the focal point, and either collage in associated pieces of drawings or photographs, or add compositional motion with blur and distortion filters. Finally, lighting or tonal effects are added to the entire piece to further delineate the forms or to homogenize disparate elements. The sources are all my own photographs or drawings.

John S. Banks
Rising Star Ltd.
445 East Illinois 345
Chicago, Illinois 60611 USA
jb@r-star.com

Untitled 10, Iris print, 20" X 24", 1995

SHERIANN KI-SUN BURNHAM

Originally I produced mixed media paintings and wall constructions, combining traditional media with computer images. Most recently, my works have been paintings solely created on the computer. These works are a continuing exploration in the formal aspects of abstracted space and form. My paintings invite the viewer to explore this visual space, finding their own interpretation.

Since an early age, I have been interested in the layering of pattern, texture, and form. This fascination has guided me through experiments with watercolor, pen and ink, stone lithography, and ultimately the computer.

Whether representational or abstract, I delight in the interplay between negative and positive spaces and the juxtaposition of geometric and biomorphic form. With the computer, I can also enhance the visual complexity within these spaces. The computer's immense texture- and pattern-generating capabilities enable me to create images that cannot be created easily in other media. I believe the computer as an artist's tool expands the imagination and extends the possibilities of what can be achieved in artistic expression. I hope the works represent a step in the development of computer art that utilizes the computer's strengths, without losing the human touch.

Sheriann Ki-Sun Burnham was born in Seoul, Korea in 1959. She holds a BA in Art from California State University, Long Beach. She has been a professional graphic designer/illustrator since 1980 and has been involved in computer graphics since 1981. Currently, she owns a freelance art and design business. Her fine art has been presented in many exhibitions and publications in the US and abroad, including the SIGGRAPH 88 and SIGGRAPH 89 Art Shows, the 1989/90 ACM SIGGRAPH Traveling Art Show, 1990 Artware – Art and Electronics in Germany, 1995 and 1996 Fractal Design Art Expos, and 1989 and 1997 Connecticut College Biennial Symposiums for Arts and Technology.

Nomad, Iris print, 22.25" X 22.25", 1996

Using scanned images of anything from rice paper to previously photographed computer textures, I create custom textures to paint with in Fractal Design Painter. The images in Ongoings are representative of a series begun in late 1994. I build images by mirroring and altering areas as I go along. These images are then used alone or as grounds for additional painting.

Sheriann Ki-Sun Burnham
227 Ancona Drive
Long Beach, California 90803 USA
kisun@earthlink.net

Cape Flora, Iris print, 28" X 28", 1996

ANNA M. CHUPA

The historical sources for my use of compressed space, intricate surface, horror vacui, and valenced imagery are medieval manuscripts and reliquaries, Kongo minkisi, and Fon bocio. As different as they may be in form and media, the Celtic carpet pages and minkisi/bocio share a common aesthetic impetus of revelation and concealment, sensuous surface and mystical presence.

Fon (Republic of Benin) and Kongo (Zaire) artist-priests create bocio and minkisi respectively as objects of personal empowerment. These power objects are assembled with a variety of layered objects, each alluding to medicine, healing, patron spirits, and the dead. Empowered with the forces of the spirits and the dead, the bocio/minkisi counter danger and hostility, promoting well-being in times of stress, (Blier,1995:73-74) and healing psychologically induced illnesses. "Peacock" contains imagery designed for the protection of my children, while "Aengus" is more immediately self-referential.

In "Aengus," the border functions as a binding device that evolved as a personal journey to find containment and integration to counter memories of dissolution. The title alludes to W.B. Yeats "Song of the Wandering Aengus," where the apple blossoms and the quest for the glimmering girl are a quest for reclamation of a sense of self and lost faith.

Peacock, Iris print on Translite lightbox, 17" X 17", 1995

Aengus, Iris Print on Translite lightbox, 19 1/2" X 13 7/8", 1996

The remaining boxes combine personal narrative with imagery inspired by African Vodun, popularly known as Voodoo. American Voodoo evolved as a transformation of a number of African religious influences, Catholicism, and Spiritualism. Out of this, an aesthetic of spiritual objects and personal altars evolved.

The hand-held altar is a gris-gris, created to be carried as a personal protection. My altar installations extend the reliquary metaphor to create a place for a communicative exchange between the spiritual world and the world of everyday life.

Assumption, Iris Print on Translite lightbox, 18 3/4" X 15 1/2", 1996

Brain Cell, Iris Print on Translite lightbox, 20" X 13 1/2", 1996

"Brain Cell," "At the Gates 2," "Descanso," and "Assumption" are images dedicated to Esu and Gede. Esu is the guardian of the gates. As such, he plays an important role in all significant moments in life when an individual or community is at a crossroads, and important decisions need to be made or actions taken. Esu is also the Loa (spirit) of communication between human and divine forces. Finally, Esu is a trickster and a patron saint of rebel heroes who disrupt the status quo in order to bring about a greater and fuller social harmony. He is often represented as a mischievous child who likes things he can't have (cigars, cigarettes, rum, matches) as well as toys and candy. Keys for Esu refer to his association with St. Peter. Conical figures with a cowrie shell face are found in altars from Benin to Brazil, Trinidad, and the United States. Esu's association with systems and networks is iterated in RJ45 connectors and similar items left on contemporary altars.

SPONSORS
Cone Editions Press
Priestess Miriam Chamani
Mississippi State University

Anna Chupa received her Master of Fine Arts degree at the University of Delaware and a Master of Arts in Liberal Studies at Dartmouth College. Her primary artistic disciplines prior to working in digital media were painting, textiles, printmaking, and performance art. She has published a book and several essays on Jungian archetypes in African-American fiction. Her digital photography and mixed media installations have been exhibited at SIGGRAPH, the Digital Salon, and the Silicon Gallery in Philadelphia.

At the Gates 2, Iris print on Translite lightbox, 18" X 21", 1996

Gede is closely related to Esu and is also associated with the crossroads, but more so with the junction between life and death. Gede imagery almost always includes cemetery crosses and skulls. His ability to see into two worlds positions him as the master of all healers. Gede is also the protector of infants and children. Together, these images are about defining moments and crossroads. They address issues of healing, empowerment, change. They are invocations, reflections.

Anna M. Chupa
Mississippi State University
Box 5182, Department of Art
Mississippi State University
Mississippi State, Mississippi 39762 USA
amc11@ra.msstate.edu

Descanso, Iris print on Translite lightbox, 19 1/2" X 22", 1996

DIANE FENSTER

The Hide and Seek Series: An Archaeological Excavation of Memory

This autobiographical body of work addresses issues of self, gender, and intimacy using the concept of an archaeological excavation of memory as a metaphorical structure.

My involvement with digital imaging began 12 years ago. I soon discovered that computer technology provided me with the opportunity to manipulate, edit, and expand the photomontage format that I felt most suited my personal artistic expression. My work reflects my interest in both the Dada and Surrealist art movements, primarily in the use of the juxtaposition of seemingly unrelated visual elements. This methodology enables me to present an almost "cinematic" storyline based on the relationship of each of the vignettes within a particular piece. The computer has now offered me an even wider range of possibilities within the photomontage format. The technology has actually freed my range of expression and allowed an even more personal shaping of the symbolic elements I use in my work.

Canto Five/Union of Opposites, Iris print, 34" X 47", 1995

In my earlier work, I utilized "found" vintage or family photographs as a starting point for the final photomontage. In my more recent works, I experiment with different types of image processes using my own photography as a means to further strengthen the "finding of my own voice" through the presentation of "landscapes" that are charged with symbolism and emotion.

Canto Six/In the Shadow of the Cathedral, Iris print, 47" X 34", 1995

My art is a combination of myth, spirit, science, and technology. I see myself as a modern alchemist, using silicon chips as a tool to transform electrical patterns into art. My attempt to portray an element of mystery is the guiding factor in these works. The juxtaposition of the image elements hopefully serves as a catalyst for the viewer's recognition of her/his own inner processes. The computer does not destroy your soul, as I once thought, but rather has liberated a creative aspect of the self that might have otherwise remained undiscovered.

Canto Seven/The Path of Lightning as it Descends from the Sky, Iris print, 47" X 34", 1995

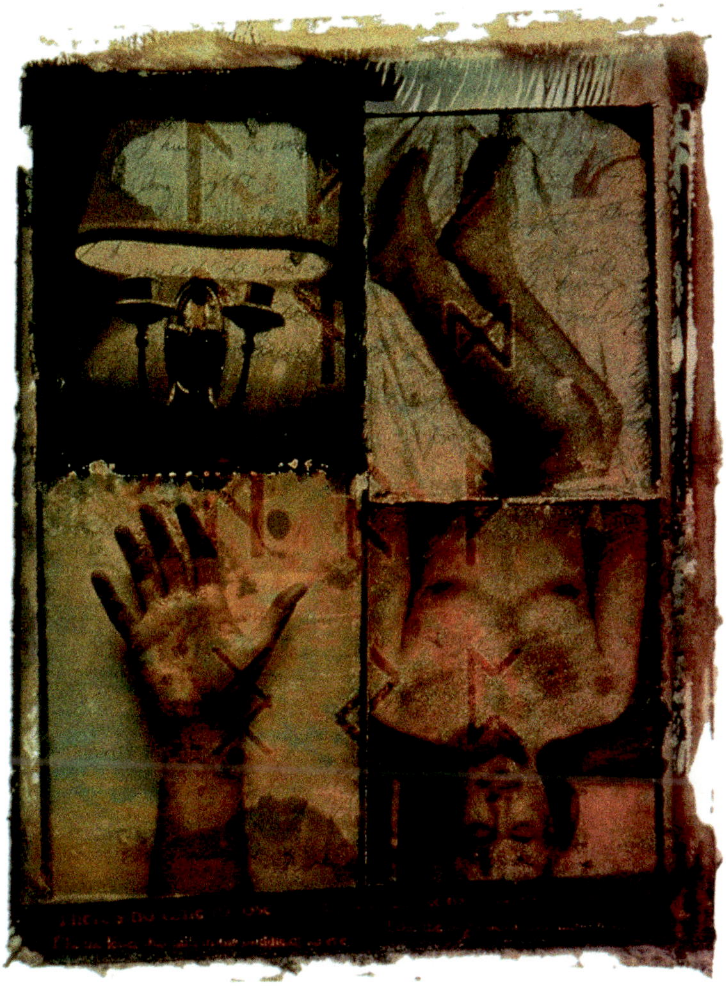

Canto Nine/Nine Nights I Hung on a Windy Tree, Iris print, 47″ X 34″, 1996

In this series, slides of the model and the objects (primarily furniture from motel rooms I have stayed in) are taken with a traditional 35mm camera. These are imaged with a slide printer using normal and transfer techniques. Resultant images are scanned and composited in Photoshop with text and other elements.

Diane Fenster creates both fine art and illustration using a Macintosh computer. Her style is an innovative combination of her own 35mm photography, video, still video, and scanned imagery. Fenster's fine art has been exhibited internationally, and her images appear in numerous publications and CD's on digital art including the APERTURE monograph "METAMORPHOSES: PHOTOGRAPHY IN THE ELECTRONIC AGE."

She is guest lecturer at many seminars, conferences, and art schools. Her illustration style is an outgrowth of the explorations she has taken with her personal work, and her commissions range from editorial to advertising to Web sites. Fenster's clients include Apple Computer, Inc., IBM Corporation, Dell Computer Corporation, Adobe Systems, Inc., Oracle, Inc. and Silicon Graphics, Inc.

Canto Ten/Perhaps You Might Remember Me, Iris print, 47" X 34", 1996

Diane Fenster
287 Reichling Avenue
Pacifica, California 94044 USA
fenster@sfsu.edu
http://www.art.net/Studios/Visual/Fenster/ritofab_Home/fenster.html
http://www.sirius.com/~fenster

Canto Thirteen/The Interior Life of the Dead, Iris print, 47" X 34", 1996

PHILLIP GEORGE

Mnemonic Notations 1990-1997

The original "Mnemonic Notations" series of images was developed from one computer file that has been continuously modified in an intuitive manner. At various stages, the computer file has been down-loaded and displayed as an artifact for the spectator.

The ongoing process that constitutes this work emerges from a reflection on the correspondences between mind, memory, our experience of the land, and the social constructions of religions and philosophies that have a major impact on humanity's perceptions of the world and consequently on the way that it is remembered.

I am currently working on a body of work that includes the use of seahorses. This work has developed from the "Mnemonic" suite of images. I am interested in the ambiguity and the outright strangeness of these creatures, in that the male becomes pregnant and carries the young in a brood pouch. Seahorses also mate for life, and when one is caught without the other, the captured one will not breed.

These images can be interpreted in many ways, but one that amuses me is that they represent the ultimate in political correctness – pregnant males! Here in these images, the Yogini with serpentine female energy manifests from the stomach of the male seahorse: a Tantric manifestation of many possible worlds embodied in the one time and incarnation. The

Phillip George was trained as a painter at the National Art School, graduating with a diploma in art in 1979. He received a masters degree with 1st class honours in painting and digital imaging from the University of New South Wales in 1996, and he is currently a lecturer in digital imaging at the University of Western Sydney Macarthur. Phillip George has also been a practitioner of Chinese yoga (Shaolin Ch'uanfa) since 1986.

Tangent @ 23 X, mixed media on canvas, 130 cm X 100 cm, 1996 works can be seen as artifacts secured from an imposing archaeological site of the future: a form of mutant androgynous specimen evolving out of memory into a theoretical future. They come with their baggage in tow.

This new work is seen as running in "Tangent" to the older "Mnemonic Notations" body of works, but in the new work, the parallel processing that is under way at the time of writing is underlined by the process of the practice. The images are created and produced as two-dimensional images on canvas, and at the same time are moved into a QuickTime VR interactive environment for use in immersive environmental works.

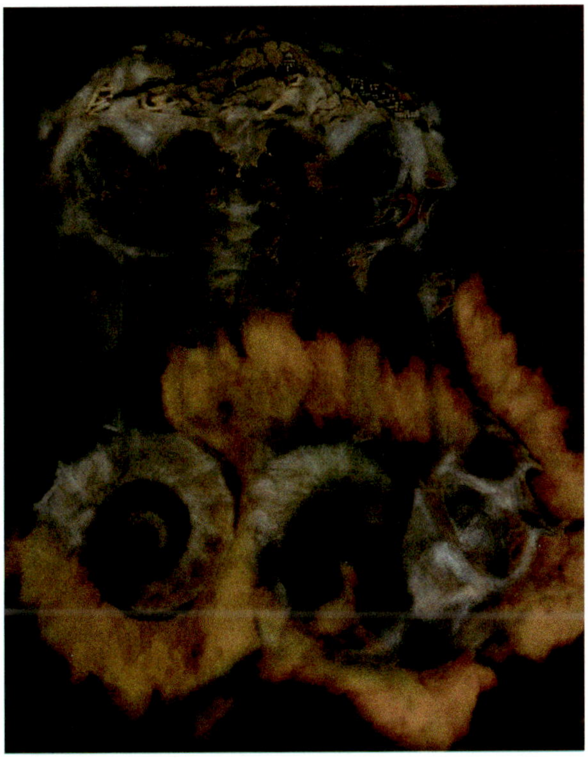

Phillip George
11 Miller Street
Bondi, Australia
p.george@uws.edu.au

Tangent @ 23 Fire, mixed media on canvas, 130 cm X 100 cm, 1996

MADGE GLEESON

I am extremely interested in the role of new technology in shaping our cultural environment. The computer is both the means and indirectly the content of many of my pieces. If Dick and Jane are still out there, they would be quite shaken by the information society that we are creating. I struggle with the social issues raised by all of this but at the same time am fascinated by the new possibilities. As artists before us have been buffeted by fin de siècle psychology, we are certainly tasting the fin de millennium.

Most of these pieces involve a scanned object that has been enhanced and then greatly enlarged. Despite their hyperreal texture, the black and white fictionalizes them. Most are printed on mylar, which is transparent or frosted and then displayed over wood veneer, formica, aluminum foil, and other materials. Hardware is repurposed from the local scrap metal yard, and the framing material is custom made by a furnace contractor. There is an intended slurring of the real and artificial, of the digital and tactile.

Artist's Garden, laser print/mixed media, 22" X 36" X 6", 1996

"Artist's Garden" captures a bar-coded leaf in an oversized specimen box with wheels and tail lights. The piece, which is meant to hang crookedly on the wall, deals with the uneasy relationship of humans to the natural environment.

In "Endangered Species," real leaves are displayed in glassine envelopes, each sequentially bar coded. All of the plants are commonplace, suggesting that everything is endangered.

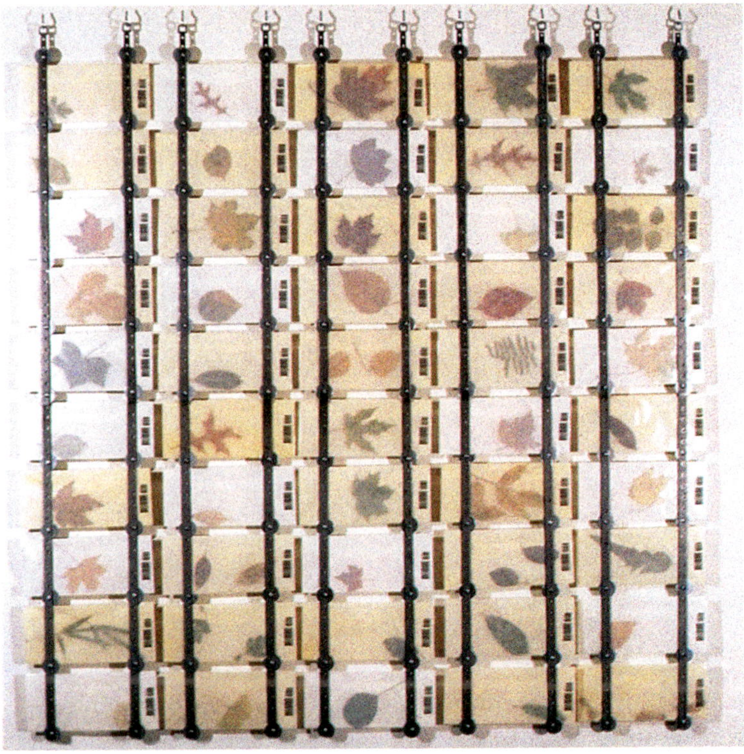

Endangered Species, mixed media, 48" X 48", 1995

"Golden Parachute" is also about money, power, and the environment.

"High Flyer" is imprinted with a tracking bar code, implying an exchange between sender and receiver, and also suggesting the potential scarcity of the commonplace. This piece is environmental in theme.

Golden Parachute, laser print/mixed media, 23" X 25", 1996

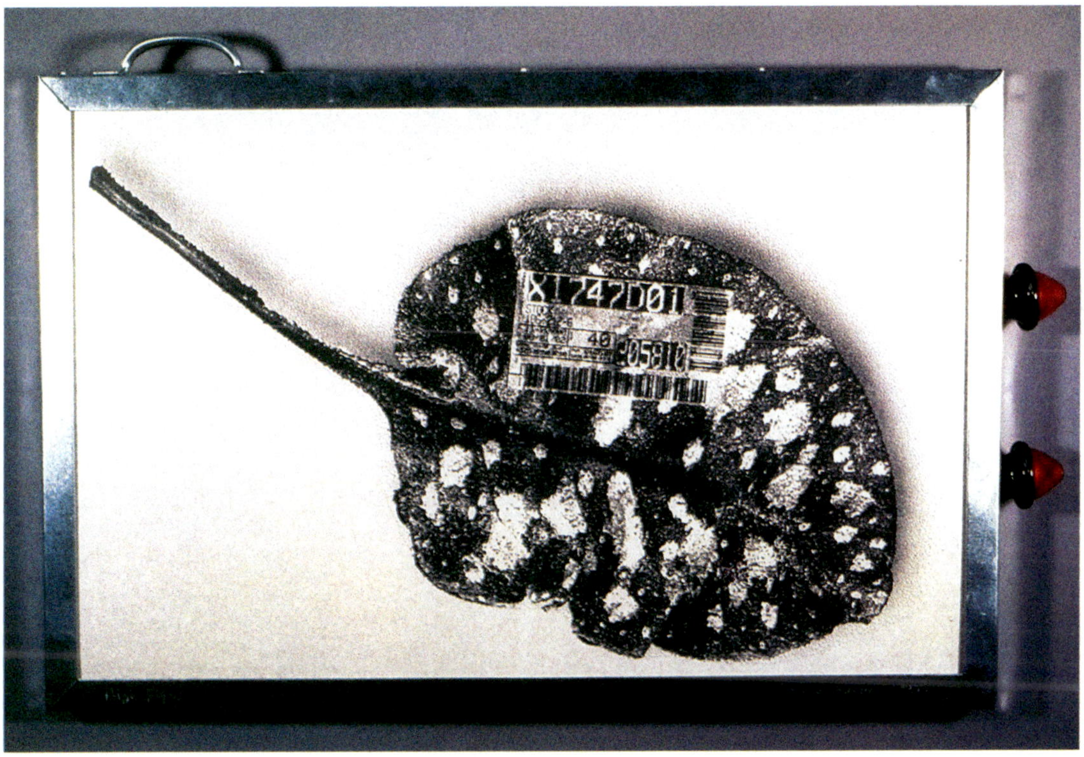

High Flyer, laser print/mixed media, 22" X 35", 1996

"Road Warrior" uses a motorcycle metaphor, including tail reflectors and a mud flap. The maple spinners are going nowhere unless someone gives them a lift. The meaning and value are, of course, altered by the predicament.

"Mirror, Mirror" is about letting go of privacy, one seemingly innocent question at a time.

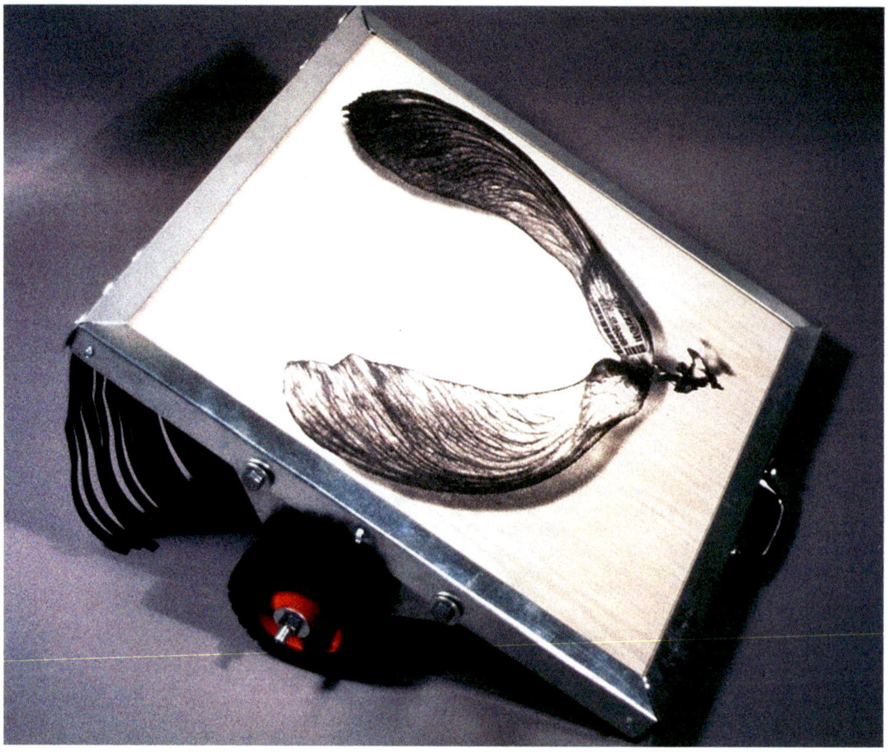

Madge Gleeson lives and works in Bellingham, Washington, a college town on the banks of Puget Sound with a view of Vancouver, British Columbia. She teaches at Western Washington University and has maintained a studio in Seattle for the past decade. Born in Chicago, she holds degrees from Brown University and Washington State University. Most of her exhibition work in the past decade has been computer-related. She has shown a number of times at both SIGGRAPH and ISEA.

Road Warrior, laser print/mixed media, 22" X 25" X 10", 1996

Madge Gleeson
Western Washington University
Department of Art
Bellingham, Washington 98225 USA
mgleeson@henson.cc.wwu.edu

Mirror, Mirror, laser print/mixed media, 30" X 30" X 5", 1996

KEN GONZALES-DAY

"The Museum of Broken Identities" takes Goya's "Black Paintings" as a point of departure. The idea is to draw attention to the fact that artists have always been engaged within a social discourse, and it is only with the emergence of a global society that the artist's role becomes increasingly unstable. This exhibition seeks to suggest a new potential for artists located within digital technology.

The themes of the work are taken from specific paintings by Goya and reference his skepticism of the social and political milieu of his day. Using digital technologies, this fictitious museum directly addresses issues concerning the artist's role in society, as well as in new technologies, and as such, enters into contemporary debates surrounding the historical instability of identity per se – an instability accentuated by the presumed

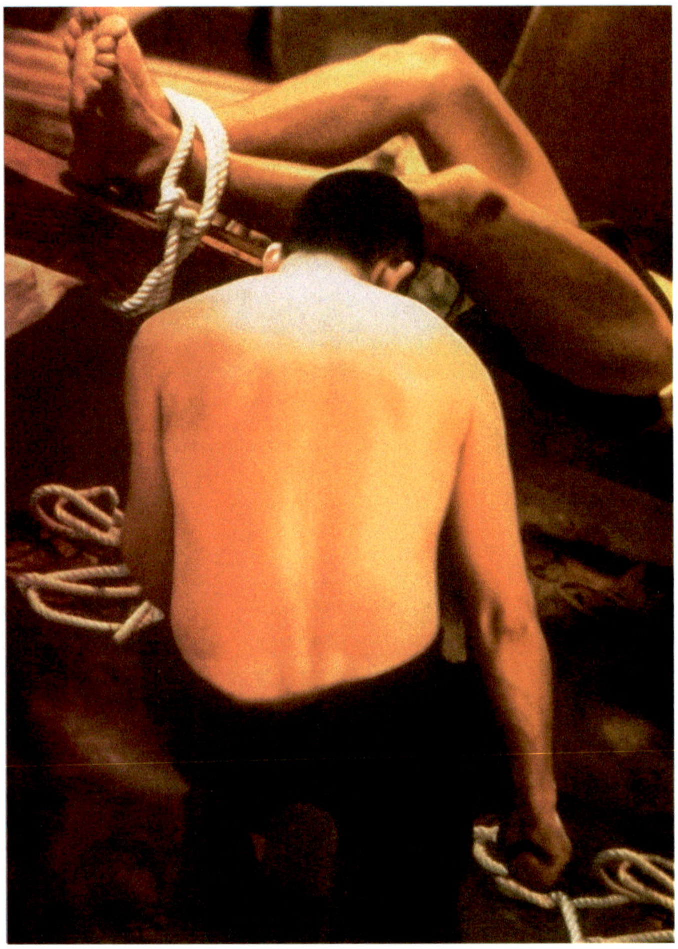

Currently an Associate Professor at Scripps College, Ken Gonzales-Day received a WESTAF/NEA award in New Genres in 1996. In 1995, he received an MFA from the University of California, Irvine. In 1993, he was a Van Leer fellow in the ISP at the Whitney Museum of American Art. He holds an MA in Art History from Hunter College, C.U.N.Y. and a BFA from Pratt Institute in Brooklyn.

He has exhibited at: White Columns & Christinerose Gallery in New York, the New Orleans Contemporary Art Center, Los Angeles' Foundation for Art Resources at Full Moon Gallery, L.A.C.P.S. Re:solution Gallery, Spaces in Cleveland, the Hallwalls Contemporary Art Center in Buffalo, and the New Museum of Contemporary Art, among others.

Untitled #33, From the Museum of Broken Identities (After Goya's Black Paintings),
C-print from digital negative, 40" X 30", 1996

Content: no; Intent and invitation: yes.

The work is abstract by choice.

Mathematics is an inspiration and a path in the search for the spiritual, an inspiration and a powerful means in the conception and execution of the work. Each one will interpret abstraction at one's own inclination and whim: so it is hoped that the work will set the viewers' thoughts, imaginations, dreams, and meditations free.

Jean-Pierre Hébert
4647 Via Huerto
Santa Barbara, California 93110 USA
jph@solo.com

Gris de Payne & Ochre, ink on paper, 56 cm X 36 cm, 1996

Deux Lignes Ochres, ink on paper, 60 cm X 46 cm, 1996

CHRIS S. JOHNSON

There was a lifeguard. Given the lives of hundreds of children, but too young to vote or drink, the lifeguard was searching for his/her identity, where it belonged in the world. His/her soul was held out like a decorated cake constructed from the basic elements of life. The lifeguard continues on a journey not knowing what it will encounter next. Symbols of society bombard the lifeguard, and stories are told.

My images use a modern saint: the lifeguard. Through the journeys of the lifeguard, the images discuss the intricate connections holding our lives together. There are things that surround us, and contradictions abound in our society. Today, we no longer pray to a god, but to computers. They have become our new religion. We rely on the machines for the lifeblood of our society. Why is it that we are so fascinated by the computer?

I use computer art to not only question our society, but to question the viewer's belief in the art object. Computer art exists not on any known natural plane. An image is reached by entering a maze of directories. I find this similar to cave painters who searched their way back to the sacred images. Once there, the image is almost alive.

After the Ache, Duratrans, fluorescent lights (lightbox), 36" X 28", 1996

Today, the computer stores a 3D rendering, a multimedia piece, an installation, a movie special effect, a scientific picture of an organism, and two-dimensional images until the moment when it is given life. It may exist only for a brief moment on the screen, or sometimes longer when printed. Computer images appear on the screen, on celluloid, and in printed form.

My work embodies a zealous devotion to computer imaging. Each piece brings a new discovery. Duratrans in lightboxes project light toward the viewer, recreating the journey from the monitor to the eye. Light engulfs the room, leaving a powerful and beautiful effect on the viewer.

I was interested in art long before I can remember; my interest in computers began in the fourth grade. That year, I programmed squares and lines to create images not unlike an etch-a-sketch. On a Tuesday in 1984, we got a Macintosh 128k computer and MacDraw. My interest in computers and art continued into college. I took printmaking, painting, sculpture, and photography. In 1991, I began using Fractal Design Painter and the WACOM tablet to create my images. They closely simulated the feeling that I was used to.

My images and discourse matured during two years of graduate work at The School of the Art Institute of Chicago. I create images that incorporate metal, wood, fabric, and an eclectic mix of output options. Now, in teaching digital art at Northern Arizona University, I constantly challenge myself and my students to embrace this new medium to the fullest.

Chris S. Johnson
Northern Arizona University
1385 West University Avenue #164
Flagstaff, Arizona 86001 USA
c.s.johnson@nau.edu

Cabrito, Duratrans, fluorescent lights (lightbox), 13.5" X 30", 1996

TAMMY KNIPP

Through the interdisciplinary medium of computer-aided video/kinetic sculptures, I create interactive, performative installations. Both visual and audio elements are simultaneously experienced in the physical domain (kinesthesia), challenging perceptions of reality through illusion. By altering perceptions and creating multi-sensory experiences, the lines between 2D, time-based imagery and 3D, tactile experiences are blurred.

These sculptural installations are assigned a CASE STUDY number (title). Each CASE STUDY encompasses three, multi-dimensional formats: the original installation; a video documentation capturing an interactive, performative aspect in which viewers become unbeknownst performers; and a mixed-media compositional design of text, image, and a nine-inch video monitor. This format depicts the work in its entirety, from concept to construction to the documentary response.

Influenced by the cognitive processes of dyslexia and its relationship to art-making, each CASE STUDY focuses on the characteristics that surround a haptic learner. In a technologically driven culture, the reality is virtually perceived.

Tammy Knipp is an artist and a Professor of Art at Florida Atlantic University. She holds an MFA degree in Imaging and Digital Arts from the University of Maryland, Baltimore County and an MFA degree in Sculpture from Washington University, St. Louis. She was a 1995-1996 fellow recipient of Art Matters. Her work has been shown in New York, Indianapolis, Austin, Los Angeles, Chicago, and the Alexandria Museum of Art, Alexandria, Louisiana.

Tammy Knipp
Florida Atlantic University
Art Department, Room 106
777 Glades Road
Boca Raton, Florida 33431-0991 USA
tknipp@fauvms.acc.fau.edu

CASE STUDY 118 (documentation), mixed-media collage/9" video monitor, 3' X 5' X 1', 1996

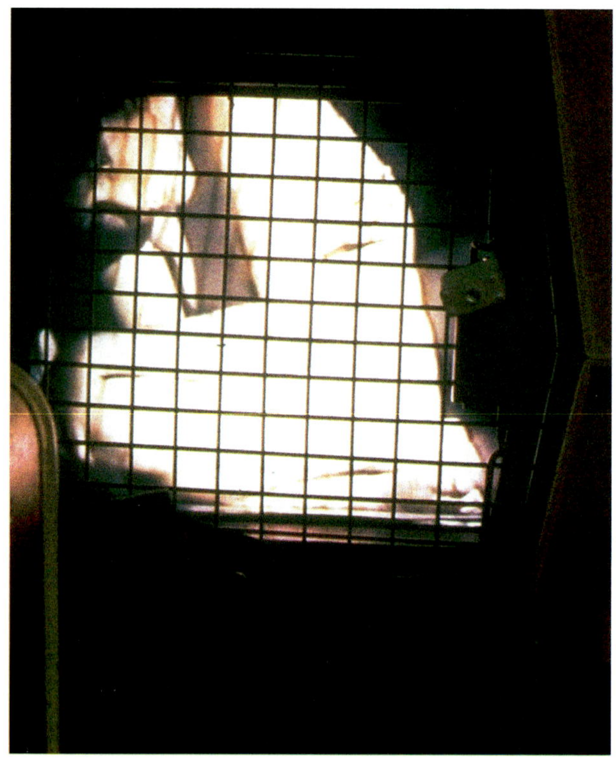

CASE STUDY 2442, computer-aided video/sculpture,
5′ X 4′ X 6′, 1994

CASE STUDY 2442 (detail view), computer-aided video/sculpture,
5′ X 4′ X 6′, 1994

CASE STUDY 2442, mixed-media collage/9" video monitor, 4' X 4' X 1', 1996

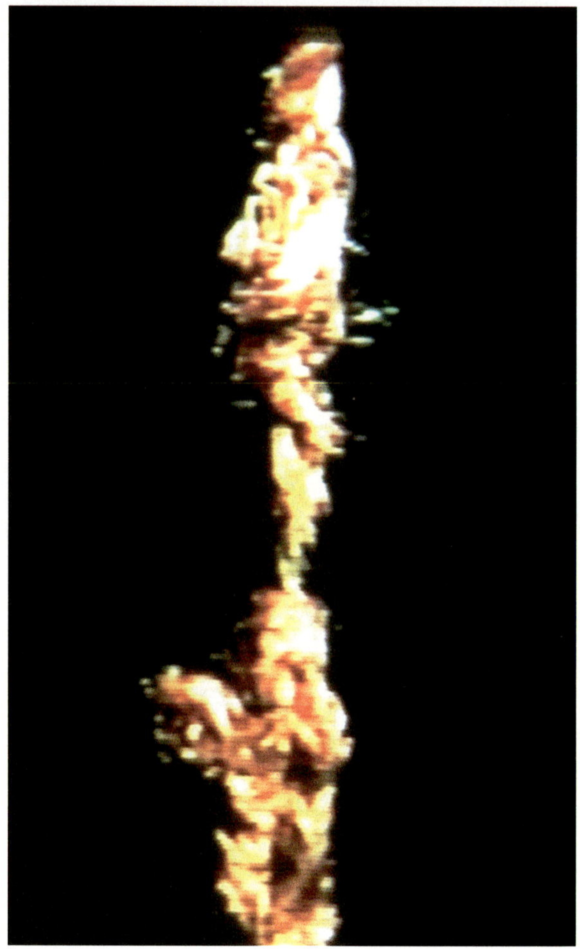

CASE STUDY 107, computer-aided video/sculpture, 1994

CASE STUDY 107 (detail view), computer-aided video/sculpture, 1994

CASE STUDY 107 (detail view), computer-aided video/sculpture, 1994

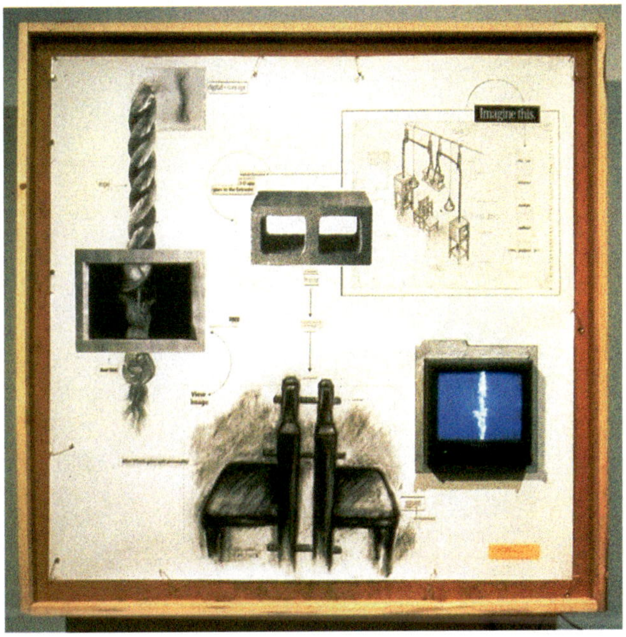

CASE STUDY 107, mixed-media collage/9" video monitor, 4' X 4' X 1', 1996

MICHAEL O'ROURKE

I think and feel most clearly and understand my world most clearly through my eyes. I tend to notice and remember the way things, places, people look. Later, when I try to think about these things, I find myself thinking most clearly when I think visually. And to help myself make sense of the complexities of the world, I attempt to represent these complexities in a visual format – as pictures, as sculptures, as moving images. This is how I try to understand my life, my experiences, life in general. This is my artwork. I am especially attuned to the spatial aspects of the visual world – to the way things are arranged in space, to the emptiness of spaces, to the clustering of objects within spaces, to the emotional resonances of space.

What first allowed me to represent space as I was perceiving it was my encounter, in 1978, with three-dimensional computer graphics. I had already been making sculpture in traditional media and becoming more and more conscious of the space of the sculpture rather than its volume. When I stumbled upon three-dimensional computer graphics, I discovered a way of visualizing space without any volume. I composed lines – of no thickness – in an empty space, now made perceptible by the lines. These first compositions were interactive. I called them "virtual" sculptures.

À La Recherche du Centre Exact: Amsterdam Ave, Iris print on paper, 43" X 35", 1997

À La Recherche du Centre Exact: Arastradero, Iris print on paper, 43" X 35", 1996

Space is emotional. The space of a cathedral can be imposing. A corridor can be threatening. The enormity of a night sky may be awe-inspiring. The spaces of these first computer compositions had their origins in emotional states. Trying to understand, to "get a handle on," to create a handle for my feelings – about death, about what was passing back and forth between a woman and myself.

À La Recherche du Centre Exact: Portola Valley, Iris print on paper, 13" X 10", 1996

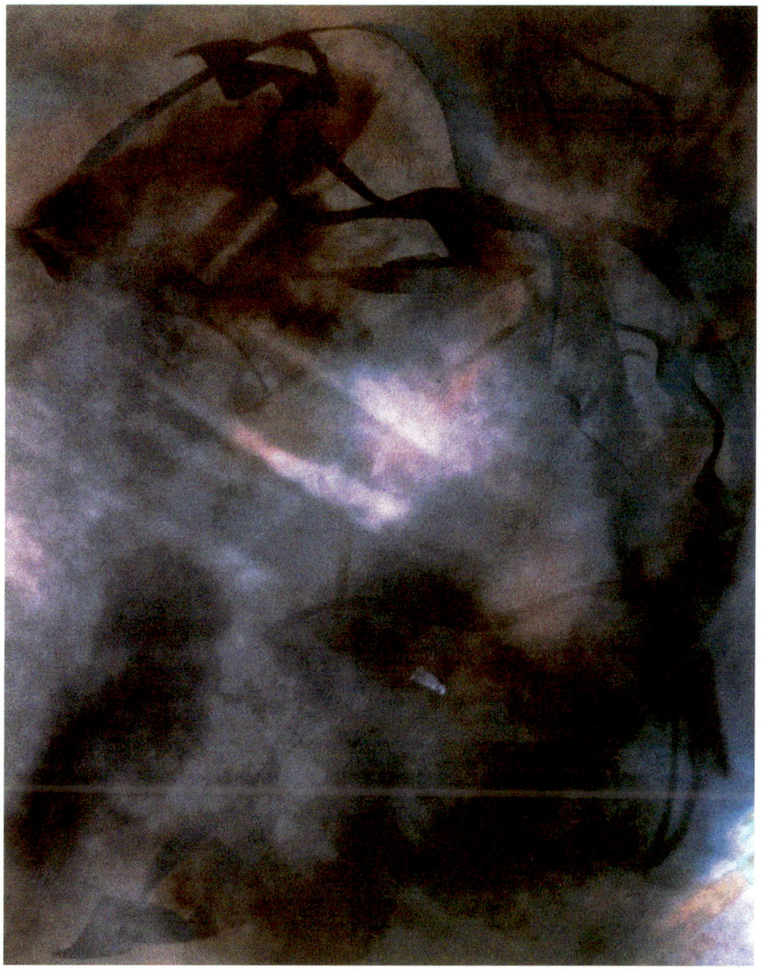

À La Recherche du Centre Exact: Santa Cruz, Iris print on paper, 43" X 35", 1996

Twenty years later, I am still thinking visually, still concerned with space, and still making spatial compositions that help me understand the world and my/our emotional reactions to it. More recently, emotional issues predominate in my work, even while the underlying perceptual issues continue. When a man and a woman come together, what is happening? What is this powerful emotional urge we feel to unite with another? What is the nature of the almost overwhelming feeling of one-ness we can feel with another? And the profound feeling of alone-ness we can feel when we lose that sense of union?

Throughout all of this work, I have always worked in a variety of media, both computer-generated and traditional. The technology of the work is significant to me only in so far as it stimulates new ways of seeing or understanding things. The computer has consistently had that effect for me for 20 years. But I also work, with equal enthusiasm, in non-computer media. The interplay that happens as I move from one medium to another, from one way of thinking about the issues to another, has always been fruitful for me. The goal is always the same: to understand my world.

Michael O'Rourke studied sculpture and computer graphic art for his MFA at the University of Pennsylvania, producing both physical sculpture and real-time interactive virtual sculpture between 1979 and 1982. He subsequently worked for seven years as a Senior Research Staff Artist at the New York Institute of Technology, where he produced computer-aided sculpture, animation and graphics. He now teaches at Pratt Institute, and continues working in a variety of media, both digital and traditional, producing graphic works and animation. His work has been exhibited widely and internationally since 1983.

Icon #1, ink, charcoals, pastels on paper, 22" X 30", 1987

Michael O'Rourke
Pratt Institute
44 Tompkins Place, #1
Brooklyn, New York 11231 USA
morourke@interport.net

Icon #4, ink, pastels, chalks on paper, 22" X 30", 1987

ANNA ULLRICH

My body of work seduces. I scan objects such as fabric, newspaper, and rope to create folds, crevices, and hidden spaces. I literally create fabricated landscapes whose tactile imagery urges one to touch the surface of the print.

No image completely retains its original value or meaning after I've transformed it in montage. A newspaper article becomes a hilltop or a corn husk. A plastic cosmetic case becomes a wind turbine. A photograph of a nurse becomes a pirate ship's sail. I am interested in how the viewer is able to follow these fantastic translations through allusions to familiar forms. The combination of real objects, photographs, and completely computer-generated imagery produces a hybridized landscape that is surreal in its incongruities and yet remains grounded because of references to the familiar.

My artwork expresses a desire for mastery and control over the male subject. Rather than being concerned with (re)gaining control over imagery of the female subject, I am fascinated with the cultural control inherent in creating imagery of the "other," in my case, the masculine experience. I imbricate the sexual within the visual through fetishizing the inorganic and invest every object with a throbbing life vein. The subjects within my layered narratives are surrounded by a landscape and objects burgeoning with desire, threats, and anxiety.

I use Photoshop, for image manipulation, along with an object-oriented and vector-based program, RIO, for laying out my compositions within a PC. My visual sources have included traditional photography, appropriated and computer-generated imagery, and images of objects captured using a flat-bed scanner. This last method, scanning objects on a flat-bed, has

Anna Ulrich earned her BFA in photography at the University of Washington in Seattle and is now a graduate student of photography at the University of Notre Dame. She teaches Web design at Andrews University and introductory workshops on Photoshop and the World Wide Web at Notre Dame. In November of 1996, she and six other artists opened the Steelhead Gallery in South Bend, Indiana with their first exhibition. She expects to receive her MFA in the spring of 1998.

The Decorative Arts of the Mariner, Cibachrome print, 35" X 77" X 1", 1996 been very important in defining my visual style. My interest in using the flat-bed to capture the various perspectives of objects and to achieve a dramatic three-dimensional quality (due to the modeling effects created by the light source) has drawn me to three-dimensional modeling programs. I now use 3D Studio MAX to create three-dimensional objects and incorporate this imagery alongside my other visual sources. I am currently exploring the possibilities of creating a hybrid between my normal output method, inkjet and cibachrome prints, and a projected animation that appears within the static print.

Anna Ullrich
P.O. Box 975
Notre Dame, Indiana 46556 USA
Ullrich.1@nd.edu
http://www.nd.edu/~aullrich

The Judgement of Lyon, Cibachrome print, 35" X 93" X 1", 1996

ROMAN VEROSTKO

My work represents 50 years of exploring worlds of unseen form. The procedures evolved from early 20th century artists who pioneered the fine art of painting and sculpting "unseen form" known as "abstract art." With the advent of computers, this adventure led to composing instructions (software) for generating worlds of form that are accessible only with extensive computing. By joining software form generators with fine arts practice, I create aesthetic objects to be contemplated much as we contemplate the wondrous forms of nature. The software, written with Basic and Digital Microprocessor/Plotting Language (DM/PL™), automatically generates work that follows the artist's instructions.

A fine art form generator specifies the procedures for initiating, developing, and improvising an artist's art-making idea. Such a form generator may be likened to a biological genotype, since it contains the coded information for generating the form. The procedure for executing the code, somewhat analogous to biological epigenesis, grows the art form. The creation and control of these instructions provide an awesome means for an artist to visualize form-growing concepts. Such routines provide access to an infinity of visual worlds never before seen by the human eye. It is noteworthy that such procedures hold much in common with processes associated with crystallization and genetics.

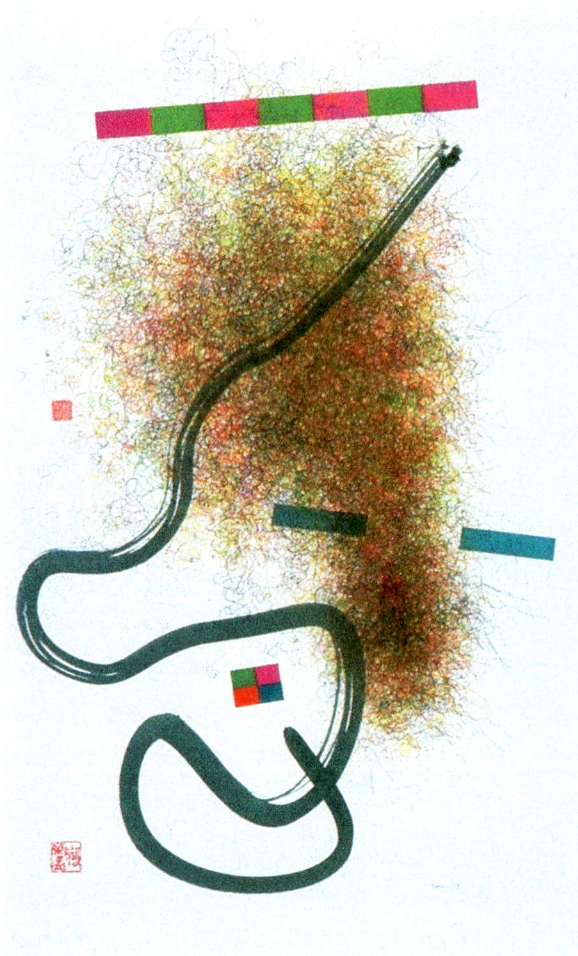

Carnival, Pathway Series, ink on paper, 36" by 24", 1989

Pathway series, ink on paper, 44" by 30", 1993

Works are executed with a multipen plotter coupled to a PC driven by the software. The plotter, choosing from an array of pens loaded with inks mixed in the studio, draws each individual line. Most works require thousands of lines and frequent pen changes, which are software controlled. An optional brush routine allows the occasional substitution of a brush for a pen. All brush strokes are plotted using Chinese brushes adapted to the machine's drawing arm. One recent series of illuminated digital scripts is reminiscent of medieval manuscripts. Many of these works are enhanced with a touch of gold or silver leaf applied by hand. However, the design elements illuminated with gold are always code-generated and machine-plotted.

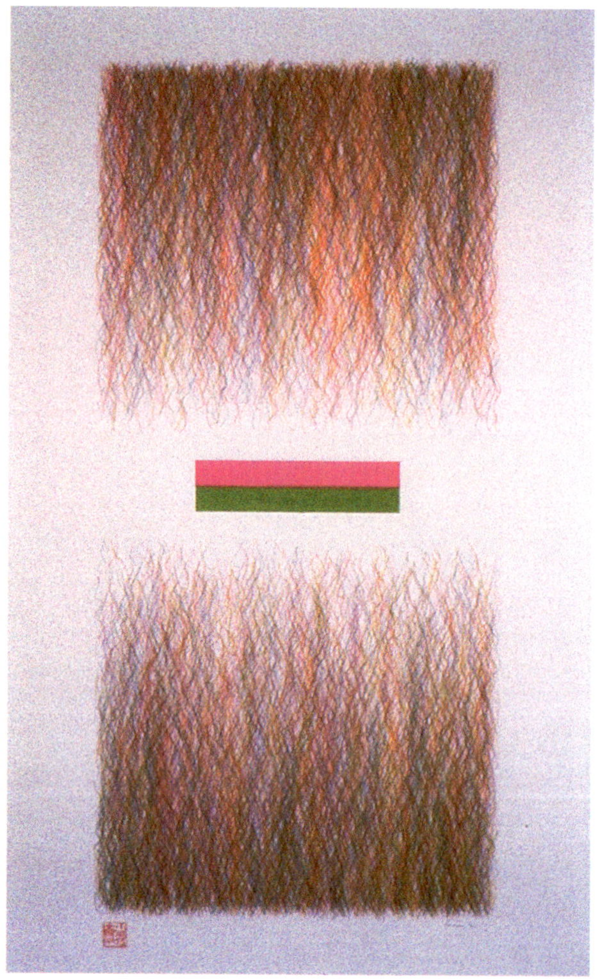

Heaven and Earth, ink on paper, 36" by 24", 1991

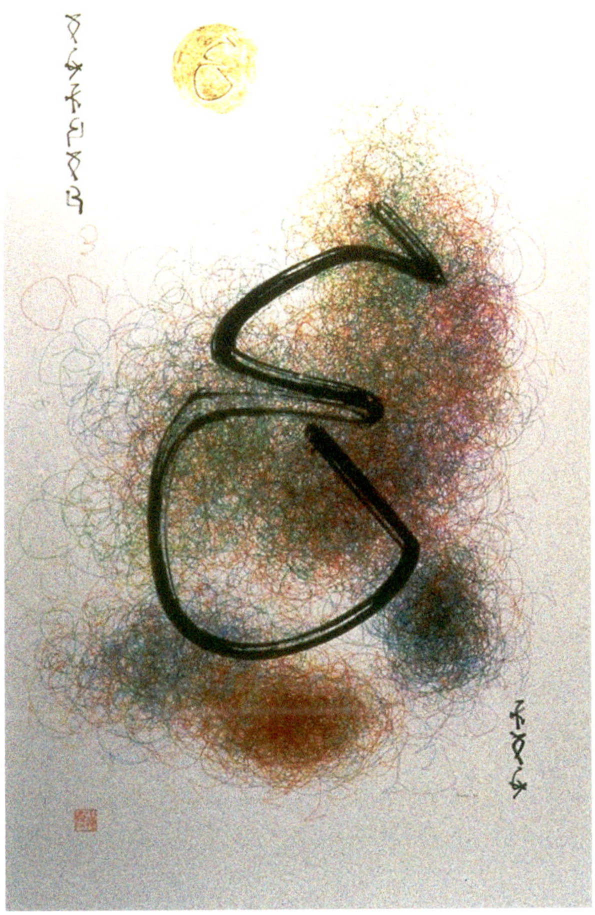

Nested Swallow, ink on paper, 44″ by 30″, 1995

Over the years the software has evolved by stages, yielding a series of works for each stage – Pathway, Gaia, Glyph, Scarab, Apocalypse, and Ezekiel. Each of these series has distinctive formal qualities associated with its form generators. None of the works are made with intentional representations in mind. Rather, each work presents one more adventure into a world of forms that have never been seen before. This art does not represent some sort of subject or object. Just as one might label this or that flower, so also I label this or that art form. Titles are therefore arbitrary and often derived from evocative qualities associated with the work.

The art works are visual manifestations of the dynamic procedures by which they grew. They may be viewed as visual celebrations of the information processing procedures embedded in today's culture. The finished works invite us to savor the mystery of their coded procedures, whose stark logic yields a surprising grace and beauty. These procedures provide a window on those unseen processes from which they are grown. By doing so, they serve as icons illuminating the mysterious nature of our evolving selves.

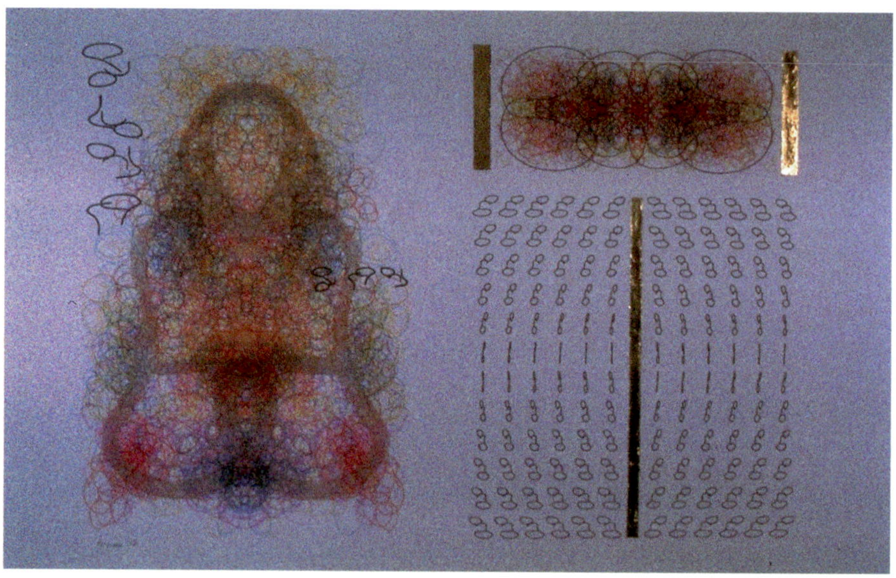

Roman Verostko has pioneered the development and creative use of an artist's personal expert system. Recipient of the Golden Plotter First Prize (1994, Gladbeck, Germany) and an Ars Electronica honorable mention (1993), his work has been exhibited in major art and technology exhibitions on five continents. A past Board Member of the Inter-Society for Electronic Art and Program Director for the Fourth International Symposium on Electronic Art, Verostko has published articles and lectured internationally on the subject of Art and Algorithm. Recent work includes a binary version of a Universal Turing Machine illuminated with algorithmically generated designs. A Professor Emeritus of the Minneapolis College of Art and Design, he currently resides in South Minneapolis, where he maintains an experimental studio with one work station reserved for research and development.

Diamond Lake Apocalypse: Buddha, ink on paper, 22" by 30", 1992

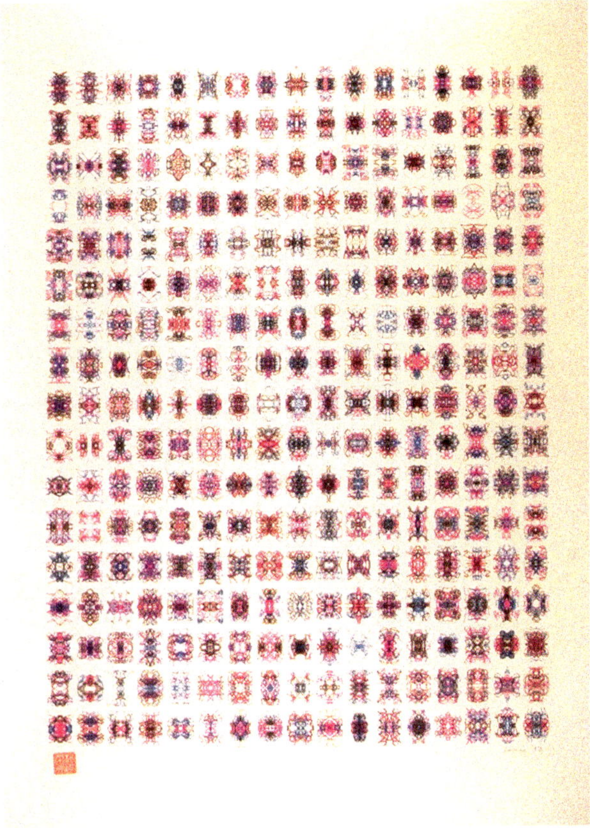

Roman Verostko
5535 Clinton Avenue South
Minneapolis, Minnesota 55419 USA
roman@mcad.edu
http://www.mcad.edu/home/faculty/verostko/roman.html

Scarab Series, ink on paper, 30" by 22", 1993

ROBERT MALLARY 1917-1997

Ongoings: the Fine Arts Gallery is dedicated to the memory of my mentor and friend, Robert Mallary.

Lynn Pocock
CHAIR, Ongoings: the Fine Arts Gallery

I am one of the pioneers of computer art, having worked continuously in this now increasingly popular field of art and technology since 1967, the year I learned of the computer's remarkable ability to generate and transform images. But my interest in the creative integration of science, technology, and art goes back to the early fifties, when my ground-breaking experiments with polyester and other plastic materials eventually gave rise to the series of assemblage relief constructions, wall sculpture, and "tuxedo" figures for which I became known during the brief halcyon days of Neo-Dada and assemblage art in the early sixties.

My contributions to computer art over the years include: learning to write and use my own computer programs; developing the first program, TRAN2, for the computer-aided design of sculpture; developing the first program, ECOSITE, for the design of land reclamation and earth sculpture; developing a series of large programs oriented to the lineal character of computer-driven pen plotters; developing a large library of tutorial programs and subroutines (over 150 in all) to support my creative work and teaching; and creating and exhibiting a large oeuvre of computer-graphic art that has drawn upon the resources of this library. I have also written articles and lectured extensively on computer art.

Robert Mallary
1917 - 1997

Photo: Paul Barube

Work by Robert Mallary

And all you touch and all you see
Is all your life will ever be.

Pink Floyd
Dark Side of the Moon

CONTENTS

I like to think
(right now please!)
of a cybernetic forest
filled with pines and electonica
where deer stroll peacefully
past computers
as if they were flowers
with spinning blossoms

David Greene
Gardener's Notebook
Archigram

Electric Garden model

In 1961, Archigram published a series of experimental projects that began to explore the new and emerging technologies of the period. This small group of British architects adopted audio/visual display systems, projection television, computer technology, entertainment facilities, exhibits, gantries, and electric lights as the building blocks of their designs.

They imagined temporary cities of activity and light.

Through their projects and proposals, they predicted a blurring of boundaries and a convergence of technologies. They realized that these technologies would begin shaping and altering the world in ways that they could only begin to imagine.

The Electric Garden at SIGGRAPH 97 is inspired by this group.

Over 30 years later, Archigram's vision of the future is being realized through the inventors, artists, programmers, and designers of today. The fabulous machines they imagined and the wonderful speculations they engaged in are now becoming a reality. As they predicted, these machines are shaping and altering our world in many ways.

The Electric Garden is an instant city that celebrates new and emerging technologies. Our garden is full of beautiful technology that we can experience today. There are remarkable things to see, hear, and touch in this rich, sensual environment.

Computer-generated images displayed by a variety of 2D and 3D systems provide color, motion, and beauty in the garden. Motion-capture systems and electronic cameras capture your gestures and expressions, and allow you to manipulate a synthetic world. Computer-controlled electric motors and machines provide surface information, telling us about the density, weight, and texture of a virtual object.

In the garden, you experience the power of a volcano or the cool breeze of a mountain glacier. You can play basketball in cyberspace and feel the weight of the virtual basketball. You can travel to another planet and hover in its atmosphere. Visit Berlin, Tokyo, or a remote part of Finland and learn about their cultures. Digitally transport your body into a computer-generated world by walking in front of a camera array and laser range finder.

The Electric Garden is a place where we can experience and celebrate our spectacular new electric toys.

It delights and amazes us.

It challenges all that you know.

It allows you to forget convention and law.

It seduces us.

The projects described in these pages are the life of the Electric Garden. Contributors from around the world have come to SIGGRAPH 97 to show us their wonderful creations. They have filled the Electric Garden with sights and sounds. For a few days, we can see their inventions and experience all they have to offer.

We are delighted by the possibilities and we thank them for sharing their flowers with us.

RICK HOPKINS
CHAIR, Electric Garden

The Selection Process

On 1 March 1997, the Electric Garden jury met at Sony Pictures Imageworks in Los Angeles for a full day of discussion, debate, review, and selection. Seventy-two proposals from four continents were reviewed on the basis of creativity, technical innovation, quality of content, presentation, and potential cultural significance. The proposals were numbered sequentially and ranked on a scale from A to F in a three-stage jury process:

1 Unanimous Rejection

- The chair cited the proposals one by one and asked the jury whether any of them received unanimous F (unacceptable) rankings. Six were rejected at this stage.
- Projects were rejected if they were considered incomplete, poorly presented, or inappropriate because they did not meet the criteria defined in the Electric Garden Call for Participation.

Selected comments on unanimously rejected proposals:

- "This one is not appropriate for the Electric Garden."
- "Number 20 is incomplete. It's not a proposal. It's just an abstract of a paper."
- "This is a product demo, and I don't see any interesting technology here that should be in the Garden."

2 Unanimous Acceptance

Another proposal-by-proposal review revealed the projects that received unanimous A (outstanding) rankings. Eleven were selected as "must-haves."

Selected comments on unanimously accepted proposals:

- "This one is either an A or an F. But we should select it just to see if it works."
- "Very cool. But I don't know if they can pull this off, and there are some liability issues here. Is this legal?"
- "It has a large Internet component, and Steve will make it happen!"

3 Debate

Before they debated the remaining proposals, the chair noted that, with its unanimous decisions in stage 2, the jury had allocated about 25 percent of the 50,000 square feet planned for the Electric Garden. "But one project is very large, so if we keep them in, we are implicitly saying that some of those remaining can't be accepted."

In stage 3, jury rankings were averaged to create a priority list of remaining projects. Those with the highest average rankings were assured of acceptance. Those at the low end of the average rankings would be accepted only if space was available at the end of the jury process.

Selected comments from the stage 3 debate:

- "The Call for Participation specified that we were looking for fun projects, and seductive projects. This one will be a real crowd pleaser."
- "I've been trying to do this kind of thing for the past year. I'd like to see if they can do it."
- "This is an interesting project, but it's largely arrogant and dumb."
- "Why do we need the violence? This is a technology in search of an application."
- "This one tells me that I don't matter. The piece is going to do what it does no matter what I do. There's no interaction."
- "But I gave it a higher ranking because it involves people outside the conference, via the Web."
- "I have a moral question about this project. All the sounds and reactions of the image seem to be painful, as if the image is being tortured. If I'm forced to participate in something that disturbs me, then I feel exploited by the process."
- "Yes, the content is strange, but it's the producer's vision. Are we censors?"
- "This one is pure SIGGRAPH. It's interesting. It's fun. And it's attacking a new problem."
- "Is this new? They've been at SIGGRAPH for several years. Is it the same as last year or not?"
- "Here's an A! I love this. They have some big technical problems to overcome. It's high risk, but compelling."
- "Another one where you're irrelevant. Confusion without learning does not lead to insight."
- "There's a gazillion dollars worth of technology behind this, and this is all they can come up with?" (Verdict: unanimous Fs.)
- "Very rich data, but there's no way to know if they can finish this project by August. If it works, it's very, very cool." (Verdict: unanimous As.)
- "We need to remember that we have a particular bias in this room, and it's not consistent with the larger SIGGRAPH audience."
- "Technologically, this is very basic, but artistically, creatively, it's pretty wonderful."
- "Very impressive VRML work. We don't have much VRML so far, and this illustrates the state of VRML right now."
- "I started out at D-plus for this one. I'll move up to B."

The jury also considered a proposal from its own ranks: Frank Foster's summary of a proposed multi-company collaboration, showing the potential of the new IEEE 1394 standard (Firewire). After some debate, the jury unanimously recommended, "outside the jury process," that SIGGRAPH 97 install this "glimpse of the digital video future."

In the course of its deliberations, the jury decided to reject all proposals that received a unanimous ranking of D or below. Final decisions on which projects would make the final cut, and where each accepted project would be located in the Electric Garden, were referred to the chair.

Adele Newton, Rick Hopkins, David Newton, Cheri Stacey,
Rosemary Ratkaj, Craig Applegath

The Electric Garden Committee

Adele Newton
Public relations, student volunteer coordination, selection committee, planting and weeding

Rick Hopkins
Design, direction, production, care, and feeding of the garden

David Newton
Database master, Web boy, and person responsible for watering the plants

Cheri Stacey
Office management, coordination, travel, and everything-under-the-sun department

Rosemary Ratkaj
Model maker, trimming, and pruning

Craig Applegath
Project manager, architect, and all things bright and beautiful

Rob Pringle
Research and growth formulas

Greg Papp
Organically grown CAD systems

The Electric Garden Jury

CHAIR
Rick Hopkins
Side Effects Software, Inc.

JURY
J. Craig Applegath
Architect

Tom Brighton
Landmark Entertainment

Frank Foster
Sony Pictures Imageworks

Andrew Glassner
Microsoft Network

Rob Hennigar
DreamWorks

Adele Newton
Side Effects Software, Inc.

Special Thanks to:

Kim Davidson, Greg Hermanovic, and the entire **Side Effects Software staff** for their patience and support.

Frank Foster and **Sony Pictures Imageworks** for their donations and generous support.

Sony for their donations and their snapshot of the future.

Clark Dodsworth and **Brian Blau** for their assistance, guidance, and excellent example.

Laura Hopkins for her help and understanding.

The **SIGGRAPH 97 committee members** and **contractors** who have helped make The Electric Garden a reality.

Last but not least, I would like to thank the **Electric Garden Selection Committee** for donating their time and expertise.

Contact

Rick Hopkins
Side Effects Software, Inc.
477 Richmond Street West, Suite 1001
Toronto, Ontario M5V 3E7 CANADA
rick@sidefx.com

Toco the Toucan: A Synthetic Character Guided by Perception, Emotion, and Story

Deb Roy, Michal Hlavac, Marina Umaschi, Tony Jebara, Justine Cassell, and Sandy Pentland

Toco the Toucan is a synthetic creature created at the MIT Media Laboratory. Participants can walk up to the display, sit down, and begin interacting with the toucan using a combination of speech and gesture. A constrained, but not entirely predetermined, story ensures that the highly interactive experience includes some structure and an overall plot.

An underlying emotion model drives Toco's facial expressions, sounds, and body motions. Changes in the creature's emotional state are determined by four factors:

- Speech and other sounds produced by the participant.
- Hand and body motions produced by the participant.
- Constraints from an underlying story-based interaction.
- Innate tendencies toward certain emotional states (personality).

This exhibit demonstrates the integration of several key technologies including behavior-based animation, interactive storytelling, robust computer audition and vision, and affective computing.

CONTACT
Deb Roy
Perceptual Computing Section
MIT Media Laboratory
20 Ames Street, Room E15-388
Cambridge, Massachusetts 02139 USA
dkroy@media.mit.edu

The Grimm Show (or The Story of the Youth Who Went Forth to Learn What Fear Was) is a 60-minute multi-media performance/interpretation of the parable by the Brothers Grimm. The story recounts the experiences of a youth who goes forth into the world to learn the meaning of "shuddering in fear." The performance incorporates pre-recorded video, live camera feeds, animation, text, and sound. The pre-recorded and live video, as well as the animation, are mixed live. Video and animation events are triggered by a continual midi/music soundtrack, which is both pre-sequenced and performed live on midi keyboards, drumpads, and wind instruments. Midi is also used to trigger a variety of sound samples and create abstract audio beds. The video (both individual sources and the live mix) appear on multiple monitors and video projectors.

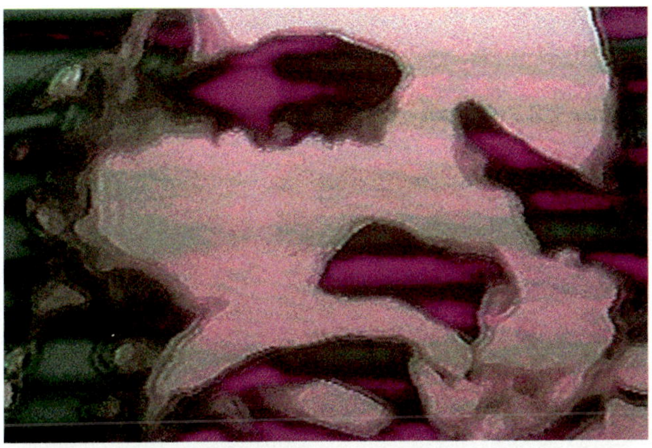
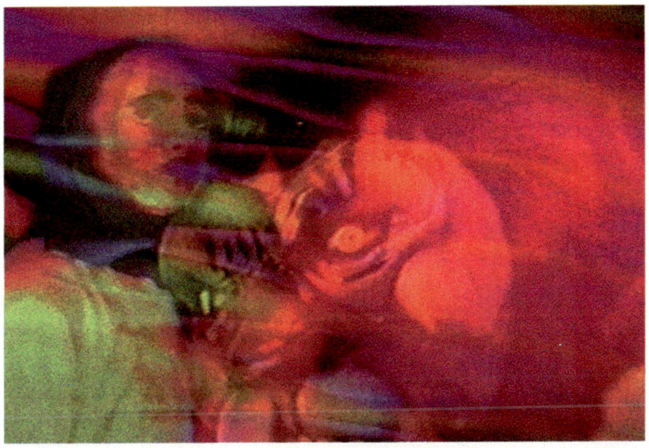
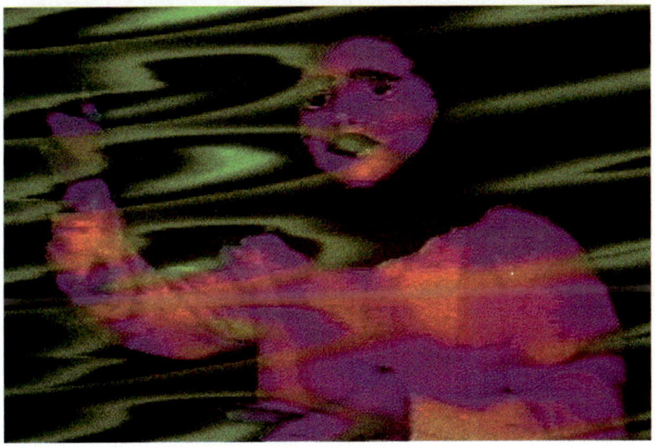
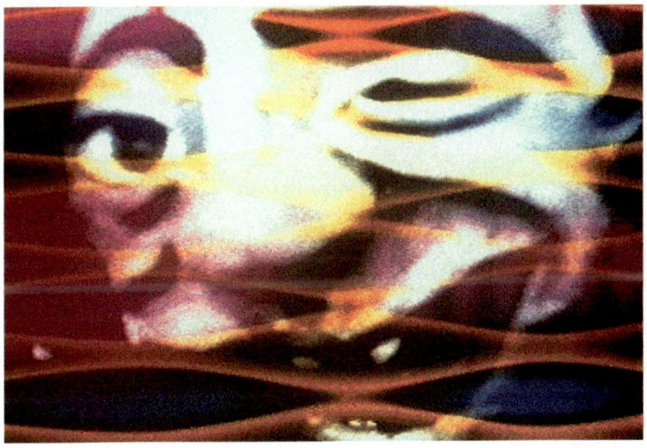

CONTACT
M.R. Petit
104 Suffolk Street, #3
New York, New York 10002 USA
petit@echonyc.com

COLLABORATOR
Jeremy X. Halpern

The JPL Space Garden features systems in current use at JPL for processing and visualization of science data returned by instruments flown on various NASA spacecraft:

1 The Science Analysis Graphics Environment (SAGE), a graphical interface used to control processing of imaging data returned by solar system exploration spacecraft, including the Galileo spacecraft currently returning data from Jupiter.

2 Mission operations support software used by the Mars Pathfinder mission that landed on Mars on 4 July 1997, providing stereoscopic mission planning tools that support rover navigation on the Martian surface.

3 Animated "fly-over" sequences produced from data of the Earth and other planets.

4 VISTAS, an interactive tool for query/retrieval of earth observations data acquired by the TOVS sensor.

5 A prototype of software for processing Atmospheric Infrared Sounder (AIRS) data.

6 Internet-accessible image database browsers and navigators that provide public access to space mission image archives.

7 Other examples of processing operational data.

CONTACT
William B. Green
Jet Propulsion Laboratory
Mailstop 168-527
4800 Oak Grove Drive
Pasadena, California 91109-8099 USA
Bill_Green@iplmail.jpl.nasa.gov

COLLABORATORS
Ray Bambery, Kris Capraro, Steve Carpenter, Jerry Clark, Bob Deen, Eric DeJong, Dave Freda, Jeff Hall, Tom Handley, Danika Jensen, Sue LaVoie, Justin McNeill, Mike Mueller, Vadim Parizher, Vince Realmuto, Allan Runkle, Mark Sarrel, Ken Starr, Tom Thaller, Charles Tompson, Felix Vanshelbaum, Bob Vargo, and Pam Woncik

Nerve Garden

Bruce Damer and Todd Goldenbaum

How can we forget the fascination that our terrariums, aquariums, or chemical crystal gardens held over us when we were children? Watching beautiful and functional structures emerge and then decay taught us a great deal about life and our own ultimate destiny. The Nerve Garden allows users to plant seeds in a digital terrarium and witness the growth of familiar and strange plant and animal structures. Through an artful combination of L-systems, VRML, neural networks, Java, the Web, and a mouse and dataglove interface, participants sow seeds in cyberspace. Participants leave the Nerve Garden proud of their petunias or unnerved by the realization that life may find a way into digital space.

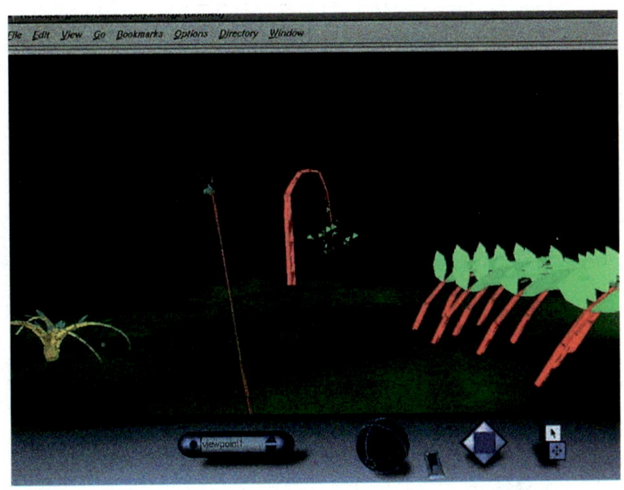

CONTACT
Bruce Damer
BIOTA Special Interest Group of the Contact Consortium
P.O. Box 66866
Scotts Valley, California 95067-6866 USA
bdamer@ccon.org

COLLABORATORS
Peter Hughes, Charles Ostman, Tim Riley, Patrick Mahoney, John Shiple, David Story, Dominic Sagolla, Ben Vigoda, Laurens Lapre, Ales Holecek, Pavel Slavik, Christopher Blohm, and Todd Goldenbaum

Daniel Schwartz

"...Decisions of time and space were out of my hands... I could become tied into another person's time and space... " Vito Acconci

d-rhum (drum room) is a room that responds to the presence and movement of its occupants. Computers translate sensor data into commands sent to motors. The motors stretch, push, strike with mallets, and move sections of the walls or the walls themselves. The walls are built of malleable materials such as latex and silicone.

As participants enter and move around the room, they notice that the walls move, change shape, and emit percussive sounds. Upon further investigation, they discover that they can interact with aspects of the movements and sounds of the room by coordinating their own movements. They are

encouraged to play the room like drums with random and/or deliberate movements around the sensors.

The spatial configuration of d-rhum and its participants is dynamic and constantly evolving. Within this fluid environment, participants begin to see that their personal boundaries are fuzzy. As they move, so do the walls, thus blurring the traditional limited expectations of architectural space. Certain combinations of movements cause deformations and sound emissions, but it is never clear which movements generate which reactions.

Our intentions in creating d-rhum are to explore two related issues. First, we wish to create an environment in which the understanding of one's boundaries is examined. Second, we wish to create an environment in which the biases of learned language can be overcome.

Movement and percussion are basic modes of communication that evolved from the most primitive cultures. By overlaying d-rhum's technological apparatus on such basic human communication techniques, we connect the participant to the long history of cultural evolution.

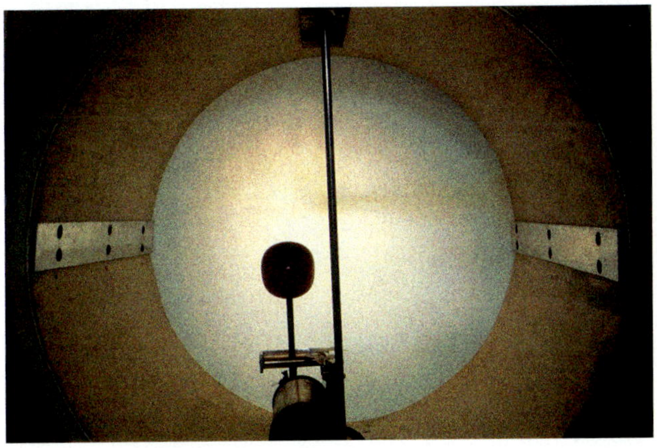

CONTACT
Daniel Schwartz
RomeBlack, Inc.
180 Varick Street, Suite 12A
New York, New York 10014 USA
dls@romeblack.com

COLLABORATORS
Peter Franch, Richard Hughes, and Eugene James Flotteron

Bodymaps: Artifacts of Touch
(The Sensuality and Anarchy of Touch)

Thecla Schiphorst

Bodymaps: Artifacts of Touch is a computer interactive sound and video installation. The piece uses a specially designed sensor surface embedded with 15 electric field sensors, which operate very much like 15 theramins, and 8 force-sensitive resistor sensors, which detect touch, pressure, and the amount of force applied to the surface.

These sensors lie beneath a white velvet surface upon which are projected images of the artist's body. The surface yearns for contact and touch. Its rule base is complex and subtle, impossible to decode. The effect is disturbing, erotic, sensual, and subjective.

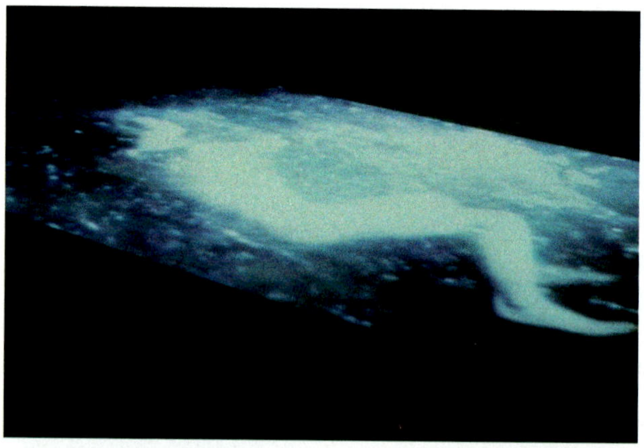

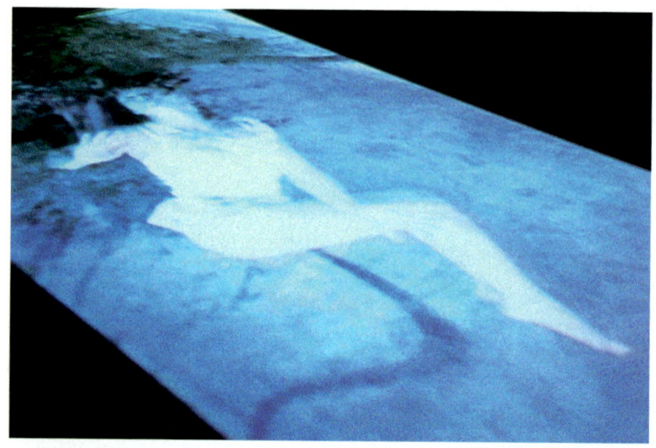

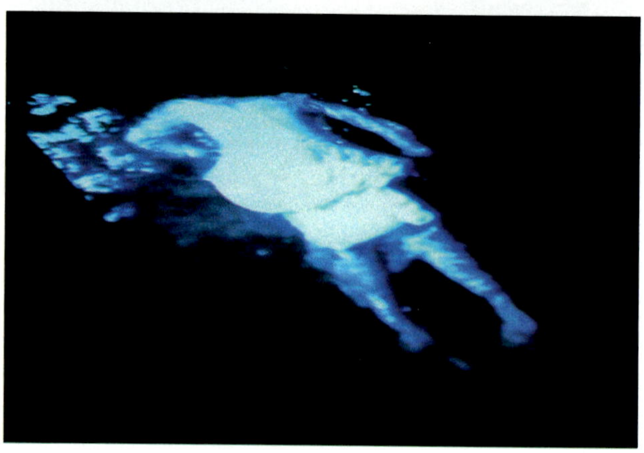

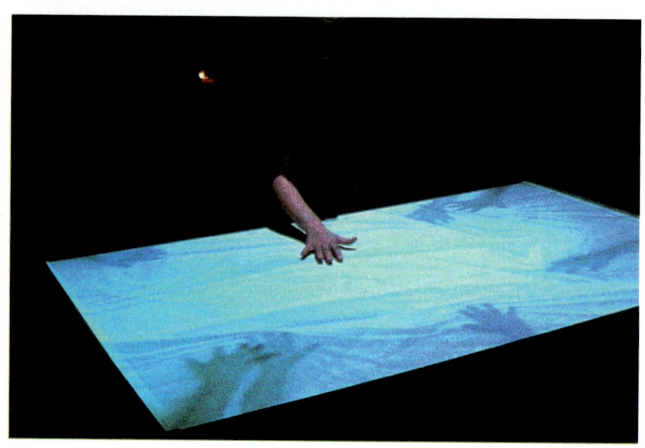

The intent of the work is to subvert the visual/objective relationship between the object and the eye, between click and drag, between analysis and power, to create a relationship between participant and technology that transgresses rules of ownership and objectivity, and begs questions of experience, power, and being.

The piece and interface were designed by Thecla Schiphorst, researched and engineered by Infusion Systems, programmed by Ken Gregory and Grant Gregson, and constructed by Hanif jan Mohamed and Ewen McNeil.

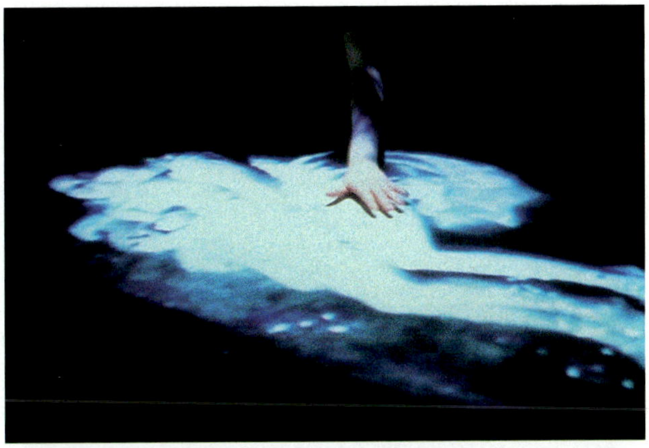

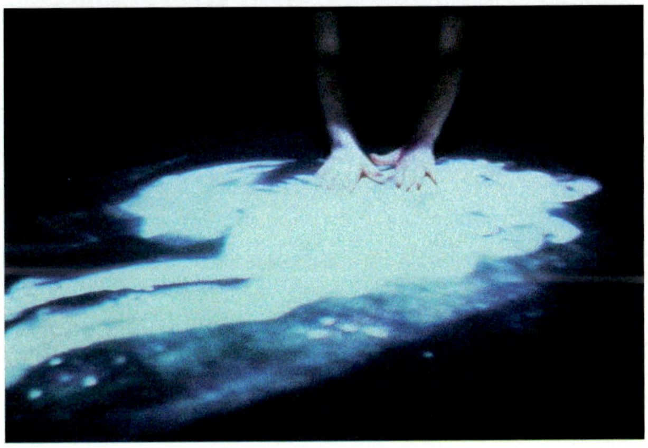

CONTACT
Thecla Schiphorst
Digital EARTH
1128 Rose Street
Vancouver, British Columbia V5L 4K8 CANADA
thecla@cs.sfu.ca

COLLABORATORS
Ken Gregory, Grant Gregson, Hanif jan Mohamed, and Ewen McNeil

Multiple Identities is a digital map of New York City that incorporates avatars (visual embodiments of concepts, personas, identities, or intelligence in virtual reality) acting as urban guides who lead travelers through unique experiences in the metropolis.

Maps have traditionally been commissioned to accumulate "detached" observations and "impersonal" facts regarding a physical location. Unlike typical navigational tools, the Multiple Identities Map acknowledges and reports on urban quantities that are less quantifiable. It collects and dispenses information that is inherently qualitative and subjective. Inspired by the research of Howard Gardner (The Theory of Multiple Intelligences, Leading Minds) and others, we have identified unique personae that emphasize multiple viewpoints as a way to identify and digest information. Each identity renders a personal experience and fashions stories that reflect unique observations and challenges.

The Multiple Identities Map does not intend to chronicle the city with efficient facts, but instead formulates compelling experiences that render the richness of a metropolis like New York.

CONTACT
Richard Yelle
Parsons School of Design
66 Fifth Avenue
New York, New York 10011 USA
yeller@newschool.edu

COLLABORATORS
Richard Yelle, Sven Travis, Richard Day, Edward Lucero, and Christopher Kirwan

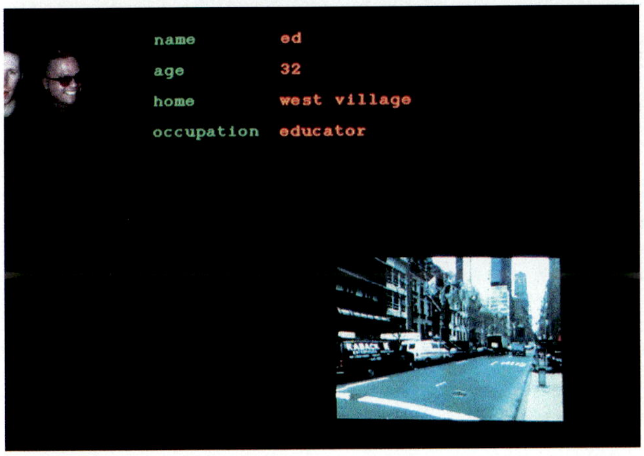
name ed
age 32
home west village
occupation educator

This interactive project introduces a multimedia experience using an interactive kaleidoscope. The Iamascope uses a video camera lens as the eye of a kaleidoscope and projects a kaleidoscopic image of the participant onto a large screen. A vision subsystem is coupled to the electronic eye to control musical tones using a sustain algorithm. A wireless microphone produces echoes corresponding to the audio analogue of the kaleidoscopic reflections.

Once inside the Iamascope, participants can gesture, dance, sing, and speak to control and choreograph the imagery and music in real time. Novices can easily produce beautiful images and music, while experts can continue to refine their skills for complex forms of expression. Both the audience and the participant engage in a rich aesthetic interactive experience.

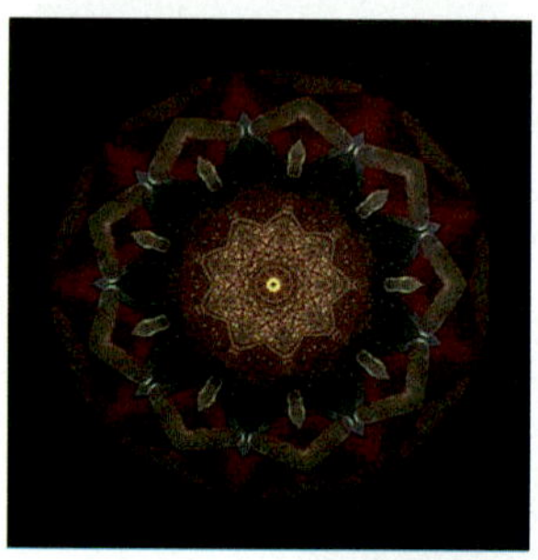

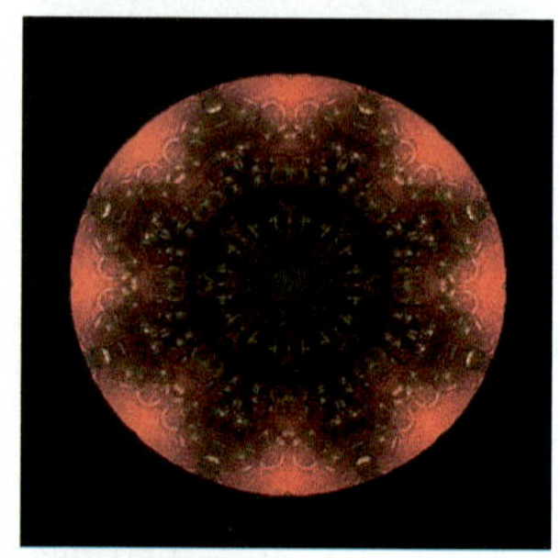

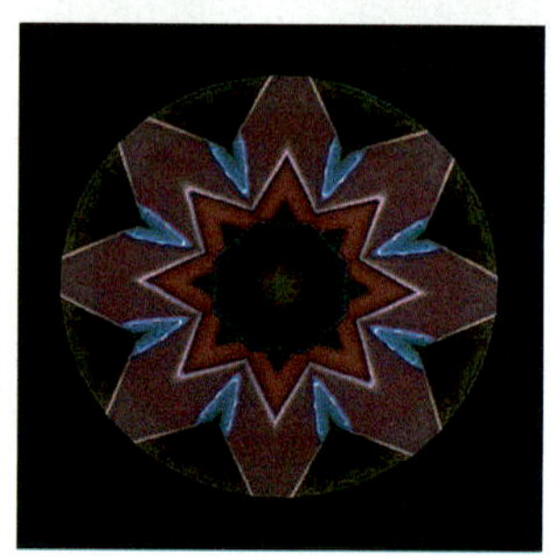

CONTACT
Sidney Fels
ATR Media Integration & Communication Research Laboratories
Seika-cho, Soraku-gun
Kyoto 619-02, JAPAN
fels,mase@mic.atr.co.jp

COLLABORATORS
Dirk Reiners and Kenji Mase

Makoto Sato

In this cave-like virtual space, participants use visual, auditory, and tactile sensations to perceive and interact with objects. A new human-scale haptic device, Big SPIDAR, couples haptic sensations with vision and audition, and displays various aspects of force feedback associated mainly with contact, weight, and inertia.

In Virtual Basketball, players feel the weight and the spherical shape of the virtual ball at any position inside the playing space and experience the illusion of natural control over the ball.

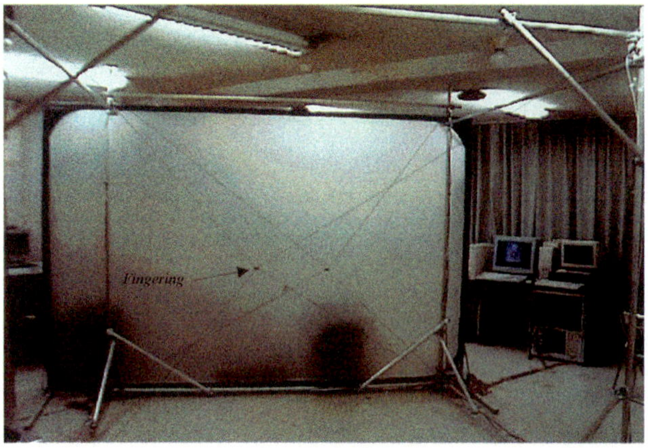

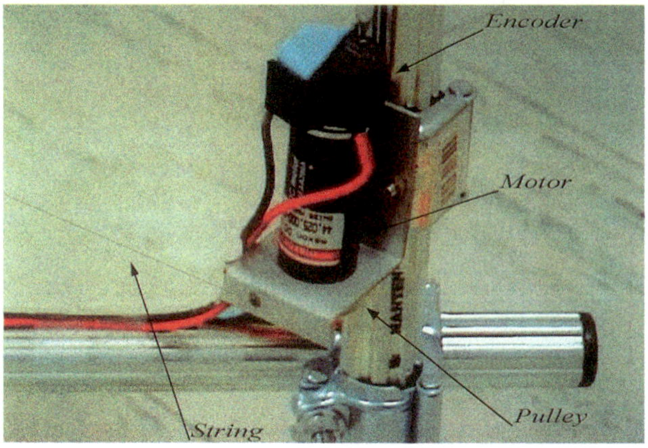

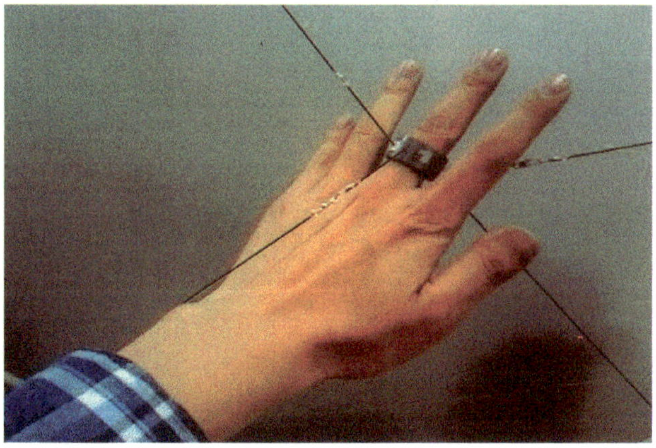

CONTACT
Makoto Sato
Precision and Intelligence Laboratory
Tokyo Institute of Technology
226 Yokohama
4259 Nagatsuta-cho
Midori-ku, JAPAN
msato@pi.titech.ac.jap

COLLABORATORS
Iguchi Yasuo, Hatano Ken, and Laroushi Bouguila

In perceiving an event, we alter that event to suit our own purposes. In making an image of an event, we apply this alteration of the real to the image-making process. Thus, in perceiving an image of a non-fictional event, we generate a perception that is twice removed from the actual event. How much of the meaning perceived in a non-fiction image is derived from the subject matter, and how much is derived from formal visual elements? Where does the real become abstract?

ants under a mushroom, an interactive collage in which the participant "paints" with moving and still images, addresses these issues by examining the relationship between the formal elements of a non-fiction image and its content, and in the process examines the notion that an image can be real (non-fictional, representational) or non-real (abstract).

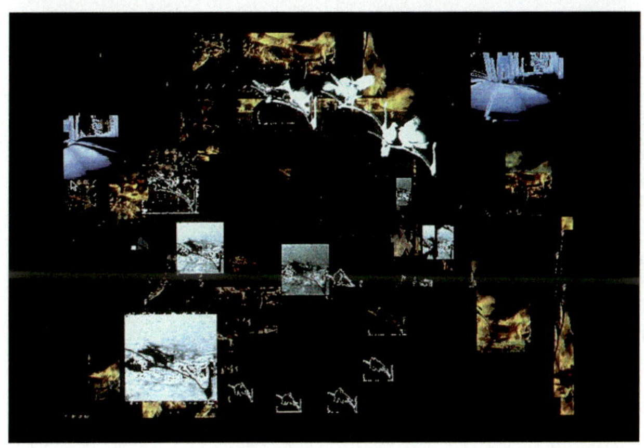

CONTACT
Amy Alexander
School of Film/Video
California Institute of the Arts
24700 McBean Parkway
Valencia, California 91355 USA
amy@emsh.calarts.edu

There has been a recent proliferation of video cameras on the World Wide Web. Ordinary people and places are instantly subject to becoming part of the mass culture and are also potentially subject to cultural recycling. The Multi-Cultural Recycler puts a tongue-in-cheek spin on this phenomenon.

When a visitor accesses the Multi-Cultural Recycler, the Recycler selects two or three camera Web sites at random and captures the live or latest image from their cameras. The Recycler then performs digital image processing on these images to "recycle" them into a new image. Since the actual process used is also selected at random, each access to the Recycler site produces a unique image.

Visitors can also look in "The Recycling Bin" to see the source images that comprise their recycled image and link to the images' original websites to learn their original context.

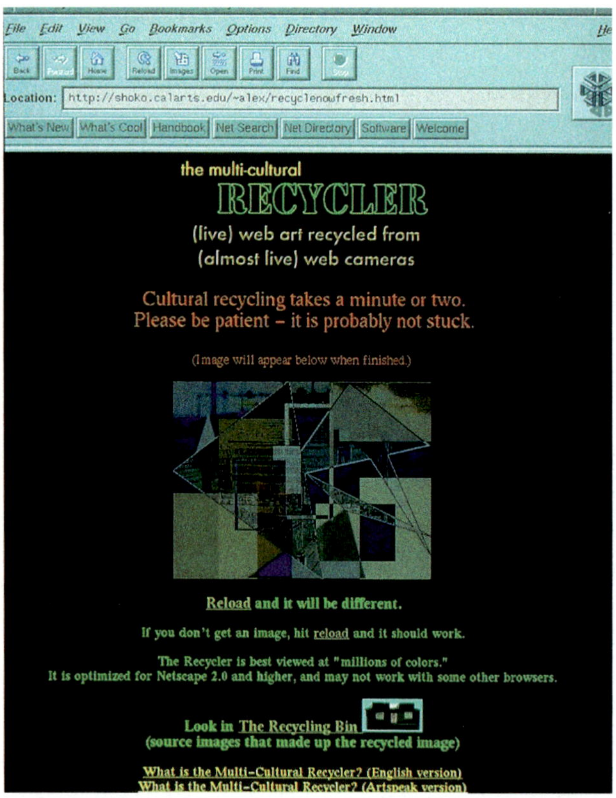

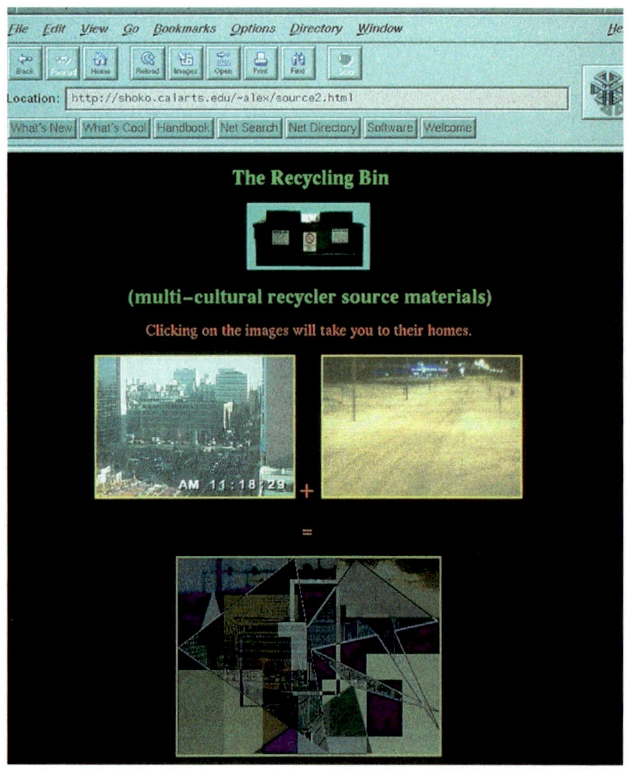

CONTACT
Amy Alexander
School of Film/Video
California Institute of the Arts
24700 McBean Parkway
Valencia, California 91355 USA
amy@emsh.calarts.edu
http://shoko.calarts.edu/~alex/recycler.html

COLLABORATORS
Tom Erbe, Palle Henckel, Sara Roberts, Steev Hise, Michael Scroggins, and Jeff Ballard

In a room with large-screen walls, where animated virtual players hold different musical instruments, the visitor, wearing data gloves, conducts a musical performance, leading the tempo with one hand and, with the other, directing aspects of the performance (a string crescendo, for example). The players show features of human behavior: they pay attention when the conductor begins, and they continue playing for awhile if the conductor ceases, but they soon return to playing nonsense. Through amplified speakers, the visitor can also experience the acoustics of the surrounding virtual concert hall. Alternative acoustic environments (open space, concert hall, church) and pieces in different musical styles can be selected from a menu.

Various techniques are used to produce this fully synthetic experience: rule-based agents for players' behavior, neural networks for response to the conductor, physical instrument modeling for the sound synthesis, real-time reverberation simulation for the hall acoustics, and auralization filters for 3D sound.

CONTACT
Tapio Takala
Department of Computer Science
Helsinki University of Technology
02150 Espoo, FINLAND
tapio.takala@hut.fi
http://www.cs.hut.fi/~tta/

COLLABORATORS
Jarmo Hiipakka, Rami Hånninen, Tommi Ilmonen, Hannu Napari, Tapio Lokki, Lauri Savioja, Jyri Huopaniemi, Matti Karjalaninen, Tero Tolonen, Vesa Vålimåki, Seppo Vålimåki, and Tapio Takala

This virtual reality application is used as a testbed for Intelligent Vehicle Highway Systems and virtual prototyping. One of its main goals is to investigate the level of fidelity required for various human factors studies.

Vehicle dynamics are computed by a 13-degree-of-freedom vehicle simulation with over 130 parameters. The vehicle is controlled by inputs obtained from a steering wheel, an accelerator pedal, and a brake pedal. From these inputs, the vehicle dynamics provide visual, aural, and haptic feedback to the driver. The simulation also uses the inputs to update the vehicle's positions, speed, and orientation in the virtual world. A unique low-speed algorithm allows the vehicle to come to a stop without the singularity caused in classical vehicle dynamic simulations.

To provide drivers with a realistic steering feel, control loading (haptics) has been carefully implemented. Real-time vehicle dynamics generate the torque applied to the steering wheel, which greatly enhances the driver's immersive experience and creates a more compelling driving scenario for testing and evaluation

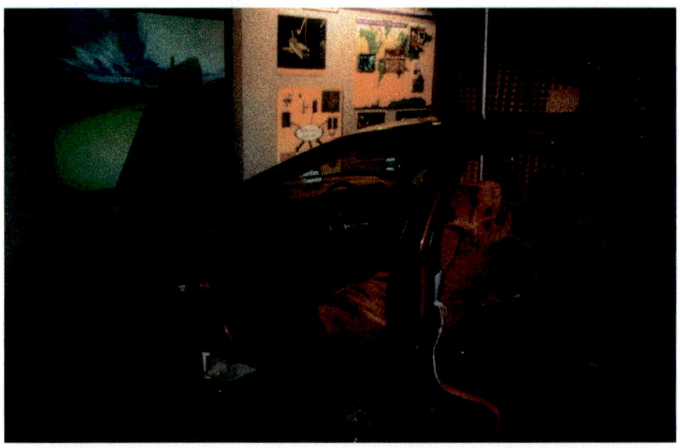

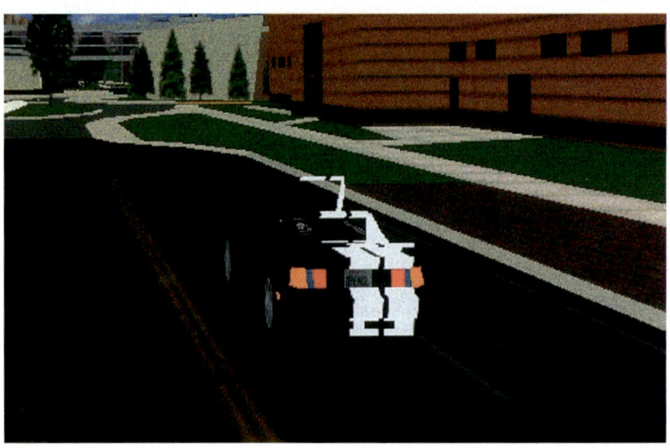

CONTACT
James Gruening
Iowa Center for Emerging Manufacturing Technology
Iowa State University
2062 Black Engineering
Ames, Iowa 50011 USA
honyamda@iastate.edu
http://www.icemt.iastate.edu

COLLABORATORS
James Gruening
Chris Clover
James Bernard
James Oliver
Iowa Center for Emerging Manufacturing Technology

ACKNOWLEDGEMENTS
Uli Lechner
Allen Bierbaum

Hiroo Iwata

Visual immersion plays an important role in virtual environments. A head-mounted-display (HMD) provides full solid-angle views of virtual space. However, the HMD's optical system limits its field of view. One alternative display system is a large screen. Another alternative is a dome screen or a cubic screen. But those alternatives require large theater-like spaces, which restricts their general use for computer-human interaction. Moreover, existing configurations of large-screen systems do not provide full solid-angle perspectives around the viewer.

In Garnet Vision, the emphasis is on how to build a full solid-angle display in a limited space. Two criteria were established to optimize space utilization:

1 Pixel efficiency (how many pixels are projected on each polygon of a polyhedral screen).

2 Space efficiency (the ratio of displayed polyhedra to overall dead volume of the rear-projection screen).

Thorough examination of these criteria led to selection of a rhombic dodecahedron. The dodecahedron screen, in which a viewer can stand, was built with 12 projectors in a space the size of a normal room. Each projector also has a speaker that generates sound.

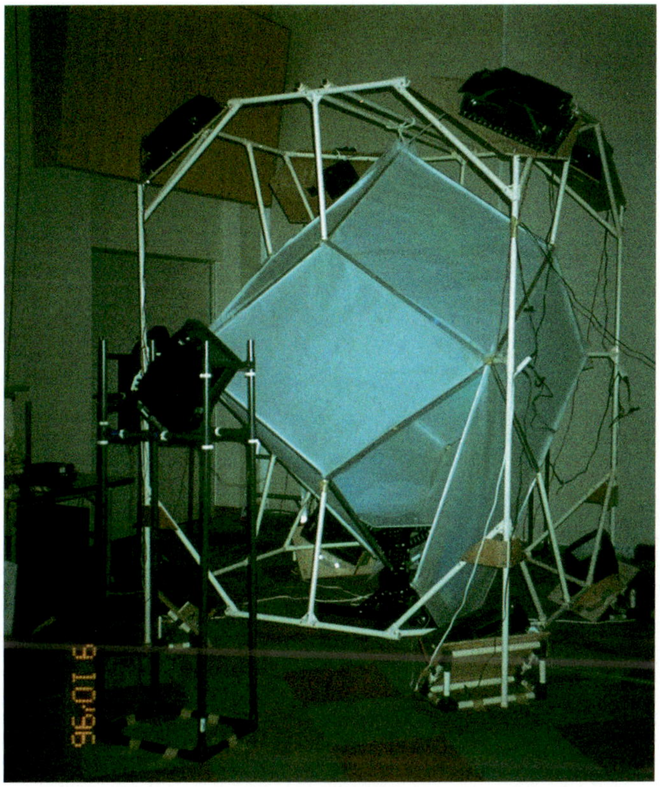

CONTACT
Hiroo Iwata
Institute of Engineering Mechanics
University of Tsukuba
Tsukuba, 305 JAPAN
iwata@kz.tsukuba.ac.jp

COLLABORATORS
Wataru Hashimoto, Atsuro Zchigaya, and Yoshinori Asada

Journey into the Brain is a story-based interactive CD-ROM funded by a research grant from the National Institute of Mental Health. It takes children between seven and 11 years of age on an adventure inside the most complex and mysterious organ of all: the human brain.

It's the year 2050, and something inside the brain of your best friend Celeste is causing her to act strangely. You must find out what it is and solve the mystery. Your guide and vehicle for this adventure is an advanced computer mouse that uses nanotechnology to shrink you for travel into Celeste's brain.

You collect bits of memory scattered throughout the various parts of the brain to solve the mystery. Twelve landscapes and twenty characters representing diverse facets of brain structure provide the backdrop and content for your journey. The program has three parts: a story/game, six activities, and a Brainarium filled with fascinating neuroscience material.

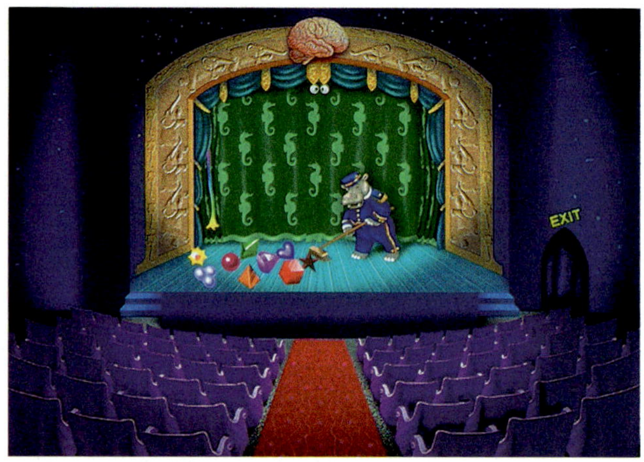

CONTACT
Karen G. Littman
Morphonix
94 Windsor Drive
San Rafael, California 94901 USA
KMorphonix@aol.com

COLLABORATORS
Jay Leibold, Mary Brewer, Christine Gralapp, Madeline Preisner, John Allison, Gerald McDermott, Floyd Bloom, Steven Glotzbach, Margo Nanny, Richard Manzullo, Morgen Smith, and Andrea Silvestri

F.A.B.R.I.CATORS

The Multi Mega Book is an up-to-date electronic book sculpture – a magic and stimulating journey through some of the most intense moments of media, technology, science, architecture, culture. It was developed as a fully immersive interactive installation with high-resolution stereoscopic images.

Users explore and freely experience the different dimensions of the 15th Century and the 20th Century through virtual reality, stereoscopic 3D sound, and holophonic effects that generate a magical interactive navigation technique.

The past and the future converge on a unique, interactive, and navigable present as users walk, interact, and live in the revolutions of two very different eras: the Renaissance world and the cyber world, integrated in one unique environment.

The ambiance of the 15th Century features Italian buildings of the epoch (the Tempietto, the Laurentian Library, the New Sacristy, the Campidoglio, Il duomo Santa Maria del Fiore, Palazzo Pitty, Loggia degli Uffizi, etc.) integrated in one unique space. Sculptures extracted from their original context appear in imaginary squares. Paintings are displayed as gigantic scenery. Users explore the revival of the classics, the heliocentric theory, movable type, the printing press, and the printed book.

CONTACT
Yesi Maharaj Singh
F.A.B.R.I.CATORS
Via Fratelli Bronzetti 6
20129 Milano, ITALY
fabricat@galactica.it

COLLABORATORS
Dave Pape, Josephine Anstey, Daniele Marini, and F.A.B.R.I.CATORS staff

Alice is a development environment for creating interesting and interactive 3D worlds. It is designed for ease of learning and use by non-engineering high school and undergraduate students.

The typical state of the art in interactive 3D graphics development environments requires the author to know a high-level programming language such as C or C++, and to understand fairly high-level mathematical concepts like linear algebra and the behavior of 4x4 homogeneous transformation matrices. The goal of the Alice project is to lower these stiff entry requirements by providing an easy-to-learn toolkit and a set of powerful abstractions that cover a wide variety of interactions and behaviors across a broad range of 3D graphics application domains.

This latest version of Alice runs on Pentium PCs. It offers attendees the chance to gain some hands-on experience with the development environment, build their own worlds, and try their hands at both desktop and virtual reality applications built with Alice.

Alice is available free for Windows 95 platforms from:
http://alice.virginia.edu

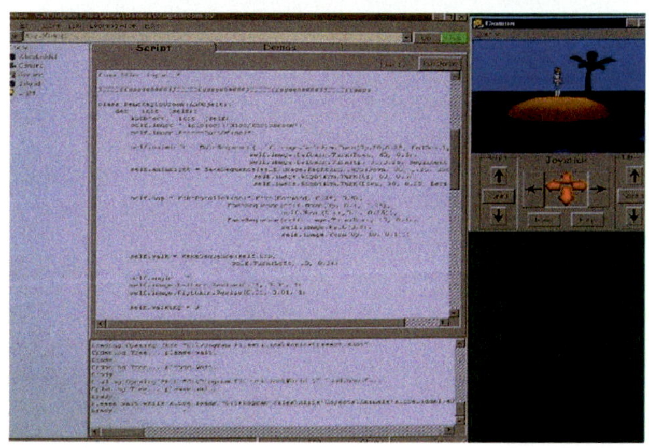

CONTACT
Jeff Pierce
User Interface Group
Carnegie Mellon University
5000 Forbes Avenue
Pittsburgh, Pennsylvania 15213 USA
jpiercet@cs.cmu.edu

Bunraku, the traditional Japanese puppet show, was originally established as one of the most popular entertainments in Japan a few hundred years ago. In a Bunraku play, a puppet is manipulated by three puppeteers: one for facial expressions and the other two for body movement.

Cyber Bunraku is an experimental system that supports manipulatior. of CG characters in real time. A facial expression tracker is used by the facial performer, while the puppeteering device for body movement is used by a traditional Bunraku puppeteer. The two performers create the 3D CG character's movements, behaviors, and emotions, which allows the audience to enjoy a brand-new traditional art form. The system was developed by Hitachi, Ltd. and Fuji Television Network, Inc.

CONTACT
Kiyoshi Arai
Central Research Laboratory
Hitachi, Ltd.
1-280 Higashi Koigakubo, Kokubunji
Tokyo 185, JAPAN
arai@crl.hitachi.co.jp

COLLABORATORS
Ken-ichi Anjyo, Yasuhiro Higashide, and Hiroshi Sakamoto

Tomas J. Filsinger

Ensconced in a structure suggesting an Aztec ceremonial temple, participants discover a richly detailed, interactively evolving map illustrating the rise and fall of civilizations in the Valley of Mexico over 3,000 years and the ensuing ecological transformation of the basin. Throughout the map, portals allow virtual visits to selected sites as they are believed to have looked at the heights of their development and as they appear today. Prehispanic music, performed on period instruments, provides an aural accompaniment to the visual experience, and the subtle scent of capal augments the sensation of presence in a different time and place.

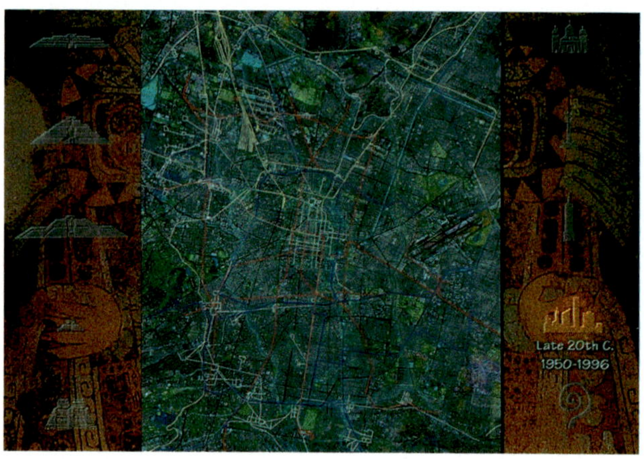

CONTACT
Tomas J. Filsinger
Apartado postal 5-325
Las Palmas
Cuernavaca, Morelos C.P. 62051 MEXICO
http://www.emersis.com.mx

COLLABORATORS
Antonio Gonzalez Cuesta and Luis Perez Ixoneztli

With the support of the National Science Foundation, this project explores the utility of physical immersion and multisensory perception to enhance science education. One objective of Project ScienceSpace is to investigate whether sensorially immersive, constructivist learning can remediate typical misconceptions in the mental models of reality held by many students. Another is to study whether mastery of traditionally difficult subjects (relativity and quantum mechanics, for example) is enhanced through learning-by-doing.

These subjects are difficult to teach because learners cannot draw analogies to personal experiences that provide metaphors for many science phenomena. ScienceSpace enables learners to experience these phenomena and inculcates an instinctive, qualitative understanding as a motivation and basis for future study. ScienceSpace now consists of three virtual worlds that address Newtonian mechanics, electrostatics, and molecular structure. So far, research has shown significant learning gains (compared with traditional approaches) on the part of both high school and college science students.

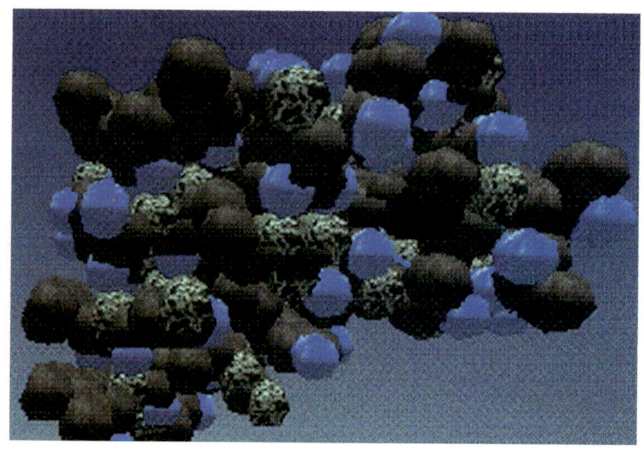

CONTACT
R. Bowen Loftin
Virtual Environment Technology Laboratory
University of Houston
4800 Calhoun, MS CSC-3475
Houston, Texas 77204-3475 USA
bowen@uh.edu

COLLABORATORS
Chris Dede and the National Science Foundation

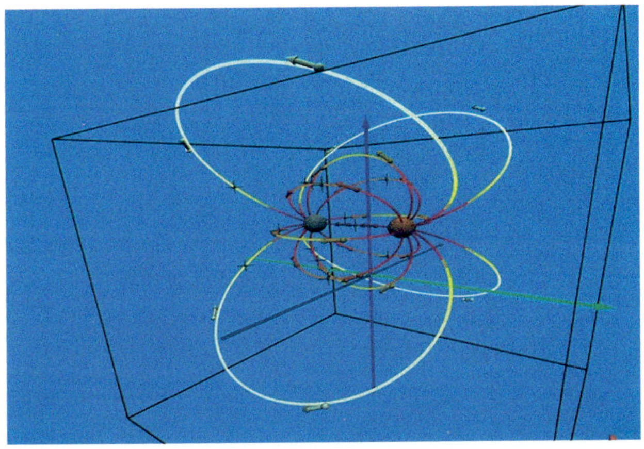

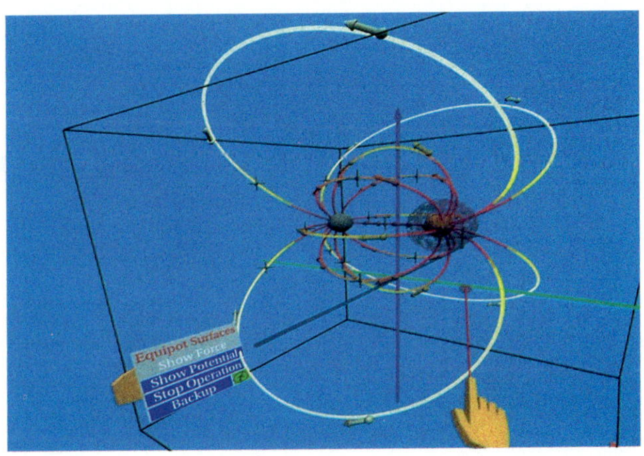
Equipot Surfaces
Show Force
Show Potential
Stop Operation
Backup

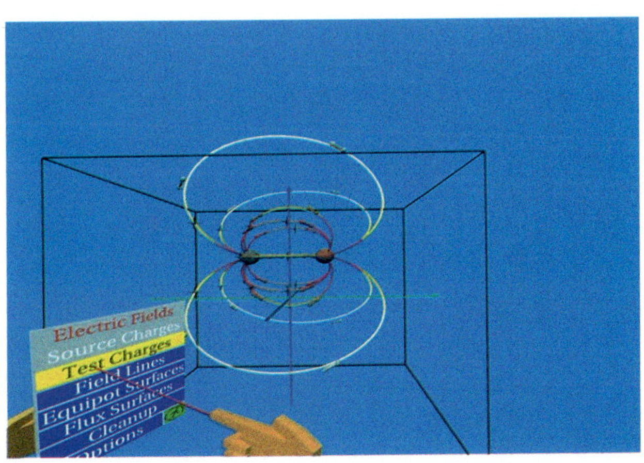
Electric Fields
Source Charges
Test Charges
Field Lines
Equipot Surfaces
Flux Surfaces
Cleanup

Paras Kaul

Mind Garden is a three-dimensional audio, visual, and neurolinguistic journey through a fractal garden environment. Using MindSet, a state-of-the-art interactive brainwave software, human brainwaves activate fractal forms, sounds, and words as objects in this VRML world. Growth in the Mind Garden is viewable on the World Wide Web and can be monitored at the Mind Garden Web site:

http://www.leonardo.net/virtualdesign.

The project combines the technologies associated with EEG, digital brainwave analysis, system design, the World Wide Web, and the synthesis of digital audio, visual, and linguistic media. Participants are asked to relax and focus their attention, which generates frequency variations in their brainwave signals, which in turn determine forms, sounds, and word objects.

The journey is determined by the brainwave activity derived from each user's own imagination. Participants who predominantly signal theta wave activity will experience a journey of greater complexity and focus, and participants experiencing beta brainwave activity may find the journey confusing and/or uneventful. The challenge is to experience the garden as controlled by theta and delta brainwave activity, thus perceiving a deeper and more complex view of the simulated reality. The goal is to achieve the ultimate experience in the Mind Garden by tuning one's frequencies to the deepest level.

The journey is best when participants have no food or alcohol in their digestive systems prior to their interactive experience.

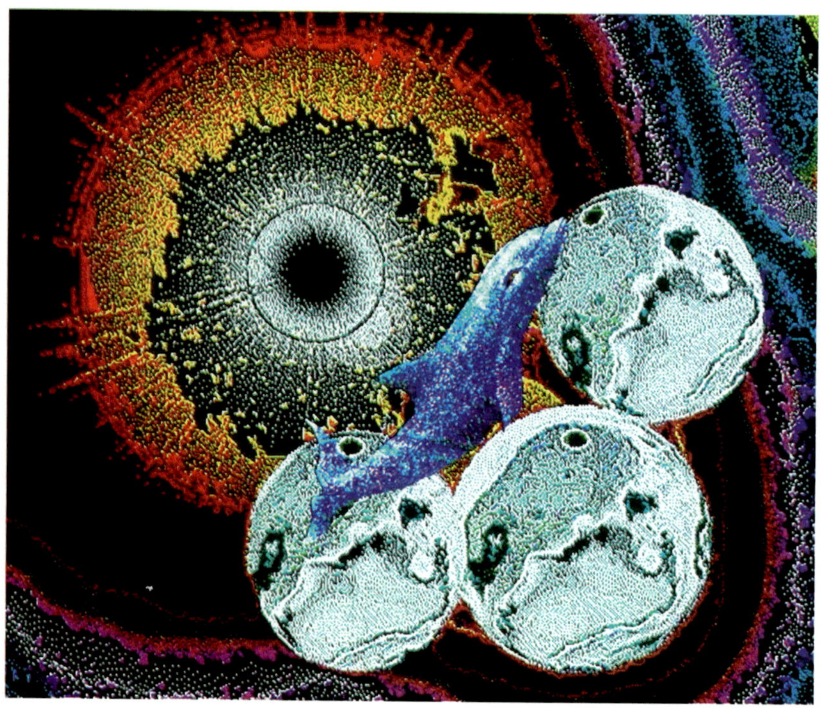

CONTACT
Paras Kaul
Paras West Productions
University of California, Santa Barbara
11714 Goshen Avenue, #204
Los Angeles, California 90049
parasw@well.com

COLLABORATORS
kf.Oe, Create Studio/University of California, Santa Barbara; Barry Keys; Crystl Peritore; Chris de Giere; Sergio Robledo; and Curtis Kosky

SPECIAL THANKS TO:
Terence McKenna, Shaman Au, Dave Cole, and Sunil Gupta

Wango: COMPOST (Compost) is an interactive system that places the audience in control of live video and audio feeds while they navigate through a real-time interface. The Wango Compost Processing Center (WCPC) combines data generated by portable recording technology attached to human vehicles called Decomposing Agents. At SIGGRAPH 97, these agents transmit audio/video information back across the Internet via the WCPC. Hosted by a virtual cyber-presence, both live and virtual attendees explore new ways of controlling media types through live interaction. The primary goal is for people not physically in Los Angeles for SIGGRAPH 97 to be able to experience as much interaction as a person attending the conference.

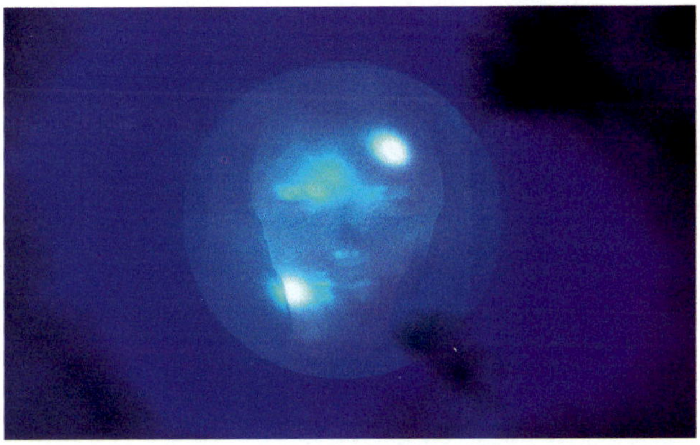

CONTACT
Cassandra Lehman
The CADRE Institute
San Jose State University
One Washington Square
San Jose, California 95192 USA
cas@riverview.com

PROJECT LEADER
Jeffery Cheung

PROJECT MANAGER, FINANCE COORDINATOR, CYBERHOST ANIMATOR
Paul Leuvano

WEBMASTERS
Thad Jones
Lamberto Alvaro

DIGITAL VIDEO DIRECTOR, TECHNICAL DIRECTOR
Sean Roach

DIGITAL VIDEO AND TECHNICAL ASSISTANTS
Tony Troung
Gerald Willie

AGENT AGENDAS
Mike Covington
Tony Troung

COMPOST PROCESSING, VIDEO TRANSMISSION
Mike Covinton
Jack Furlow
Mike Pyrch

CYBERHOST ANIMATOR
Will Ogden

COLLABORATORS
Ian Atchison, Jeffery Cheung, Corrine Jew, Lamberto Alvaro, Monica Arman, Don Hart, Thad Jones, Candy Murillo, Ed Muyco, Anthony Scannel, Lorena Vidrio

This simulation program was developed as a children's attraction for a municipal science museum. The scale of the venue did not permit a 60-fps projection system or computer-controlled moving seats. The system uses a network of personal computers to create a simulated experience that involves children in imaginative team play in an exciting space adventure.

Participants choose one of two roles. They either join a team of astronauts on an interstellar voyage or stay in Mission Control here in our Solar System, where they help the spaceship crew look for the secrets of the universe.

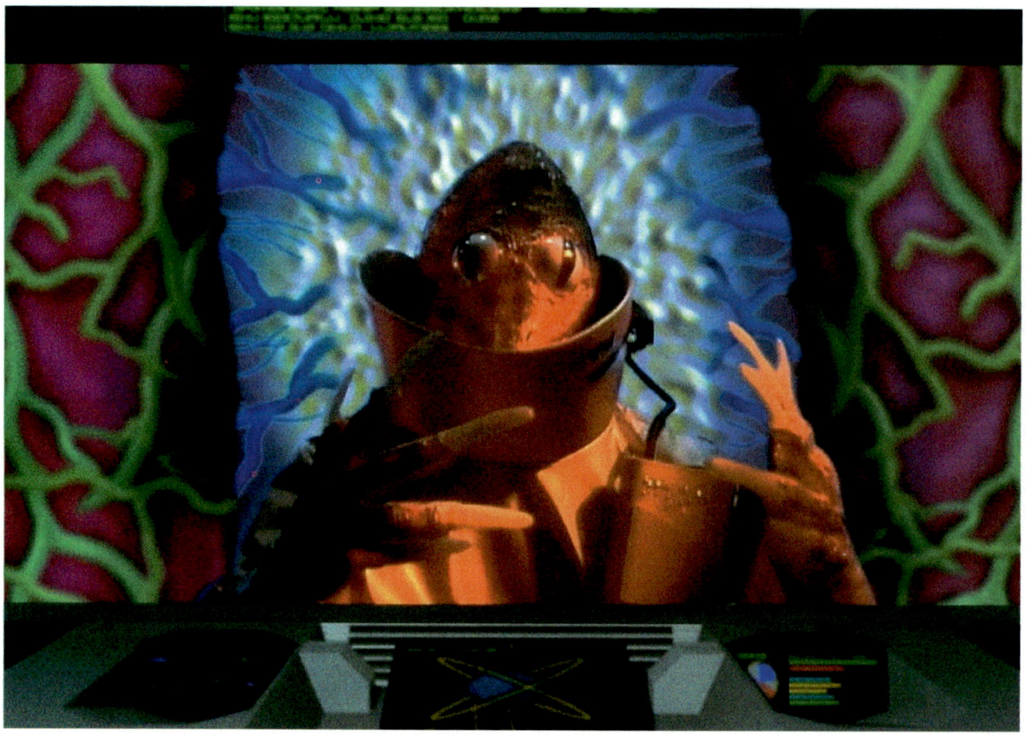

CONTACT
Yuichiro Kamata
Cyber Network Co., Ltd.
4th Floor, Shio-Seven Building
7-4 Honshio-cho
Shinjuku-ku, Tokyo 160, JAPAN
you@cyber-net.co.jp

CONTACT
Nobu Masuda
Cyber Entertainment, Inc.
5111 Denny Avenue, #10
North Hollywood, California 91601 USA
masuda@cyber-net.co.jp
CYBERENTER@aol.com

COLLABORATORS
Tanseisha Co., Ltd.
Yaizu Discovery Park

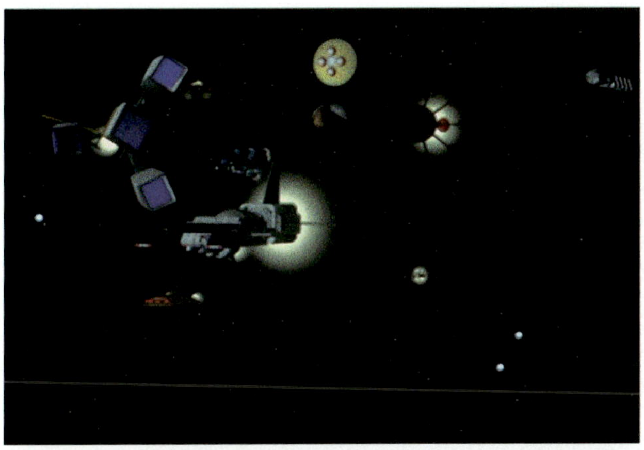

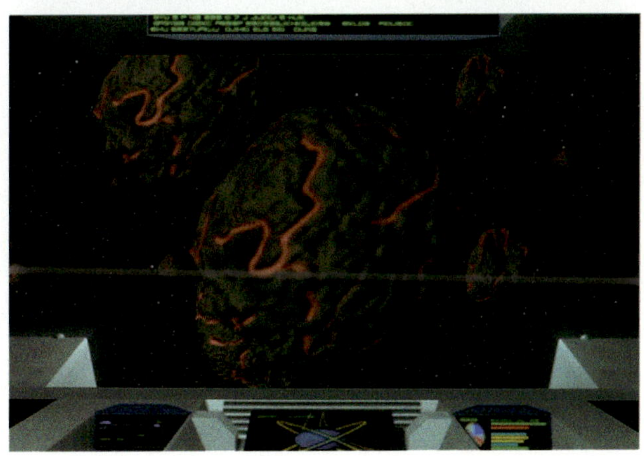

Dancing Fire and Water is an artistic expression of sounds and images of two of the earth's great energies: Norway's Jostedal glacier and Japan's Owakudani volcano. It is an encounter between fire and water, two of the four fundamental elements in the universe. Live communication via ISDN is maintained between Jostedalsbreen, a growing glacier; Owakudani, an active volcano in Japan's Hakone; and SIGGRAPH 97 in Los Angeles.

The essential dilemma for artists is how to involve themselves with humans' inner feelings in life beyond terminals. There are digital and analog networks in the human world, and there are two kinds of worlds: virtual reality and authentic reality. Like a dream, these networks come and go between the space-time of these two realities. These worlds also generate new, imaginative, and creative art. These circumstances will radically change human existence in the future.

CONTACT
Vigdis Holen
Vig's Kunstlab
Firdavegen 22
68960 Sandne, NORWAY
vigdis@axp1.vestdata.no

COLLABORATORS
Keigo Yamamoto, Jaroslaw Hollan, Ole Johnny Devik, Akihiko Shibata, Junji Tsudada, Ayuka Yamazaki, Tomoko Shibata, Kazumi Kinoshita, Sachiko Kurihara, Hisashi Wakabayoshi, Tadahiro Tazumi, Chiaki Matsumura, and others

Fantasy^3

J. Michael Moshell, David Haxton, Charles E. Hughes, Mark Kilby, and Jerry Gardner

Theme parks, movies, and virtual environments have much in common. Some have even claimed that simulated experiences will render theme parks obsolete. A partnership between the University of Central Florida and Disney i.d.e.a.s in Orlando is experimenting with the concurrent creation of an animated movie and a Web-based virtual experience above a theme park: Disney/MGM Studios. The key question: how can virtual world-building and animated film-making inform each other?

Fantasy^3 is a year-long Senior Design Project involving 30 undergraduate students from six academic departments, four faculty members, and several graduate students. The animated film concerns a group of aliens in a tour bus/spacecraft who visit the park and have typical tourist experiences, with a twist. The virtual world is similar, and some of the same experiences are available, but the story may turn out differently.

CONTACT
J. Michael Moshell
University of Central Florida
Computer Science Department
Orlando, Florida 32751 USA
moshell@cs.ucf.edu

COLLABORATORS
The students of the CREAT Program

PRoP: Personal Roving Presence

Eric Paulos

In the rush into cyberspace, we leave our physical presence and our real-world environment behind. The Internet, undoubtedly a remarkable modern communications tool, still does not empower us to enter the real world of the person at the other end of the connection. We cannot look out their window, admire their furniture, talk to their office mates, tour their laboratory, or walk outside. We lack the equivalent of a body or Personal Roving Presence (PRoP) at the other end with which we can move around in, communicate through, and observe with. However, by combining elements of computer graphics, the Internet, and tele-robotics it is possible to transparently immerse users into navigable real remote worlds filled with rich spatial sensorium and to make such systems accessible from any networked computer in the world, in essence: globally accessible tele-embodiment.

We have populated the Electric Garden with several special tele-robots including several ground-based surface cruisers and a few space-browsing airborne blimps to provide the sensation of tele-embodiment. Drivers and pilots control these PRoPs and experience their remote world through live two-way audio and video. Attendees can also control and interact with separate virtual PRoPs inhabiting a simulated world that exhibits realistic physical and dynamic behavior.

CONTACT
Eric Paulos
University of California, Berkeley
Computer Science Department
387 Soda Hall
Berkeley, California 94720-1776 USA
paulos@cs.berkeley.edu

COLLABORATORS
John Canny and Francesca Barrientos

Mary Whitton, Gary Bishop, Fred Brooks, Nick England, Henry Fuchs, Anselmo Lastra, Dinesh Manoch, John Poulton, and Russell Taylor

Walkthrough
Interactive visualizations for design of complex environments containing millions of primitives, such as those of houses and ships, are severely limited by the frame rates obtainable using current graphics workstations. Use of advanced model-management techniques to reduce model complexity, while retaining essential visual information, makes interactive walkthroughs feasible. In this interactive experience, the user walks through a very large, complex model. It illustrates a variety of model-management techniques, such as visibility culling, dynamic tessellation of higher-order surfaces, static and dynamic model simplification, and textured impostors, to enable rendering at interactive rates.

http://www.cs.unc.edu/~walk

nanoManipulator
The nanoWorkbench adds a PHANToM force-feedback device to a rear-projected display to allow the user to touch the objects that are displayed. This overlay of the visual with haptic spaces provides the sense of a solid object that can be prodded and molded by the user. The nanoManipulator system is connected to an atomic-force microscope to allow participants to move, bend, and stack "bucky tubes" on a sub-micron playing field.

http://www.cs.unc.edu/Research/nano.

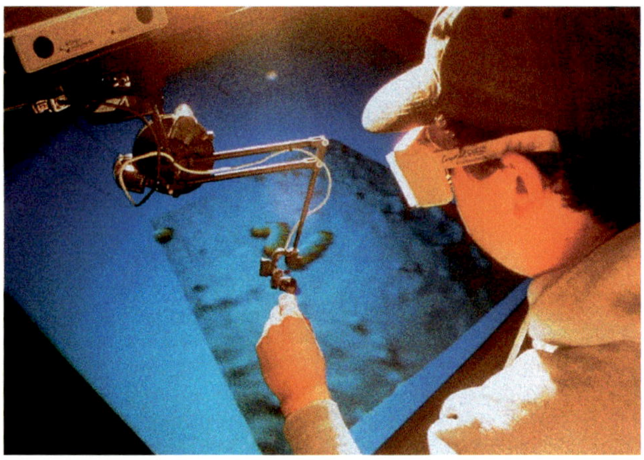

CONTACT
Mary Whitton
Department of Computer Science
University of North Carolina
Chapel Hill, North Carolina 27599-3175 USA
whitton@cs.unc.edu

Image-based Rendering

In the past few years, a new method of rendering has received a great deal of attention. This new approach, image-based rendering, uses one or more reference images as the basic primitive in contrast to the geometry used in traditional rendering. Since the reference images may be directly acquired from the environment through photography or video, image-based rendering promises to deliver a level of realism that has, so far, been unobtainable using traditional rendering. In this experience, the user walks though a real-world scene rendered from a set of captured reference images, rather than from traditional geometric models.

Sunset Boulevard

Margaret Crane, Dale MacDonald, Scott Minneman, and Jon Winet

Interactive narrative hits the street. Motorists on Hollywood's legendary Sunset Boulevard activate and control a drive-by soap opera playing on two outdoor billboard-sized TVs at Billboard Live, a high-tech nightclub.

Two ubiquitous consumer technologies (radio car-security keyfobs and garage-door openers) allow the story to be steered by radio signals from the passing vehicles of this driven metropolis. Viewer participation ignites curiosities about quotidian dramas and life behind closed doors as the electronic garage door, on the screen, opens to reveal unexpected secrets. A soundtrack is transmitted on an ultra-low-power radio station associated with the displays.

Viewers at the Los Angeles Convention Center also observe and participate in the Sunset proceedings.

CONTACT
Scott Minneman
Xerox PARC
3333 Coyote Hill Road
Palo Alto, California 94304 USA
minneman@parc.xerox.com

This is an experience of being in a fey place with an active population of "little people." You are standing in a fairy ring of mushrooms in a tiny valley surrounded by bushes and rock walls, lit by the golden glow of the late afternoon sun. The bushes are real, the rock walls are cloth, the golden glow comes from the far end of the valley, which is a virtual reality projection wall. In the real bushes around you, you hear the rustle and squeak of tiny people, busy with their unseen lives. In one of the real side walls is a tiny grotto in which tiny virtual shapes are dancing to bright music. When you approach, they "poof" in alarm. In the other side wall is a tiny virtual waterfall that "splashes" off your hand when you reach out to touch it. In the virtual end of the garden, you see small people who go about their errands until you get too close, when they squeak in dismay and hide.

Faery Garden uses virtual reality, MIDI sound, theatrical techniques, and real world objects to blur the real and imaginary worlds together into a compelling visit to a magical place.

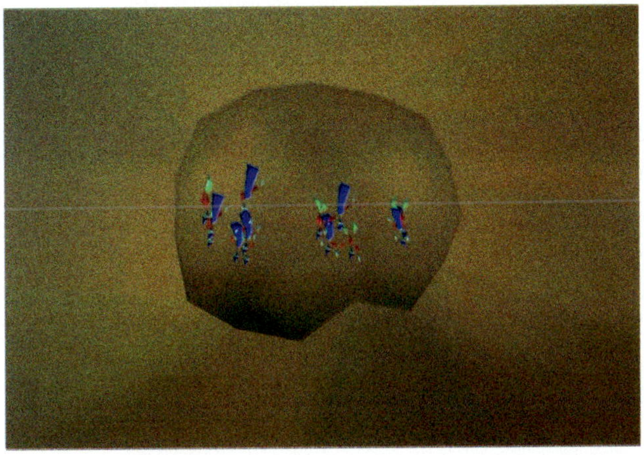

CONTACT
Eben Gay
2 Moore Road
Southboro, Massachusetts 01772 USA
eben@ergeng.com

COLLABORATORS
Eben Gay, Amatul Hannan, Brenden Maher, Colin Owens, Eric Pierce, and Ann Powers

The Land of Time is a 3D puzzle that consists of two different stages. In the game part, a puzzle is presented. Clock parts are delivered onto the stage. When dragged, they move, snap, drop, and bounce. By solving the puzzle, or just playing with it, the user creates the other stage: the result stage. At first, the result stage is just blank. As the clock is assembled piece by piece, the result stage accumulates more and more elements. When the puzzle is completed, the clock starts ticking, and "time starts to flow" in the result stage.

The images and/or animations in the result stage are personal impressions of time and people. We are all bound to time; there are no exceptions. While time itself is rather hard for us to feel, a clock provides the illusion that it is controlling us with its own power.

CONTACT
Youn H. Lee
11215 Research Boulevard, #2168
Austin, Texas 78759 USA
youn@sva.edu

Chuck Lexa

The VEAT is a three-dimensional interactive tutor designed to teach and refresh students on the fundamentals of air traffic control. It utilizes virtual environments, voice recognition, 3D sound, and artificial intelligence (AI) to provide a complete adaptive training system. AI allows the tutor to adapt to individual students, which ensures that they receive proper training without the presence of an instructor. In addition, the virtual world can be made specific to an airport, providing on-site training and allowing for faster site certification while reducing training costs.

CONTACT
Chuck Lexa
Human Resources Directorate
Armstrong Laboratory
7909 Lindbergh Drive
Brooks Air Force Base, Texas 78235 USA
lexa@alhrt.brooks.af.mil

COLLABORATORS
Jim Fleming, Iler, James Marvin, Amn Shan Pomeroy, and Wes Regian

MEDIA^3: the Virtual Hologram

Masahiko Inami, Naoki Kawakami, Taro Maeda, and Susamu Tachi

The MEDIA^3 (MEDIA CUBE) consists of liquid crystal displays arranged in the shape of a cubic body. In coordination with the motion of an operator's head and the MEDIA^3, synthesized images of virtual objects (an insect, a tropical fish, artworks, a medical image, etc.) located inside the MEDIA^3 appear on each LCD. The effect is exactly the opposite of that generated by an OMNIMAX or CAVE system. Instead of an operator located inside the virtual world, operators of the MEDIA^3 see an inner virtual world from outside. In other words, the MEDIA^3 is an object-oriented display.

CONTACT
Masahiko Inami
Tachi Laboratory
MEIP Faculty of Engineering
University of Tokyo
7-3-1 Hongo, Bunkyo-ku
Tokyo 113, JAPAN
minami@star.t.u-tokyo.ac.jp

COLLABORATORS
Fumihiro Endo and Toshitomo Ohba

A revolutionary, entirely new prototype, Big Head Racer has been created with the objective of personalizing video racing entertainment experiences. It allows participants to see a live video image of themselves in the cockpit of a futuristic racing machine, competing against other drivers (whose heads also appear in their cars) in a race for the finish line!

For the first time, players pilot their own machines! Unlike games that provide generic heroes (or no driver at all), Big Head Racer does not require users to imagine that they are in control of the vehicle, because they're right there on the screen! Big Head Racer modules are linked for the ultimate in competitive experiences, so players can go head to head for the checkered flag!

CONTACT
Valerie Dunford
VIVID GROUP
317 Adelaide Street West, Suite 302
Toronto, Ontario M5V 1P9 CANADA
valerie@vividgroup.com
http://www.vividgroup.com

COLLABORATORS
David Bennett and Jim May

Hiroshi Usuda

Currently, the personal computer is the core of most intelligent, integrated consumer electronics and communication systems. Like GUI's in the computer industry, these intelligent audio/visual, computer/communication (AVCC) systems lack a standardized, truly intuitive user interface. This presents a serious problem for novice users.

Ultra Magic Paper Interface is a new type of user interface based on tactile input on plain paper, featuring ease-of-use and unified operation for AVCC systems. The system's ease of operation and extensibility have been enthusiastically received by test users.

CONTACT
Hiroshi Usuda
Architecture Laboratories
Sony Corporation
6-7-35 Kitashinagawa, Shinagawa-ku
Tokyo 141, JAPAN
usuda@sys.ptg.sony.co.jp

COLLABORATORS
Mitsuhiro Miyazaki, Ikuhiko Nishio, Motohiro Kobayashi, Takashi Hosoda, Yuko Tsukamura, and Ken Kubota

The Virtual Explorer project seeks to create highly interactive virtual environments for stimulating, immersive science learning experiences that are not possible with textbook-based approaches. The current system provides a realistic and content-rich environment for teaching basic immunology.

Students navigate through the bloodstream, the lymph system, and infected tissue of a patient, performing the assigned tasks and functions of the immune system from various first-person points of view, and enhancing their integrated understanding of its complex processes.

The virtual environment simulates the viewscreen of a nanobot that has been injected into a human body. It includes detailed, biologically accurate models of cells and proteins of the immune system and bloodstream, which are rendered in real-time during the simulation.

Eventually, the Virtual Explorer project will be extended to include additional fields of science education.

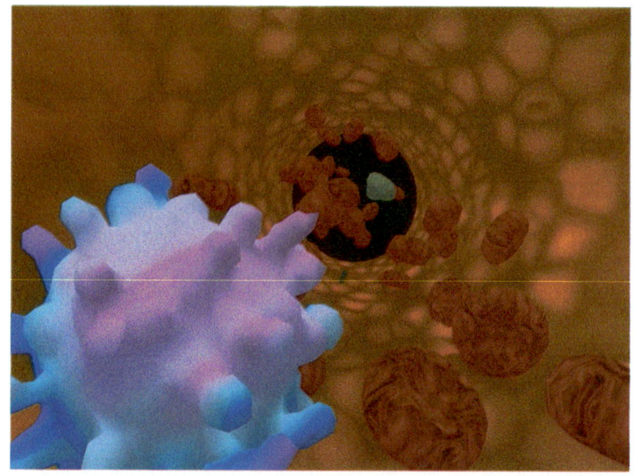

CONTACT
Kevin Dean
Senses Bureau
University of California, San Diego
9500 Gilman Drive, 0339
La Jolla, California 92093 USA
kld@chem.ucsd.edu
http://www-wilson.ucsd.edu/ve/

COLLABORATORS
Kevin Dean, Evan Finn, Jeremy Friesner, Bret Naylor, Sarah Wustner, Kent Wilson, and Scott Fisher

WonderSpace is a browser for visualizing a virtual world in cyberspace, where lifelike creatures act according to VRML 2.0 and a specification for skeleton animation. Through human-like avatars, WonderSpace realizes voice or sound communication in multi-user cyberspace. Technical features include compression/decompression of shape data and motion data, modified motions generated from a base motion, motion connecting, and synchronizing motion with sound.

At SIGGRAPH 97, WonderSpace technology provides three interactive experiences:

1. DayDream is the virtual-life world for voice chats via human-like avatars.

2. Wonder KARAOKE is a virtual KARAOKE world with dancing avatars.

3. Wonder ShrineOmikuji is a virtual Japanese shrine with interactive avatars that seek to attain "Omikuji," a Japanese technique for predicting the future.

CONTACT
Toshiya Naka, Yoshiyuki Mochizuki
Multimedia Development Center
Matsushita Electric Industrial Co., Ltd.
1006 Kadoma, Kadoma-shi
Osaka 571, JAPAN
naka@isl.mei.co.jp
Mochik@isl.mei.co.jp

COLLABORATORS
Shigeo Asahara (Team Director) and Michiharu Katsuda (Programmer)

Direct Manipulation Scene Creation in 3D: Estimating Hand Postures from Multiple-Camera Images

Akira Utsumi

In virtual reality systems, virtual objects and scenes have so far been created manually, or semi-automatically, by a variety of computer graphics utility software. This approach, however, is time consuming and demanding.

In this alternative approach, the system allows users to create different colors and shapes of virtual objects in 3D spaces by direct manipulation. It is based on a proprietary, multiple-camera-based hand posture estimation method, in which palm poses are estimated from multiple-camera images by a statistical approach regardless of finger bending. Then, hand gestures associated with commands for direct manipulation are recognized by verifying the finger bending.

With this system, participants create virtual 3D scenes by giving predefined commands with their own hands, to which no sensing devices are attached. Since the virtual scenes are displayed on a 3D display, participants feel as though the virtual scenes are real 3D spaces, even though they are not encumbered by technological equipment.

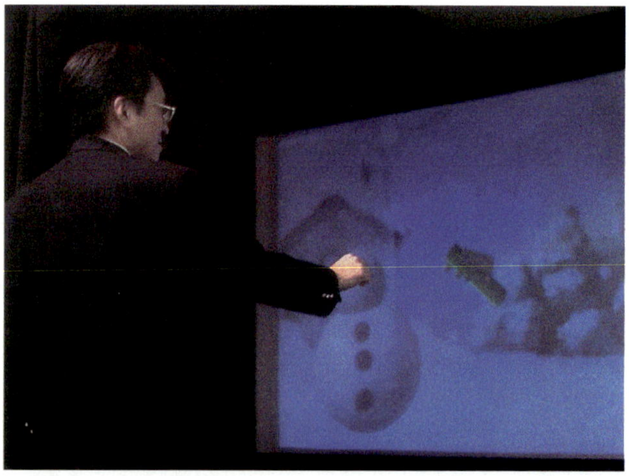

CONTACT
Akira Utsumi
ATR Media Integration & Communications Research Laboratories
2-2 Hikaridai. Seika-cho, Soraku-gun
Kyoto 619-02, JAPAN
utsumi@mic.atr.co.jp

COLLABORATORS
Jun Kurumisawa, Takahiro Otsuka, and Jun Ohya

Robert Dunn

In a studio atmosphere extending across time zones, students imagine and filter realities and cultures, and offer personal views on life potentials. They share art, visions, experiences, and adventures through creative efforts in animation, multimedia, Web site development, and telecommunications.

Works flowing from HORIZONS represent destinations and directions, expand understanding through new knowledge and contact, and reference or interpret explorations and discoveries of the past, present, and future.

Regional and international sites support experimentation in CG animation, interactive and object-oriented multimedia, QuickTime movies, dynamic Web site production, and Internet videoconferencing. Artists and mentors collaborate with young students in networked studio environments alive with concepts and conviviality, where narratives and realized works are communicated to remote partners via the Internet and a dedicated server.

Participating sites include:

- Duquesne University School of Education, Pittsburgh, Pennsylvania USA
- YBG Studio for Technology & The Arts, San Francisco, California USA
- New Orleans Center for Creative Arts, New Orleans, Louisiana, USA
- Local high schools, Los Angeles, California USA
- Israel Museum Youth Wing, Jerusalem, Israel
- K-bit Institute and CGT Kids World, Japan

CONTACT
Robert Dunn
Arc Vertuel, Inc.
School of Education
Duquesne University
111 The Oaks
Pittsburgh, Pennsylvania 15215 USA
rd1s+@andrew.cmu.edu
http://www.telecommunity.org

COLLABORATORS
Melanie Carr, Rachel Gerstein, Susan Hazan, Carrie Lee, Sim Graves, Bill Weinman, Nathan Fullerton, Sergio Ferdman, Alex Leltchouk, Gunhan Danisman, Andrew McCain, Keigo Yamamoto, Nobuo Yoshikawa and students from Pittsburgh, San Francisco, Los Angeles, Jerusalem, and Japan

Atsushi Yokoyama

This project presents two 3D imaging systems:

1. A stereo camera system that acquires a dense z-map for a scene. The prototype system demonstrates compositing of motion video and other real or even virtual segments, with full depth information and interaction between elements/actors in each segment. New algorithms considerably minimize occlusion and boundary overreach problems.

2. A real-time rangefinder that utilizes a dual-laser and single camera to calculate and display range information at video frame rates. A specially developed VLSI sensor with photodiodes integrated at the pixel level function as analog/digital micro-rangefinders, processing range data from an emitted laser for all pixels in parallel. The prototype demonstrates real-time range quantification of objects randomly selected by a user.

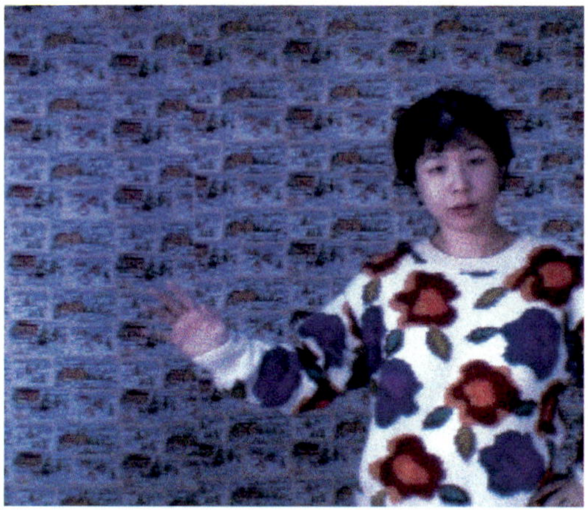

CONTACT
Atsushi Yokoyama
Hashimoto Signal Processing Lab
Sony Corporation
6-7-35 Kitashinagawa, Shinagawa-ku
Tokyo 141, JAPAN
ayoko@ius.ptg.sony.co.jp

COLLABORATORS
Jun Kurumisawa, Kazuyoshi Hayashi, Shinichi Yoshimura, Hideki Oyaizu, Takayuki Yoshigahara, and Yoko Miwa

In these two installations, participants enter two different rooms (which can be kilometers apart from each other) and virtually interact with each other in real time.

Point of Vue, Point of You

Images from two cameras, each one aimed into a separate space, are combined on two screens. By touching the screen, participants in each space select information from either of the two closed-circuit video cameras and, to a certain extent, create and organize their own images in real time and see them realized on the screen. In its constant displacements, the crowd in each space generates a group portrait and creates its own representation, which fills the space of each screen. The installation undermines the idea of belonging. Everybody's images is everybody else's. It is a visual mixture.

Body to Body

Participants' images are superimposed on images of others. Liberated of all technologies, they move freely to catch virtual objects that actually control their movements. As the participants' interaction evolves, the image of the others progressively vanishes from the screen, leaving viewers confronted only with their own images, as in a mirror.

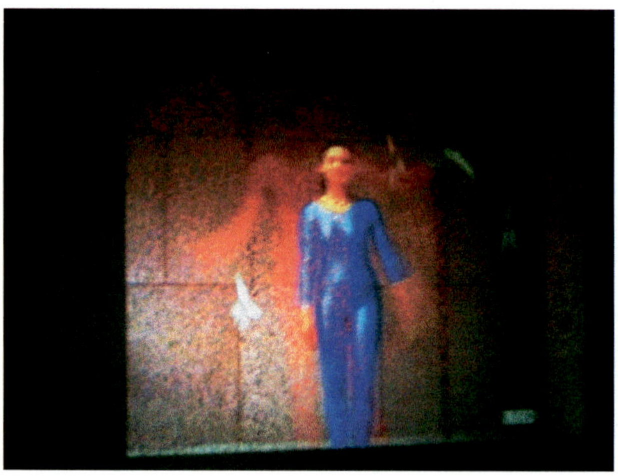

CONTACT
Elsa Mazeau
89, passage Emile Boutrais
94120 Fontenay sous Bois, FRANCE

COLLABORATORS
LTCM laboratory (University Paris VIII)

Optical Gesture Recognition System

Seiji Kobayshi

In this real-time human gesture recognition system, video images of a person are sent to a recognition module. The system does not require any sensors or cables to be attached to the subject's body. The key technology here is optical information processing. In the recognition module, video images taken by a CCD camera are presented to a holographic device that generates a vector representation of the gesture. The vector is then analyzed electronically to determine the gesture in real time.

CONTACT
Seiji Kobayashi
Advanced Development Laboratories
Sony Corproation
6-7-35 Kitashinagawa, Shinagawa-ku
Tokyo 141, JAPAN
seiji@devom.crl.sony.co.jp

COLLABORATORS
Yong Qiao, Ajay Chugh, Holoplex Corporation

Talking Head is a prototype product for a new generation of video conferencing. Video images projected on a bust give participants a true three-dimensional impression of their conversation partners, and implemented compensation algorithms generate eye-to-eye contact during the communication.

The effect is very interesting. At first, communication seems a little irritating, and astounding. But after a few moments, the user typically accepts the artificial "Talking Head" and feels comfortable with the communication. After some time, the user "forgets" about the fact that the communication partner is not real.

CONTACT
Gesellschaft für Mediales Gestalten GmbH
"The Virtual Company"
Kantstrasse 165
10623 Berlin, GERMANY
chris@well.com

Through virtual reality, Traffic Control offers a unique, interactive, highly entertaining, and completely new way of understanding traffic in urban environments. Users navigate in a very detailed model of Berlin, interactively choose their viewpoints (birds-eye, driver, bicycle, walking adult, little child), and interactively control traffic lights, signs, and vehicles.

A state-of-the-art simulation kernel shows highly realistic (chaotic) and complex traffic behavior in an environment of high-quality images generated by a Silicon Graphics Onyx2. Traffic Control is also suitable for real data input from street sensors.

CONTACT
Gesellschaft für Mediales Gestalten GmbH
"The Virtual Company"
Kantstrasse 165
10623 Berlin, GERMANY
chris@well.com

Magic Morphin Mirror: Face-Sensitive Distortion and Exaggeration

T. Darrell, H. Baker, F. Crow, G. Gordon, and J. Woodfill

From an early age, the image of one's face in a mirror evokes a quality of being connected and disconnected at the same time. One sees an "other," but knows it is one's self. This project explores the boundary between these qualities through a virtual mirror with face-specific image manipulation.

The system combines real-time special effects such as image morphing and texture synthesis with new advances in computer vision for face tracking and expression analysis. By distorting one or more aspects of a user's face in real time, Magic Morphin Mirror creates a self-referential experience with an image that is clearly neither really oneself nor entirely synthetic nor autonomous.

Faces are central to human communication and yet machines have been largely blind to their presence. This project demonstrates that it is now possible to track and analyze faces in real time for interactive displays.

CONTACT
T. Darrell, H. Baker, F. Crow, G. Gordon, J. Woodfill
Interval Research Corporation
1801 Page Mill Road, Building C
Palo Alto, California 94304 USA
trevor@interval.com

ART & DESIGN

TECHNICAL

SESSION: Imaging

SESSION: Animation

SESSION: Fur, Film, and Textures

SESSION: Level of Detail

SESSION: Hardware

SESSION: 3D UIs and VE

SESSION: Artistic Rendering

SESSION: Display Tools

CONTINUED ▶

APPLICATIONS

SESSION: Visualizations

SESSION: Virtual Environments

SESSION: Education and Information

SESSION: Art Applications

ANIMATIONS

SESSION: Full Body Animation

SESSION: Visual Styles

SESSION: Dynamics and Character Motion

SESSION: Mutts, Machines, and Molten Monsters: The Making Of...

SESSION: Tracking and Talking

Welcome to SIGGRAPH 97 Sketches! This is the fourth year for the Sketches program, and it is evolving like a large, collaborative sketch or drawing. Each year, the contributors and Sketches committee members add new vision and form, redefine pieces, and add more detail to the drawing.

Andrew Glassner created Technical Sketches in 1994. Art & Design Sketches were added in 1995, and, in 1996, Animation Sketches. This year, Applications have become a type of Sketch, instead of a separate program.

Sketches have something for everyone and provide an opportunity for intermixing ideas among people from all areas of the SIGGRAPH community. Just like the Creative Applications Laboratory, Sketches provide a common tie between the technical programs, Ongoings: The Fine Arts Gallery, and the Computer Animation Festival, bringing artists, animators, designers, programmers, technical directors, and researchers together.

Building upon the success of the SIGGRAPH 96 Sketches program, we received 215 submissions this year – almost double the number of submissions in 1996. The four Sketches juries selected 100 Sketches for inclusion in this year's program.

In Art & Design Sketches, you will see innovative uses of computer graphics for art and design, new artistic tools, explanations of the use of technology for creating art, and social provocation. There are also two Art & Design sessions featuring panel discussions by the artists featured in Ongoings: The Fine Arts Gallery.

In Application Sketches, you will see innovative uses of computer graphics technology for visualization, virtual reality, Web-based applications, interaction, education, and art.

Animation Sketches feature examples of new research in animation techniques, commercial use of motion capture and special effects techniques, character animation, tracking technology, dance, and illustrative Sketches describing the process of commercial production and movie special effects. Several Animation Sketches were solicited from the Computer Animation Festival, to explain how the animations were created.

Technical Sketches feature a wide range of new graphics techniques and early ideas, including realistic rendering, non-photorealistic rendering, modeling and simulation, shading, illumination, graphics hardware, and virtual environments. Technical Sketches allow presentation of both early results (late-breaking research) and small, useful results that may not warrant a full technical paper.

This year, one-page abstracts of all Sketches are published in the Visual Proceedings. The choice of short abstracts was deliberate to allow documentation of techniques and ideas, but not to prevent future publication of full-length papers based on further development of these techniques.

The Sketches program is continuing to evolve, and its success is largely derived from those who contribute their work to it. I encourage you to attend Sketch presentations, participate in lively Sketch discussions, and, most importantly, submit a Sketch next year. Sketches are a great opportunity to contribute to the annual SIGGRAPH conference, whether you are a seasoned contributor or a newcomer.

Finally, I would like to thank the Sketches committee members for their hard work and incredible contributions to this year's Sketches program.

DAVID EBERT
CHAIR, SIGGRAPH 97 Sketches

Sketches Committee

ANIMATION SKETCHES
Jonathan Luskin Franz, Inc. CHAIR
Pauline Ts'o Rhythm & Hues Studios
Chris Wedge Blue Sky Studios

APPLICATION SKETCHES
Roger Crawfis The Ohio State University CHAIR
Chuck Hansen University of Utah
Lloyd Treinish IBM TJ Watson Research Center

ART & DESIGN SKETCHES
Diane Gromala University of Washington CHAIR
Thecla Schiphorst Credo Multimedia Software Inc.
Tim Binkley School of Visual Arts

TECHNICAL SKETCHES
Rick Parent The Ohio State University CHAIR
Steve Feiner Columbia University
Andrew Glassner Microsoft Network
Holly Rushmeier IBM TJ Watson Research Center

SKETCHES ADMINISTRATIVE ASSISTANT
Susan Wrights University of Maryland Baltimore County

Using Video to Create Avatars in Virtual Reality

The VideoAvatar Library is a collection of functions that works in conjunction with the CAVE Library and can be used to add static, photo-realistic, three-dimensional representations of remote users, as well as other objects or agents, to virtual reality applications. The process involves obtaining views from 360 degrees around the person, then selecting two of these images, one for each eye, to represent the user in 3D space.

To acquire these images, the person stands on a turntable placed in front of a blue screen at a distance of 10 feet from a video camera, which is at eye level. We preview the images and set the levels of the various parameters that are to be used in calculating the chroma key to drop out the background. Once these values are set, we record one revolution of the person turning on the turntable and capture the chroma key settings. Recording at 30 frames per second for the 15 seconds required for one revolution generates a movie file consisting of 450 frames. A configuration file can later be used to specify the maximum number of images that should be used, as well as other pertinent information. This allows individual users to adjust parameters based on the specific hardware and memory capacities of their machines.

From this series of images, a different image is selected to represent the person to each eye. Which two images are to be used is calculated based on the positions of both the local and remote users in the space, and the direction that the remote user is facing. These images are then texture mapped onto two separate polygons, each of which is rotated around the vertical axis toward the eye which is meant to see it.

As we are not actually creating a three-dimensional model, but using two two-dimensional images to represent the avatars, not all depth cues are supported. Among those supported are convergence, binocular disparity, horizontal motion parallax, and occlusion. The proper perspective of the VideoAvatar is maintained in relation to the other objects in the modeled environment.

Despite the limitations of using image-based versus model-based rendering techniques for the VideoAvatars, the results are stunningly realistic. The goal is to supply a range of avatars with varying capabilities. Future versions of the library will incorporate multiple positions within the avatar model and real-time live video in order to fulfill this goal.

Joseph A. Insley, Daniel J. Sandin, Thomas A. DeFanti
Electronic Visualization Laboratory
University of Illinois at Chicago
851 South Morgan Street, Room 1120
Chicago, Illinois 60607 USA
insley@evl.uic.edu

The authors wish to acknowledge **Dave Pape, Javier I. Girado, and Terry Franguiadakis** for their valuable input to this research.

The process of designing multi-user virtual environments (VE) is similar to the process of designing code or imagery, in that it is necessary to passionately maintain a catalog of ideas and references. VE design combines these passions to construct a consistent graphical user interface (GUI) with metaphors for exploration and self-reflection in a collaborative team effort.

Dream Grrrls, a VE created in the CAVE, focuses on the immersive nature of dreams. A typical GUI has elements or icons that function as navigational tools and sit on the periphery. VE icons do not operate like a toolbox, but are spatially based, like the galleries in an art museum. *Dream Grrrls* is a journey through five different environments presented in a labyrinth filled with paths and three-dimensional objects or "icons."

Much as art attempts to convey insight, *Dream Grrrls* attempts to generate a new awareness based on interaction and immersive experience in order to create an exciting new level of communication beyond verbal know ledge. Dream imagery presents itself in a way that makes the real uncertain. On one path, the participant can ignore the warnings ("Don't go up there!") and enter a commanding head. Inside, the navigational wand becomes a flashlight to reveal walls made of whispering faces and creatures. The light provides illumination – a gateway to another level of consciousness and ultimately, the many sides of ourselves.

In a world inhabited by large vessels, the user approaches the unfamiliar territory like a desert island of loneliness. One vessel has imposing eyes that follow the participant wherever she goes. She comes face to face with what could be her psyche. If she chooses to confront it, she finds herself unable to move, rattled by the world around her, only to awaken back where she came from (the labyrinth), the same, yet somehow different.

Dream Grrrls allows users to experience their world in a new and dynamic way, much like an active or lucid dream. Participants "cooperate" with the computer in such a way that one is uncertain of the action/reaction hierarchy. *Dream Grrrls* becomes a medium to create a personal performance by learning to interact with the environment and recognize its plasticity.

Dream Grrrls could not have been possible without the artist's library of images and the focused dedication on software by Grit Sehmisch. Audio consultation was provided by Joe Reitzer, and programming consultation was provided by Marcus Thiebaux, Dave Pape, Bor-Tyng Lin, and an Electronic Visualization Laboratory of sages. Special Thanks to Dan Sandin, Tom DeFanti, Maxine Brown, Dana Plepys, Jim Costigan, and Maggie Rawlings.

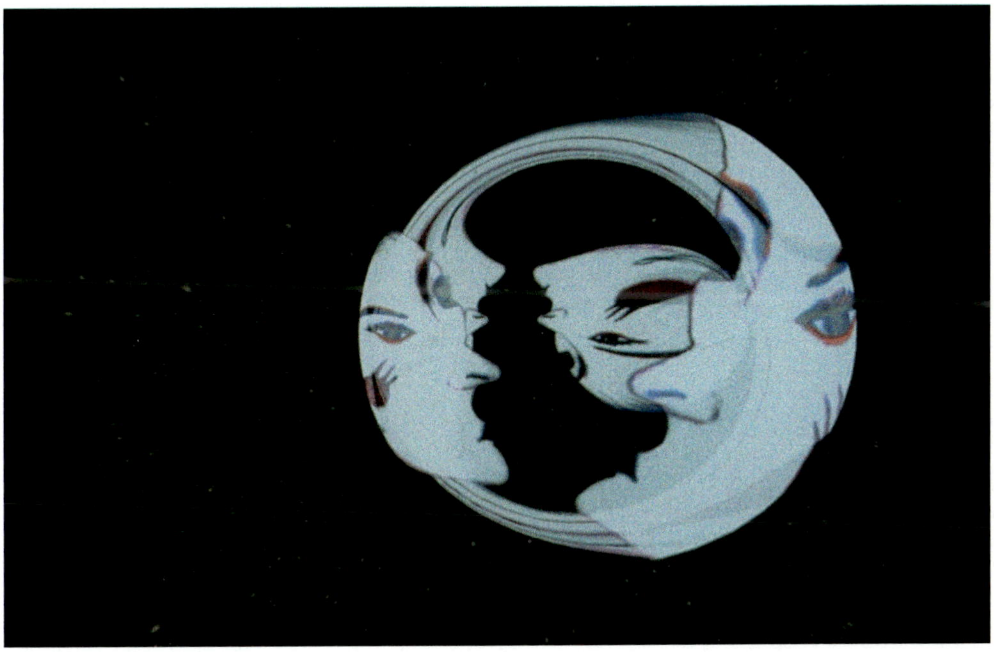

Margaret Dolinsky, Grit Sehmisch
Electronic Visualization Laboratory
University of Illinois at Chicago
851 South Morgan Street, Room 1120
Chicago, Illinois 60607 USA
dolinsky@evl.uic.edu

CyberHuman Dances Series: An Articulation of Body, Space, and Motion in Performance

The CyberHuman Dance Series is an experimental dance work exploring simulations of physical and virtual phenomena in the context of performance. By integrating innovative digital technology with the choreographic and design process, this work investigates all aspects of design and performance in cyberspace, with particular emphasis on issues of real and perceived boundaries between virtual space and real space, and the possibility of a blurred distinction between two intersecting worlds.

Questions are raised as to possible metaphors for construction of virtual spaces and the bodies that inhabit them, leading to new ideas about the behavior of the body and its expression through motion. What, for instance, are the ways in which the cyberdancer begins to claim a virtually constructed space through movement? What kind of relationship (physical, emotional, psychological) can be established between real dancers and their cyberspatial counterparts? How can narrative identities be exchanged, modified, or made explicit? Finally, how can these investigations be brought to performance as a means of formulating an appropriate language for dance in the virtual age?

An analysis of the work in progress offers an opportunity to discuss design issues related to the development of cyberspatial environments and virtual bodies. Issues of space, time, physicality, and gravity are visited, as is the question of how the body is to be represented and inhabited within a virtual space. What is the connection between humans and their representational presence in cyberspace and what, exactly, does it mean to be cyberhuman? How can an articulation of the process of the design of the cyberfigure provide an answer to this question? What is an appropriate representation for a physical figure in a space that lacks physicality? How can a sense of bounded space be accommodated within an environment defined through its lack of edges?

In offering an analysis of the design and performance process, and the questions raised in the development of both cyberfigure and environment, a model for collaboration is proposed between individuals and across technologies. This model illuminates how a collaborative technological investigation infuses the work with a concern for methods of expression in virtual spaces and how innovative digital processes can be explored through experimentation with choreographic software, three-dimensional rendering programs, and their combination into output to digital video.

The creative process of making the work is examined in the collaboration between choreographer, designer, composer, and video artist. The conclusion argues that integration of the working methods of a group of individuals trained in different aspects of the arts offers insight into the range of methodologies available for study and infuses the series with an energy of human discovery.

Katie Salen, Yacov Sharir
Department of Art and Art History
University of Texas at Austin
Austin, Texas 78712 USA
zed@mail.utexas.edu

Disability in the Arts

Life with a physical disability has allowed me a unique and humbling perspective that has manifested in my art work. I create art with and for people who live with various types of physical and/or mental limitations.

Because my work deals with issues of accessibility, it is essential for me to make my work accessible to people with a range of different abilities. The use of non-traditional materials and technology in my installations allows me to incorporate the senses of smell, taste, sound, and touch in addition to providing the more traditional visual experience.

Because I live with a wheelchair, collaboration has been an essential element in my work and life. Using the computer as an art medium has allowed me the freedom and access to create virtual worlds that would have been impossible in my life. No longer do I need assistance to move a block of marble or build a room. The computer has given me all the tools I need to accomplish these tasks. Imagination is now my limitation.

My work is often referred to as interdisciplinary because I often use more than one medium to provide additional access to communication. Often the work is interactive, so the participant can experience art rather than just see it. The focus in my studies lies in educating and encouraging participants – regardless of prior experience, physical limitations, age, or ethnicity – to examine the relevance of art and accessibility in their own lives. For example, by incorporating a medium like Braille into an installation, I can attempt to change an art piece to be more inclusive for a visually impaired audience.

I believe art is fundamentally a communicative experience that can be and should be shared by all. My research method includes a hands-on approach, working collaboratively with several different groups and individuals to create art pieces that have been specifically designed to incorporate more than the traditional visual experience.

What one person might feel is important or beautiful another may not. I have found that by displaying work without an emphasis solely on the visual aspect, artistic integrity is still maintained. By including elements such as a wheelchair, Braille translations, and audio descriptions, individuals without mental or physical limitations may re-evaluate and gain a deeper appreciation for their own abilities by not only seeing art but experiencing and interacting with it.

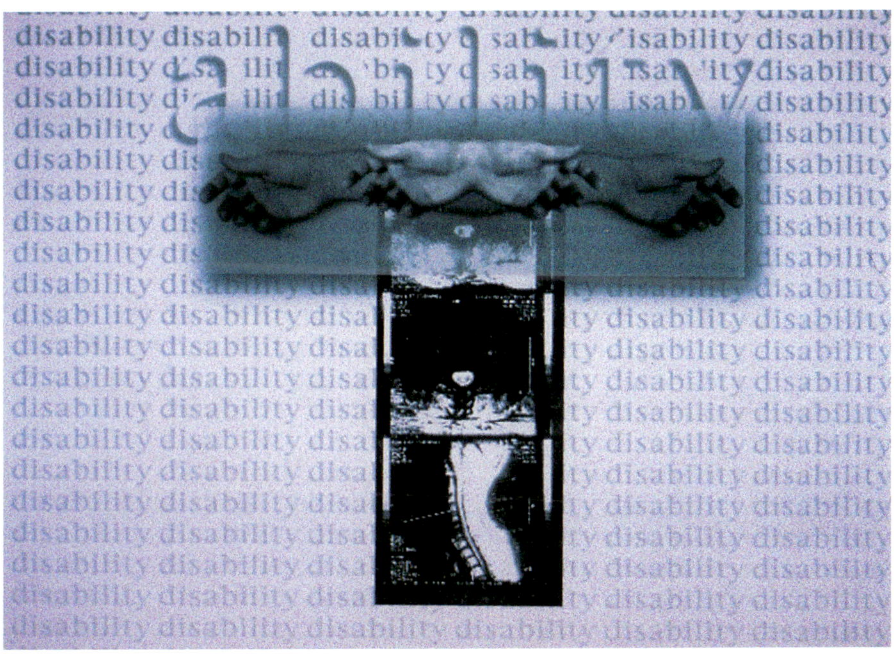

Jon Berge
Department of Fine Arts
The Ohio State University
753 Oak Street
Columbus, Ohio 43205 USA
+1.614.224.9477
jberge@cgrg.ohio-state.edu

Multi-Media Metamorphosis (or making the medium shoe fit)

A large portion of my work has entailed taking a theme or story and giving it life in a variety of media. *The Mutant Gene & Tainted Kool-Aid Sideshow* CD-ROM (completed October 1995) is a navigable interpretation of a series of performances I staged in 1994, by the same name. The performances incorporated live and pre-recorded, multiple-monitor and projected video; animation; text; both sequenced and live instrumental music; and dramatic artifacts and performance elements such as masks and dance.

Beginning with the psycho-dramatic confession of an extraterrestrial, the piece journeyed into a series of multicolored, entropic landscapes. My intent with the performances, and the use of technology, was to create alternate or augmented realities for an audience. I wanted the audience to be immersed in an environment of sound, light, and motion, which often paralleled the content – in essence, making certain fantasy states real. The CD-ROM emerged from a desire to break down the linear constraints of a performance to create a more personal "circular" experience, where an individual can explore the environment in any order, without being guided as a collective "audience" through various states.

Similarly, *The Grimm Tale (or the Story of the Youth Who Went Forth to Learn what Fear Was)* began as a Web site. Clay puppets were created to represent each of the characters in the tale. Hours of footage were shot, keying the characters on top of beds of analog video patches. Then, after the video was digitized, dozens of small loopable gif animations were made, and a continual MIDI soundtrack was constructed. In its second incarnation, *The Grimm Tale* is a performance, similar to *The Mutant Gene*, with MIDI triggering multiple video and animation events.

Taking a piece and creating a work as a performance, CD-ROM, or Web site presents fascinating progressions and developments. Each of these media has individual advantages, limitations, opportunities, and constraints, all of which have to be worked within, taken advantage of, and manipulated to make the piece a wholly new and unique work in its own right, in its new form.

This presentation examines the implications of traversing media, the technical issues involved in crossing medium boundaries, and related conceptual issues.

M.R. Petit
104 Suffolk Street, #3
New York, New York 10002 USA
petit@echonyc.com
http://www.weirdos.com
http://www.echonyc.com/~mrp
http://www.somewhere.org

Technophobia is a collection of original multimedia art in an interactive exhibition. In addition to the original multimedia artwork, the CD-ROM includes a studio visit with each artist.

The Vision Behind the Project:

I think that this new technology offers the most exciting, perhaps the only exciting thing happening in contemporary art today. I'm using the technology to transcend the limitations of physics and history inherent in other art methods.

From the creative point of view, working in a new medium is both exacting and liberating. On this CD-ROM, I worked with other artists who covered the whole gamut from those with no computer experience at all to those who had training in specialized tertiary institutions.

I've felt for a long time that art has to go outside itself, that deconstruction has worked itself out as a modus operandi. For me, working with digital technology provides the freedom to create something that is almost indefinable but reflects the obsessions of my generation: cinema, popular culture, cutting-edge art, and electronic culture.

Of the greatest interest to me is how digital culture will alter human experience – in practical day-to-day matters, in the deployment of corporate information, in entertainment, and in the art of the next phase of human and technological development.

The artists on this CD-ROM are not coming from a naive position, and the artworks we've made represent a highly considered position from the point of view of making art with new technology.

The Artists

Judith Ahern
Bill Albertini
Huma Bhabha
Joseph Ferrari
Alan Koninger
Tim Maul
Christian Perez
Troy Innocent
Guillaume Wolf and Genevieve Glaucker
Jody Zellen
Lynne Sanderson
Dooley Le Cappellaine

Electronic and Ambient Music

David Barnes and Charles Cohen
Moniek Darge
Joshua Fried
The Happy Jacks
Fugitive Pope
Phil Niblock
Mike Hovanscek with Pointless Orchestra
John Hajeski with Post Prandials

Dooley Le Cappellaine
284 Mott Street #9K
New York, New York 10012. USA
dooley@thing.net
http://www.thing.net/dooley

izzy bombus and the story of flight

izzy bombus and the story of flight is a prototype CD-ROM consisting of an animated story with associated games and educational activities for children ages four through seven. Izzy, a young bumblebee, discovers that according to the laws of aerodynamics, the bumblebee cannot fly. Dismayed but undeterred, izzy collects implements from a kitchen drawer to build a flying machine and asks her viewers for help with the construction. With izzy in the cockpit, the viewer pushes the launch button, the countdown begins, the smoke swirls... lift-off!

What happens next? izzy bombus is a story of resolution and innovation in overcoming obstacles. Izzy is a girl bumblebee involved in activities not traditionally considered the domain of girls, such as aerodynamics, flying, building, and exploration. The adventure is accompanied by original delta blues music by Blind Mississippi Morris. Ten games and educational activities are linked to the story and can also be accessed directly from a menu screen.

The story is complete and fully interactive to the point where it branches to the various endings. A short animated introduction leads to a menu where viewers choose between the story or the games menu. The "know-it-all-bug" serves as a guide, offering instruction and advice. Games and activities can be accessed as the viewer progresses through the story or directly from the menu.

Through this project, I am attempting to make connections between my experience as a designer of traditional print graphics and new media. My goal is to produce a viable commercial product for the children's CD-ROM market as well as to incorporate the experience into the planning and implementation of coursework in multimedia. Work began on the project in January 1996 and is continuing.

In crossing the boundaries between graphic design for print and graphic design for new media, I explored and considered the possibilities and at the same time dealt with the realities and limitations of desktop multimedia. As a graphic designer, my interest is in innovative design that combines an understanding of traditional principles of visual communication with the unique possibilities offered by the interactive experience.

With this project I have employed a collage method of assembling the illustrative elements of the story in an eclectic style. Elements are painted, drawn, and assembled from old engravings. Traditional methods are used for parts of the illustrations, while others are entirely computer-generated. The combination of techniques produces a rich, textural quality and unexpected combinations.

Another unexpected aspect of the project is the music. The blues, a part of the unique cultural heritage of the South, has gained an appreciative audience throughout the world. Although this type of music is unusual in the domain of children's products, the connection between the sound and the movement and activities of the bumblebee makes it an appropriate choice.

Sandy Lowrance
Art Department
Campus Box 526715
The University of Memphis
Memphis, Tennessee 38152 USA
sllowrnc@memphis.edu

Manifest destiny: In "Excerpts from the Vancouver Lectures," Jack Spicer relates the story: Yeats, 1918, a train bound for Los Angeles. His wife in a trance, automatic writing, taking dictation from "spooks." Yeats poses the question: "What are you here for?" And the spooks reply: "We are here to give metaphors for your poetry."

Poetry, according to Ezra Pound in *The ABC of Reading*, is language concentrated, condensed. Pound postulates that poetry "is the most concentrated form of verbal expression." It is this metaphorical (or possibly malaphorical) condensation, this condensed cultural automatic writing, or dictation, that I strive for.

Throwing Apples at the Sun and *Eye Sling Shot Lions* are enhanced CDs that consist of integrated multimedia compositions of sound, images, poetry, and QuickTime movies. Each disc also contains 30 minutes of original music and spoken-word poetry.

The 1995 release of *Throwing Apples at the Sun* could best be typified by the substitution of referential density for narrative coherence. The linear logic of story telling gives way to the field of intertextuality and the beauty of sliding signification. With the release of *Eye Sling Shot Lions*, this impulse is extended and elaborated through the incorporation of a series of loosely structured micro-narratives. This confluence of overt referent and micro-narrative weaves an open text, mirroring the archetypal patterns in tragic poetry.

Both discs are the direct result of the semantic experimentation begun while I was at the Cranbrook Academy of Art. These early syntactic and formal explorations of typographic form, image, and music serve as the foundation for both discs. In the most basic thematic terms, both discs are attempts to construct meditations on power, religion, language, and culture through construction of computer "applications."

Utilizing Allegiant Technologies' Supercard allowed me to examine the idea of the work of art through the filter and language of a standard computer application. Specifically, the ability to easily adhere to Apple Computers' human interface guidelines allowed for an interesting semantic slippage between the language of the "application" and the language of the artwork proper. I involved myself in the process of mapping upon this desktop terrain, with its familiar menus, windows, and dialog boxes, a series of home movies, poetic sound fragments, typographic experiments, photo-montages, and spoken word texts. During the construction process, there was a constant interplay between intent and a sense of natural wholistic growth.

The formal construction of both pieces, and the thrust of all of my work, has been based upon a series of related concepts dealing specifically with macro-procedure. On a macro-procedural level, we may, with a little effort, reduce all creative acts down to a two-step process consisting of analysis and synthesis. Obviously, this process may be extended with the introduction of numerous other processes, including analysis, selection, definition, ideation, implementation, and evaluation. And while this collection of processes represents an abstraction of the actual physiological creative process, it is this "mapping" that allows us to begin to understand the complex, non-linear, and interrelated acts that comprise all creative endeavors.

The first phase of construction for both discs, could most easily be categorized as the creation of individual, traditional media that was informed by their respective disciplines. For instance, during the creation of the fonts for *Throwing Apples at the Sun*, typographic tradition, history, and formal principals were examined in a semi-rigorous analytical phase, only to yield to a a synthetic phase that dealt primarily with cultural association and marginalized typographic forms. The second phase was typified by hybrid processes. For instance, pieces of music were written, composed, and constructed utilizing some of the primary principles of digital video editing, or utilizing ideas borrowed from photography. This phase yielded typography constructed as poetry, prose generated as if it were music, and video edited with an intimate awareness of haiku. The third and final phase of design and construction continued to blur the distinction between the media. At this point, the design and construction process became extremely wholistic, kinetic, and organic. Disparate media were brought into the authoring environment, and the process of finding commonalities and themes began.

As in traditional Western music composition, theme gave way to modulation and finally recapitulation. As in non-traditional Western music composition (rap), flow, rupture, and looping structures were emphasized. As in traditional English composition, the four master tropes of figurative language – metaphor, synechdoche, metonymy, and irony – were articulated. And as in the Russian Formalist movement, the process of "defamiliarization," or strange making, was a primary focus.

Throwing Apples at the Sun and *Eye Sling Shot Lions* have given me the opportunity to involve myself in a process of over-simplification or mapping. I have made maps of the varied terrain of self expression. I have attempted to rigorously approach and understand the fundamental principals underlying different artistic disciplines and then use the rules, not be used by them. I strive to see the big picture, to understand the method and means by which a human being can express something deeply personal. *Throwing Apples at the Sun* and *Eye Sling Shot Lions* represent these honest attempts.

Elliott Peter Earls
The Apollo Program
82 East Elm Street
Greenwich, Connecticut 06830 USA
elliott@theapolloprogram.com

Design Speech Acts: "How to do things with words" in Virtual Communities

Cyberspace is language-based (cf. Cicognani, 1996, 1997; Winograd, 1987), and so are virtual communities. The author argues that virtual communities are ideal places to experience and enhance a language for design, and for designers.

Design in virtual communities can actually be performed using speech acts that in real life wouldn't perform any design: we will call these acts "design speech acts." For example, the command "@create wall" issued in a MOO environment corresponds to the creation of a (virtual) wall in that environment.

Beyond the interest of computer-mediated communication researchers (cf. Cherny 1995), who deal with the content of the communication in text-based virtual realities, there is a possibility for designers to finally employ speech acts for the purpose of designing cyberspace, for cyberspace's sake. Speech act theory has been applied as a way of designing computer systems and feedback processes to natural language interaction. It is interesting to observe that these applications have been abandoned, mainly for two reasons: on the one hand, the intentionality and on the other, the meaning of utterances, which create ambiguity in the interpretation.

To "perform" with natural language, there is the need to consider the context in which the speech act is uttered, and how that speech act is going to be interpreted by the hearer(s). The theory, then, has been restricted to the analysis of speech acts as content of messages issued in a computer-mediated environment, rather than commands issued to "make the computer do things with words," to actually create virtual things.

The author argues that the coincidence of functionality and appearance in text-based virtual realities can be an advantage for design in these environments, through the application of speech act theory. CAD system interfaces are not considered as relevant in the scheme of definition of design speech acts in a text-based virtual community, due to their lack of correspondence between appearance and functionality. It is in fact this discrepancy that the application of speech act theory tries to fill. Even though graphic interfaces seem to be the only actual solution to computer-based design representations, text-based virtual realities can become a relevant area of study and application for alternatives to those interfaces.

This sketch presents an hypothesis and a methodology for structuring and defining design speech acts, so that a language and interface for design in a virtual community can be subsequently developed. The author has selected and categorized a list of design verbs that can be used in a virtual community for design. A first model of this categorization is also presented and discussed. The author has developed a specific virtual community in which designers can articulate their needs and produce text-based design objects.

Anna Cicognani
Faculty of Architecture, G04
University of Sydney
New South Wales 2006 Australia
anna@arch.usyd.edu.au
http://www.arch.usyd.edu.au/~anna

Agree to Disagree Online

Any collaboration is a negotiation. While most artistic teams hide the filibustering, intellectual posturing, and shifting alliances that lie behind their decisions, *Agree to Disagree Online* brings these facets of collaboration to the fore.

Especially designed for the World Wide Web, this interactive work charts an argument among the three artists that begins with the inflammatory statement "In the future, books will be replaced by maps." *Agree to Disagree Online* maps this negotiation in time and space. Viewers can navigate through an individual argument by clicking one at a time on the participants' responses to each other. These responses are represented both in words and by a series of arrows that indicate agreement or disagreement in spatial terms: if the negotiation is nearing consensus, the arrow moves toward a central point between the artists' three initials. If the discussion is becoming more divisive, the arrow moves toward the periphery of the screen. In this way, the cumulative overlay of arrows expresses the shape of the argument, and viewers can trace this final trajectory in animated form.

The larger-scale structure of *Agree to Disagree Online* is determined by digressions from one argument to another, which the viewer is free to pursue. The forking paths that result from these digressions wander into such absurdly unrelated topics as Watergate, the way buffalos roam, and the efficacy of the Evelyn Wood speed-reading course.

The authors have been agreeing to disagree since their first adversarial collaboration in 1992. Unlike most artistic teams, they emphasize the conflict inherent in collaboration by basing each work on a particular competitive event, such as marking territory by spitting pins, targeting an opponent with projectiles, or evaluating each other's ideas for an artwork.

Janet Cohen, Keith Frank, Jon Ippolito
345 Greenwich Street, #5A
New York, New York 10013 USA
cohen@interport.net
http://www.interport.net/~gering

Is there a way to make a meaningful shape from a collection of the individual words of the English language? What would that shape look like? Why would this approach be preferable to a traditional representation – a printed dictionary, for example? These were among the questions we asked when we set out to visualize the English language as a single entity.

The first assumption we made was that our daily interaction with three-dimensional objects would give us leverage in establishing meaning through familiarity. We set out to create an object that would, as a result of regular observation, begin to afford the same level of information about its state as the plant you observe on your breakfast table each morning.

The initial step in the process of developing the formal attributes of the object was the identification of salient ways to categorize our data (individual words). Because the intent of the project was to propose a system that would function primarily as a reference tool, the dimensions we chose were tailored both to enable the retrieval of a particular word and to facilitate the recognition of broad trends throughout the base of data. Presumably, we are all used to locating words in a dictionary by wading through an alphabetic ordering. Based largely on this familiarity and the efficiency this familiarity affords, we chose alphabetic organization as our first axis of description.

The remaining axes of description, or "descriptors," were chosen for their perceived ability to contribute to the overall expressiveness of the resultant form: word familiarity and temporal etymology. Determined on a word-by-word basis, the most likely methodology to be used in the measurement of the familiarity of a particular word would be based on the number of times that word appeared in a statistically significant corpus. Temporal etymology would be determined by the first recorded use of a word. Once plotted along the axes, the polygonal representations of the words would be packed along their vectors to the origin. Additional expressiveness would be added to the resultant form through the assignment of color to a particular word based on the national origin of that word: for instance, words with a Germanic root would share a common hue.

The interface to this reference tool would allow the user to extract information specific to a particular word such as its definition, etymology, or illustration (if appropriate). One could also use *Gradus* to browse synonyms and antonyms, replicating the essential functionality of a thesaurus. The emergent form would be tornado-like – relatively few words at the tail of the object (the beginning of the language) and a burgeoning of words following the industrial revolution through the 20th century. Herein lies one of the major advantages of this approach over traditional means: unlike printed dictionaries, *Gradus* offers information about its content through its form.

Gradus, as an expressive, sculptural representation of the English language offers an efficient way to develop an understanding of the nature and the history of specific words and the language as a whole.

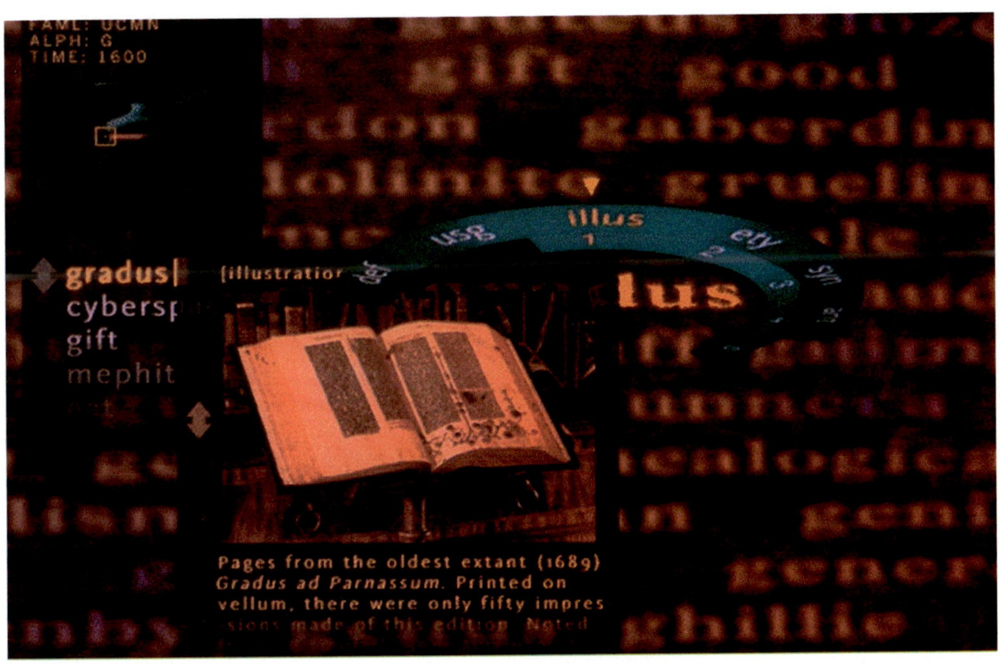

Matt Grenby
MIT Media Lab
20 Ames Street
Cambridge, Massachusetts 02139 USA
grenby@media.mit.edu

Computer Graphics as Stainless Steel Output

Project Description

A history of hand-held graphics might include Tarot cards, playing cards, the *carte de visite*, business cards, credit cards, and more recently telephone cards. While each of these subsets has a differing history and function, they also have shared attributes that continue to attract our interest. Proportions, scale, content, cost, and techniques of production all merge with more recent communication functions. Borrowing from these physical and conceptual traditions suggests possibilities for an artist using digital typography to create a kind of permanent ephemera. Incorporating stainless steel output offers an option for the designer to employ a technology similar to computer chip technology and to investigate the conversion of digitized art to artifact.

The cards examine the discrepancy between the technology of chemical machining, high-resolution digital output, non-corrosive steel material, and the language of the street: doggerel, the vernacular, the pun, a japer, or the sadness of an epitaph-in-waiting. The computer unleashes the typographic possibilities. Reversing type, customizing the fully etched openings in the metal, low embossed textures, shaping the perimeter, and scaling graphic elements are just a few of the options made possible by the digital process.

Procedure

A template was created in Freehand 7.0 that defined the format for 21 traditional business cards arranged in a grid on a tabloid-sized sheet. A space 1/8-inch wide was used to separate the individual cards. The final design was proofed on the laser printer before being used to create the film output on a Linotronic film recorder. Two tabloid-sized pieces of positive film output were generated, one emulsion down for the front side of the cards and one emulsion up for the back side exposure of the .007-inch stainless steel metal plate. After exposure and development, the metal plate was submerged in acid for chemical machining. The final etched sheet contains the cards, held in place by tiny sprews or connecting points. At this point, the cards are broken out of the sheet by hand and touched up with 600-grit emery cloth to smooth the edges.

Conclusions

A computer equipped with graphics software can be used to facilitate design and execution of art that combines text and images for output on metal surfaces using chemical machining technology. Further applications are likely – for example, limited-edition artist books with metal pages, light fixtures with metal shades that project light and shadow through the openings, and folded-metal, free-standing sculpture with surface engraving. Text and design are used to evoke expressive and conceptual issues such as: material as metaphor, the vernacular context, new cards of identity, and corporate hand-held art. A blueprint for a miniature samizdat ... or maybe just another business card.

Ronald Carraher
Photography Program
School of Art, Box 353440
University of Washington
Seattle Washington 98195-3440 USA
rgc@u.washington.edu

If computers are tools for manipulating information, they have been notoriously poor at using the hands of the people who use them. By engaging the hands of the user, it is possible to get a literal handle on complex visualizations of information. In this project, the goal is to design a more practical, productive, and fluid kind of interface.

A Mathematical Twist

This project was inspired by a model of a hyperbolic paraboloid in the Collection of Historical Scientific Instruments at Harvard University. Built of brass and wood, with strings held taut by lead weights, it allowed students to create and examine a variety of hyperbolic paraboloids. We built a scale model with potentiometers mounted at key mechanical points. The change in resistance at those points is used to determine the state of the model as users modify it in real time. On the computer display, a synthetic model is shown, along with dynamic equations that show how variables such as volume and surface area change in tandem with the model.

The goal is to match the real and virtual model smoothly so that users feel as if they are the same object. Future work on this project will include using better graphic representations of the underlying math in the virtual space, which should clarify the connection between the form and the equation.

Talmudic Typography

This project was built around an essay by the philosopher Emmanuel Levinas, whose commentary on a tract of the Talmud, which itself is a complex, nested series of references to the Torah, forms an intricate web of text and connections. A visual representation of these interconnected texts should construct a space for discussion and argument in which scholars can pull and push the words as they dissect the intellectual issues posed by the text.

The Talmud is traditionally read by two people, so that it can be argued and debated. The controls were designed to facilitate this style of polemic. While discussing some fine point of logic, either reader can grab a control and modify the visual relationships between the texts in order to support an argument.

Conclusion

If you hold a hammer in your hand, everything in the world begins to resemble a nail. Likewise, we tend to get stuck in the conventional mouse-windows paradigm. By designing new interfaces, we can bridge the gap between the space people inhabit in front of the computer and the abstract landscapes inside the computer.

David Small
MIT Media Lab, E15-443
20 Ames Street
Cambridge, Massachusetts 02139 USA
dsmall@media.mit.edu

Dynamic3: Interactive Physics and Physicality In Three Dimensions

We lose the joy of pliability in our interactions with the computer when we get lost in a cacophony of visual iconic references. There is no grace. *Dynamic3* emphasizes the subtleties of interaction. Not what is seen, but what is felt. A physics-based computational model and a fluid physical interface amplify the expression.

Two physical cubes control a malleable, hierarchical data structure represented as abstract objects on a virtual stage. The external appearance of the physical cubes mimics the simple geometrical forms on the screen. By using interactive particle physics, virtual objects react in ways that correspond to our existing assumptions about our physical world.

The two physical cubes control the position and orientation of their virtual counterparts. A change in position of one of the physical cubes exerts a force on the parameterized particle physics model. By variably weighting various data objects, a new paradigm is introduced, by which the dynamic/motive reaction of information structures gives subtle cues as to the contents of the object.

Through repeated exploration, users are able to feel differences in reactivity and modulate their decisions accordingly, without sacrificing aesthetic or metaphorical continuity.

A firm gesture towards the rear of the virtual stage allows the user to view more detailed information about the contents of the abstract data objects. The camera tracks and pans to a position behind the translucent rear stage. From this position, it acts much like an X-ray machine, revealing the information structure within each data object. The objects' shadows transform into projections of their corresponding data.

Today's supercomputers and tomorrow's desktop machines have tremendous capabilities for display of three-dimensional information in real time. A great deal of work has been done in realistic creation and display of bodies of information, yet navigation and manipulation of these spaces remains frustratingly rigid. Using advanced visualization techniques and traditional design principles, this project creates visceral, intuitive methods for modulation of 3D space for both commercial and design purposes. The physical underpinnings of the interface architecture allow for the possibility of functionally and aesthetically graceful interactions.

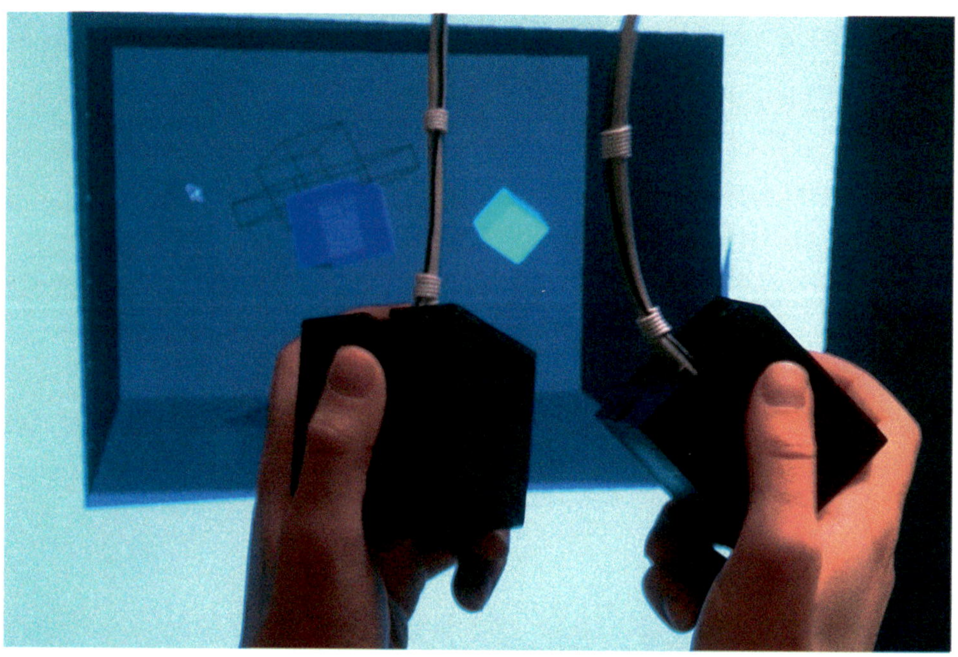

Reed Kram, John Maeda
MIT Media Lab
20 Ames Street
Cambridge, Massachusetts 02139 USA
kram@media.mit.edu

Pad++, a general-purpose zoomable substrate for creating and interacting with structured information, is under development by researchers at the University of New Mexico and New York University. All Pad++ objects support zooming, and there are mechanisms for navigating through a multiscale space using panning, zooming, and hyperlinks. Pad++ includes a number of efficiency mechanisms that help maintain interactive frame-rates with large and complicated graphical scenes.

Applications based on Pad++ attempt to tap into our natural spatial ways of thinking by supporting views of information at multiple scales. These applications move beyond the simple binary choice of presenting or eliding particular information and present a continuous context in which information is encountered. Arrangement, proximity, size, and scale-based representation may be used to present semantic information in manners unique to zooming interfaces. Very large amounts of information may be embedded at successively deeper levels, making it easier to provide effective access to a structure of information much larger than the available display.

PadDraw is a sample application that supports many of the features found in drawing and hypermedia programs, but it adds a zooming component. Zooms are smooth and continuously animated, much like using the zoom controls on a video camera, so users always retain a sense of context. When a link is followed in PadDraw, the system automatically pans and zooms the view, taking the user to the appropriate piece of data. Readers are left with the sense that the starting information point is "up to the left" or otherwise in an intuitive relationship with their current view. This helps readers to orient themselves in a complex hypermedia document.

Gray Matters is a collaborative, multiscale hypertext artwork/fiction. Using a subset of the PadDraw functionality, it creates an environment for multiscale reading and exploration. Fifteen images from *Gray's Anatomy* are tinted and arranged in a patchwork body. Each image has two representations: a scanned and manipulated bitmap, and a simplified vector graphic. The bitmap is seen when the view is zoomed out, and this cross-fades into the the vector graphic as the view moves closer. At the same time, color-coded labels representing texts fade into visibility. As the view zooms in further, the labels dissolve away, and the full texts are displayed against the color fields of the vector graphics.

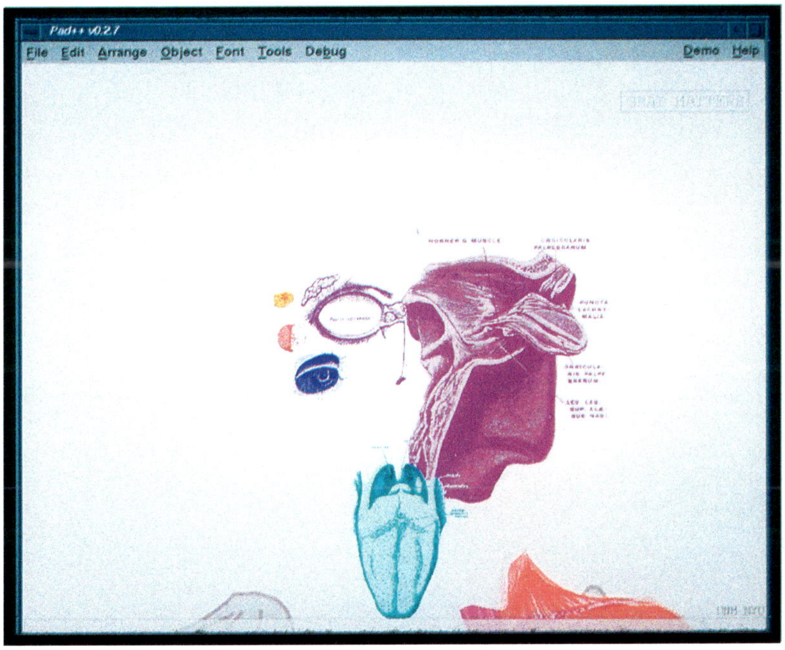

Noah Wardrip-Fruin, Jon Meyer, Ken Perlin
NYU Center for Advanced Technology
719 Broadway, 12th Floor
New York, New York 10003 USA
noah@cat.nyu.edu
http://www.cat.nyu.edu/graymatters

Ben Bederson, Jim Hollan
University of Mexico
http://www.cs.unm.edu/pad++

Multimedia Interactive Artist's Archive and Retrospective

Creative options and challenges: a digital art archive grows into a dynamic showcase with new views of the art.

This archive is an independent, solo production that gauges the efficacy of CD-ROM publishing for, and by, individual artists as well as for groups, galleries, and other larger institutions. The set of discs is more similar to an artist's portfolio than a commercial product and is intended primarily for art and educational institutions, rather than for distribution through strictly commercial channels.

The art included in "The Art dimension: an artist's archive and retrospective" (an overview of a half-century in the fine arts) and "The Image Circle: a life in photography" was digitized using one of two methods: scanned on a flatbed scanner or transferred to Photo CDs. Such scans require a considerable amount of "tweaking" or retouching before their appearance is acceptable. In this process, many aspects of an image can be adjusted or altered: color, contrast, sharpness, and even composition.

Sometimes this leads to creation of entirely new versions of the earlier work, and rediscovering the work in its digital form with its new options to alter and create new versions of the original renditions at will constitutes one of the most creative and exciting parts of the task.

The process of developing a digital portfolio provides a whole new view of the art vis-a-vis the potentials of the new media. Creating animated versions of once-static traditional collages has also led to Dada-esque moving image/sound collages and numerous other dynamic variations of the original art. The possibility of combining simple motion with the existing art has also added a new dimension to the current work: new animations that utilize and recombine parts of earlier imagery into new meaning and a new dynamic creation.

More advanced techniques include such explorations as "mapping" photographic work onto dynamic 3D structures to explore new(ly) anomalous content as well as spatial relationships.

Josepha Haveman
A/PIX computer art center
P.O. Box 9063
Berkeley, California 94708 USA
JosephaH@aol.com
http:www//illuminated.com/JH_ArtArchive/

This presentation reviews three works: *Genderbender, Smart Stall* (exhibited in The Bridge: SIGGRAPH 96 Art Show), and *The Automatic Confession Machine* (exhibited in Machine Culture, SIGGRAPH 93).

Genderbender 1.0, loosely based on the Bem Sex Role Inventory (BSRI) (1974) and the Turing test for artificial intelligence, scavenges the trash heap of psychological testing in pursuit of the "Virtual Personality." It allows a user to self-administer a gender test of 20 masculine, feminine, or neutral traits. The Morph-o-meter and the Tile-o-matic give instant feedback on whether masculine or feminine characteristics predominate in the user's personality by morphing towards identifiably male or female visual representations and revealing the user's digitized image. Based on the user's input, the "psychologist" displays: "You are a man!" or "You are a woman!" or "You are androgynous!"

Smart Stall is the Master/Slave Duchampian Telecommunications Interface. It is conceived as an immersive, interactive theatrical experience inspired by Antonin Artaud's "Theatre of Cruelty." The user's motion triggers "orders" and "instructions" from an abusive semi-intelligent agent suffering from multiple personality disorder. In homage to Duchamp's avatar, R. Mutt, this installation looks like a public toilet stall, but it actually is a telecommunications terminal. Two non-functioning bathroom toilet stalls are equipped with digital white boards, which digitize handwritten graffiti and transmit the messages to remote stalls where the messages are projected. *Smart Stall* is especially interesting in light of Roger Penrose's lawsuit alleging that Kimberley Clark Corporation infringed a copyright when it sold toilet paper bearing the Penrose Tiling pattern, a demonstration of a class of non-computable problems that forms a key part of Penrose's argument that "human understanding and insight cannot be reduced to any set of computational rules."

The Automatic Confession Machine: A Catholic Turing Test is a stand-alone kiosk that resembles an automatic banking machine. Users must kneel and confess committed sins, after which they receive a printout indicating how many Hail Marys and Our Fathers must be said for digital absolution and silicon salvation. This work is inspired by Alan Turing's test for judging whether or not a computer can be said to think.

These three installations use technology to question our infatuation with the brave new world of AI, VR, and ubiquitous computing. They put users "on the spot" by requiring a commitment or a theatrical suspension of disbelief and forcing them to make choices that require examination of their own beliefs and biases. As Brenda Laurel has noted, the potential of the computer is "not in its ability to perform calculations but in its capacity to represent action in which humans could participate."

Genderbender can be viewed at the Transverse Worlds web site:
http://142.232.132.45.80/dedocs

Users can go to confession at the Lightfactory web site:
http://www.lightfactory.org/artists.html

Gregory Patrick Garvey
Department of Design Art, VA-246
Concordia University
1455 de Maisonneuve Boulevard West
Montréal, Québec H3GA 1M8 CANADA
ggarvey@vax2.concordia.ca

The Virtual Harvester Project

The Virtual Harvester project is an effort to address the need for global commitment and action to fight one of human society's most basic problems: food insecurity. The United Nations Development Program (UNDP) created the Poverty Clock to illustrate how quickly poverty grows. Each successive digit on the clock indicates another person living on less than $1.00 (U.S.) per day. Synchronized to the Poverty Clock's ticking, one new plant sprouts on the virtual corn field; yielding approximately 47 plants each minute.

In *The Virtual Harvester,* one new plant sprouts on a virtual cornfield with each tick of the clock, yielding approximately 47 plants each minute. Proposed to be experienced in the harbour simulator facility in Rotterdam, the project surrounds viewers with virtual corn plants, each representing a person living in poverty. Instead of a ship's bridge, the platform displays a fictional harvester cabin. In front of the viewers, virtually attached to the pilothouse, is an enormous virtual harvesting device. The device produces a loud mechanical noise (amplified by the harbour simulator's 3D sound), vibrating the pilothouse from side to side while it reaps the harvest. As the yield is blown into virtual storage trucks moving slowly alongside the pilothouse, viewers become aware of the scent of fresh grain rising from a thick layer of yellow maize that covers the entire inside floor of the simulator. As they stand protected inside the pilothouse, viewers will be able to steer the virtual combine through green virtual cornfields, leaving a trail of scorched earth behind the harvester's reaping blades. Protruding from the fields are gigantic communication towers, which serve as beacons amidst the vast virtual landscape. While viewers "play the game," it is subtly revealed (via incoming messages on the harvester's two-way radio system) that the virtual cornfields are in fact 3D visual data fields that represent the number of people living in absolute poverty across the globe.

The Virtual Harvester questions the motives of the Western world's immersion in information technology as it constructs "the global village." The work asks if the Western world is not paradoxically isolating itself even further from the social and economic realities of its impoverished neighbors.

"Alongside the ever-widening social divisions, another apartheid is being created between the 'information-rich' and the 'information-poor.'" (excerpt from *The Californian Ideology*, Barbrook & Cameron)

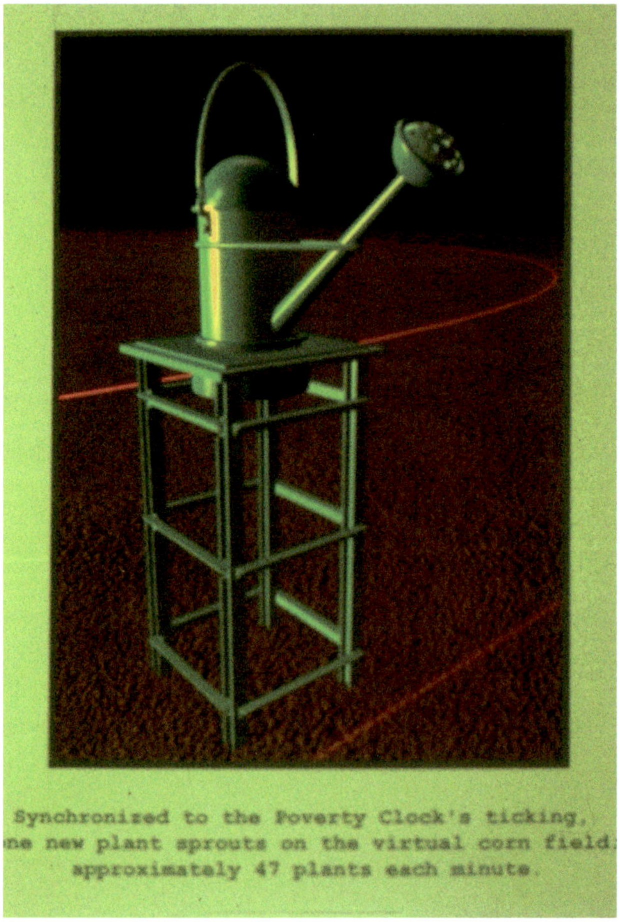

Johann van der Schijff
MEDIA-GN
Hoendiepskade 23 A
9718 BG Groningen, THE NETHERLANDS
schijff@scan.media-gn.nl
http://www.media-gn.nl/people/johannvdS/index.html

The talent of a caricaturist is important when using traditional media such as pencil and paper. Since traditional media are not interactive, caricaturists must complete the caricatures in their minds before starting to draw. Since this ability does not exist in most people, it has always been considered some sort of magical talent of a gifted few.

I have noticed that when using an interactive morphing tool, there is no need to have the special talent of a caricaturist. Based on my experience as a professional caricaturist, I have developed a procedure to make caricatures from photographs by using morphing tools. With this method, people need only have the ability to recognize others from their caricatures. Judging from the popularity of caricatures, I expect that most human beings have this ability.

Procedure for Making Caricatures

1 Use an extremely simple template. Thinking it will give them greater control, most people, when using morphing tools, tend to start with complicated templates. However, in this case less is more. The templates should be extremely simple and they should include only the essential features of the face: nose, eyes, mouth, and outline.

2 Exaggerate only one feature at a time. Concentrating on only one feature forces the caricaturist to understand its importance relative to the face.

3 If exaggeration creates a likeness, continue to exaggerate. If it does not create a likeness, make the exaggeration in the opposite direction. If neither direction gives a likeness, return the feature to its original position.

4 Start again with another feature until satisfied with the result.

In this work, I am proposing a simple procedure for making caricatures. I believe that anybody who can recognize a likeness can make caricatures by using this procedure. I made the caricatures of six presidents and many other people following this procedure. To further enhance the results, I created a painted look by smudging the images in Photoshop. The figure shows the caricature of President George Bush. The photograph I based this caricature on is a 417x460 greyscale image, which I obtained from the Presidential Portraits Web page of the Library of Congress.

Ergun Akleman
Visualization Laboratory, 216 Langford Center
Department of Architecture
Texas A&M University
College Station, Texas 77843-3137 USA
ergun@viz.tamu.edu
http://www-viz.tamu.edu/faculty/ergun/artworks/artworks.html

ACKNOWLEDGEMENTS
I am grateful to **Quintin King** for developing the morphing program. I also would like to thank both **Donald H. House** and **John Ferguson** for their helpful suggestions.

Visual Simulation of Waterfalls and Other Water Phenomena

Accurate physically based rendering of complex phenomena such as the flow of water is an unrealistic aim: computational fluid dynamics simulation is a compute-intensive task, even for simple flow regimes, and is far beyond current knowledge for complex flows such as waterfalls. Our goal here is to develop a simple yet flexible simulation system that models a rich variety of scenes and behaviors, and provides the basis for visually convincing rendering. The simulation system aims to provide a convenient set of facilities for an animator to construct a scene and control the flow of water in that scene.

Whereas other authors[1,2,3] have simulated flows such as rivers, we have concentrated on falling water. Our system draws on observations of a large number of real waterfalls. A standard collection of objects such as spheres, planes, and polygons is used to model terrain or other solid objects such as fountains. More elaborate terrain models as in[4,6] are intended, but the current focus is on behavior.

Falling water is modeled using a three-dimensional particle system[5]: sections of falling water consist of a collection of relatively small particles that obey gravity. Each particle contains data relating to position, velocity, and size (including mass). Drops may influence one another, depending on the outcome of a simple particle-particle intersection test. As two particles approach, their relative velocity is examined. If this is above a certain threshold, the particles bounce away from one another, but if they are moving slowly they coalesce into a single blob of water (Figure 1 shows a fountain with coalescing columns). Intersection tests between particles or particles and solid objects are evaluated efficiently because the velocity of the particles and the simulation time step enable a localization optimization to be employed. Where a particle collides with a solid object, reflection about the surface normal takes place, but the normal is perturbed by a random amount to simulate surface irregularities and roughness. The reflection velocity is dampened by a factor based on the incident angle: if the angle is near 0°, then minimum loss occurs, but if the angle is near 90° then almost all energy is lost in the collision, thus slowing down the particle. If the impact velocity exceeds a given threshold, the particle splits into two equally sized particles. Figure 2 is a typical example.

Whilst falling, water is influenced by a number of factors. It can slow down and spread out due to air resistance and have its position affected by wind, sometimes dramatically. In our system, when wind is encountered, the number of nearby particles in the plane of interest is counted. This value is used to dampen the effect of wind on the volume of water falling, on the principle that dense particles mask the effects of wind, whereas sparse particles are more susceptible to being blown around. Multiple winds from multiple directions are used.

Mist/water vapor surrounds any section of falling water, contributed to by collisions with objects, deceleration, splitting, and small droplets of vapor escaping from the main volume. For example, a particle moving above a given velocity emits much smaller mist particles. Figure 3 demonstrates this effect. The behavior of mist differs from water particles in that it is very light, so it does not fall at the same rate as a normal section of water due to air resistance. Mist is particularly susceptible to influence both from the main body of water and external effects such as wind and may rise as well as fall. Mist also expands, contracts, and is even less predictable than its liquid counterpart. Rendering the final image in our simulation is currently straightforward, as our goal is not realistic rendering but visualization of the dynamics of the simulation. Each particle is initially assigned a blue colour, and a vector is drawn at the end of each time step based on the distance travelled in that time step (i.e. we draw velocity vectors). On striking an object, the colour of the particle is changed. The sound that water makes is emulated by generating random noise when particles strike solid objects.

In our future work, we plan to explore the turbulent actions of the splashdown area of a waterfall. We will also apply the ideas developed in the study of falling water to other water phenomena such as rivers and puddles. The goal is to provide an animator system that allows the construction of water-based scenes and effects based on the ideas that evolve during this research.

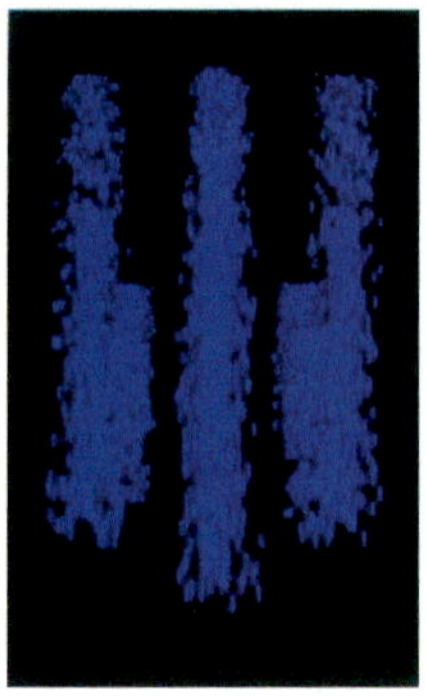

FIGURE 1 Fountain with coalescing columns (still)

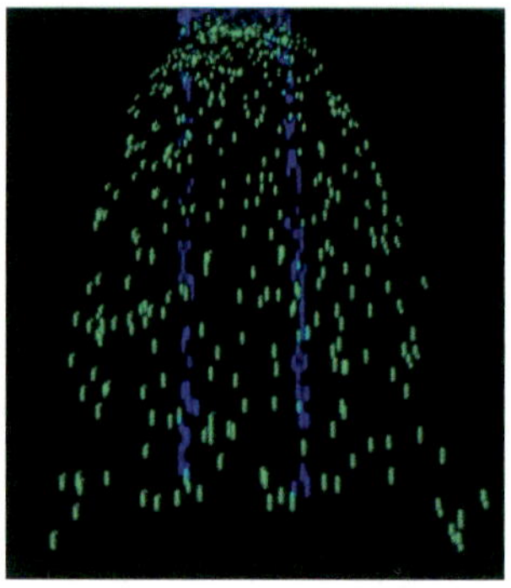

FIGURE 2 Water striking obstacle (still)

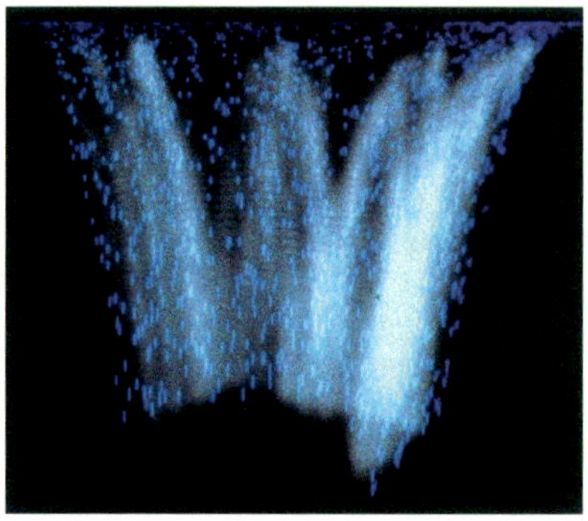

FIGURE 3 Horseshoe Falls with mist (still from video)

Ashley T. Howes, A.R. Forrest
Computational Geometry Project
School of Information Systems
University of East Anglia
Norwich NR4 7TJ, UNITED KINGDOM
ah,forrest@sys.uea.ac.uk

REFERENCES

1 N. Chiba, S. Sanakanishi, K. Yokoyama, I. Ootawara, K. Muraoka & N. Saito. Visual Simulation of Water Currents Using a Particle-based Behavioural Model, Journal of Visualization and Computer Animation, Volume 6, Issue 3, July-September 1995, pages 155-171.

2 N. Foster & D. Metaxas. Realistic Animation of Liquids, Graphical Models and Image Processing, Volume 58, Number 5, September 1996, pages 471-483.

3 M. Kass & G.S.P. Miller. Rapid, Stable Fluid Dynamics for Computer Graphics, ACM SIGGRAPH Computer Graphics, Volume 24, Number 4, August 1990, pages 49-57.

4 H. Mallinder. The Modelling of Large Waterfalls using String Texture, Journal of Visualization and Computer Animation, Volume 6, Issue 1, January-March 1995, pages 3-10.

5 W.T. Reeves. Particle Systems – A Technique for Modelling a Class of Fuzzy Objects, ACM Transactions on Graphics, Vol. 2, No. 2, 1983, pages 91-108.

6 K. Sims. Particle Animation and Rendering Using Data Parallel Computation, ACM SIGGRAPH Computer Graphics, Volume 24, Number 4, August 1990, pages 405-413.

Volumetric modeling is vital for realistic simulation of many natural phenomena, including water, clouds, gases, and fire[1]. Unlike traditional surface-based approaches[3], volumetric models allow you to capture the entire three-dimensionality of the phenomena. There are two general classes of techniques to simulate these natural phenoma: physically based simulation and non-physically based solutions. This sketch describes a new procedural technique for modeling and animating volumetric objects, which combines implicit function modeling, procedural turbulence simulations, and volume rendering to produce a powerful, easy-to-use, realistic volumetric modeling system for natural phenomena. The use of implicit functions (blobs, metaballs) as a modeling primitive allows the user to take advantage of smooth blending of primitives, sketetal modeling elements[4], and more natural animation control.

Volumetric procedural modeling (VPM) techniques have many advantages, including data amplification and parametric control[2]. However, the definition of overall volumetric shape through procedures can be a difficult task, especially for non-programmers. By combining implicit functions with VPMs, a natural, flexible, powerful animation and modeling system can be built. The advantages of both techniques can be harnessed to enhance the design and animation of volumetric objects.

An Example Procedural Volumetric Implicit Function

This new technique can be used to create realistic volumetric clouds that can be rendered with low-albedo and high-albedo physically based illumination and atmospheric attenuation. Figure 1 shows a cumulus cloud created by positioning nine implicit spheres with varying radii and blending amounts to define the overall shape of the cloud.

The turbulence-based[5] volumetric procedures add natural detail and allow control of the density and edge sharpness of the cloud. User-defined parameters control the blending of the implicit function density and the turbulence-based procedural density, the overall denseness of the cloud, and the sharpness of the density fall-off. The algorithm below describes the general cloud procedure:

```
cloud(pnt)
  perturb point using noise and turbulence
  density1 = implicit_function(perturbed_point)
  density2 = turbulence(pnt)
  blend = blend% * density1 + (1 - blend%) * density2
  returned density = power(blend*max_density, exponent)
end cloud
```

Cloud formation and evolution can be simulated by adding time as a parameter.

Conclusion

This sketch shows that implicit functions can be combined with procedural models to model and animate complex volumetric objects and phenomena. The addition of implicit functions provides natural blending of primitives, use of skeletal models, and ease of modeling and animation. More examples of this technique and resulting animations can be found at: http://www.cs.umbc.edu/~ebert/cloud

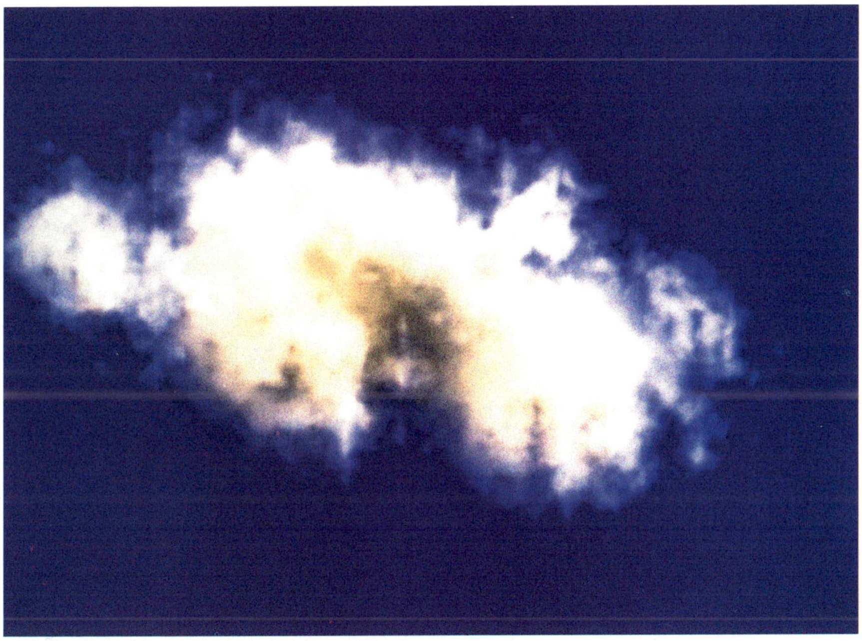

FIGURE 1 Procedural volumetric implicit turbulent cloud

David S. Ebert
Computer Science and Electrical Engineering Department
University of Maryland Baltimore County
1000 Hilltop Circle
Baltimore, Maryland 21250 USA
ebert@cs.umbc.edu
http://www.cs.umbc.edu/~ebert

REFERENCES

1 David Ebert, Ken Musgrave, Darwyn Peachey, Ken Perlin, and Steve Worley. Texturing and Modeling: A Procedural Approach, Academic Press,October 1994, ISBN 0-12-228760-6.

2 David S. Ebert. Advanced Modeling Techniques for Computer Graphics. In CRC Handbook of Computer Science and Engineering, chapter 56, CRC, 1997.

3 Gardner, Geoffrey. Visual Simulation of Clouds, In B.A. Barsky, editor, Computer Graphics (SIGGRAPH '85 Proceedings), volume 19, pages 297-303, July 1985.

4 Andrew Guy and Brian Wyvill. Controlled Blending for Implicit Surfaces, In Implicit Surfaces '95, April 1995.

5 Ken Perlin. An Image Synthesizer, In B. A. Barsky, editor, Computer Graphics (SIGGRAPH '85 Proceedings), volume 19, pages 287-296, July 1985.

In 1992, Pat Hanrahan and Don Mitchell introduced[3] a new algorithm that allowed an exact computation of the reflected illumination from curved mirror surfaces onto other surfaces (see Figure 1). That superb work was based on Fermat's principle, which says that this computation is equivalent to finding extremal paths from the light source to the visible surface via the mirrors. Once pathways were found, irradiance was computed from the Gaussian curvature of the geometrical wavefront. Another approach is bi-directional ray tracing[4], but it has as a major drawback: the inherent high computational cost of ray tracing.

In this sketch, I present a high-speed scan-line based algorithm to achieve the same effect. The key ideas on which the whole work is based are:

- There is no light-reflecting mirror that is not "seen" by the light sources.
- We can think of the whole process as if each curved reflector that receives light acts as a secondary light, that is, transforms itself into a non-isotropic extended light source.
- We can perform Phong-like interpolation, within a certain error, of any quantity that can be pointwise obtained, such as the intensity (Gouraud Shading), the surface normal (Phong Shading) or even its curvature.

Armed with these three ideas, we can introduce our scan-line based solution. As we build the shadow maps, we store the reflected illumination info within the mirror (see below), and later, when performing the final rendering step, we treat it exactly as any other light source. To do so, we only need a data structure to hold the illumination information in an efficient and accurate way. But that structure was already developed. It's a modification of the Environment Map[1] called Z-Buffered Environment Map[5]. It is very similar to the Light Buffers[2], where, for each pixel in the map, a complete sorted list of all the surfaces seen through it is stored (Figure 2). However, instead of storing the surface ID, we store its distance from the map center, its material ID, and the light intensity accumulated on it. Given a reflection ray in the map coordinate system (given by the position on the reflector, W, and the reflection direction, R), we only need to search in the line given by the intersection of the Env. Map and the plane determined by the Center of Projection, W and R; checking only the lists stored in the pixels that are between W and R, in order to find the closest to the desired intersection point.

So, the first step of our algorithm proceeds as follows (see Figure 3): Firstly, compute the Z-buffered Env. Map for each reflector. Then, when computing the shadow buffer for each light source, scan-line the mirrors as usual, but linearly interpolating the curvatures (stored with their respective vertices) as we use to do with the color or the normal. For each point of the surface rendered, calculate the light ray to it from the source and reflect it. With the Z-Buffered Env. Map, compute the intersection of this new ray with the environment, leaving the intensity information (computed exactly as described in Hanrahan, P & Mitchell) in the corresponding entry of the map.

During the final rendering, we must transform any point to be shaded to all the light sources' spaces and to all the mirrored objects own spaces, too. With the second ones, it's just a matter of taking the illumination information from the corresponding entry from the right pixel and computing the illumination (see Figure 4). If the object being rendered is the mirror itself, I use the indirect illumination stored in the first entry, along with the position (and coordinates of the pixel) to get the direct component, treating the surface as a pure lambertian one.

If we take into account that the original images were rendered in an eight-processor Silicon Graphics Iris in about 10 hours and that a small image (200*200) only took 10 minutes in a 486DLC PC, we would see that scan-line algorithms are just as capable of generating sophisticated lighting effects as ray tracing, at noticeably lower computational costs.

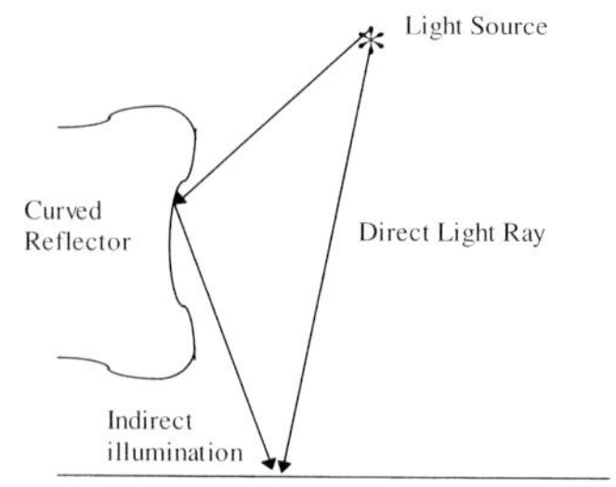

FIGURE 1
Direct and Indirect illumination to be computed at a surface.

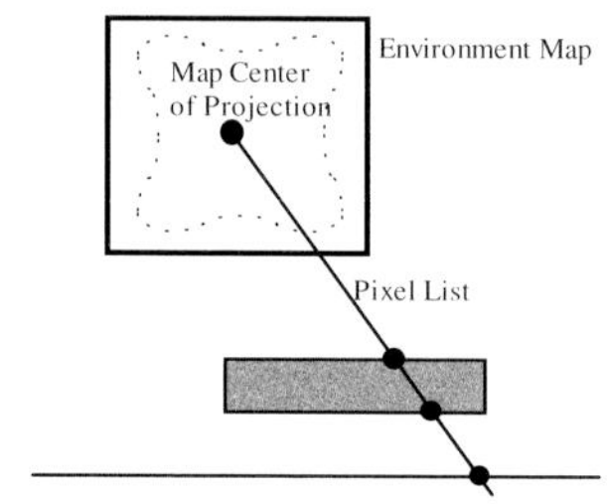

FIGURE 2
The Z-Buffered Environment Map geometry: A pixel list is shown with the three intersection points it contains marked as black dots.

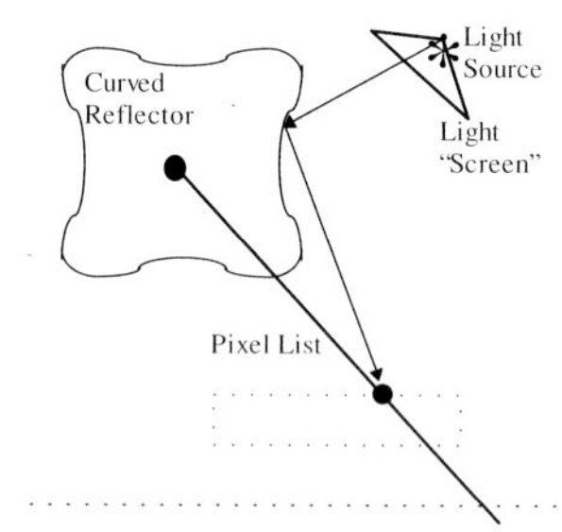

FIGURE 3
Storing the reflected illumination into the Environment Map. When computing the shadow buffer, each light ray that reaches the mirror surface is reflected and stored in its respective intersected list item.

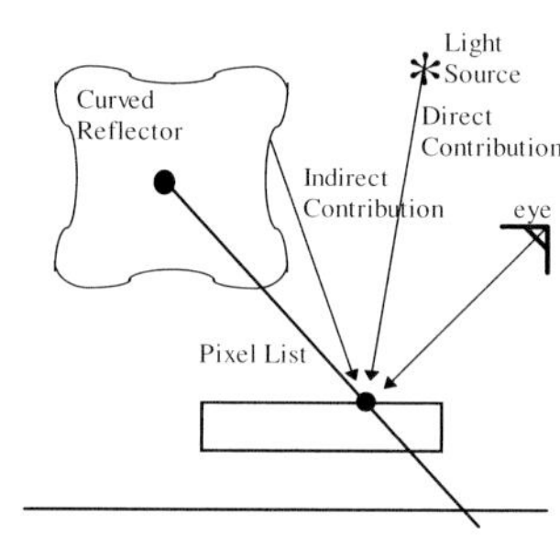

FIGURE 4
The final illumination step: the shading of the point seen by the observer is computed both from the light sources and from the curved reflector.

Gustavo A. Patow
LIFIA - UNLP - ARGENTINA
La Plata
Buenos Aires 1900 ARGENTINA
dagush@sol.info.unlp.edu.ar

REFERENCES
1 Blinn, J. F. & Newell, M. E. Texture and Reflection in Computer Generated Images, Comm. ACM, 19(10), October 1976, pp. 542-547.
2 Haines, E.A.. & Greenberg, D.P. The Light Buffer: A Shadow-Testing Accelerator, CG & A, 6(9), September 1986, pp. 6-16.
3 Hanrahan, P & Mitchell, D. Illumination from curved reflectors, Computer Graphics (Proc. SIGGRAPH 92), 26(2), July 1992, pp. 283-291.
4 Heckbert, P. Adaptative Textures for Bidirectional Ray Tracing, Computer Graphics (Proc. SIGGRAPH 90), 20(4) , August 1990, pp. 315-321.
5 Patow, G. A. Accurate Reflections Through Z-Buffered Environment Maps, (Proc. XV Int. Conf. of the Chilean Computer Science Society) 1995, pp. 385-392 .

We present a new method to compute the impulse response (IR) of a given virtual room based on hierarchical radiosity. Unlike previous work, our approach can treat complex geometries and is listening-position-independent. Moreover, complex phenomena such as sound diffraction are also taken into account.

The acoustical quality of a room may be evaluated from two points of view: objective criteria that can be measured and subjective appreciation by listening. These two ways, however, usually require knowledge of the room's impulse response at the listening position. The impulse response of a room may be seen as the pressure response of the room when the source emits an instantaneous impulse (Dirac signal). It is a digital filter that encodes all sound reflections through time from the source position to the listening position. By convolving this filter with a rough sound signal, the virtual sound field is made audible. This process is referred to as "auralisation".[2,3] Two standard methods for IR computation are ray/cone-tracing and image sources methods.[2,3] However, they quickly become impractical for complex geometries or high orders of reflection. They do not take into account complex phenomena such as diffraction by partial occluders. Moreover, they are listening-position-dependent, so the complete solution must be recomputed if the listener is moving, which can be limiting for virtual acoustics applications.[2,3]

We present a new approach to compute the IR of a virtual room based on a hierarchical-radiosity-like solution with general reflectance distributions.[1] We propagate energy from patch to patch as in the classic hierarchical radiosity method. Since sound propagation time cannot be neglected, we store an energy repartition through time for each surface corresponding to the list of echoes that reach the surface. This energy repartition through time (or echogram) is computed for various frequencies (generally octave bands), since reflection functions, source, and microphone directivities as well as propagation medium scattering are frequency dependent.

We approximate the attenuation factor due to diffraction by partial occluders by evaluating a frequential extended sound visibility term. This term is computed by counting the proportion of the first Fresnel ellipsoid, where most of the energy propagates, blocked by occluders. The first Fresnel ellipsoid is defined by $\{ M \in IR^3 \ / \ C_iM + MC_j = C_iC_j + \lambda/2 \}$ where C_i is the center of a patch P_i, C_j is the center of a linked patch P_j and λ the wavelength of the sound wave. We use graphics hardware for fast calculations by evaluating occlusions using the Z-buffer (Figure 1).

Phase information is also essential in order to reconstruct the IR. Thus, we represent echoes as complex numbers corresponding to modulus and phase. Once the sound radiosity solution is computed, the IR can be evaluated by re-projecting each echo stored on each surface onto the listening point. A short sampled impulse response of a basic bandpass filter is associated with each complex echo. These short IRs are then delayed and summed to obtain the final IR.

Our new method allows for using the appropriate number of patches for each frequency band, thus leading to an "optimal" usage of the computing resources. Complex propagation phenomena are taken into account, and final rendering times of less than a second make our approach promising for virtual acoustics applications. Validation of our algorithm with measured IRs of existing concert halls and rooms is currently in progress.

Nicolas Tsingos, Jean-Dominique Gascuel
iMAGIS-GRAVIR/IMAG
BP53, F-38041
Grenoble, Cedex 09 FRANCE
Nicholas.Tsingos@imag.fr
Jean-Dominique.Gascuel@imag.fr

REFERENCES
1 François X. Sillion and C. Puech. Radiosity and Global Illumination, Morgan Kaufmann Publishers Inc., 1994.
2 H. Lehnert and J. Blauert. Principles of Binaural Room Simulation, Applied Acoustics, 36, 1992.
3 M. Kleiner, B. Dalenbäck, & P. Svensson. Auralization – An Overview, Journal of the Audio Engineering Society, 41 (11), November 1993.

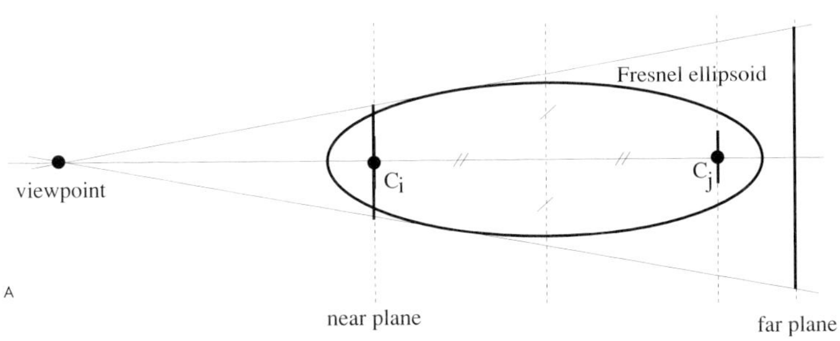

A

FIGURE 1 Using graphics hardware for sound visibility calculations
A Viewing frustum
B 3D view of microphone, source, occluders and Fresnel ellipsoids for 400 and 4000 Hz
C Visibility from microphone at 400 Hz
D Visibility from microphone at 4000 Hz
(Visibility term is the percentage of white pixels in the view)

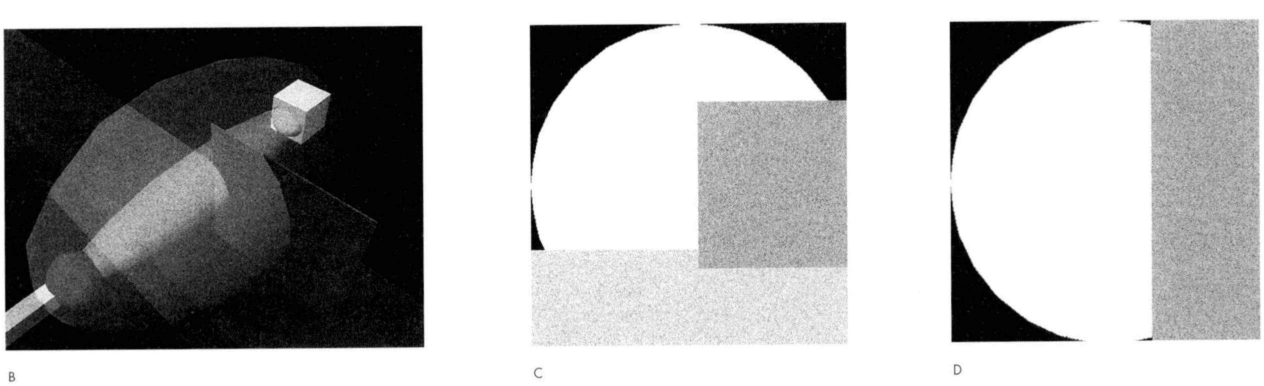

B C D

Radial Basis Function Interpolation Surface On Space Mesh

The B-spline paradigm for modeling smooth surfaces is limited by the requirement that the control point mesh must be organized as a regular rectangular structure. Ignoring this requirement by collapsing control mesh edges leads to surfaces with ambiguous surface-normals and degenerated parameterizations. Many approximation approaches have been considered for modeling surfaces of arbitrary topological type by smoothly approximating an irregular control mesh. A limitation of the polishing method is that it does not satisfy the interpolation condition. Some local interpolation methods have been discussed for constructing piecewise interpolation smooth space surfaces. These methods are based on increasing free degrees of each surface patch by using increasing polynomial order or refinement of space mesh. Generally, surface degree is not less quartic. In applying these methods, surface shapes depend on determination of parameters and estimation of gradient. It is concluded that local polynomial interplant generally produces unsatisfactory shapes.

In this sketch, we consider construction of a smooth interpolation space surface. A radial basis function interpolation surface over space mesh is generated by combining both the subdivision method and the radial basis function interpolation method. The technique's advantages include using interpolation to generate generally nice shapes.

Radial Basis Function Interpolation Surface

The interpolation surface algorithm takes a space mesh as input. A spline surface is constructed by using a subdivision method with bi-quadratic Bezier patch representation and tangent plane continuity between these patches that are in the same space triangular patch surrounded by space triangular. Then, a radial basis function interpolation surface defined on the spline surface is introduced. Radial functions are chosen to be either inverse multiquadric case or Gauss case, depending on which case will guarantee a coefficient matrix of radial function parameter equation system that is positive definite.

The radial basis function interpolation surface is constructed in two stages:

1 Construct bi-quadratic Bezier patches by subdivision algorithm.

2 Construct RBFIS defined on the collection of Bezier patches.

Input: irregular control mesh.
Output: radial basis function interpolation surface.

The purpose of using subdivision bi-quadratic Bezier patches is to isolate irregularities and smooth the entire surface shape. Any approximation surface is general enough to be used. The interpolation surface shape and smoothness order are dependent on the construction of the subdivision surface. A human face surface generated by using the algorithm is illustrated in Figure 1.

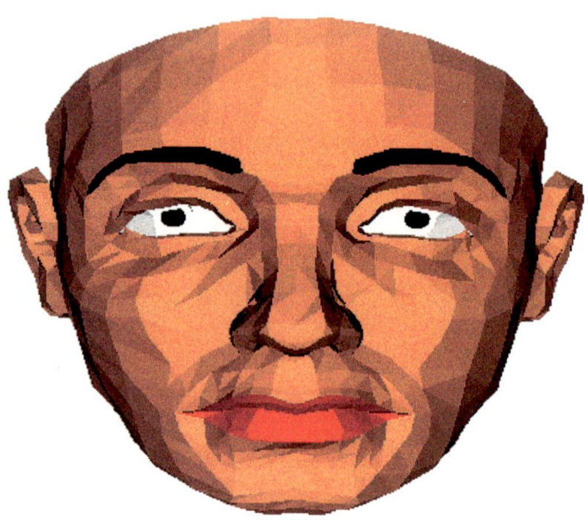

A

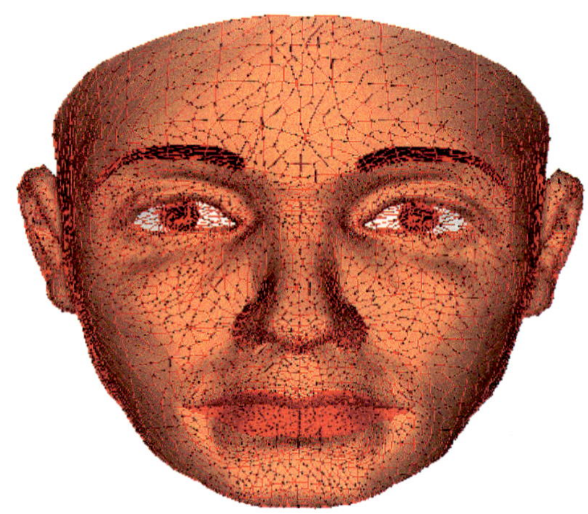

C

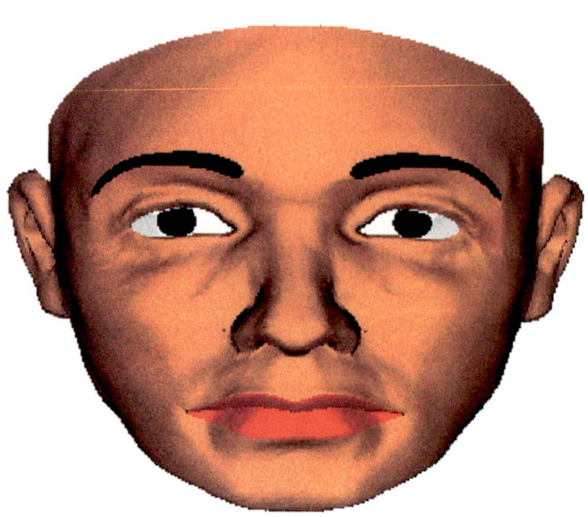

B

FIGURE 1
A A human face triangulation control mesh
B Radial basis function interpolation surface. The radial basis function is chosen to be Gaussian case: e^{-r^2}
C Control point mesh of subdivision spline surface (red color lines, only eight boundary lines are drawn for each bi-quadric Bezier path) and resulting subdivision spline surface.

Baocai Yin
Department of Computer Science
Beijing Polytechnic University
Beijing 100022, China
ybc@jdl.mcel.mot.com

Wen Gao
Department of Computer Science
Harbin Institute of Technology
Harbin 150001, China
wgao@jdl.mcel.mot.com

A 3D model construction constrained by a set of polylines provides a simple and accurate result. In particular, we provide a boundary-based model without using an irregular tetrahedra mesh, which is guaranteed to generate the triangular facets to match the surface of the 3D model. Our algorithm to generate a 3D model does not need a fine discretization on the 3D surface. However, if the model needs to be finer, recursive subdivision on the triangulated meshes can be implemented after the shrink.

Reconstruction of a 3D complex model from interpreted seismic data has been an intriguing problem during the last decade. The main motivations for solving this problem come from applications such as the study of medical imaging or geological imaging for oil exploration. Data obtained by digitization of 3D objects can be triangulated in order to represent a 3D model. When the model has a simple shape, the triangulated meshes can be easily generated. However, if a set of digitized data corresponds to a multi-valued surface, no method relying on projection can be applied.

Edelsbrunner and Mucke[1] tried to define the geometrical data structure by the notion of "shape" for a set of points. Starting from the Delaunay triangulation, an alpha coefficient is associated with each point, edge, triangle, and tetrahedron. For alpha equals infinity, the shape of a 3D object is identical to the convex hull. However, as alpha decreases, the shape shrinks by gradually developing cavities. Unfortunately, based on our experience, it is difficult to define a continuous triangulated boundary from a set of points.

Boissonnat[2] proposed a volume-based approach to build a 3D object. The first step of this approach is to implement Delaunay triangulation on the scattered data points. The second step is to successively remove the triangles or tetrahedra from the convex hull to the objective boundary of the 3D model. In both methods described above, the generated 3D model will cause an error when the data points representing the surface are not dense. Given a set of constraints such as tetrahedra, triangles, or edges, we are unable to build the tetrahedra that can be filled with those tetrahedra or triangles, if the data to represent the 3D surface are not fine enough. Therefore, to tetrahedralize a geometric structure involving vertices, edges, and triangles, Steiner points must be added in the general case[3]. Their number can be very large, resulting in a far more complex tetrahedralization. Boissonnat proposed another surface-based approach to build a 3D model by means of a local procedure[3]. However, the proposed method does not guarantee a satisfactory triangulation of a 3D surface even if the discretization is fine enough.

We propose a method to circumvent this problem by applying constrained triangulation on a 3D surface. Rather than implementing 3D triangulation and removing the tetrahedra step by step, we implement 2D Delaunay triangulation to generate the convex hull. We then implement local triangulation, constrained by the given polylines, which guarantees an efficient and accurate result surface.

By providing a set of points in space, one can build a convex hull filled with triangulated meshes. At the beginning, four triangles are built as a single tetrahedron, which contains four vertices but not any three points on a line. For any point outside the existing polyhedron, we add and locally triangulate on the 3D surface. The triangulation scheme we use satisfies the Delaunay criterion (that is, there is no point in space defined by each circumscribing sphere associated with each triangle).

After all the points in 3D space have been checked and triangulated, we are able to generate a convex hull with all the points either inside or on the surface of the convex hull, as shown in Figure 1.

A polyline is generated if a set of points in 3D space is in a sequential order. We are able to use sequential points as a guide to ensure the proper triangulation in the 3D model. The first step is to compute the normal vector from the given polylines. For each point in 3D space, we assume the vector is orthogonal to the 3D object and intersected with a specific triangle on the convex hull. The normal vector gives us the direction to apply local triangulation. Note that the lines projected from a normal vector should not intersect with its polyline. Therefore, our algorithm relies on checking of the minimum distance of query point inside the convex hull. Each time, we select a point with the minimum distance to the convex hull, and locally triangulate to the 3D surface. Rather than building Delaunay triangulated surface, we implement 2D local triangulation, constrained by polylines. This is to ensure that the edges of triangular meshes are constrained by the polylines. Figures 2 and 3 show the procedures of shrunk processing. Finally. we are able to generate a 3D model after the implementation of local triangulation on all the hidden points inside the convex hull.

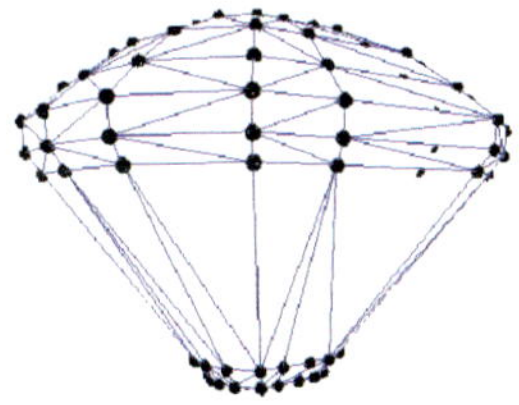

FIGURE 1

FIGURE 2

FIGURE 3

Toshi Chang, Luis Canales, Tom Ledoux
CogniSeis Development, Inc.
2401 Portsmouth
Houston, Texas 77098 USA
toshi@cogniseis.com

REFERENCES

1 Edelsbrunner, H., and Mucke, E. P. Three-dimensional Alpha Shape, ACM Transactions on Graphics 13, 1 (Jan. 1994), 43-72.

2 Boissonnat, J.D. Geometric Structures for Three-dimensional Shape Representation, ACM Transactions on Graphics 3, 4 (Oct. 1984), 266-286.

3 Nackman, L.R., and Srinivasan, V. Point Placement for Delaunay Triangulation of Polygonal Domains. In Proc. 3rd Canad. Conf. Comput. Geom, 1991, 37-40.

There have been many point-in-polygon test algorithms presented; Haines[1] gives a thorough comparative treatment of existing point-in-polygon algorithms, and the terminology that we use is based upon that work. The best of the current methods utilizing a preprocessing phase (the grid method[1]) requires a lot of extra storage in addition to the basic polygon information. We present a method based on constructive solid geometry (CSG) representations of polygons[2] requiring only two integers and three reals per edge plus an integer and two pointers per polygon (the original representation can be discarded). The only drawback to this method is that it does not support self-intersecting polygons.

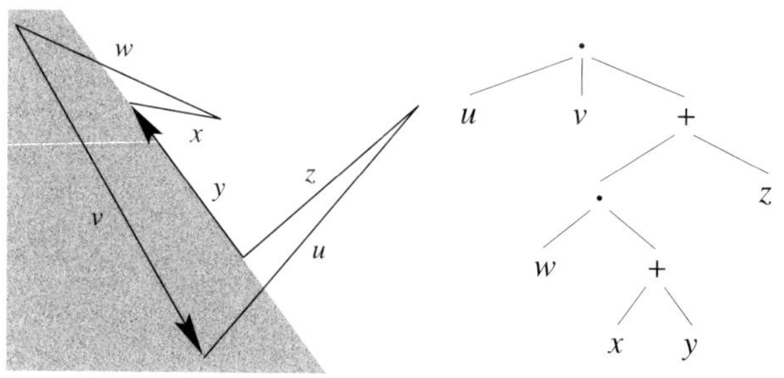

An example polygon yielding the formula uv((w(x+y))+z) (the half-plane defined by the edge y is also shown) and its CSG representation.

A polygon may be represented via CSG as a monotone Boolean formula on the half-planes bounded by the edges of the polygon[2]. If we orient the edges of the polygon in a counter-clockwise fashion, the half-planes of interest lie to the left of the edges. These formulae may be represented as directed trees in which each edge of the polygon appears only once.

The point of interest is then tested against the leaves (edges) of the directed tree in left-to-right order to determine if it falls inside (TRUE) or outside (FALSE) the associated half-planes. Since an AND-node will not be satisfied if any of its children are FALSE, as soon as we determine that one of its children is FALSE, the remaining children need not be tested; the situation is analogous with OR-nodes. The idea is then to minimize the number of tests required for points on average for a given polygon; this may be done by altering the embedding of the directed tree by swapping any two children of a given node. As a simple first step, we chose to rearrange children beneath each node by size of subtree and secondarily by length of edge. We are developing more sophisticated heuristics based upon coverage of the target plane (or bounding box) by the defined half-planes.

We confine the construction of the tree and its rearrangement to a preprocessing phase. This reduces the actual test algorithm to a series of point-in-half-plane tests, each resulting in a predetermined decision as to which edge to test next.

	3	4	10	20	50	100
Crossings	6.8	7.1	11.4	19.3	41.2	77.1
Half-plane	2.4	3.8	11.3	23.7	59.0	117.8
Spackman	3.3	4.9	13.6	27.7	74.3	137.2
Grid 20 X 20	5.1	5.1	5.3	5.5	6.2	7.0
Grid 100 X 100	4.8	4.8	4.9	4.8	5.0	5.1
CSG w/sorting	3.0	3.9	7.6	11.3	20.5	32.4
CSG w/o sorting	3.4	4.3	7.8	12.7	24.4	41.5

Average times for point-in-polygon tests (in microseconds), number of vertices per polygon vs. method. For each of 50 random polygons, 50 random points were tested. Some tests were repeated to reduce inaccuracy; see Haines[1] for discussion.

Haines' implementation of existing point-in-polygon tests[1] was augmented with our CSG method both with and without the sorting heuristics described above. Tests were as described by Haines, save that, to ensure that the polygons were non-self-intersecting, an edge-swap algorithm was used to untangle them. The tests were run on a Silicon Graphics Indigo workstation.

The simply sorted CSG representation method is faster than the basic methods for all polygons save triangles. It uses significantly less memory than the grid method and is faster than the grid method for small polygons. This method may be extended to 3D ray intersection, via the use of Pluecker coordinates, without having first to resort to determining a plane for the polygon and intersecting the ray with this plane.

Robert Walker, Jack Snoeyink
2366 Main Mall
University of British Columbia
Vancouver, British Columbia V6T 1Z4 CANADA
walker@cs.ubc.ca

REFERENCES

1 Eric Haines. Point in Polygon Strategies, In Paul S. Heckbert, ed., Graphics Gems IV, chapter 1.4, pp. 24-46, Academic Press, Boston, 1994.

2 David Dobkin, Leonidas Guibas, John Hershberger, and Jack Snoeyink. An Efficient Algorithm for Finding the CSG Representation of a Simple Polygon, In John Dill, ed., Computer Graphics (SIGGRAPH '88 Proceedings), volume 22, pp. 31-40, August 1988.

Discrete models of elastic materials have many applications, particularly in computer graphics. The driving force for the research described in this sketch was the problem of modeling skin so that it would stretch and slide realistically over an underlying body of modeled muscles and bones. Particularly on animal skin with markings, the markings should shift realistically in response to underlying limb movements and changes in muscle shape.

In two dimensions, given a discretization of a membrane as an irregular triangle mesh, the standard finite element method analyzes each triangle approximately as a membrane with specified elastic properties, computing stresses and strains. An alternative is to regard each edge as a spring, assuming the springs are connected by "pin-joints" at the vertices of the discretization.

This alternative, called a "spring mesh," offers conceptual and computational simplicity compared to the first, but it is unclear under what conditions it produces the same results.

Spring meshes have been used by numerous researchers to model elastic material, with skin, textiles, and soft tissue being typical applications. However, given a specified set of elastic material properties, the question of whether a particular spring mesh accurately simulates those properties has been largely ignored in the literature, leaving the presumption that they are all equal. As we shall show experimentally, identical spring stiffness coefficients for all edges in the mesh may lead to noticeable distortions, while varying the coefficients according to the geometrically based formula presented here provides a more accurate simulation. Because the formula is local, it extends immediately to the case of non-uniform membranes. Extension to tetrahedral meshes in 3D is work in progress.

The relationship between stress and strain depends on two parameters of elasticity, called Young's stiffness modulus (E_2 for membranes) and the Poisson coefficient (v). Timoshenko and Goodier [1951] recommend using v=0.25 for "most materials."

Consider a triangle T, with edges and angles as shown in the accompanying image, top left, which is subjected to horizontal opposing stretching forces. First, suppose that the triangle consists of pin-connected springs. Then, clearly edge c will elongate, while edges a and b will not change length (black triangle, right). Now, suppose that the triangle is modeled as a membrane. The question is, for what family of internal stresses will the lengths of both a and b not change?

This question has an elegant geometrical answer, which is indicated in the top right part of the image. The key is to transform into the coordinate frame (u,v) such that the v-axis bisects the angle γ. Now, *any* constant stress whose principal directions are the u and v axes will produce identical elongations in edges a and b, and in our case we want both to be *zero*. Applying the constraints and solving:

$$k_c = \frac{E_2}{(1-v^2)} \left(\frac{\sin\alpha \sin\beta - v\cos\alpha \cos\beta}{\sin\gamma} \right)$$

For $v = 0$, this equation is equivalent to $k_c = 2E_2\, area(T)/|c|^2$. Corresponding formulas may be obtained for k_a and k_b. The coefficient derived, k_c applies for *one* triangle of which c is an edge, but normally, c is in *two* triangles, so the two individual coefficients are added to give the total stiffness coefficient for edge c in the overall spring mesh.

The method described has been implemented for some test meshes, where the correct behavior is known from the construction. For simplicity we used $v = 0$ throughout the tests. The accompanying image shows a hexagonal membrane subjected to a constant outward radial force at the six external vertices. A regularly triangulated membrane would expand uniformly.

The irregularly subdivided membrane in which all spring k's are equal undergoes distortion, as in the bottom left of the image. However, the same geometry expands correctly when the spring k's are calculated by the formula given here, as in bottom right. One supplemental movie animates this test. The second supplemental movie shows simulated tiger skin stretching. Notice the deformation of the skin stripes on the hindquarters.

Allen Van Gelder, Jane Wilhelms
Computer Science Department
University of California, Santa Cruz
Santa Cruz, California 95064 USA
avg@cs.ucsc.edu
wilhelms@cs.ucsc.edu

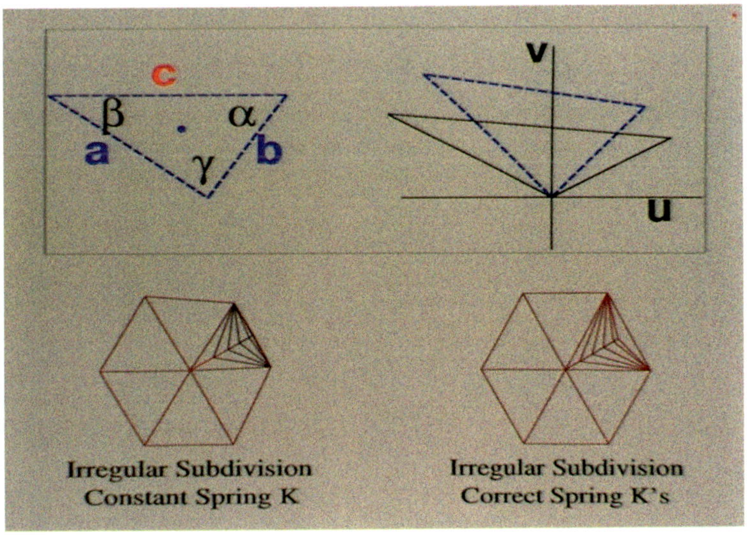

Display of High Contrast Images using Models of Visual Adaptation

High-contrast scenes and images are quite common. Scenes with dark shadows, specular highlights, or directly visible light sources may have contrasts (ratios of light intensities) of 100,000:1 or more. Images of these scenes are difficult to display accurately because their contrasts greatly exceed the range of most display devices (about 100:1). As a result, displayed image contrasts are often compressed by "gamma correction" or truncated by "clipping," which hides or destroys subtle textures and details. Unlike displays, the human eye can accommodate high-contrast scenes easily, *adapting* the visual response with no apparent loss of content or detail. This sketch presents two methods for display of high-contrast images that are based on some of these visual adaptation processes.

Layering

Humans see far more than just intensities when viewing a scene or image. We also sense shapes, textures, reflectances, transparencies, and illumination. Several researchers in disparate areas have suggested that an image is not perceived as a single entity, but as image *layers*, each of which describes an important scene quantity[1]. We propose segregating synthetic image intensities into three layers during rendering: diffuse surface reflectance R, diffuse illumination I, and image intensity due to specular reflection toward the eye, transparency, or self-luminous emission of the surface STE. Often STE is recursively subdivided into additional I, R, and STE layers to accommodate scenes containing partially transparent or mirrored surfaces.

Dividing the image into layers allows us to compress the layers independently to reduce the overall contrast in the image while preserving fine details and textures. Most of the detail is contained in the R layer, but the contrast of this layer is always small. The wide-ranging values of the I and STE layers are the cause of high image contrasts, and the layering method compresses and combines them with the unmodified R layer to create a displayable image.

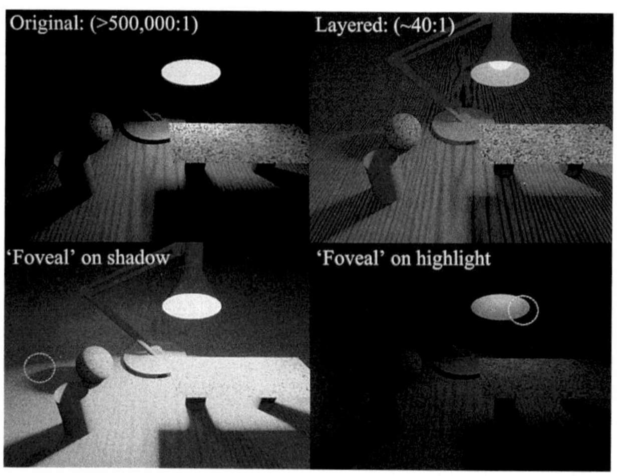

High-contrast scene (>500,000:1) displayed using layering and foveal methods: a) Original loses highlight and shadow detail to clipping; b) "layering" reduces image contrast (estimated 40:1) but preserves visible scene details; c),d) "foveal" interactively adjusts entire image for best display of a small circled region near the cursor, compressing out-of-range values. Interactive viewing of a scene resembles the familiar dynamic behavior of an automatic-exposure camera.

This approach is supported by substantial experimental evidence that shows that the visual system acutely senses surface reflectance R, but tolerates wide variations in illumination. For example, humans are often unaware of artificial changes to illumination such as "fill" lighting, which lessens shadow contrasts but does not disrupt the boundaries or other primary features of the scene. Because specular highlights within a viewed scene are predominantly used to refine estimates of surface properties such as local curvature and smoothness, the shape and width of specular highlight boundaries may be far more important than the intensity. The compression of I and STE layers preserves boundaries well but reduces overall image contrast to the range of the display device.

Foveal

The human eye is highly directional, adaptable, and nonuniform. The 2-5 degree central region of the retina, or fovea, gathers almost all the fine image detail and color information we see, and the eye preferentially adapts to the available light in the small foveal region. This changeable and localized assessment is particularly useful for high contrast images, because small neighborhoods tend to have much lower contrasts than the entire image, suggesting that neither the eye nor the image display must accept all scene contrasts at once.

Our "foveal" display program mimics this process by using a small circular neighborhood around the mouse cursor as the "fovea" and adjusting the entire image for best display of this region. Out-of-range display values are asymptotically compressed towards black or white, reducing contrasts without truncating them. Interactive viewing of high-contrast images in this fashion relies on the remarkable ability of the human visual system to form a stable and seamless impression of the entire visual field from glances at interesting scene features.

Conclusions

These two simple, effective methods show that limited display contrasts do not prevent accurate depictions of visible scene content and suggest that more perceptually motivated methods should replace clipping. Van Allsburg[2] and other skilled artists can create detailed, artifact-free drawings of high-contrast scenes such as a rocket launch at midnight (>100,000:1) using low-contrast displays such as a pencil on paper (<30:1). Clearly, the 100:1 contrast range of CRT displays should be adequate for all synthetic scenes with the development of improved display methods.

Jack Tumblin, Jessica Hodgins
College of Computing
Georgia Institute of Technology
ccsupjt@cc.gatech.edu
jkh@cc.gatech.edu

Brian Guenter
Microsoft Research
bguenter@microsoft.com

REFERENCES
1 Alan L. Gilchrist. Lightness, Brightness, and Transparency, Lawrence Erlbaum Associates, Inc., Hillsdale, New Jersey, 1994,
2 Chris Van Allsburg, The Mysteries of Harris Burdick, Houghton Mifflin Company, New York, 1984,

Human vision operates over about nine orders of magnitude, from starlight at 10^{-4} candelas/meter^2 to daylight at 10^5 cd/m^2. In any given scene, the eye can adapt comfortably over a smaller range of about four orders of magnitude. This still exceeds the dynamic range of conventional display devices and media, which at best cover a range of about 100:1 – only two orders of magnitude. The rest of the information, which would be perceived in the real world as detail in bright and dark regions, is lost above the maximum display value or below the black level. This limitation has serious ramifications for simulated imagery, especially when it is needed to evaluate visual performance or in virtual reality (VR) environments. Previous tone mapping work by Tumblin and Rushmeier[1], Ward[2], and Ferwerda et al[3] did not consider the question of local adaptation. Chiu et al[4] looked into this problem, but their solution resulted in reverse gradients and did not account for human visual response.

In this sketch, we present a new method for mapping scenes and images containing high dynamic range information to conventional (and VR) displays. The technique matches object visibility as its primary goal, meaning that objects visible in the real world will be visible on the display, and conversely, objects not visible in the real world will not be visible on the display. As a secondary goal, the method attempts to reproduce a viewer's subjective response, meaning that the impression of the displayed image should correlate well with memories of the actual scene.

The starting point of our method is a histogram of scene brightnesses, which we define as the log of luminances averaged over 1° areas. These areas correspond to foveal adaptation levels for possible fixation points in a scene or image. We then apply a histogram adjustment procedure to remove portions of the brightness population that are under-represented in the scene, since they convey relatively little visible information. We compress this unused dynamic range so that important objects in bright and dark regions can be included within the usable dynamic range of the display. The eye tends not to notice the compressed information as missing, since human vision is designed to perceive object detail, not relative brightnesses.

Once we have solved the problem of making visible world objects also visible on the display, we need to consider human visual limitations, so that objects *not* visible in the real world are *not* visible on the display. First, we adjust our brightness histogram to match local human contrast sensitivity. Next, we add veiling luminance around bright areas (e.g., light sources) to simulate scattering in the eye. In dark scenes, we also model the loss of color sensitivity in accord with measurements of mesopic and scotopic response. Finally, in very dark regions, we may adjust image resolution locally to match limits in human visual acuity.

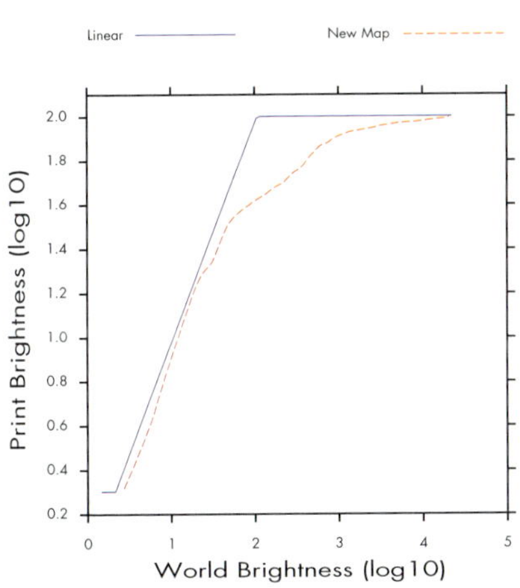

FIGURE 1 Plot of linear tone mapping used in Figure 2 versus new tone mapping used in Figure 3.

FIGURE 2 An unadjusted simulation of a bathroom scene mapped with a standard linear tone reproduction operator.

FIGURE3 The same simulation reproduced using the new tone mapping operator, which models human contrast sensitivity and disability glare.

Gregory Ward Larson (the computer artist formerly known as Greg Ward)
Silicon Graphics, Inc.
2011 N. Shoreline Blvd., M/S 07U-553
Mountain View, California 94043-1389 USA
gregl@sgi.com

Holly Rushmeier
IBM T.J. Watson Research Laboratory

Christine Piatko
JHU/APL

REFERENCES

1 J. Tumblin and H. Rushmeier. Tone Reproduction for Realistic Images, IEEE Computer Graphics and Applications, November 1993, 13(6), 42-48.

2 G. Ward. A contrast-based scalefactor for luminance display, In P.S. Heckbert (Ed.) Graphics Gems IV, Boston, Academic Press Professional.

3 J. Ferwerda, S. Pattanaik, P. Shirley and D.P. Greenberg. A Model of Visual Adaptation for Realistic Image Synthesis, Proceedings of ACM SIGGRAPH 96, p. 249-258.

4 K. Chiu, M. Herf, P. Shirley, S. Swamy, C. Wang and K. Zimmerman. Spatially nonuniform scaling functions for high contrast images, Proceedings of Graphics Interface '93, Toronto, Canada, May 1993, pp. 245-253.

Validating Global Illumination Algorithms and Software

It is relatively easy to use photorealistic rendering techniques to create images that look great. It is much more difficult to perform physically based lighting simulation and create images that match the appearance of an actual space. A direct comparison of the virtual and real-world images is an effective way to validate rendering algorithms and discover their drawbacks. Unfortunately, such comparisons are almost never performed, even for very simple environments.

In this work, we simultaneously view synthetic images and photographic images, and we vary the parameters of our perception-based image rendering software to achieve the best visual match between the virtual and real-world images. This qualitative evaluation is complemented by a quantitative measurement of lighting simulation accuracy. We investigated two different lighting simulation techniques:

1 Deterministic cluster-based hierarchical progressive radiosity.

2 Stochastic Monte Carlo photon tracing (the core algorithms of the Inspirer system from Integra, Inc.).

As a case study, we chose an atrium at the University of Aizu (left below). While the direct lighting distribution within such an environment can be easily predicted analytically, calculating the results of indirect lighting is much more involved. In fact, analytic solutions exist only for extremely simple, symmetric environments. So for quantitative validation of the lighting simulation, we examined several simple cases. (See our Web site[1] for more details on the analytic derivation of illumination values for these simpler cases).

In our work on the atrium, we began by specifying the light sources and surfaces in our model according to information from luminaire manufacturers and architectural drawings. More adequate measurement data are needed (for example reflectance functions), but in practice, it is very difficult to obtain complete and reliable data.

In the lighting simulation phase, we obtain luminance and chroma (maintained separately) values for every pixel of the final image. We then transform the stimulus luminance values to brightness values (perceived brightness predicted for the observer using Stevens' power law[2]). The brightness transformation is also performed for the range of luminances produced by the display device.

First, we confirm that we are able to present the photographic image under display conditions that give the best match between this image and the original environment. Next, we adjust the parameters of the brightness transformation until the appearance of the synthetic image (right below) best matches that of the photographic image (left below). Since we were unable to directly determine a given viewer's light adaptation level, this method allowed selection of the brightness function that worked best for that viewer under those viewing conditions.

While our atrium rendering is still far from perfect, first impressions were very favorable. In fact, many viewers who were quite familiar with the real atrium thought that they were viewing the actual photographic images when they first viewed the synthetic images. However, when the same viewers compared the synthetic images to the photographic images, they were able to find many differences and therefore were able to provide us very useful feedback.

We hope that the global illumination community will come to a more standardized approach to evaluating their algorithms and software. Toward this end, we have posted our atrium data in various formats[1]. We also provide a comprehensive description of our validation tests for lighting simulation with analytically derived luminance values.

Photograph

Rendering using the deterministic method

Karol Myszkowski
The University of Aizu
k-myszk@u-aizu.ac.jp

Andrei Khodulev, Edward A. Kopylov
Keldysh Institute of Applied Mathematics
Russian Academy of Sciences

REFERENCES
1 http://www.u-aizu.ac.jp/~k-myszk/valid (the Web page that provides more information on this work)
2 Jack Tumblin and Holly E. Rushmeier. Tone Reproduction for Realistic Images, IEEE Computer Graphics and Applications, 13(6):42-48, 1993.

Many different lighting simulation techniques have been developed for computing illumination in a virtual environment. However, many of the techniques make different simplifying assumptions and thereby restrict the lighting effects they can simulate. Multi-pass methods try to combine the advantages of each of these techniques to yield better algorithms, but they have so far been limited to static combinations of the above techniques.

In the Lighting Network approach, each lighting algorithm is considered a lighting operator, taking illumination information as input and generating new illumination information as output after having computed a part of the global lighting simulation in the scene. By formalizing the representations of illumination taken as input and generated as output, different algorithms can be combined in a data-flow network. This flexible combination allows for obtaining special lighting effects that would be difficult to compute with single algorithms or a fixed combination thereof. Light paths computed by a Lighting Network can formally be described using extended regular expressions. This allows an automatic analysis of composite lighting simulation and guarantees completeness and redundant-free computations.

The ability to restrict Lighting Operators to certain parts of the scene allows for tailoring the simulation to the needs of a user. It allows the simulation to be restricted to a small subset of the scene, thereby making it usable for simulating costly lighting effects, even in complex scenes. This brings back the control that has been taken away from users by conventional global lighting simulations.

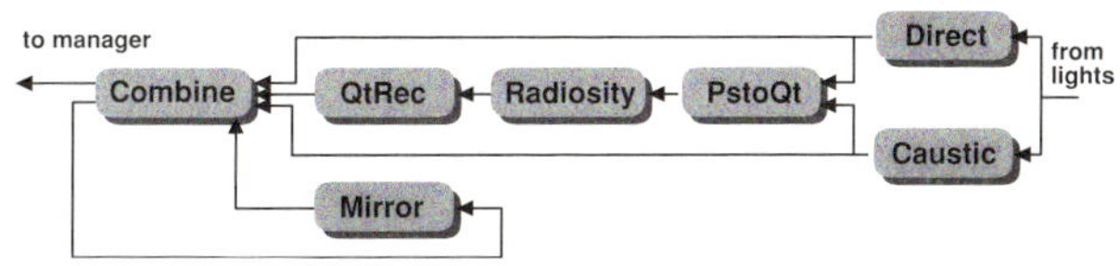

FIGURE 1 Lighting Networks: A simple example

Figure 1 shows a schematic view of the Lighting Network used for generating the images in Figure 2. The direct and caustic illumination (computed by ray tracing and photon maps, respectively) from a lamp with an internal reflector is used directly and as the input for computing indirect illumination with Radiosity. Additional lighting operators convert between and combine different illumination representations and account for perfect specular reflection and transmission.

This approach presents an open framework for composite lighting simulations, where advanced algorithms and new solution strategies can easily be integrated. While this makes Lighting Networks a versatile tool for research and development, its advantages are most useful to practitioners. Traditionally, global illumination algorithms have offered only little opportunity for configuration, tweaking, and creating special effects. With Lighting Networks, the user may select where and to which extent the features of automatic global lighting simulation are appropriate or necessary.

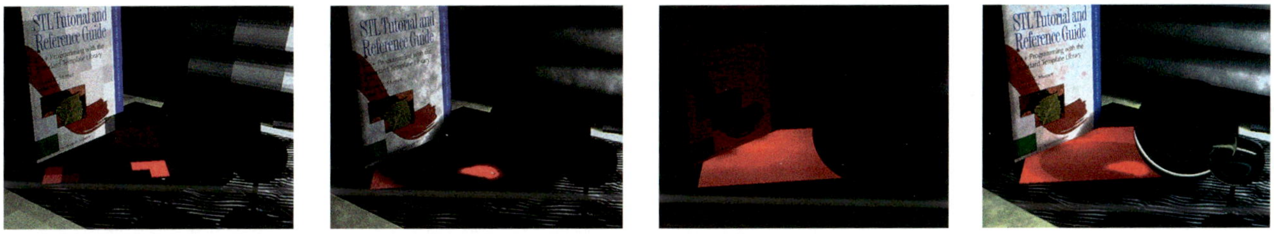

FIGURE 2 Partial results computed by the Lighting Network in Figure 1(from left: direct, caustic, indirect, and full illumination).

Philipp Slusallek, Marc Stamminger, Wolfgang Heidrich, Jan-Christian Popp, Hans-Pieter Seidel
Computer Graphics Group - IMMD IX
University of Erlangen
Am Weichselgarten 9
91058 Erlangen, Germany
heidrich@informatik.uni-erlangen.de

Live Web Stationery: Virtual Paper Aging

We propose a method to visualize a World Wide Web page's life based on the metaphor of the page. Pages are made of paper, which, over time, shows the effects of time and use: it may fade, get dusty, get stained, smudged, creased, and torn. These changes provide us with clues about that piece of paper: its age, how often it was handled, where it was placed, and even something about the people who have handled it. The type of paper and how it has been handled also provide us with clues to its content. A long document or book, a personal letter, or a list are typically produced on differently sized and colored paper with different characteristics. Although Web pages share these characteristics of age, handling, and intent, this information is not systematically integrated with the presentation graphics of the page.

In fact, there is very little we can glean about a page on the Web, with perhaps the exception of a hit counter or date of last revision. Even this information does not tell us how the Internet community interacted with the page. The hit counter of a Web page with 100 hits from one user looks just like the hit counter on a site with one hit each from 100 different users. Similarly, hits are counted as the same whether the user stays on the page or immediately follows a link to another page. A richer set of information is available, some through the current mechanisms of the web (http), but most of it requires specialized data gathering mechanisms and analysis. This information can be mapped to the characteristics of a piece of paper. The system created by Hill, et. al. represented document usage through variations in the appearance of user interface elements such as their attribute-mapped scroll bars[1]. Instead, our system integrates the visual representation of time and usage with the document itself, relying on metaphors of real-world paper aging to provide instantaneous visual cues to the relative age and popularity of the documents in the system.

Problem and Proposed Solution

Our goal is to automatically generate image files representing pieces of paper to use as background images for HTML formatted pages. Hence, we favor approximate, but speedy methods over correct, but slow, methods in order to generate the images in real time, and minimize additional downloading delays. Some elements of wear and tear are mathematically modeled, while others are drawn from a library of textures created by Cati Laporte and parametrically combined to create the desired effect. The virtual paper generated by our system is a visualization of document usage, showing what links have been followed the most, time since last visit, etc. Some of this information can be provided by linking user interaction to a collection of human-caused effects: smudges, spilt coffee stains, creasing. Other information will be provided by showing wear and tear.

We model the paper, its environment, time, and human manipulation:

- Paper attributes: color, texture, weight, wear and tear.
- Environment attributes: storage, dust, dirt, light.
- Time: creation, modification, display.
- Human interaction: retrieval attributes (user, browser, originating link, bookmarking, site-mapping, etc.) and interaction types (clicking, editing, copying, printing, etc.).

Our example, shown in Figure 1, illustrates several of these techniques. The surface deformation and edge wear depicts handling. Coffee stains are used to indicate that the page has been read for long periods of time. Smudges and fingerprints are placed over links that have been followed frequently, with cumulative wear indicating the most frequently followed links. More general smudges and stains, as well as yellowing, provide further cues to the relative age and amount of handling received by this document.

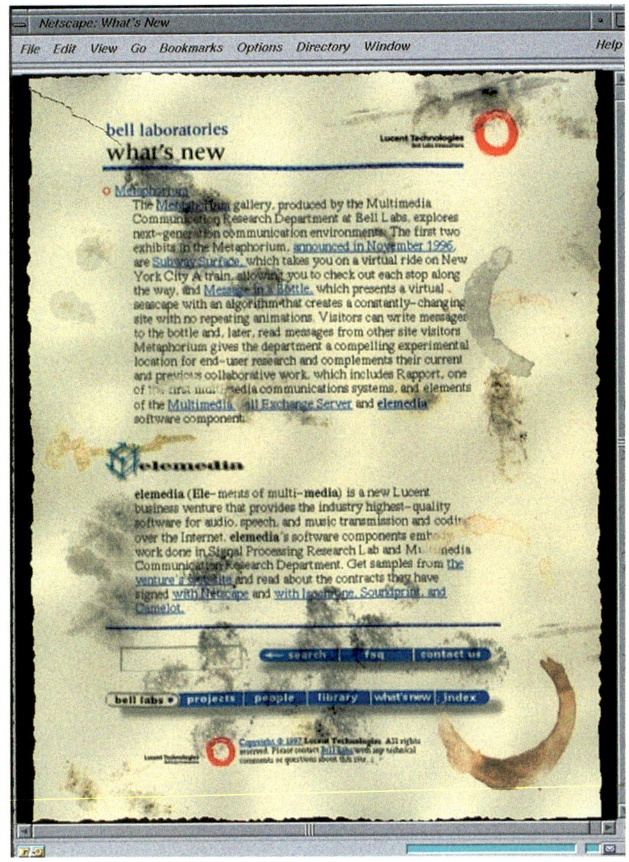

FIGURE 1

Doree Duncan Seligmann, Stephan Vladimir Bugaj
Multimedia Communication Research Department
Bell Laboratories of Lucent Technologies
101 Crawfords Corner Road
Holmdel, New Jersey 07733-3030 USA
+1.732.949.4290
+1.732.949.0399 fax
doree@bell-labs.com
bugaj@bell-labs.com
http://www.multimedia.bell-labs.com

REFERENCE

1 Hill, W.C., Hollan, J.D., Wroblewski, D., McCandless, T. Edit Wear and Read Wear, In Proceedings of ACM SIGCHI, Monterey, California, May 3-7, 1992.

In computer graphics, scan-converting (i.e., rastering) a straight line segment (or simply line) is the most basic operation. Many curves, wireframe objects, and complex scenes are composed of line segments. The speed of graphics rendering depends heavily on the speed of scan-converting a line. The ability to scan-convert a line quickly and efficiently is a very important factor in a graphical library. Bresenham's Midpoint algorithm (1965)[2] is the most important algorithm and has been widely used for line scan-conversion. In the past 30 years, many new methods have been proposed in the attempt to speed up the line scan-conversion process, and most of these new methods have been based on Bresenham's algorithm[1-7].

We observed that a scan-converted line may contain many identical pixel segments in their relative positions. We can prove that if any two points on a line repeat their relative positions in the raster grid field, the line can be cut into segments and the corresponding pixel arrangements of the scan-converted line segments will repeat also. In other words, if (x_0, y_0) and (x_0+r, y_0+s) are on the line, where r and s are two arbitrary integers, then the corresponding scan-converted pixel arrangements from $x=[x_0]$ to $x=[x_0]+r$ will be the same as the pixel arrangements from $x=[x_0]+r$ to $x=[x_0]+2r$. Therefore, multiple segments (or pixels) of the line can be replicated, or scan-converted in parallel. Furthermore, as shown in Figure 1, the repeated points on a line (L) can be decided by its translation (L_0, L_1, or L_2), of which one end point is on the raster grid. Therefore, our algorithm will not require any of the two end points of the line on the raster grid. In fact, we don't even require the line to intersect any grid point. All existing well-known line scan-conversion algorithms require at least one end point on the grid, restricting the range of the applications.

Theoretically, we can speed up any existing line scan-converting algorithms m times, where m is the number of repeated line segments. On average, we can speed up all existing methods about three times. We have integrated the Midpoint algorithm and the Symmetry algorithm with our method to prove the idea.

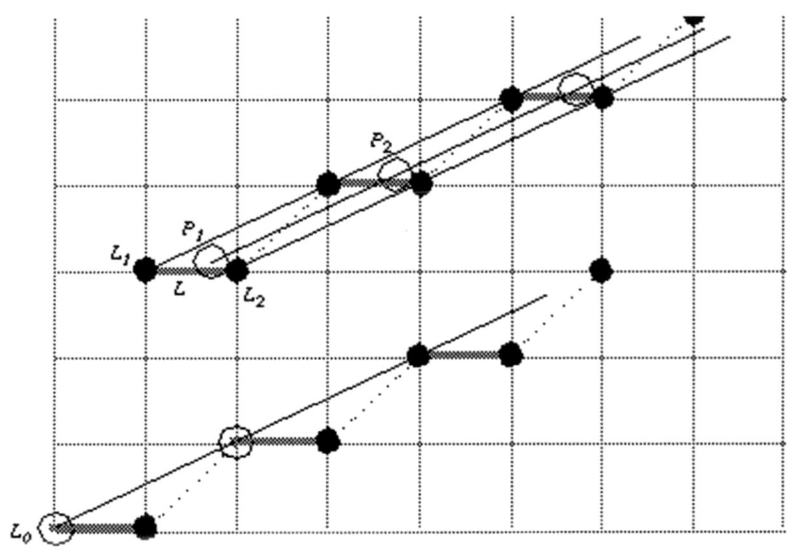

L: the line under consideration

L_1: L's left translation and one end on grid

L_2: L's right translation and one end point on grid

L_0: L's translation and one end point on grid (0,0) having the same relative location as the end point

$P_1=(x,y)$: L's end point

P_2-$(x+2, y+1)$: first point on L

P_1 in the grids

FIGURE 1 Pixel segments having the same shape

Jim X. Chen
Department of Computer Science
George Mason University
jchen@leibniz.cadsim2.gmu.edu

REFERENCES

1 Bao, G. and Rokne, J. G. Quadruple-step Line Generation, Computers & Graphics, Vol.13, No.4, 1989, 461-469.
2 Bresenham, J. E. Algorithm for Computer Control of Digital Plotter, IBM Syst. J., 4 (1965), 25-30.
3 Foley, J. D., van Dam, A., Feiner, S. K., and Hughes, J. F. Computer Graphics: Principles and Practice, Second Edition in C, Addison Wesley, 1996.
4 Gardner, P. L. Modifications of Bresenham's Algorithm for Display, IBM Tech. Disclosure Bull. 18 (1975), 1595-1596.
5 Gill, G. W, N-Step Incremental Straight-Line Algorithms, IEEE CG&A, 5 (1994), 66-72.
6 Pang, A. Line-drawing Algorithms for Parallel Machines, IEEE CG&A, 10, 9 (1990), 54-59.
7 Sproull, R. F., Sutherland, I. E., Thomson, A., Gupta, S., and Minter, C. The 8 by 8 Display, ACM Trans on Graphics, Jan. 1983.
8 Wu, X. and Rokne, J. G. Double-Step Incremental Generation of Lines and Circles, Comput. Vision, Gr. Image Process. 37, 3 (1987), 331-344.
9 Wyvill, B. Symmetric Double Step Line Algorithm, Graphics Gems, A. Glassner, editor, Academic Press, Boston, 1990, 101-104.

LiveType: A Parametric Font Model Based on Features and Constraints

Text is an extremely important data type in computer graphics. Current font models are based on glyph outlines[2,8], resulting in two major deficiencies:

1 Design intent, which is expressed using high-level typographic features, is translated to a low-level outline representation and lost.

2 The functionalities provided to font users are only resolution independent scaling and outline interpolations or extrapolation[3,4].

We present LiveType, a new font model based on features, parameters, and constraints. LiveType consists of two tightly related glyph models. One is a designer model where font designers can losslessly express their designs in high-level terms corresponding to the way they think. The other is a compressed run-time model, which font users can create font instances in different variations along typographic, aesthetic, or other axes predefined by the font designer. Changes in glyphs can also be used in real time in order to create animated-like text.

The underlying geometry of a LiveType glyph includes both outline and supporting constructs. Features are defined on top of the geometry and organized in a feature hierarchy. They are mainly used to represent typographic elements such as stems, bars, and serifs, but any desired subset of the underlying geometry can be defined as a feature.

Geometric constraints, such as distance and ratio relationships between points, are associated with the geometry of features, either automatically, using a feature detection algorithm[10], or manually by the designer. The types of constraints have been chosen to enable an expressive language for design, along with an efficient constraint evaluation algorithm that guarantees finding a single solution to the constraints graph in real time. This is done by automatically transforming the constraint graph during design stage to a direct acyclic graph that can be solved constructively in linear time.

The numbers participating in the definition of a constraint can be regarded as parameters having meaningful names such as stem width or baseline distance. Parameters can be further grouped hierarchically inside a single glyph and across the font to form font axis parameters such as weight or spikeness. When parameters are modified, some points change their position. This triggers the constraint evaluation algorithm to compute new positions for all affected points, thereby modifying the outline of the glyph. Parameter modification can result in non-linear font variations that preserve the typographical nature of glyphs or follow any other designer intent. The model can be compressed for end-user systems by flattening the feature hierarchy and retaining only the constraint and parameters structure.

LiveType introduces advanced modeling techniques into font models. This allows designers of fonts a more intuitive navigation in design space, preserving their intent using constraints and parameters. LiveType fonts enable font users to modify parameters interactively and create richer, more flexible, and more vivid text.

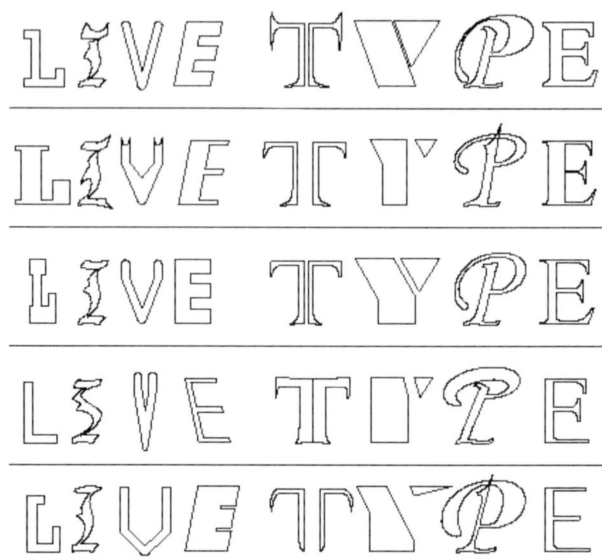

FIGURE 1

Ariel Shamir, Ari Rappoport
Institute of Computer Science
The Hebrew University
Jerusalem 91904, Israel
http://www.cs.huji.ac.il
{arik,arir}@cs.huji.ac.il)

REFERENCES

1 Adams, A.D. Abcdefg (a better constraint driven environment for font generation), in: Andre, Hersch (Eds.), Raster Imaging and Digital Typography, Cambridge University Press, 1989, pp. 54–70.
2 Adobe Systems Inc. The Type 1 Format Specification, Addison Wesley, 1990.
3 Adobe Developer Support. Adobe Type 1 Font Format: Multiple Masters Extensions, 1992.
4 Apple Computer. QuickDraw GX: Typography; Font File Formats; 1994.
5 Hersch, R.D., and Betrisey, C. Model Based Matching and Hinting of Fonts, Computer Graphics, Vol. 25, July 1991, pp. 71–80 (SIGGRAPH '91).
6 Heydon A., and Nelson G. The Juno-2 Constraint-Based Drawing Editor, SRC Research Report 131a, Digital Systems Research Center, December, 1994.
7 Knuth, Donald E. The MetaFont Book, Addison-Wesley, 1986.
8 Microsoft Corporation. The TrueType Font Format Specification, 1990.
9 A commercial system for TrueType hinting from Type Solutions Inc. (http://www.typesolutions.com)
10 Shamir, A., Rappoport, A. Extraction of Typographic Elements from Outline Representations of Fonts, Computer Graphics Forum, 15(3):259-268, 1996 (Eurographics '96).

As a work in progress, the Texture Maps from Orthographic Video project is an attempt at enhancing virtual spaces with photographic-like texture maps from real-life environments. While traditional methods of generating such texture maps for virtual worlds rely heavily on photographic manipulation, the goal of this project is to produce seamless texture maps from recorded video. The project will particularly benefit virtual environments where texture maps orthogonal to the path of travel are used to enhance the user's experience, such as those used in driving, biking, running, and other similar simulators.

In its most literal interpretation, the process of producing a texture map from video might seem quite simple. Taking into account that a field of video is captured every 60th of a second (on traditional video cameras), one might assume that the center lines of each field are thus evenly spaced in time. By extracting the center lines from each field and piecing them together, the resulting image resembles a snapshot of the environment captured by the source video. However, it becomes quite obvious that this "snapshot" is not accurate enough, and a few adjustments must be added to the theory, including: controlled camera movement, averaging of several lines from each field to produce an equivalent center line of that field, adjustment for motion in the direction parallel to the lines of video, and expansion or compression of the resulting image in accordance with the speed at which the camera moves.

In order to produce a usable texture map from video, restrictions to camera orientation and motion apply. The camera movement must be parallel to the desired environment and oriented so that the lines of video are perpendicular to the path of motion. Since the overall requirement of the project is to produce an accurate image that one may texture map along some path, such as a road, a camera was mounted to an automobile so the lines of video were perpendicular to the road surface and orthogonal to the path of travel. The vehicle was then driven through a residential neighborhood, where the roads were fairly level, maintaining an average speed between five and 10 miles per hour.

Once the video had been captured, the video was digitized and then processed using a custom Visual C++ (PC) application. This application performs the composition of the final image from the fields of video by performing such operations as averaging the lines of each field and determining the optimum correlation between fields. In order to solve the problem of the time/space mismatch that occurs when only the center line of each field is used, the program employs a gaussian average across multiple lines of each field to approximate the true center line. Further computations that adjust for such problems as bumps in the road determine the point of the greatest correlation between successive fields. The resulting offset along the lines of video is then applied to the averaged center line from each field before being added to the final image.

The next step in the project's evolution will be to affix a bike tire with an optical encoder to the moving vehicle and produce a "click track" (an audio click per unit of distance traveled) that is synced to the video and embedded in the audio channel of the video tape. This "click track" will allow the application to stretch or compress the resulting image, depending on the speed at which the vehicle is moving. Thus, in theory, an accurate image should be produced. This image may then be texture mapped on a polygon to achieve a real-life feel in the 3D space. If additional dimensions are desired, objects may be extracted from this image and arranged in a 2.5D fashion where discrete depth layers are produced. Although other problems are sure to arise, this project has a promising future in the realm of 3D simulation.

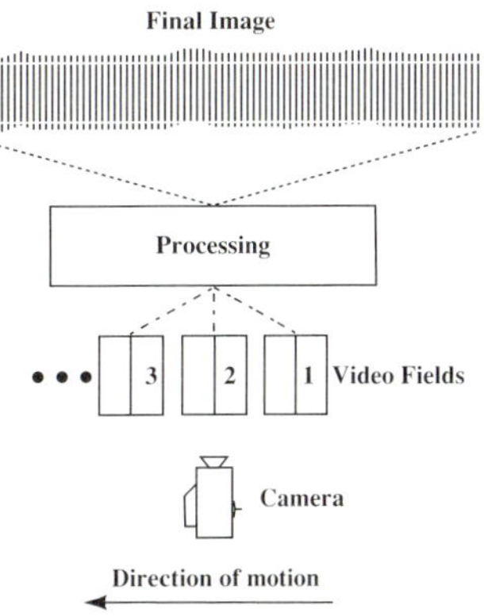

Process used in creating texture maps from video captured using a camera mounted orthogonal to some path of travel (driving, pan, track, etc.) with scan lines perpendicular to travel surface.

Portion of image produced from video captured while driving between five and 10 mph, using camera mounted orthogonal to path of travel with scan lines perpendicular to road surface.

Brian Jones
Interactive Media Technology Center
Georgia Institute of Technology
GCATT Building, Suite M14
250 14th Street NW
Atlanta, Georgia 30332-0130 USA
brian.jones@oip.gatech.edu

Disparity Morphing for Automatic Generation of Stereo Panoramas for Image-Based VR

Stereo perception is important for a truly immersive virtual reality (VR) system. Recent improvements in computer and video technology have made stereoscopic display systems more prevalent than ever. While most panoramic imaging systems are capable of displaying photo-realistic VR worlds, they still have difficulties in automatic production of high-quality stereo panoramas.

The major difficulty comes from the fact that, when taking a stereo image sequence with a two-camera set having a horizontal stereo baseline, only one camera can have its lens center located on the vertical rotation axis. In our experiment, we let the rotation axis pass through the lens center of the left camera. Hence, the position of the lens center of the right camera will move along a circle (i.e., off the rotation axis) during the acquisition process, as shown in Figure 1. Consequently, the objects in the overlapping image area will not be of the same size, and the image locations of those objects will be inconsistent in two adjacent partially overlapping images, which will make the conventional image stitching techniques fail to produce high-quality stereo panoramas, especially when the objects are near to the camera. To automatically generate a high-quality panorama from a sequence of "off-the-rotation-axis" images, we propose a new method that utilizes the FOE (focus of expansion) and block matching techniques that are familiar in the field of computer vision.

Let O_1 and O_2 be the lens centers of the cameras located at two adjacent positions, as shown in Figure 1. The 3D line connecting O_1 and O_2 is referred to as the motion baseline. We first warp each image into a cylindrical image (e.q., I_1 and I_2 shown in Figure 2) as in the conventional stitching method. However, we then dewarp the cylindrical image into a flat image whose image plane is perpendicular to the motion baseline, as IF_1 and IF_2 shown in Figure 2. Notice that the intersection of the motion baseline with the flat image plane is the so-called focus of expansion (FOE), as illustrated in Figure 3, which can be determined by using the extracted image features and their between-image correspondence.

Consider Figure 3. Let p_1 and p_2 be the projection of an object point P onto IF_1 and IF_2, respectively. Let L_1 be the epipolar line passing through p_1 and FOE_1, and L_2 passing through p_2 and FOE_2. According to the epipolar geometry, all the 3D object points seen on L_1 must be also seen on L_2, if not occluded. Hence, given an image point p_1 in IF_1, one can find its corresponding point p_2 in IF_2 along the epipolar line L_2 by using the block matching techniques. Let $\mathrm{v}=\overrightarrow{p_1 p_2}$ be the image disparity vector. Now, suppose a camera is moving from O_1 to O_2 and takes an image IF_s when its lens center stops at O_s, $s \in (0,1)$, as shown in Figure 3. However, IF_s is not really available, and we want to generate an approximation of it by using IF_1. What we have done is copy each pixel value at an image position, say p_1, of IF_1 to position p_s of IF_s, where $p_s = p_1 = s \bullet \mathrm{v}$, and then interpolate the pixels not covered by any value.

Next, suppose there are K vertical scan lines in image IF_1, we can create K_1 images, IF_s where s ranges from $1/K$ to $(K\text{-}1)/K$ with increments of $1/K$. Then, a disparity morphed image, IF_{morph1}, can be generated by letting the k-th vertical line of IF_{morph1} equal to the k-th vertical line of $IF_{k/K}$. By using the same procedure with the camera moving from O_2 to O_1, we can generate IF_{morph2} from IF_2. Then, IF_{morph1} and IF_{morph2} can be used to generate the right-eye panorama by using the regular image-seaming and image-blending techniques.

Our experiments have shown that the above method can produce high-quality stereo panoramas from a sequence of stereo images by generating an off-the-rotation-axis panorama with smooth transitions and without manual trial-and-error.

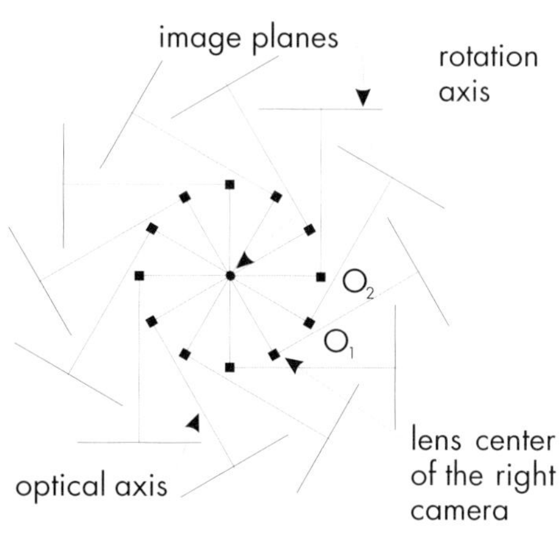

FIGURE 1

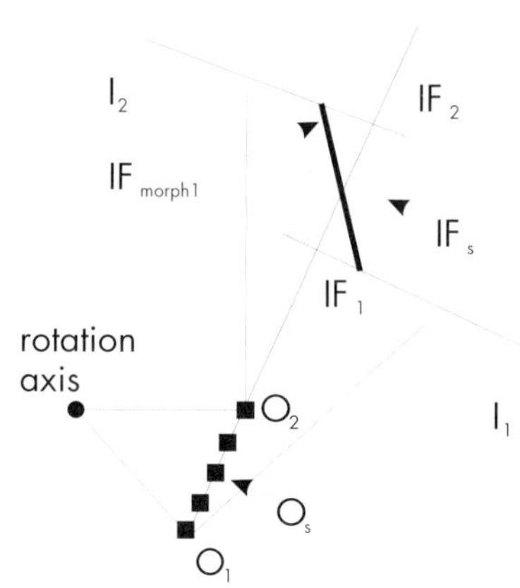

FIGURE 2

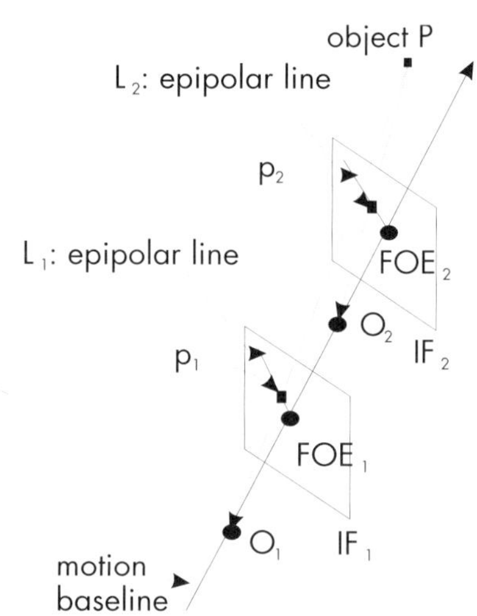

FIGURE 3

Ho-Chao Huang, Yi-Ping Hung
Institute of Information Science
Academia Sinica
Taipei, Taiwan, ROC
jet@iis.sinica.edu.tw
hung@iis.sinica.edu.tw

Interactive Contour Modeling Applied to Image Querying

Query By Sketch for indexing into an image database involves presenting the machine with a sketch of the object to be found in the database. The sketch can be of the object shape or distinct contours on the image of the object. This sketch can be made from memory or can be refined interactively in response to what the database search returns at each iteration. We introduce a family of 2D curves for this purpose and an algorithm for generating a representation that passes within small distances of a set of control points specified by the user. Control points can be placed at arbitrary locations and in arbitrary order, and can be erased by the user at will, in order to arrive at the desired shape representation.

The geometric model that we use should facilitate the efficient indexing or querying of the database. Although B-splines can represent geometric structures accurately, their effectiveness in dealing with missing data, matching of "approximately" similar shapes, and unknown coordinate transformations, at low computational cost, has not been established. We use an implicit polynomial (IP) shape model instead (i.e., polynomial function $f(x,y) = \Sigma_{i,j\{0,i+j\}n} a_{ij} x^i y^j = 0$ whose zero set represents shape).

To generate the IP model for a shape interactively, we use a linear programming (LP) approach and build the constraint matrix by choosing a number of control points and requiring the IP model to be close to these control points. Specifically, we fit a polynomial to represent a shape potential field (Figure 2, column 1) that is positive for points interior to S and negative for points exterior to S. For any control point, $p_k(x_k,y_k)$ selected by the user, impose the constraint:

$$f(x_k,y_k) = \Sigma_{i,j\{0,i+j\}4} a_{ij} x_k^i y_k^j > 0, \text{ if } p_k \text{ inside object,}$$

$$\text{and } f(x_k,y_k) < 0 \text{ if } p_k \text{ outside object.}$$

A set of control points provided by the user generates a set of linear constraints. The objective function of LP problem can be constant, quadratic, or other nonlinear functions.

Figure 1 illustrates the LP-based IP model fitting process. The user inputs a set of control points (close or far apart) on a sample image. The object shape boundary (black) is displayed with the control points (circles and squares) and the zero set of the fitted IP model (gray). The user starts with very few control points. The fitted IP model then may capture only part of the overall shape. As the user places more control points, the resulting IP model becomes closer to the object boundary and eventually captures the global structure. The degree of the polynomial is four, and constant objective function is used. The user can also function by placing a set of control points freehand, observe what is returned by the query, then modify the control points to refine the desired shape, and repeat.

Another example is illustrated in Figure 2, which shows objects automatically segmented and decomposed invariantly into parts from LADAR data. Now, given a new image, a user can interactively build models for one or more parts, and the system matches the joint geometries of the parts against those in the database to find the similar images.

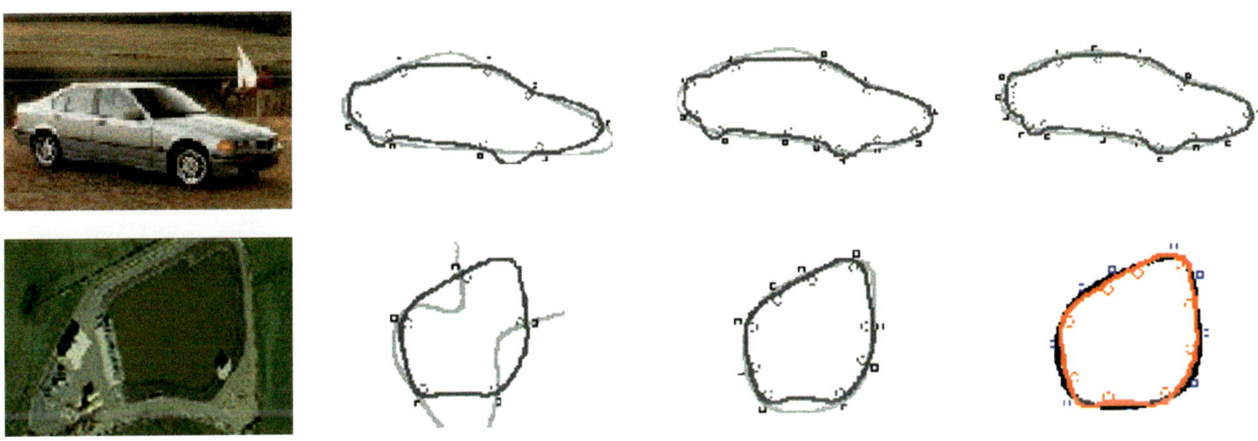

FIGURE 1 Interactive shape modeling examples

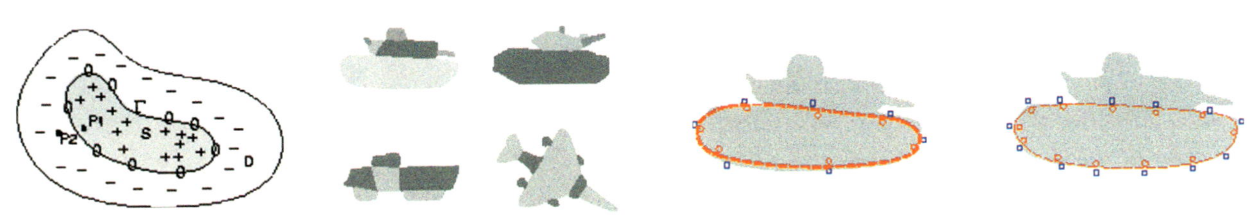

FIGURE 2 Parts database for object shapes and indexing based on the tank body part

Zhibin Lei, David B. Cooper
Division of Engineering
Brown University
Providence, Rhode Island 02912 USA
zbl@lems.brown.edu

Making Them Behave

For applications in computer game development and character animation, recent work in behavioral animation has taken impressive steps toward autonomous, self-animating characters. It remains difficult, however, to direct autonomous characters to perform specific tasks. We propose a new approach to high-level control in which the user gives the character a behavior outline, or "sketch plan."

The behavior outline specification language has syntax deliberately chosen to resemble that of a conventional imperative programming language. In terms of functionality, however, it is a strict superset. In particular, a behavior outline need not be deterministic. This added freedom allows many behaviors to be specified more naturally, more simply, more succinctly, and at a much higher level than would otherwise be possible. The character has complete autonomy to decide on how to fill in the necessary missing details. For example, with some basic background information we can ask a character to search for any path through a maze. That is, we do not initially have to give an explicit algorithm for how to find a particular path. Later, we may want to speed up the character's decision-making process by giving more detailed advice.

Although the underlying theory is completely hidden from the user, the success of our approach rests heavily on our use of a rigorous logical language, known as the situation calculus. The situation calculus is well-known, simple, and intuitive to understand. The basic idea is that a character views its world as a sequence of "snapshots" known as situations. An understanding of how the world can change from one situation to another can then be given to the character by describing what the effect of performing each given action would be. The character can use this knowledge to keep track of its world and to work out which actions to do next in order to attain its goals. The version of the situation calculus we use is inspired by new work in cognitive robotics[1]. By solving the well-known "frame problem," it allows us to avoid any combinatorial explosion in the number of action-effect rules. In addition, this new work incorporates knowledge-producing actions (like sensing), and allows regular programming constructs to be used to specify sketch plans. This has enabled us to propel our creatures out of the realm of background animation and into the world of character animation.

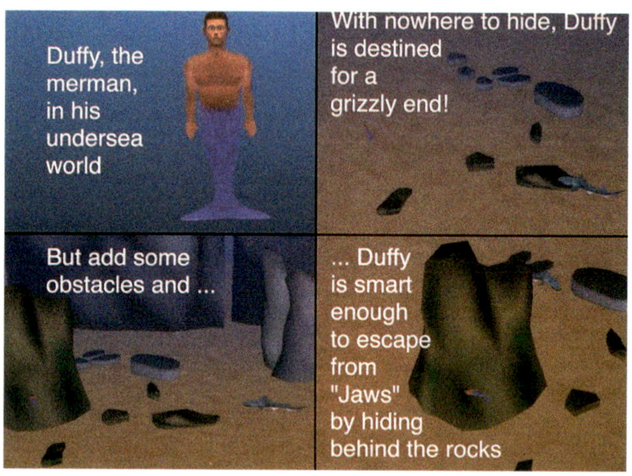

We have developed a character design workbench (CDW) that is both convenient to use and results in executable behavioral specifications with clear semantics. We can use the system to control multiple characters in realistic, hard-to-predict, physics-based, dynamic worlds. Interaction takes place at a level that has many of the advantages of natural language but avoids the associated ambiguities. Meanwhile, the ability to omit details from our specifications makes it straightforward to build, reconfigure, or extend the behavior control system of the characters. By shifting more of the burden for generating behavior from the animator to the animated characters themselves, our system is ideal for rapid prototyping and producing one-off animations.

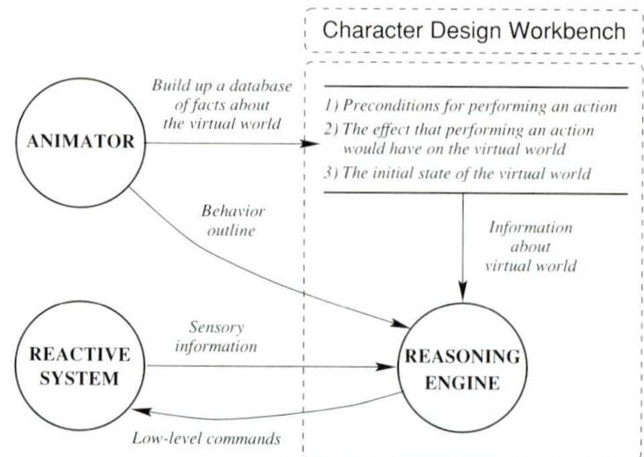

FIGURE 1 Interaction between CDW, the animator and the low-level reactive behavior system

The potential of our approach is demonstrated by some intriguing animations of physics-based "merpeople" characters engaged in pursuit and evasion behaviors. Using our system meant that without having to state exactly which one, the merpeople were able to pick any goal position that met some given specification. The animations were the result of elegantly incorporating the existing lower-level reactive behavior system, described in X. Tu and D. Terzopoulos, into CDW.

John Funge, Xiaoyuan Tu (涂晓媛)
University of Toronto
10 King's College Road
Toronto, Ontario M5S 3G4 CANADA
{funge | tu}@cs.toronto.edu
http://www.cs.toronto.edu/~funge

REFERENCES

1 H.J. Levesque, R. Reiter, Y. Lesperance, F. Lin and R. Scherl. GOLOG: A Logic Programming Language for Dynamic Domains, Journal of Logic Programming, 31:59-84, Special issue on Reasoning about Action and Change.

2 X. Tu and D. Terzopoulos. Artificial Fishes: Physics, Locomotion, Perception, Behavior, In A. Glassner, editor, Proceedings of SIGGRAPH 94, Computer Graphics Proceedings, Annual Conference Series, pages 43-50. ACM SIGGRAPH, ACM Press, July 1994.

Animation through the numerical simulation of physics-based graphics models offers unsurpassed realism, but it can be computationally very demanding. This sketch demonstrates the viability of replacing the numerical simulation of model dynamics with a dramatically more efficient alternative. In particular, we propose a radically different approach to creating physically realistic animation that exploits fast emulators implemented as neural networks, which we call NeuroAnimators.

NeuroAnimators are automatically trained off-line to emulate the actions of physics-based models, by observing the models in action. We demonstrate NeuroAnimators that have learned the motion not only of simple passive and active dynamic models, but also of state-of-the-art. physics-based models reported in the literature, including mechanical models of a swimming dolphin and a running human. Depending on the model, our approach yields physically faithful animation one or two orders of magnitude faster than the conventional, numerical simulation technique.

FIGURE 1 This plate illustrates the emulation of three different dynamical systems: a three-link pendulum, an elastic cube and a biomechanical dolphin. In each image the physical model is indicated byt he SIGGRAPH logo. In the third image the biomechanical dolphin[2] is in the background

FIGURE 2 Emulated motion produced by training a NeuroAnimator on state transition data generated by the numerically simulated (by SD-Fast) Hodgins mechanical runner model.[3]

Radek Grzeszczuk, Demetri Terzopoulos, Geoffrey Hinton
Department of Computer Science
University of Toronto
radek@vis.toronto.edu

REFERENCES

1 "Learning Internal Representations by Error Backpropagation", Rumelhart, D. E. and Hinton, G. E. and Williams, R.J., in "Parallel Distributed Processing: Explorations in the Microstructure of Cognition", MIT Press, 1986, ed. Rumelhart, D. E. and McCleland, J. L. and the PDP Research Group, vol. 1, 318-362.

2 "Automated Learning of Muscle-Actuated Locomotion through control abstraction", R. Grzeszczuk, D. Terzopoulos, *Proc. ACM SIGGRAPH 95 Conference*, Los Angeles, CA, August, 1995, in *Computer Graphics* Proceedings, Annual Conference Series, 1995, 63-70.

3 "Animating Human Athletics", Jessica K. Hodgins and Wayne L. Wooten and David C. Brogan and James F. O'Brien, *Proc. ACM SIGGRAPH 95 Conference*, Los Angeles, CA, August, 1995, in *Computer Graphics* Proceedings, Annual Conference Series, 1995, 71-78.

Combining Active and Passive Simulations for Secondary Motion

The secondary motion of passive objects in the scene is essential for appealing and natural-looking animated characters[1], but because of the difficulty of controlling the motion of the primary character, most research in computer animation has largely ignored secondary motion. We use dynamic simulation to generate secondary motion. Simulation is an appropriate technique because secondary motion is passive, dictated only by forces from the environment or the primary actor and not from an internal source of energy in the object itself. Secondary motion does not lend itself easily to keyframing, procedural approaches, or motion capture because of the many degrees of freedom that must move in synchrony with the primary motion of the animated figure.

Passive simulations have been used with great success for many systems, including water, cloth, flags, and leaves blowing in the wind. Active simulations have been used to animate the motion of running, walking, jumping, diving, and vaulting human figures. We explore the interactions between passive and active simulations by coupling passive simulations of objects in the environment with active, rigid-body simulations of humans to compute secondary motion for animated figures. We describe several examples: a gymnast on a trampoline, a bungee jumper, a gymnast vaulting onto a mat, a girl swinging while wearing a skirt, and kites in the air.

The primary contribution of this work is an exploration of three different kinds of coupling between passive and active simulations: full, partial, and one-way. To clarify the differences between the forms of coupling, we use the interaction between a basketball (primary) and the net (secondary) as an example. If the coupling is one-way, the direction and velocity of the ball are not affected by the motion of the net, and the ball continues on a ballistic trajectory. If the two simulations are fully coupled, the rotational and linear velocity of the ball will be changed by the contact with the net, the deformation of the net will be less extreme, and the motion will more closely match that of an actual basketball net. In between these two solutions are a variety of partially coupled solutions. For example, a heuristic drag constant might be applied to the velocity of the ball when it is in contact with the net.

The physics of the particular situation and the fidelity of the required motion dictate how tightly the simulations must be coupled. In some situations, substantial computational savings can be achieved with little loss of realism, but in others tight coupling is essential. The gymnast jumping on the trampoline and the bungee jumper are examples of systems where the interaction forces must be applied to both the passive and the active simulations. In contrast, the girl on a swing is an example of a system where it is sufficient to have a one-way interaction: the active simulation of the swinger affects the passive simulation of the clothing, but the passive simulation does not influence the rigid body motion. A final set of problems is amenable to the use of a simplified passive model that is fully coupled to the rigid-body model and a more complete passive model that is driven by the motion from the rigid-body system. For example, the vaulter is fully coupled to a simple model of a mat with vertical springs, and the resulting motion of the feet is used to drive a more realistic simulation of a flexible mat.

The decision about the degree to which the systems are coupled is similar to the modeling decision about the level of detail required for a physical simulation. In the physical world, all interacting objects are coupled, and movement includes a remarkable amount of perceptible detail. Each decision to ignore a potential coupling or use a more approximate model will result in some loss of realism. In the case of the basketball and net, the motion of the ball in the fully coupled simulation much more closely matches the real world than the motion produced by one-way coupling. However, with appropriate selection of the simulation parameters, either motion might be appropriate for a background element in a scene.

Although we are often not consciously aware of secondary motions, they add greatly to the perceived realism of an animated scene. While we have simulated the secondary motion of some of the objects in the scene, many objects are still motionless. In some cases, it appears that modeling some of the moving and flexible objects emphasizes the lack of motion in the others. Like the progression in models from wireframe to polygonal models, this increase in the fidelity of the modeling may increase the viewer's expectations.

FIGURE 1 Image of a girl swinging while wearing a skirt, kites in the air, and a gymnast on a trampoline

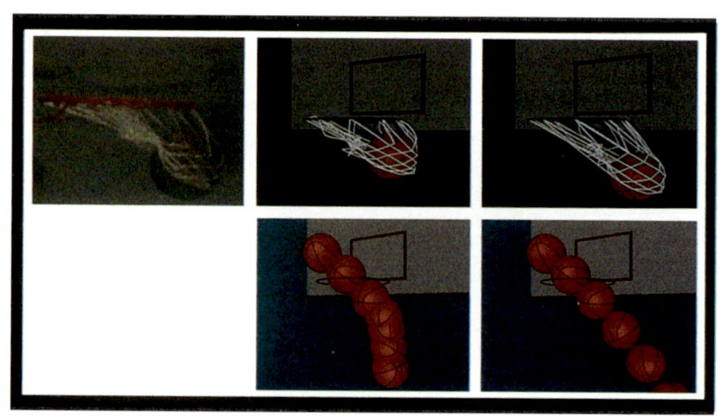

FIGURE 2 Images of a basketball and net with fully coupled interactions, one-way coupled, and an actual net and basketball for comparison (The bottom two images show the trajectory of the ball with fully coupled and one-way coupled interactions)

Jessica K. Hodgins, James F. O'Brien, Victor B. Zordan
Graphics, Visualization, and Usability Center and College of Computing
Georgia Institute of Technology
jkh@cc.gatech.edu

REFERENCE
1 F. Thomas and O. Johnston. Disney Animation: The Illusion of Life, Abbeville Press, New York, 1984.

In this sketch, we present a rendering meta-primitive called the paintstroke and develop a fast, view-adaptive method for rendering it using our implementation of the A-Buffer. Since the paintstroke's shape is that of a generalized cylinder, it is not a general-purpose tool for building arbitrary objects. At the expense of this generality, however, comes a highly optimized rendering algorithm that greatly improves over traditional methods for drawing the equivalent curved surfaces.

Paintstrokes serve as useful building blocks for a variety of finely detailed natural phenomena such as fur, hair, fine branches, wicker, and pine needles. By incorporating various view-dependent image effects into the rendering algorithm, paintstrokes can be further used for modeling streams of water, icicles, and wisps of smoke. Self-shadowing is simulated on a global scale, offering an alternative to shadow mapping.

Implementation

The standard way to render a curved surface is to tessellate it into a fixed set of three-dimensional polygons. Our algorithm tessellates the paintstroke dynamically, directly making use of the image-space projection of the generalized cylinder to obtain a desirable arrangement of polygons in screen coordinates. Capitalizing on important modeling and rendering efficiencies, the algorithm arranges the polygons so as to maximize their projected screen size, thereby minimizing their number. The resulting savings in vertex transformations, rasterization overhead, and A-Buffer fragment blending more than repay the cost of the dynamic tessellation.

After transforming the control points from world to viewing coordinates, we generate Hermite interpolants for the path and radius components, and linear interpolants for the others. The paintstroke is then subdivided along its length into segments, with a granularity that adapts to its screen-projected size and curvature. Each segment is subsequently tessellated into polygons such that the side of the paintstroke closestto the viewer is always completely covered by one, two, or four polygons, depending on the user-adjustable quality level. Quality-zero paintstrokes use a single polygon per segment and represent the most efficient tiling pattern, although they do not render correctly when viewed head-on, and the distribution of normals along their breadth, derived by linear interpolation across a single polygon, is somewhat inaccurate. Nevertheless, they are an excellent choice for fur, as shown in the bottom right figure.

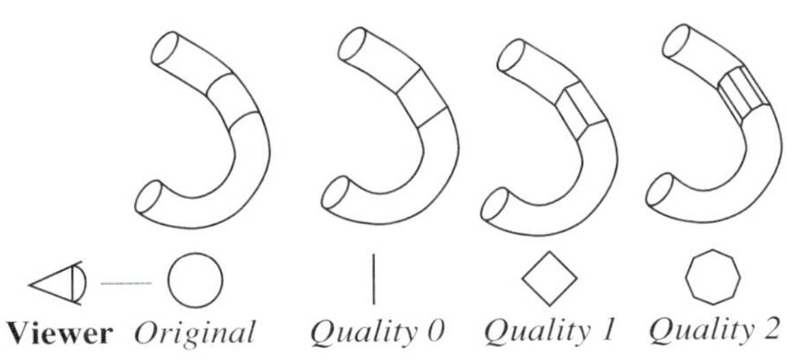

FIGURE 1 View-dependent tessellation meshes

Special Rendering Effects for Paintstrokes

The dynamic, view-dependent tessellation of paintstrokes allows for several useful rendering effects that would be difficult or impossible to achieve with a fixed polygonal model.

Lengthwise Opacity Variation

This feature simulates volume opacity, which varies according to the penetration of the light rays passing through a paintstroke segment. A simple formula involving the segment's path and the viewer's direction estimates the opacity, with a maximum value achieved when the viewing angle is along the path, and a minimum value when it is orthogonal to it.

Breadthwise Opacity Variation

The opacity of the paintstroke can also vary across its breadth, allowing the user to specify distinct opacities for the centre and for the edges. Our view-dependent tesselation scheme makes this effect particularly easy to implement. It can be used to produce fuzzy paintstrokes or to simulate the Fresnel effect for transparent fluids, as shown in the top middle figure.

Global Lighting Algorithm

This algorithm works well when a large number of control points are fairly uniformly distributed over a convex volume. Each control point of a paintstroke contains a user-specified global normal and depth value. The former indicates the normal of the global shape to which the control point belongs, and the latter the relative depth from the surface. The estimated amount of light penetration at each control point is computed using the depth, global normal, and average light direction. The control point's reflectance is then scaled accordingly. The left and top right figures are good examples of this effect's efficacy.

Thanks to Michiel van de Panne for the original idea and motivation for this research, and for the many useful discussions about it.

Animal (bottom right) modeled by Nick Torkos using approximately 12,000 quality-zero paintstrokes and as many polygons, rendered at 640x480 resolution in six minutes on a 250MHz R4400. Torus (top right) modeled using 1,250 hybrid quality (level zero/one) paintstrokes, rendered at 256x192 in 15 seconds on a 200MHz 604e. Water (top middle) modeled with four paintstrokes (three for tap, one for stream), rendered at 256x192 in four seconds on a 200MHz 604e.

Ivan Neulander
University of Toronto
ivan@dgp.utoronto.ca
http://www.dgp.utoronto.ca/people/ivan/ivan.html

The concept of motion tracking has attracted a lot of academic and industrial attention in the last few years, and it is gradually being applied to special effects in the film industry. Tracking is already used in nearly all special effects shots for camera stabilization and smoothing of object motion. It is also necessary when composing multiple layers of images taken from different positions, when adding new computer-generated objects to the scene, and when mapping textures or reflections onto moving objects. Most of the existing 2D and 3D tracking algorithms are designed and tested to work with video-resolution data, and are too slow and imprecise for film resolution sequences. The reasons for this are: a significantly larger number of pixels in film production, the huge physical size of pixels on the film screen (higher precision requirements), and film grain (high noise level).

We propose an advantageous architecture for tracking and describe novel algorithms for fast and accurate camera/object 2D/3D transform recovery. These algorithms cover most tracking needs in the industry. Some of the techniques are improved versions of existing ones and some are completely new. The proposed algorithms could be successfully used on video sequences, providing a significant improvement in precision and efficiency.

Architecture (see figure below)

- Optic flow calculation is expensive and noisy for film sequences. Tracking of high-frequency features is preferable.
- 2D and 3D tracking is separated so the user can choose the best features for 2D tracking, define an optimal set of parameters (gamma correction, color transformations, reference of tracking), check the results, and repeat the process if necessary.
- The accuracy of 2D tracking is crucial. A high-precision sub-pixel algorithm is required.
- The 2D results from the set of features are used to calculate the 3D transformation. The main factor for choosing 3D tracking algorithms is the ability to work with precise but limited data.
- Two different methods of 3D tracking are used. When the camera parameters are known, and some information on the tracked object is available, precise frame-to-frame 3D transformation can be recovered. When no pre-measurements on the object can be done, a different transform recovery method should be used. In this case, tracking is known to be extremely sensitive to noise, and object/camera translation is defined only up to a scale factor. Therefore, the motion will be only approximated.

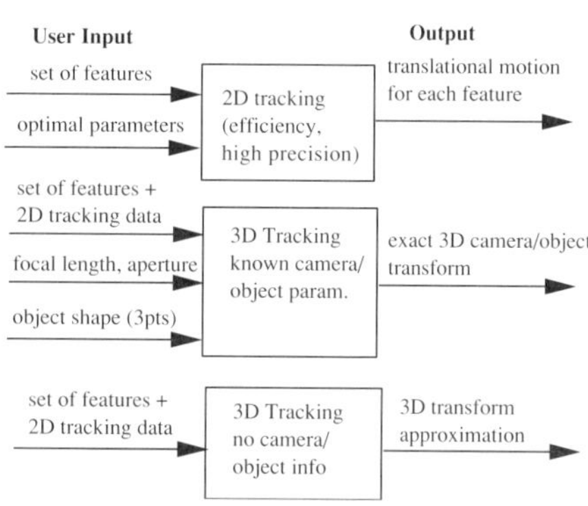

Description of Algorithms

2D tracking module. The following combination of techniques provides the high-precision and efficiency that are necessary for film industry applications. We subsequently perform a small radius multi-resolution search on the Gaussian Pyramid. The Sum of Square Differences (SSD) algorithm is used on each pyramid level to find the best match. For each pair of frames, the translation from the previous pair is used as an initial motion guess. High-precision sub-pixel data is then obtained by fitting a paraboloid to the best SSD results and calculating the minimum of this function.

3D tracking with known camera and object parameters. The standard 3D transformation has 12 (9+3) unknowns that could be computed by a least-square technique with six data points. We are limiting the number of points to only three by assuming small frame-to-frame rotations and using an antisymmetric matrix to represent rotation[1]. After each step, the matrix is converted[2] into the standard rotational matrix that is used to define object depth. Initial object/camera position is obtained by iterating this process and rotating the relative features position according to the transformation until the algorithm converges. This technique allows a precise reconstruction of the camera/object transformation using only the minimum possible number of features.

3D tracking with no camera/object information. Two main standard approaches exist for this type of 3D tracking: epipolar and bilinear constraints. Both of them are extremely unstable for a small number of points, especially for small motions. We propose a new algorithm, created on the basis of a three-frame-based technique recently introduced by Shashua and Avidan[3]. This technique is more simple and robust than others, and has no degenerate cases. The proposed method has been shown to give accurate results with as few as five features, a significant improvement over existing algorithms.

Our tracking module has been successfully used to track objects as complicated as clouds, to achieve excellent stabilization results, and to precisely recover complex transformations using only a few object points.

Maria Lando
BOSS Film Studios
13335 Maxella Avenue
Marina Del Rey, California 90292 USA
maria@boss.com

REFERENCES

1 O. Faugeras. Three-Dimensional Computer Vision, The MIT Press, 93.
2 K. Shoemake. Graphic Gems II, 351-354, Academic Press, 91.
3 A. Shashua, S. Avidan. The Rank 4 Constraint in Multiple View Geometry, ECCV, 96.

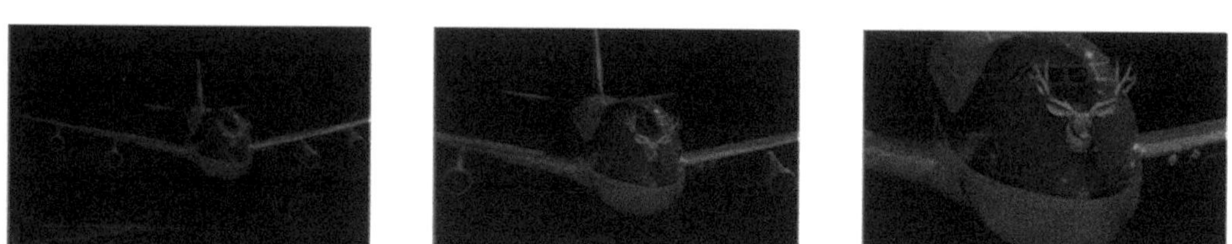

FIGURE 1 Demonstration of the synthesis (according to the recovered motion) of a computer-generated object in a film sequence.

In designing or examining free-form surfaces or polygonal objects, there is often a need to display linear dimensions of the object, especially when the object must fit with other objects, as in the case of mechanical or industrial design. The standard technique of underlaying axis-aligned grids for measurement is convenient only in an orthographic view. In a perspective scene, a shadow of the object can be orthographically projected onto surrounding walls that contain a grid[1]. One measurement at a time can also be provided by an inquiry function, where the user temporarily attaches a measurement widget to the desired objects, but the widget will obscure the objects. For general angle measurement, almost the only choice is a three-point measurement widget that will obscure part of the scene while reading out the angle.

The approach suggested in this sketch is simply to mark the surface directly with texture-mapped measurement tools.

In a similar technique, Silicon Graphics has a demo that maps a regular grid texture onto a bicubic patch to show its (u,v) parameter space. The main advantage with this approach is that input clutter is eliminated, because there are no widgets to avoid clicking. Instead, the surface is painted with measurements that can be turned on or off as a rendering attribute. Output clutter is also reduced because the measurements occupy the identical space as the object being measured, meaning that the measurements cannot occlude other objects in the scene. Because images are textured onto the surface, potentially hundreds or thousands of measurements are available simultaneously to the user, who simply has to look at the points of interest to learn the dimension of interest.

To measure the edge lengths of polygon P, a bilevel ruler texture is applied to each edge. An inner inscribed polygon is generated in the plane of P, and for each edge a four-sided ruler quad is generated to hold the texture.For example, a triangle would be divided into an inscribed triangle and three ruler quads.

For angle measurement, the bilevel arc texture map is used, which is essentially a protractor with heavy tickmarks at 10-degree intervals (Figure 1). For each angle of the polygon to be measured, the axis of this protractor image (at the center of the bottom edge) is placed at the vertex, with the line marked 0 located along the edge lying counter-clockwise from the vertex. To apply the arc at each vertex, the polygon must be cut into subpolygons with the arc texture applied to each, as shown schematically in Figure 1. For a triangle, each subpolygon is a quadrilateral that is made up of the main triangle's vertex, the midpoint of each incident edge, and the centroid of the main triangle. Both arcs and rulers can be displayed at the same time, in which case the texturing occurs using the inscribed vertex values for the edge and centroid calculations.

This new scheme of textured annotations on the surface of objects is quite effective at providing users with ready access to salient metrics on the surface. In an experiment that required subjects to build a simple object to precise dimensions, subjects were readily able to visually access linear measurements provided by the texture-mapped rulers. Subjects could quickly tell that they had reached the correct length.

In a surface with hundreds or thousands of quads in the mesh, each quad can be textured with rulers and arcs, making the linear dimensions of each quad visually available simultaneously without cluttering the scene with auxiliary measurement dialogs. This new texturing method eliminates input clutter and reduces output clutter.

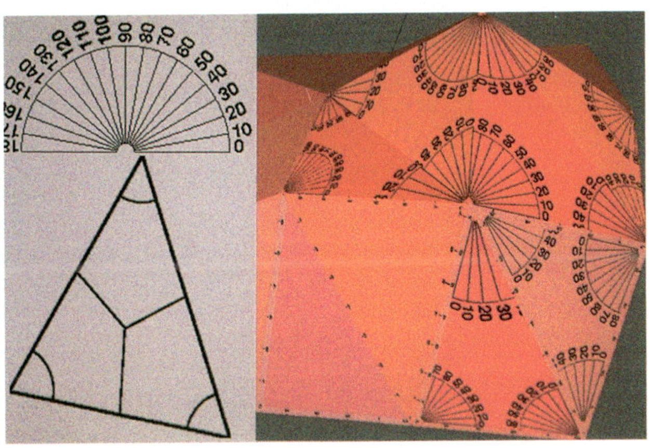

FIGURE 1

TOP LEFT Protractor texture applied at the vertex of each triangle

BOTTOM LEFT Subdivision of a triangle into 3 subpolygons so that the arc texture can be drawn at each vertex

RIGHT An example surface CLOCKWISE FROM TOP LEFT Two quads with arcs applied to each vertex of each component triangle, a quad with rulers and arcs, and a quad with just rulers.

Chris Shaw
Department of Computer Science
University of Regina
3737 Wascana Parkway
Regina, Saskatchewan, S4S 0A2 Canada
cdshaw@cs.uregina.ca

REFERENCES

1 K P Herndon, R C Zeleznik, D C Robbins, D B Conner, S S Snibbe, and A van Dam. Interactive Shadows, In UIST 1992 Proceedings, pages 1–6, 1992.

Texturing Implicit Surfaces with Particle Systems

We describe an intuitive yet effective method to apply bidimensional textures onto implicit surfaces. The main idea is to simulate the motion of particles starting on the surface and moving along the gradient vector field until the particles reach a support surface, where a texture is defined. This approach is a good alternative to the use of solid texture, allowing effective application of arbitrary 2D image textures onto implicit surfaces. Moreover, our method is enhanced by a set of tools for controlling how the texture is mapped.

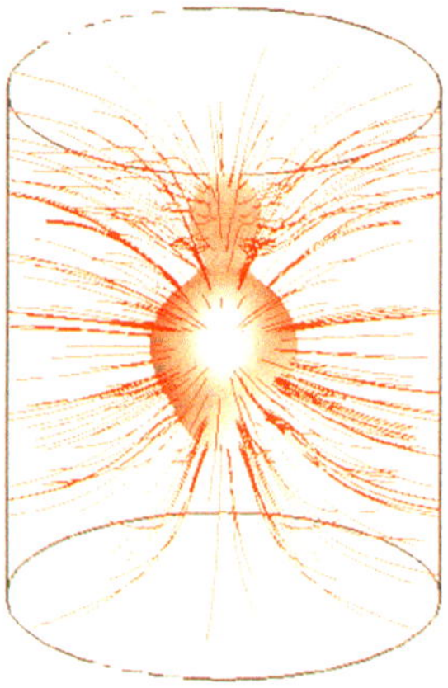

The Method

The method is based on inherent properties of implicit models. Let S be an implicit surface defined by a function $F:\mathbf{R}^3 \rightarrow \mathbf{R}$, i.e., $S=F^{-1}(0)$. We interpret the gradient vector field ∇F as a force field defined in the ambient space, and we use it to guide the particles that are initially at rest on S. The motion of a particle is governed by the differential equation $d^2x/dt^2 + \gamma dx/dt + \nabla F = 0$ where γ is a viscosity constant. This particle system establishes a correspondence between points on the implicit surface and points on a support surface T, where the texture is defined: the texture attribute for each point on the surface is "read" at the intersection of the corresponding particle trajectory with T. The support surface T should be simple enough so that it is very easy to define texture coordinates on it (e.g. cylinder, sphere etc.).

Computation

We start the simulation with particles placed at the vertices of a simplicial approximation of the implicit surface. Next, particle trajectories are generated by numeric integration of the motion equation. At each integration step, we test whether a particle trajectory has crossed the support surface. If it has, then we obtain the texture coordinate for the corresponding point on the implicit surface from the intersection point on the support surface. Once the simulation is over, texture coordinates are available for each vertex of the polyhedron approximating the surface. Linear interpolation of texture coordinates on each face then completes the texturing of the implicit surface.

Control

The dynamic behavior of a particle system allows us to create a set of tools for controlling the placement of the texture onto the surface. Global control is done by positioning the implicit and support surfaces relative to each other. Local control is achieved by introducing external forces in the system, such as attractive and repulsive point, curve, or surface sources.

Example

The figures below demonstrate how the method accurately applies an image onto a blobby surface. A cylinder is chosen as a support surface for the texture, and the particle system is generated from a blend of the blobby and support surfaces gradient vector fields. More examples, including animations, can be seen at:
http://www.visgraf.impa.br/Projects/dtexture

This project is sponsored by CNPq, FAPERJ, FINEP, and IBM Brasil.

Ruben Zonenschein, Jonas Gomes, Luiz Velho
Instituto de Matematica Pura e Aplicada
Estrada Dona Castorina, 110 - Jardim Botanico
Rio de Janeiro, Brazil
ruben@visgraf.impa.br

Luiz Henrique de Figueiredo
Laboratorio Nacional de Computação Cientifica

REFERENCES
1 G. Wyvill, C. McPheeters, B. Wyvill. Solid Texture of Soft Objects, IEEE CG&A 7 (1987) 20-26.
2 A. Barr. Decals, in: State-of-the-Art in Image Synthesis, SIGGRAPH Course Notes (1983).

We present a new data structure and algorithm for fast, flexible computation of static levels of detail. Our algorithm extends previous work by Jarek Rossignac and Paul Borrel[1].

Vertex clustering is a fast, robust technique for generating static levels of detail. However, the results can be crude and unpredictable. The user has very little control over the properties of the output simplifications (e.g. number of triangles, size of triangles, topology, surface properties, preservation of features). Furthermore, the existing algorithms compute only isolated simplifications, rather than the continuous range of simplifications needed for many network applications today.

A quick review of basic vertex-cluster simplification is in order. Cluster the v vertices of an object and choose a representative vertex in each cluster. Translate each facet of the object to a facet of the simplification by mapping its old vertices to new ones. Eliminate degenerate and redundant facets by comparing the new vertex indices. This process can be accomplished in $O(v \log v)$ time, and various enhancements can be made without increasing the cost. Note that the translation and elimination steps are independent of the clustering algorithm. This observation is the key to our new method.

We present a new data structure called a vertex cluster tree from which a particular vertex clustering can be extracted quickly and adaptively. The tree can be used to simplify to a desired number of triangles or to optimize a wide variety of other geometric and topological properties.

In general, the tree is built by defining a hierarchy of clustering functions C_i, one for each level i of the tree. C_i must be hierarchical: if two vertices are in the same cluster at level i, then they must be in the same cluster at level $i+1$; and an upper bound on the number of possible clusters should decrease by a constant factor at each level. For example, let C_0 be a spatial binning into a regular grid of cells with 2^k cells, $k=\lceil \log v \rceil$m, along each dimension of the grid. Let $C_i, 0 < i <= k$, be a similar binning using a grid 2^{k-1} cells wide. In this example, the same type of clustering is used at each level, but this need not be the case.

To build the tree, we cluster the vertices at each level of tree, up to a single cluster at the root. If a vertex is assigned to a cluster at level i in time $O(T_i)$, the number of clusters generated at level i is c_i, and the tree has d levels, then the entire tree is built in time $O(vT_0 + \Sigma_{i=i}^{d} c_{i-1} T_i)$. With the regular spatial binning described above, for which $T_i = O(1)$ and $d=k=\lceil \log v \rceil$, this reduces to $O(\Sigma_{i=0}^{k} \min(v, 2^{3(k-i)})) = O(v \log v)$.

We grade the importance of each cluster in the tree by propagating value up from the leaves. The properties we use to grade the tree will determine the properties we can optimize in our simplifications. For example, if we want to use the tree to simplify to a target number of triangles, we can grade each cluster with the number of triangles of the original object that would collapse if all of the vertices in the cluster were collapsed into a single vertex. This grading can be accomplished in time $O(td\Sigma_{i=1}^{v} G(i)$, where t is the number of triangles and $G(i)$ is the complexity of the local grading function. Note that in the case of spatial binning, the tree can be built and graded in time $O(v \log v)$.

By selecting a set of nodes that cover every path from the root to the leaves, we define a clustering of the vertices. For any interesting criteria, choosing the optimum clustering is a complex problem, but we have found that a greedy approach gives good results in practical cases. Initialize the clustering to the root and repeatedly choose the child of a node in the current clustering that increases the desired property by the largest amount. Stop when the target is reached. This step can be accomplished in $O(\log v \Sigma_{i=1}^{d} c_i) = O(v \log v)$.

Note that we can record a vertex clustering at any point in the last stage of the algorithm, and use it immediately for translation and elimination to produce a simplified object. Thus, we can very quickly extract many levels of detail with a single pass through the tree. In particular, we can generate a hierarchy of levels of detail using spatial binning in $O(v \log v)$ total time.

To consider more complicated properties of the object, we modify the algorithms for grading the tree and choosing clusterings. Essentially any local property of the data can be incorporated into these stages of the algorithm. Cluster grading could be based on topological complexity (to control topology and identity of separate objects), triangle size (to refine relative to the amount of detail in the object), angles between facets (to preserve features), importance of vertices (to maintain silhouettes), or any geometric or surface property.

Joshua D. Mittleman, Jai Menon
IBM TJ Watson Research Center
Yorktown Heights, New York 10598 USA
{mittle,menon}@watson.ibm.com

REFERENCE
1 Multi-Resolution 3D Approximations for Rendering Complex Scenes. Modeling in Computer Graphics, B. Falcidieno and T. L Kunii, Eds., Springer-Verlag, pp.455-465, 1993.

Model Simplification Using Directional Clustering

We are developing a clustering algorithm whose simplification metric minimizes changes to the final image rather than changes to the input model topology. This allows significant simplification of difficult models such as trees and plants, and it allows inter-model simplification for collections of objects. Most simplification algorithms attempt to produce compressed models that closely approximate the topology of the original model. Our algorithm takes advantage of recorded geometry compression generated in an off-line precalculation routine that runs on the order of minutes while the real-time object generation routine adapts to motion parameters and the demands of different graphics system hardware to ensure the fastest balance between rendering and simplification. This enables the algorithm to be used for a number of applications, including games, motion previews, and large-scale virtual environments.

The Approach

Many of the methods that have been used to reduce the complexity of object geometry perform reduction or re-triangulation of an input mesh based on some criteria, usually progress towards simplification and minimization of changes in the topology of the original mesh. Our approach is inspired by a clustering algorithm[1], in which any two vertices can be merged whether or not they share an edge or polygon. This allows the algorithm to introduce significant topological changes during simplification.

We introduce a metric for selection of mesh simplification steps based on their impact on the final image. The metric estimates the eventual screen distance of pairs of vertices and the color and normal differences of adjoining polygons. In Schaufler & Sturzlinger[1], the set of merges can be pre-calculated and used as geometry compression. However, in the course of an animation, a metric based strongly on eventual screen position can wildly change the order of compression and the underlying simplification data structure. Our method uses a hybrid of precalculated non-directional simplification and real-time simplification using our image-dependent measure.

The algorithm takes as much advantage of pre-calculated non-directional clustering as possible. This minimizes the amount of directional clustering in any given frame. For any frame, initial work is derived from the pre-recorded clusters, while a smaller set of easily changeable directional clusters are subsequent. Directional clusters are determined from a weighted average of global and screen distance in order to avoid pathological merges. The weight is determined from the rotation speed of the object. The ratio between a system's rendering speed and processor speed is also used to determine the profitability of (and thus determine how much effort to expend on) directional clustering. Animations with relatively static scene segments run on machines with a low ratio will spend more effort in eliminating polygons, while a wildly spinning scene calculated on a powerful graphics station gracefully degrades to the simplest version of geometry playback using the original metric and an algorithm similar to geometry compression.

A key feature of our new algorithm is the ability to control the amount of topological modification. Coarse models (which can be smoothly interpolated if needed) can be generated for motion previews and polygon-limited systems. Topological changes can be limited to sub-pixel merges for accurate renderings or turned off altogether so that the algorithm can still be used to eliminate redundant data from laser range data.

The advantages of directional clustering include near-back side surface removal and profitable results for distant slow moving objects like trees, terrain, and buildings. Results thus far show that in combination with a static, precalculated simplification hierarchy, our new approach is very effective in further reducing the cost of image synthesis without a significant loss of quality. Our scheme dynamically adapts to changes in viewing characteristics and automatically adapts to various display architectures.

Dana Marshall, A.T. Campbell III, Donald S. Fussell
Department of Computer Sciences and The Applied Research Laboratories
The University of Texas at Austin
Austin, Texas 78712 USA
dane@cs.utexas.edu

REFERENCES
1 G. Schaufler, W. Sturzlinger. Generating Multiple Levels of Detail for Polygonal Geometry Models, in Virtual Environments '95, ed. G l bel, Springer Verlag, pp. 33-41.

We study the use of wavelet compression of a volumetric representation of polyhedral surfaces. The surface is first represented by the zero set of a distance function. We apply wavelet multiresolution analysis to this function. This allows us to represent a polyhedral object of arbitrary topology to a variable level of detail. By reducing the number of detail coefficients, we can achieve very high compression ratios of the geometry data with little loss in image quality[1]. Secondly, this method allows change of the genus of the object as level of detail is decreased. Most current methods of surface simplification[2] (and many others) do not allow variations of genus as resolution is lowered. This is a significant drawback when used for the purpose of low resolution approximations of object for rapid rendering. Indeed, if we are given a grid of n intersecting cylinders, the number of triangles necessary for a genus-preserving representation is necessarily greater than n^2. The method of J Rossignac, P. Borrel and T.He, et al. are an exception. In the former, simplification is done by merging surface vertices. Our method uses a volumetric representation, as in T.He, et al. where a low-pass filtering method is used on a different representation.

We combine several techniques, and proceed as follows. Given a polyhedral surface S, we define a distance function $d(x,y,z)$ on 3D space such that S is the zero set of d. The function d will be the distance from the point (x,y,z) to the surface for points outside the object, and the negative of the distance for points inside. This function is piecewise linear and discontinuities occur at the faces, edges, and vertices of the Voronoi diagram of the polygonal object surface.

We sample this function at a regular 3D grid (the sample interval is a function of curvature and triangle size), and perform three-dimensional wavelet analysis[4] using an orthogonal filter bank. See below for the type of wavelet used. We now have a multiresolution representation of the distance function: a series of wavelet coefficients. Next, we apply wavelet compression: the number of largest wavelet coefficients we keep depends on the desired level of detail and accuracy. At this point, the object has a very compact representation which can be efficiently stored or transmitted.

To reconstruct the surface, the distance function is approximated by wavelet reconstruction using a synthesis filter bank. The next step is to reconstruct the polygonal surface. This is accomplished by using the classical marching cubes algorithm. Using the function d instead of the classical "volume inside voxel" function reduces the blockyness of the reconstructed surface.[3] The final step involves simplifying the resulting surface. We employ a triangle decimation method. An alternative to our last two steps is to use the methods of R. Shekhar, et al., which produces an already simplified triangular mesh.

In Figure 1, we give an example of the results obtainable by our method. We used Daubechies wavelets for their ability to approximate piecewise linear functions. The original object is shown in Figure 1a. In b., keeping 0.5% of coefficients yields a compression of 36:1 without much loss of image quality. In c., we show an intermediate resolution, and in d., we use Haar wavelets, keep 0.1% of coefficients, and obtain a reduction of genus.

In summary, we achieve high compression ratios of polyhedral surfaces. Other advantages of our method are that it allows simplifying and possibly merging several objects. In addition, this method can be used for progressive transmission of surfaces. We plan to continue the study of this type of object representation including using different distance functions, studying different types of wavelets, and comparing to other simplification algorithms.

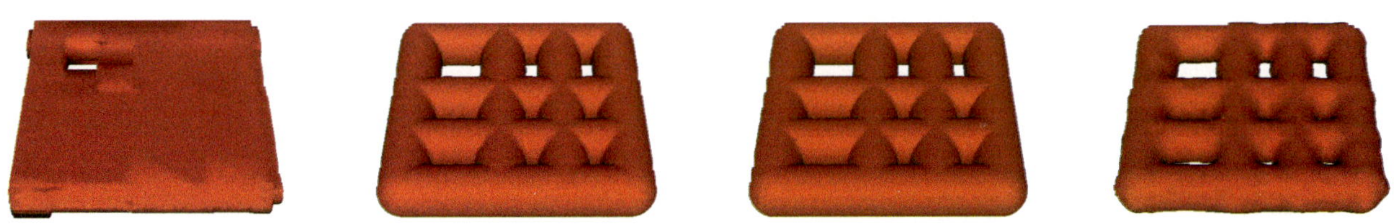

FIGURE 1a, 1b, 1c, 1d

Mike M. Chow, Marek Teichmann
Computer Graphics Group
Massachusetts Institute of Technology
(mchow, marekt)@graphics.lcs.mit.edu
http://graphics.lcs.mit.edu/~mchow

REFERENCES

1 M. Deering. Geometry Compression, Proc. SIGGRAPH 95, 13-20.
2 M. Eck, T. DeRose, T. Duchamp, H. Hoppe, M. Loundbery, W. Stuetzle. Multiresolution Analysis of Arbitrary Meshes, Proc. SIGGRAPH 95, 173-182.
3 M. Jones. The Production of Volume Data from Triangular Meshes Using Voxelisation, Computer Graphics forum, vol. 15, number 4, 311-318.
4 T. He, L. Hong, A. Kaufman, A. Varshney, S. Wang. Voxel Based Object Simplification, Visualization 94, 85-92.
5 S. Muraki. Volume Data and Wavelet Transforms, IEEE Computer Graphics and Applications, vol. 13, 4, 1993, 50-56.
6 J. Rossignac, P. Borrel. Multi-Resolution 3D Approximations for Rendering Complex Scenes, Modeling in Computer Graphics, Springer-Verlag, 1993, 455-465.
7 R. Shekhar, E. Fayyad, R. Yagel, J.F. Cornhill. Octree-based Decimation of Marching Cubes Surfaces, IEEE Visualization '96.

Several authors have recently described novel approaches to the problem of generating multiresolution representations of 3D models[1,2,4,5]. This sketch presents a flexible and simple framework that can utilize such representations to offer improved Level of Detail (LOD) management in VRML. The framework can accelerate the rendering of VRML scenes by progressively transmitting and rendering selectively refined models of every object in the scene. Such models are constructed from small fragments of polygonal approximations to the objects, and hence the resolution of rendered meshes can be varied on a per-facet basis. When combined with our method for specifying the resolution required in a displayed scene, this gives an extremely flexible and accurate approach to the problem of polygonal LOD management.

Key Components of the Framework

Resolution Control Function: The RCF is an "oracle" which, when passed a facet, assesses whether the facet meets user-specified resolution criteria. These criteria can depend on client-side parameters (e.g. view frustum extent and object- and screen-based Areas of Interest). By using an inverted form of Cohen's "simplification envelopes"[3], the geometric precision required in the displayed surfaces can be specified simply by indicating volumes within which the surfaces' resolution must be enhanced.

Continuous Resolution Model Representation: A pre-processing step produces a representation of a VRML model from which selectively refined versions can be obtained. The CRMR consists of a base mesh together with a history of the refinements required to improve the base mesh with respect to some object-space resolution metric.[1,2,5] An RCF-classified object-space measure is associated with each refinement fragment. Our CRMR can be generated from many existing approximation techniques, such as Hoppe's Progressive Mesh approach.[4]

Algorithms: Selection of the regions to be transmitted and reconstruction of the selectively refined surface is performed as described in.[2] These routines identify the refinements that must be passed to the client in order to satisfy the RCF and produce a complete surface from a consistent set of such fragments.

It is necessary to geomorph[2,4] between displayed selectively refined surfaces in order to prevent "popping" artifacts. This can be performed efficiently with minimal alterations to the surface using the algorithm in.[2]

Advantages

During transmission, progressively better approximations to each object in a scene can be rendered on the client. In addition, the amount of scene information transmitted and rendered is directly proportional to the perceived quality of the displayed image.

Results

Figure 1 illustrates the structure of our selective refinement framework together with its application to a Progressive Mesh representation[4] of Viewpoint Datalabs' Cessna model. The resolution of the model displayed on the client has been reduced in the background of the view (i.e. the plane's tail and the wing on the left) such that the rendered polygon count is approximately 50 percent of the original VRML model.

Peter J.C. Brown
Computer Laboratory
University of Cambridge
Pembroke Street
Cambridge CB2 3QG UNITED KINGDOM
Peter.Brown@cl.cam.ac.uk
http://www.cl.cam.ac.uk/users/pjcb2/

REFERENCES
1 P.J.C. Brown. A Fast Algorithm for Selective Refinement of Terrain Meshes, In COMPUGRAPHICS 96, pages 70-82. GRASP, December 1996. To appear in Computer Networks & ISDN Systems.
2 P.J.C. Brown. Selective Mesh Refinement for Interactive Terrain Rendering, Technical Report TR No. 417, Computer Laboratory, Cambridge University, CB2 3QG, UK, February 1997.
3 J. Cohen, A. Varshney, D. Manocha, G. Turk, H. Weber, P. Agarwal, F. Brooks and W. Wright. Simplification Envelopes, In SIGGRAPH 96, Computer Graphics. ACM SIGGRAPH, August 1996.
4 H. Hoppe. Progressive Meshes, In SIGGRAPH 96, Computer Graphics, pages 99-108. ACM SIGGRAPH, August 1996.
5 E. Puppo. Variable Resolution Terrain Surfaces. In 8th Canadian Conference on Computational Geometry, August 1996. Ottawa..

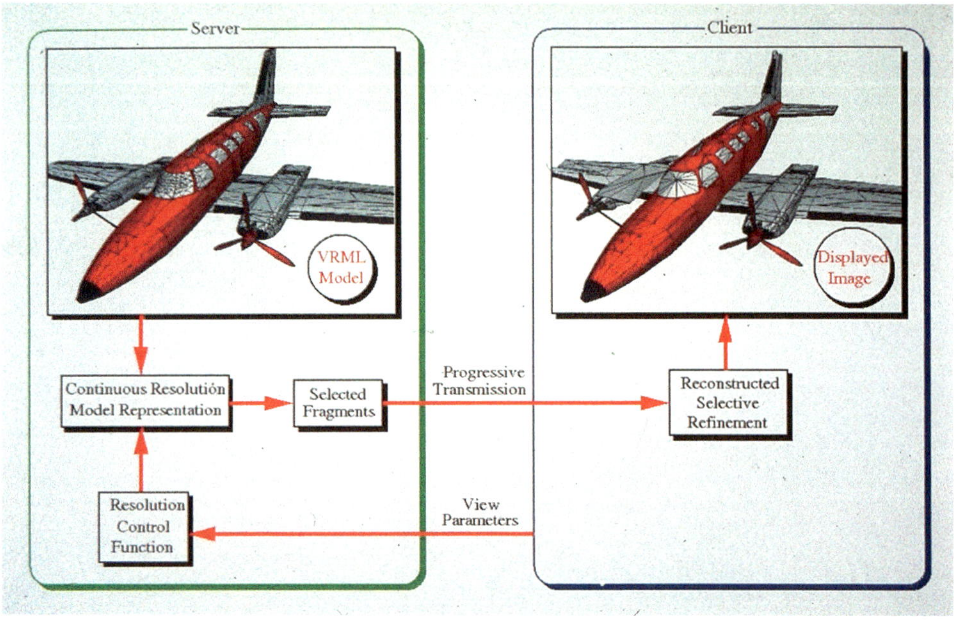

The goal of the Talisman program is to dramatically improve the graphics and multimedia capabilities of a Windows PC. Talisman introduces both innovative hardware and an innovative merging of DirectDraw and Direct3D APIs to deliver multimedia performance and quality equal to or better than workstations that cost much more.

A key element of the Talisman architecture is scaleability – the ability to implement Talisman-consistent versions of hardware for motherboards to high-end, add-in cards for the PC. Microsoft has defined two implementation concepts that span the scaleability range for Talisman. This sketch discusses specific elements of a version called Wizard, which is specified to meet the requirements for volume PC applications of the Talisman architecture. Development of products based upon this version of Talisman was made possible beginning in January 1997, when the Talisman Technology license was commercially offered by Microsoft. Specific concepts for scaling the Talisman architecture to enable cost-effective Talisman 3D solutions for the motherboard and ~ $200 add-in card are presented.

In the Talisman reference design, the graphical functions are distributed across four ASIC chips with a targeted PCI add-in card BOM exceeding $200. The goal of the Wizard program is to provide Talisman quality at a motherboard or add-in card equivalent BOM cost of less than $100. This is only possible by increasing integration and lowering the chip count of the implementation. This sketch describes the results of on-going design work that demonstrates how this can be accomplished and delivered in real products in 1998.

The fundamental design goal for the Wizard version of Talisman was that it be fully architecturally compliant with the original Talisman concept. This means that the implementation had to include composited image layers, image compression, chunking, and multi-pass rendering. High-quality features such as anisotropic filtering, shadows and reflections, alpha blended transparency, and anti-aliasing must be supported.

The approach taken was to construct a super engine capable of performing the functions of both the Polygon Object Processor and Image Layer Compositor of the original reference design. In the reference design, these two chips were characterized by duplicated processing engines running independently and in parallel. The Wizard approach features time domain multiplexing of a common super-set engine. The Wizard is further designed to operate with a host CPU providing front end pipeline calculations in lieu of a DSP. However, the Wizard does include a setup engine to offload the processor and increased overall polygon throughput. The Compositing DAC of the reference design is eliminated by the addition of an external buffer and compositing directly into the on-chip color buffer. The LUT/DAC functions and a VGA/2D core are both integrated into the design as well. In order to accommodate both motherboard and add-in card designs, the chip interface supports both AGP and PCI interfaces.

The results of this sketch clearly demonstrate the viability of the Talisman architecture for volume PC applications and project a promising view of the quality of 3D that will arrive soon on the desktops of virtually all PC users.

Rick Humphrey
Fujitsu Microelectronics, Inc.
3545 North First Street
San Jose, California 95134 USA
rhumphre@fmi.fujitsu.com

Agha Ahsan
MultiDimensional Consulting, Inc.

Practical SIMD

Sun's VIS instruction set has been integrated into all UltraSPARC processors shipped since December, 1995. SIMD extensions accelerate algorithms by partitioning a 64-bit register into smaller registers and executing a single instruction against each value simultaneously.

Documented Accelerations

APPLICATION AREA	ALGORITHM	SPEEDUP
Medical Imaging	Maximum intensity projection (MIP) Multiplanar reformatting (MPR)	4X
Video Encoding	Distance between vectors	4.6X
Image Processing	16-bit 1K x 1K convolution	1.7X
Audio Processing	FIR and IIR filters	2.8X and 1.4X
Printer	Color conversion look-up table	6X
Networking	Fletcher1s checksum (0.5 and 4 kB packets	4.3X and 5.9X
Mass Storage	XOR 64 kB blocks	3.75 X
Genome Sequencing	Sequence comparison	2X
Cryptography	Bit matrix multiplication	11 to 14X

VIS Summary

- 30 three-operand RISC-instructions, additions, subtractions, multiplications, and comparisons on four pairs of 16-bit values, or two pairs of 32-bit values at a time.
- Pdist (pixel distance), for motion estimation and cross correlation, compares eight pairs of 8-bit values at once, using a sum of absolute values of differences. Can provide a 20-50X performance boost for the inner loop for MPEG decompression or decode.
- Single-instruction commands move 64 bytes of data directly between eight 64-bit registers and system memory, bypassing cache.
- 3D data blocking for efficient handling of volumetric data. A 3blocked byte2 addressing scheme loads cache with cubes of data, rather than lines of data.

SIMD Impacts Coding, Requires Libraries

SIMD code, while faster-executing, is generally longer and more complex than a pure C code implementation of the same function, so libraries are essential. Examples:

	STRAIGHT C	VIS SIMD	LIBRARY
7 by 7 convolution	386 lines	4,984 lines	mlib_ImageConv7x7()
Image addition	177 lines	903 lines	mlib_ImageAdd()
RGB-HSV color space conversion	360 lines	565 lines	mlib_ImageColorRGB2HSV()

Sun's mediaLib Application Library

At the time this sketch is being written (Spring, 1997), Sun appears to have the first low-level application library for its SIMD extensions. (Intel has ported some existing libraries to MMX, but all libraries we have seen are coded in assembly language. Higher level MMX tools are available from Microsoft.) Sun developed its mediaLib library functions at the lowest possible level, to be inserted into the inner loops of the most demanding applications. The library consists of two sets of functions. One is VIS-accelerated, for the UltraSPARC platform, the other consists of highly tuned C functions that can be compiled on any platform. Portability enables developers to write to a common, low-level interface and run their applications on several high-performance platforms. Both versions provide access to the functions from C, C++, or Java.

mediaLib Functions

Imaging: Data format conversion, spatial operations, image generation and copying, arithmetic and logical operations, color space conversion, geometric and radiometric operations, image statistics, Fourier domain processing, volumetric data processing, and volumetric visualization.

Linear Algebra: Vector and matrix algebra.

Audio/Video: Digital signal filtering, signal generation, transformations, and the basic elements for JPEG and MPEG processing.

Graphics: 2D and 3D primitives, rendering and texturing

William Bryant
Engineering Manager, New-Media Software
Sun Microelectronics
2550 Garcia Avenue, MSSUN02-104
Mountain View, California 94043-1100 USA
william.bryant@eng.sun.com

We have developed a low-cost hardware and software device to enable the real-time visualization of the haptic sense of pressure. The device and supporting PC-based software enable the visualization and documentation of certain forms of tactile input for applications such as robotic end-effectors, medical palpation, 3D digitizer, and a novel 3D input device resembling clay.

The sensor is actually a low-resolution 3D surface digitizer. It consists of an easily compressible elastomer bounded on one side by an opaque white deformable membrane and on the other side by a clear rigid face plate. An intrinsically clear elastomer is evenly colored throughout its volume during manufacture by an optically attenuating with low dispersion gray dye, imparting an optical neutral density. Pressing a 3D object against the white membrane while observing it through the elastomer, one sees a black and white image representing a 3D range map of the applied surface. The gray value at each 2D image location represents a monotonic function of the distance from the membrane to the face plate. The closer the white membrane is pressed to the face plate, the less gray elastomer the light has to pass through, the less attenuation to the image of the white membrane, and hence, the lighter that part will appear.

Using a video camera (a Connectix digital camera was used) and even illumination, a real-time digitized range image representing the 3D surface in contact with the membrane is produced. This is then converted to a real-time rendered 3D surface with special software. A function relating the Z-value of the membrane deformation [Z_def(x,y)] returns an approximate (and relative) compliant force at that location [Z_force(x,y)]. Multiple Z_force(x,y). iImages, taken at different average forces, can be used to generate a "modulus map" of an object exhibiting varying material densities, such as a body part. Thus, tissue density contrasts (difference between skin and bone, for example) can be characterized, documented, and visualized.

Initial problems encountered were minor but can be eventually overcome for real applications. The first device built consisted of an optically dense fluid instead of the elastomer. Even though this was less useful in a final product (potential fluid leaks), it facilitated sensing of the average internal vessel pressure through a connected pressure transducer. This pressure value is added to the 3D spatially modulated pressure to yield the absolute restoring force at any x,y location on the membrane, resulting in absolute and repeatable data. Accuracy of the range image is dependent on eveness of illumination, color and clarity of the fluid or elastomer, and color of the membrane. Also, reflections from the on-axis illumination source must be reduced so as not to corrupt the image. Cross-polarized filters were used to reduce these reflections. The focal length of field of view of the camera lens also affects the range image, particularly off the optic axis.

Applications include haptic sensors for robotics, medical palpation, telemedicine, a 3D "digital clay" input device, and a low-cost 3D digitizer, among others. For the palpation application, a physician can objectively document the size, shape, area, modulus, and volume of a skin-level anomaly (such as a sub-cutaneous cyst), tracking its evolution over time. By superimposing a color texture map of the object over the 3D surface, one can produce a 3D computer model of the original object as shown in the picture.

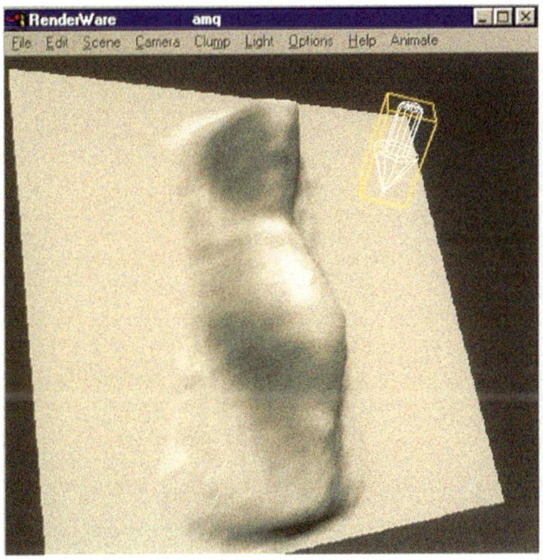

Real-time 3D Surface Visualizer (thumb pressed into haptic lens)

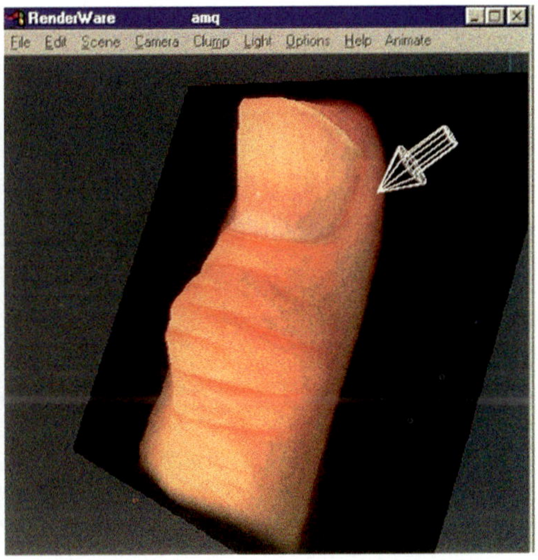

Real-time 3D Surface Visualizer (color texture map added)

Michael Sinclair
Interactive Media Technology Center
Georgia Institute of Technology
250 14th Street NW
Atlanta, Georgia 30332-0130 USA
michael.sinclair@oip.gatech.edu

Panoramic photography has become a popular medium since the advent of the Internet and software presentation technology such as Apple's QuickTime Virtual Reality (QTVR). The combination of a well-commercialized and low-cost digital scanner with some simple modifications can net a high quality digital panoramic camera.

The immersive qualities on observers of wrap-around video and the compelling nature of the ability to interactively pan around in a fixed-eyepoint environment are well known. Unfortunately, production of these images is presently either very tedious or the camera is very expensive. If film is the original medium, it must then be digitized for computer use.

Enter the digital hand scanner, a relatively low-cost collection of lens, mirrors, linear color CCD sensor, electronics, mechanics, and software. In its off-the-shelf form, it is intended to connect to a special input card or to the PC's parallel port and allow users to carefully drag it across a piece of paper or artwork and transfer the image digitally to the computer. Though not as useful as a flatbed scanner for normal scanning, the hand scanner's portability and small size makes it a natural for use as a camera. Through modification (some call it butchering) with a knife, file, saw, and some electronics, it becomes a 360-degree digital panoramic color camera capable of producing remarkable images exceeding 27 Mbytes, which are directly importable into presentation technologies such as QTVR.

The unit chosen for modification is a Logitech Scanman2000 hand scanner because of its low cost, parallel port connectivity, and availability. The initial modification consists of focusing the lens at infinity, disconnecting the fluorescent lamp, cutting the circuit trace to the internal encoder, and wiring the encoder input to an external scan pulse source. A geared stepper motor with a battery-operated driver provides the external pulse source and a constant speed panning function of approximately 0.5 rev/minute with 6,000 motor steps per revolution. The camera is completed by mounting the modified scanner vertically on the geared motor output shaft and adjusting the motor speed so as not to exceed the data acceptance rate of the computer. While panning through one revolution (with this setup, it takes about two minutes, so a tripod is a must), it produces a 27 Mbyte image or approximately 1500 x 6000 x 3 RGB pixels. The scanner lens provides approximately 90 degrees of vertical field of view. Using Apple's PANOTOOL, one can produce a QTVR source image in just a couple of minutes.

Additional modifications consist of relocating the internal RGB adjustments to the outside, moving the bow-tie aperture closer to the lens, removing all mirrors, and adding two counter-rotating polarization filters. The adjustments on the outside facilitate exposure and color correction: moving the bow-tie aperture reduces vignetting when the lens is re-focused, and the polarization filters function as a variable neutral density for further exposure control (the lens has no adjustable aperture).

There are some problems with this technique, most of which can be eventually overcome. The eight-bit dynamic range of most scanners is not usually sufficient for normal outdoor images without some form of exposure compression. You lose detail in shadows and/or highlight areas. Also, the hand scanner's CCD color filters, fluorescent lamp, and software combination were made for a particular color temperature, not necessarily daylight. With low-cost, single-CCD sensor scanners, there may also be color banding problems, though this appears to be minimal. The images indicate some of these problems, mainly the lack of dynamic range. The white areas are generally caused by the saturation of the RGB sensor and analog-to-digital converter range limitation. But... for an investment of approximately $250, there seems little reason to complain.

Michael Sinclair
Interactive Media Technology Center
Georgia Institute of Technology
250 14th Street NW
Atlanta, Georgia 30332-0130 USA
michael.sinclair@oip.gatech.edu

To digitize curved, especially organic shapes, current systems require that the user trace very dense and regular meshes on the surface. Such work is tedious and time-consuming. Our system allows the user to casually specify the most important features and let the computer fill in the regular gaps. The system can also automatically infer features such as creases and corners.

Prototyper: Boxing-Up and Outlining the Shape

We implemented an efficient volumetric clay modeling scheme (or metaballs, soft objects, blobby models). Gesture recognition is used for fast modeling without clicking the menus or icons. If more than three strokes are sketched, an ellipsoid is generated; if two strokes, the closed (or almost closed) stroke is taken as cross-section and classified into a square or an ellipse in 3D space, and the other stroke is used as the sweeping direction for the cross-section.

Refiner: Adding Details to the Prototype

The user needs to improve the surface by adding more detail strokes. In our system, the user randomly sketches over a region where corrections are needed, and the surface adapts to the new strokes to yield a better shape. The user can also trace the crease edges and mark corners on the object for the model to align with. Finally, a smooth surface with preserved and aligned creases and corners will be obtained.

Since the clay parts are solid models (blobs, plates, sticks) and lack local details, we treat the prototype as a surface model for local refinement by adjusting the positions of control points. The triangle mesh is upgraded to a quadratic triangular Bezier surface then to a triangular B-spline surface. Each datapoint contributes a negative spherical potential field that decays with distance, and thus three potential fields are generated by surface points, crease points, and corner points, respectively. Energy minimization is performed to deform the surface and align its edges and corners. Using potential fields makes surface fitting fast enough for interactive modeling. In some previous work, the distances from datapoints to the triangle mesh are computed many times during the iterations, and the program runs for hours. By contrast, the potential field is only computed once for each datapoint, and is incrementally updated with new sketching strokes.

autoTracer: Automatic Inference of Creases and Corners

The autoTracer module can automatically infer creases and corners from random strokes over smooth regions, and the user does not need to manually trace the edges or mark the corners. Then the Refiner module is called to perform the energy minimization that deforms the smooth surface and better aligns the inferred creases and corners. Drawing smooth surfaces is easy, but the singular points and boundaries are problematic. The autoTracer module reduces such difficulty.

Mathematically, each datapoint contributes a vector field in a 3D volume (grid), and we compute at each voxel a 3x3 covariance matrix (or second-order moments, or scatter matrix) of all accumulated vectors, and the three eigenvectors defining the major, medium, and minor axes of an ellipsoid. In other words, we build a dense structured tensor field from the sparse unstructured stroke data, and thus, surfaces, edges, and corners can be inferred from the shape of the ellipsoid. A stick-like shape indicates a surface passing through this position. A large plate-like shape has two salient directions, indicating an intersection of two surfaces. And a ball-like shape indicates a corner due to three salient directions.

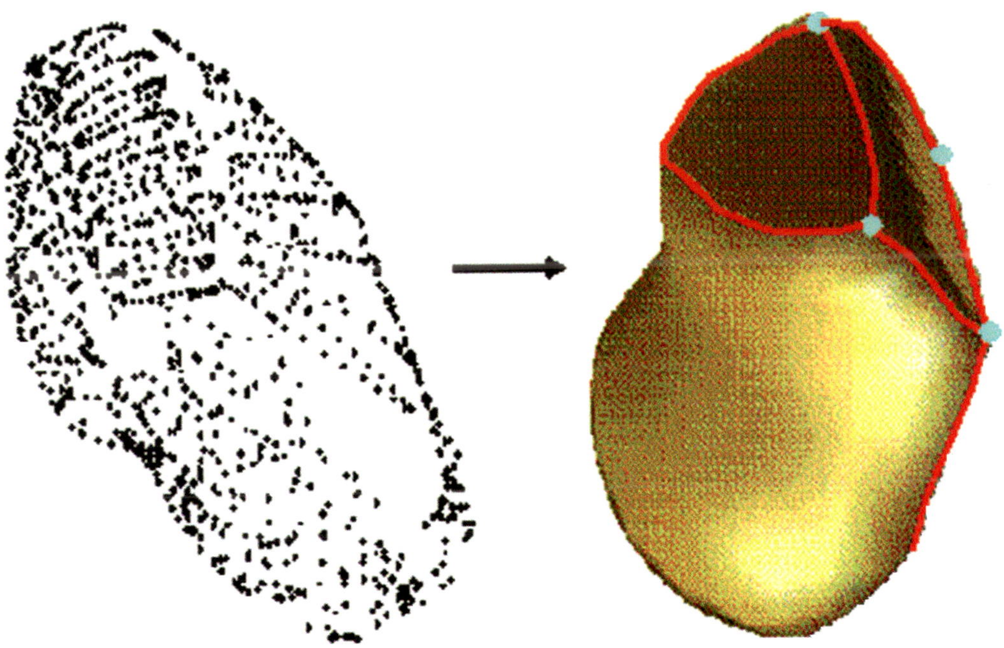

Song Han, Gerard Medioni
Integrated Media Systems Center and
Institute for Robotics and Intelligent Systems
University of Southern California
Los Angeles, California 90089 USA
han@seer.usc.edu

3D I/O devices, long awaited in computer-aided design (CAD) systems, are finally available as force feedback devices such as PHANToM (SensAble Devices, Inc.). This paper presents Feature Based Haptic Rendering (FBR), which provides haptic feedback of a more accurate shape required by the haptic man-machine interface for surface CAD than intermediate representation (IR).[1,2]

Figure 1 shows the FBR architecture. The virtual surface modeling process is connected to a haptic rendering loop using a single asynchronous TCP/IP socket stream. As Mark et al[2] state, decoupling the haptic rendering process is indispensable to obtaining high haptic fidelity that requires device control latency of ~kHz, since shape modelling (e.g. NURBS knot insertion) may take time. IR is data exchanged between decoupled processes, which actually is a plane in Adach & Ogino[1] and to which Mark et al[2] added a few more primitives. Because only received IR is used in haptic rendering, the haptic process does not need a geometry database. The database coherency problem that arises with such architecture, in that each process has its own geometry database copy, can thus be avoided.

FBR generalizes the idea of IR to a feature, which is the unit of communication and can be categorized into two groups: data and commands. The data feature includes local haptic properties of virtual objects, such as shape (Figure 2), texture, stiffness, and position. Command feature is used to control other processes (e. g., switching interpolation strategies of received shape features in the haptic rendering loop). FBR provides a communication protocol to exchange features. A feature is split into one or more fixed-length packets from which the receiver reconstructs the original feature. The haptic renderer has force feedback calculation algorithms and interpolation strategies for features.

FBR can be used by any point-contact type force feedback device as IR and can be easily extended to multiple-contact type devices by introducing an object momentum feature. Haptic volume rendering is also easy: shape features can be constructed as local iso-surfaces by the Marching Cube algorithm,[3] for example. Physically correct haptic rendering of a thin, elastic object is then possible, which is important for surgical simulation but is difficult with the voxel density field algorithm.[4] A virtual surface modeler with force feedback has been implemented with FBR, whose modelling and graphic rendering run on a SGI Indigo2 Elan (200 MHz R4400), and the haptic display is PHANToM (6 DOF input and 3 DOF force output) on a PC (200 MHz Pentium Pro). The user can touch, trace, and deform a B-Spline and a triangular surface directly[5] with virtual tools catching haptic feedback (Figure 3). Rich shape features display the surface shape accurately. A 5-10 kHz device control latency has been achieved with 20-30 Hz communication and graphics refresh rate. Quantitative and qualitative evaluation of FBR using psychophysical methods is underway.

Juli Yamashita, Cai Yi, Yukio Fukui
National Institute of Bioscience and Human Technology
1-1, Higashi
Tsukuba, Ibaraki, 305 Japan
juli@nibh.go.jp
fukui@nibh.go.jp
ycai@nibh.go.jp

REFERENCES

1 Adachi, Y., T. Kumano, and K. Ogino. Intermediate Representation for Stiff Virtual Objects, in Proc. of IEEE VRAIS'95, 1995.
2 Mark, W. R. et al. Adding Force Feedback to Graphics Systems: Issues and Solutions, in Proc. of ACM SIGGRAPH 96, 1996.
3 Lorensen, W. E. and H. E. Cline. Marching Cubes: A High Resolution 3D Surface Construction Algorithm, in Proc. of ACM SIGGRAPH 87, 1987.
4 Avila, R. S. and L. M. Sobierajski. A Haptic Interaction Method for Volume Visualization, in Proc. of Visualization Conf., 1996.
5 Yamashita, J. and Y. Fukui. A Direct Deformation Method, in Proc. of IEEE VRAIS'93, 1993.

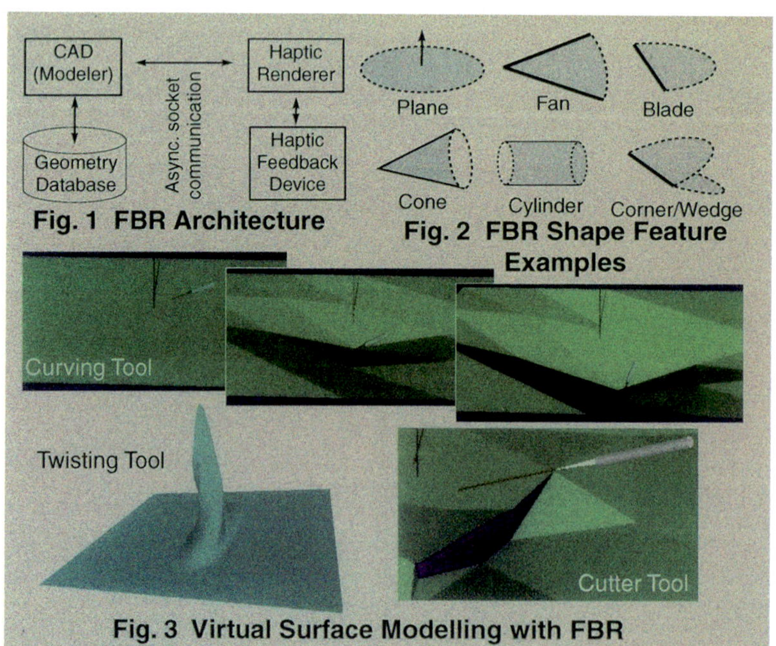

Fig. 1 FBR Architecture

Fig. 2 FBR Shape Feature Examples

Fig. 3 Virtual Surface Modelling with FBR

The three-dimensional models used for computer graphics display are becoming so large and complex that they cannot be rendered at interactive speeds. As a solution to this problem, researchers have introduced the concept of level of detail (LOD). With this approach, model complexity is varied to ensure that interactive display speeds are maintained, instituting a tradeoff between LOD and interactivity. Two complementary lines of LOD research exist. The first, object simplification, introduces methods that allow variation in LOD, and has been the focus of much recent research effort. The second, LOD management, introduces methods for managing the LOD vs. display speed tradeoff. This sketch describes such an LOD management method.

The human visual system perceives the world at a high LOD in the center of its field of view, and a low LOD in the periphery of its field of view (FOV). This suggests an LOD management technique that mimics this characteristic of the visual system, and reduces LOD in the periphery of displays with relatively large (60 degrees or more horizontal) FOVs. We call this technique peripheral degradation. Previous experiments[1] have shown that this technique can work well, allowing reductions in detail that do not harm user performance on search tasks. With the increases in display speed that accompany these detail reductions, user performance should improve.

Use of peripheral degradation requires knowledge of user gaze direction, including both head and eye movements. Head tracking hardware is widely available and is used in many existing systems. However, there are a number of reasons to avoid eye tracking. Eye tracking technology can be expensive and often requires calibration for each new user. It is unwieldy and often unpleasant to use. Finally, sampling the eye tracker with each iteration of the rendering loop can actually reduce interactivity. We did not use eye tracking in our implementation of peripheral degradation.

Psychophysical research[2] shows that when the head can move freely, eye motion relative to the head is almost always restricted to a 15-degree central horizontal band. This suggests that LOD in a head-tracked display (without eye tracking) need only be high within this band. We performed an experiment to verify this hypothesis and to see if a similar detail degradation could be introduced in the vertical dimension. Eight participants performed a complex search task using head-mounted displays with varying degrees of horizontal and vertical peripheral degradation (Figure 1), or with no degradation at all. Search space was four times larger than total display FOV. Peripheral detail was degraded by using pixels roughly two degrees x two degrees in size.

Results, presented in Table 1, confirmed the hypothesized 15-degree horizontal detail constraint and indicated that a vertical 15-degree constraint could also be introduced. Displays with at least 30 horizontal and vertical degrees of central high detail did not differ from an undegraded display. This indicates that designers of head-tracked interactive graphics need only maintain high levels of detail within a 30 degrees x 30 degrees central display area. In CAVE systems that may have a 270 degrees x 270 degrees FOV, this high detail area may occupy only 1.25 percent of the display area. In our continuing research, we are attempting to isolate an appropriate LOD for the degraded periphery.

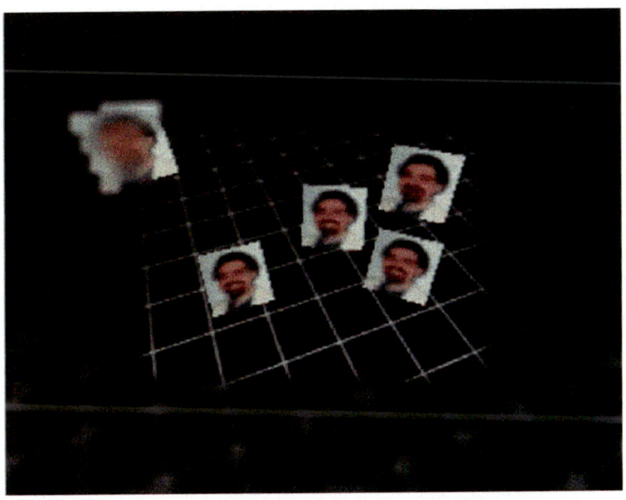

FIGURE 1 View with a degraded display with a 40 degrees x 30 degrees central detail area. Subjects located the face with its mouth closed.

	10°	20°	30°	40°
10°	4.147	4.150	4.058	3.538
20°	3.721	3.552	3.398	3.448
30°	3.601	3.451	2.876	3.147
40°	3.808	3.105	3.281	3.061

TABLE 1
Mean search times in seconds for differently sized high-detail areas. Rows have the same horizontal extent, columns the same vertical extent. Mean search time for the undegraded 75 degrees x 58 degrees display was 2.85 seconds.

Benjamin Watson, Larry Hodges, Neff Walker
Graphics, Visualization & Usability Center
Georgia Institute of Technology
801 Atlantic Drive
Atlanta, Georgia 30332-0280 USA
watsonb@cc.gatech.edu
neff.walker@psych.gatech.edu
larry@cc.gatech.edu

REFERENCES
1 Watson, B., Walker, N. , Hodges, L. F., & Worden, A. Managing Level of Detail through Peripheral Degradation: Effects on Search Performance with a Head-Mounted Display, GVU Technical Report 96-04, Georgia Institute of Technology.
2 Barnes, G. R. Vestibulo-Ocular Function during Coordinated Head and Eye Movements to Acquire Visual Targets, J. of Physiology, 287, pp. 127-147.

Virtual Backdrops

Large and complex 3D models are required for architectural walk-throughs, flight simulators, and other applications of virtual environments. It is not possible to render all the geometry of these arbitrarily complex scenes at highly interactive rates, even with high-end computer graphics systems. This has led to extensive work in 3D model simplification methods.

We have been investigating dynamically replacing portions of 3D models with textures. This approach is similar to the old stage-trick of draping cloth backgrounds in order to generate the illusion of presence in a scene too complex to actually construct on stage. A texture (or backdrop) once created, can be rendered in time independent of the geometric complexity it represents. Consequently, significant frame rate increases can be achieved at the expense of memory and image quality. Properly handling these last two tradeoffs is crucial to a successful texture-based simplification algorithm.

Previous work has approached these tradeoffs by requiring a large number of texture samples in order to guarantee a maximum per-pixel error. While for some ranges of applications and models this provides a good solution, we have found that in our domain (architectural models, CAD models, and other indoor models) the simplification benefits are overwhelmed by the large number of textures that need to be precomputed or dynamically rendered.

A successful algorithm for dynamically replacing geometry with textures must provide solutions for the following three major problems:

1 Geometric Continuity: a texture contains an image of a portion of the model. The image is only perspectively correct when viewed from the same viewpoint used to create it. Thus, when the eye moves from the texture's original viewpoint, the geometry adjacent to the texture appears discontinuous with the image of the texture. Previous systems addressed this issue by either allowing a small discontinuity or restricting the texture locations to fully contain entire "objects."

2 Temporal Continuity: when the eye approaches a texture (or recedes far enough from a subset of the model), we need to switch the texture to geometry (or vice versa). During this motion, the viewpoint will not be at the same position from where the texture was created. This sudden transition will cause an effect commonly known as "popping."

3 Automatic Placement: the texture-based simplification system will need to choose where in the model to place textures in order to achieve the desired speedup and image quality.

Solutions have been proposed[1] for the geometric and temporal continuity problems (see Figure 1). We have been focusing on the automatic placement aspect. For our purposes, we can loosely classify indoor models into two categories:

1 Single-Room Models: models where most of the geometric complexity is visible from the typical viewing locations (few large occluders are present).

2 Multiple-Room Models: this category fits well with the cells and portals framework used by some visibility culling algorithms.

The special characteristics of the cells and portals framework were used to solve the automatic placement problem for cell-partitioned models (see Figure 2)[2]. We are currently exploring solutions for the texture placement problem in general 3D models.

FIGURE 1 Geometric Continuity Two textures outlined in red (adjacent geometry warped to match the textures)

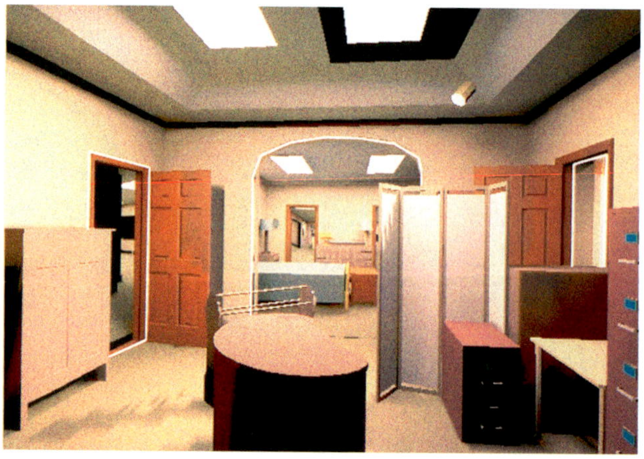

FIGURE 2 Portal Textures The portals have been replaced with textures

Daniel G. Aliaga, Anselmo A. Lastra
Computer Science Department
University of North Carolina at Chapel Hill
Chapel Hill, NC 27599-3175
aliaga@cs.unc.edu

REFERENCES
1 D. Aliaga. Visualization of Complex Models Using Dynamic Texture-based Simplification, IEEE Visualization '96, pp. 101-106, 1996.
2 D. Aliaga, A. Lastra. Visibility Culling using Portal Textures, to appear in IEEE Visualization '97, Oct 19-24, 1997.

The use of lines of contour to depict 3D surfaces has a centuries-old tradition in printmaking, reaching its peak in the technical virtuosity of the Italian Renaissance engravers (see Kemp[1]). Their techniques, being essentially manual, relied upon skill, experience, and intuition acquired through long years of apprenticeship. Since that period, several painters have also employed contouring, but with the addition of colour.[2,3] Current understanding of our perceptual mechanisms confirms that one of the most immediate and important depth cues is object surface contour information.[4]

Dissatisfied with existing methods of rendering 2D images of (projected) 3D computer models, some researchers have lately turned their attention to non-photorealistic (NPR) rendering techniques, in which the drawn line or mark replaces the pixel as the basic unit of depiction. Winkenbach and Salesin[5], for example, have developed sophisticated programs to generate monochromatic line-hatchings, modulated in weight and density, for rendering surfaces in a way that conveys spatial as well as tonal information. (A comprehensive review of NPR to 1995 is given by Schofield and Lansdown.[6])

To overcome the limitations of monochromatic contouring, the author has devised a specialized form of colour contouring using a restricted colour palette to facilitate transcription to fine art printmaking media, especially screenprinting. This method arises from his earlier work with techniques of optical colour mixing using dots and intersticed lines, and offers the creative artist new opportunities for control and intervention in making this type of "divisionistic" image.

An original 3D composition comprising an arcaded structure from a Sassetta painting housing a range of curved solids (including a greatly enlarged eye from Michelangelo's David) was used as the testbed for successive versions of the contouring procedure, designed and implemented by the author in AutoLISP (the LISP language extension to AutoCAD). Under user control, the procedure traces sets of lines across selected surface meshes. The contour lines are formed by contiguous "platelets" of cyan, magenta, yellow, or black whose relative widths, overlaid combinations, and spacing are computed to give the required balance of colour.

On each triangular facet, three bands of contours are constructed, one band for each of the (user-specified) HSV parameters: hue, saturation, and tone or value. The method depends upon the phenomenon of optical colour mixing, and since the colour of each surface region is set interactively, the colour composition of the resulting image is entirely under the (intuitive) control of the artist/user, who may use a conventional rendering of the same scene and/or direct observation as reference. Contour direction is generally chosen to be sympathetic to the underlying object structure, although line direction and width can also be used to introduce textural variation and contrast. In this way occlusion effects, for example, can be accentuated.

Each contour line thus produced is assigned by colour to one of four AutoCAD layers, facilitating the production of separations for imagesetting or plotting onto polyester drafting film at any size. Using a drafting pen to add or erase as required, the artist enjoys an additional level of control, which again differentiates this method from conventional photomechanical processes. Separations are transferred to screens using normal photostencil methods, ready for (manual) editioning using high quality process colours. A detail of a completed four-colour screenprint is shown.

Initial results demonstrate how this kind of contoured 2D representation conveys considerably more spatial information than a conventional colour rendering. The viewer also experiences various optical phenomena depending on proximity to the image surface.

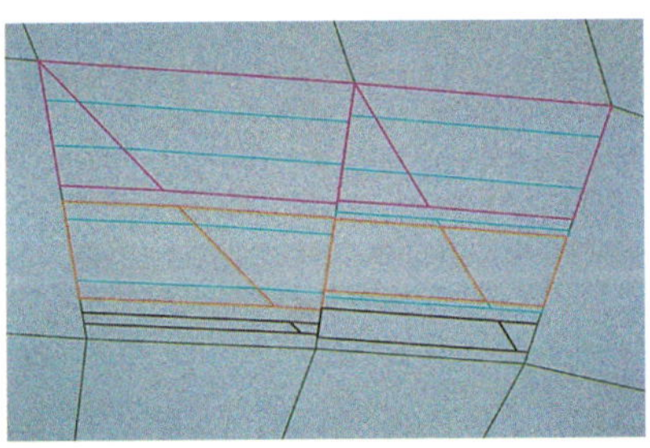

FIGURE 1 Surface contour lines built from coloured "platelets"

FIGURE 2 Plotted cyan separation (detail)

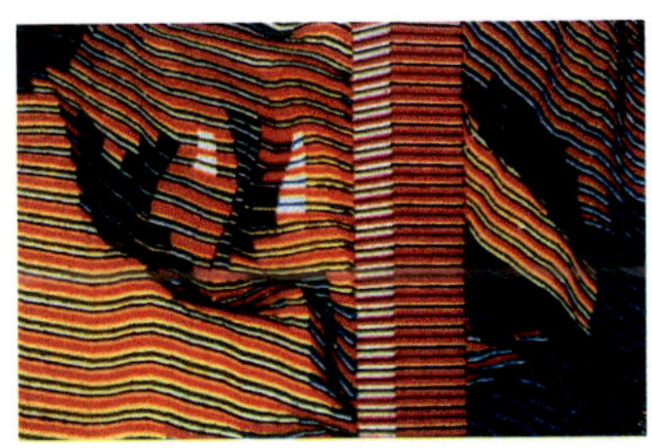

FIGURE 3 Four-colour screenprint (detail)

Peter Lee
15 Mayhill Road, Charlton
London SE7 7JG United Kingdom
george@camwell.demon.co.uk

ACKNOWLEDGEMENTS
The author would like to thank the research group at Camberwell College of Arts for their assistance, especially George Whale for his 3D graphics expertise, help with AutoLISP programming, and with the preparation of this sketch.

REFERENCES

1 M. Kemp. Coming into Line: Graphic Demonstrations of Skill in Renaissance and Baroque Engravings, Sight and Insight, Essays on Art and Culture in Honour of E. H. Gombrich at 85, ed. J. Onians, Phaidon Press, London, 1994, pp. 221-244.

2 M. W. Martin. Futurist Art & Theory, Oxford University Press, 1968.

3 D. Petherbridge. Studies for the Monumental: the Work of Victor Newsome, Architectural Review UK, Vol. 69, No. 1009, March 1981, pp. 167-169.

4 R. Gregory, J. Harris, P. Heard & D. Rose. The Artful Eye, Oxford University Press, 1995, pp. 57, 61.

5 G. Winkenbach and D. H. Salesin. Computer-Generated Pen-and-Ink Illustration, Computer Graphics (SIGGRAPH 94 Proceedings), Vol. 28, No. 4, October 1994, pp. 91-108.

6 J. Lansdown and S. Schofield. Expressive Rendering: A Review of Nonphotorealistic Techniques, IEEE Computer Graphics and Applications, May 1995.

Integrating Digital Media and Autographic Fine Art Printmaking

As a painter-printmaker – a maker of art objects – my concern is integrating digital technologies with traditional processes such that formal and material concerns are not denied the fine art printmaker who uses digital processes. Some recent and current work includes the following objectives:

1 Independence of printed colour from the computer and the constraints of both the CMYK and standard custom colour sets.

2 Using overprinted layers of inks, not dots in close proximity, allowing real physical planes of colours to create complex visual spaces. Wresting colour creation and manipulation from the "device," back to the printmaker, to be modified as the process develops in response to earlier stages.

3 Independence from the limitations imposed by the halftone dot.

4 Finding a durable image creation process that utilizes the computer's capacity for exploration and manipulation but which is susceptible to intervention by the hand of the artist at any point during the process, not simply during the process of compositing in non-real space.

5 Making a cheap, accessible method for artists and students, so they can work at manageable resolutions without high-end equipment.

6 Development of a process into which drawing (and/or other non-digital manipulation) can be re-integrated at any point without the work suffering a sense of intrusion.

Images to be transferred to photolitho plate are created from grayscale scans. Using alpha channels as selections and transparency masks, the image is made across a number of visual layers. Actual layers could be used in Photoshop 3.x and later to composite the entire image before committing parts to their destination channels, but this is not essential. Alpha channels can give an indication of the overprinted inks, if not their precise mixing requirements. Colours may be assigned to channels to simulate the eventual print, but, on RGB monitors, this is restricted and inaccurate. With suitable gamma settings and understanding of printmaking inks, this can be minimized. Outputting split channels using diffusion dither allows image scaling without succumbing to screen angles and rulings.

Colours may be mixed by the printmaker, using traditional inks, tested directly on the papers, and, significantly, may be modified in response to previous plates as the work proceeds. The printing of such works is thus time-based, the artist being free to leave the fixing of colours to the last conceivable moment. Given other processes, such as direct work on the plate, a great degree of flexibility and adaptation after output from the computer is still possible. The image can be almost infinitely variable and may be overworked right up until the artist decides to fix the process. These are all attributes of an autographic process.

Source scans are grayscale, as they need only work on alpha channels. The only expensive equipment used in my prints was a Novajet large format inkjet printer, but all other equipment would certainly be available in any art school's print workshops. The most recent pieces use five channels per image. Work is continuing on prints using up to 12, with direct physical intervention and/or drawing re-introduced at the stage of plate-making.

The images are details from offset litho prints on Fabriano Artistico Ivory 200gsm, using five plates rolled in hand-mixed printmaking inks.

Raz Barfield
28 Monkridge
Crouch End Hill
London N8 8DE United Kingdom
george@camwell.demon.co.uk

Why colored pencil drawings?

In general, traditional synthetic images tend to cause eye fatigue for the viewer, since all of the points are in focus, which gives the impression that they were painted uniformly. As a solution to this problem from an artistic point of view, "colored pencil drawings" (CPDs) should attract more attention also from the CG community, because of their intrinsic ability to produce a gentle appearance for human eyes. One of the salient features of CPDs is that high-level depiction and controllability can be achieved by a proper choice of papers and pencil holding, sharpening, and movement.[1] Therefore, it is becoming commonly acknowledged that CPD has become an artform in its own right, and is considered to be a challenging theme of advanced CG modeling in the area of digital painting. CPDs could be emulated on screen by combining various functions provided by existing commercially-available digital paint systems. At present, however, there exists no system that directly supports the CPD techniques.

Modeling Paper Microstructure

As the appearance of CPDs stems primarily from the "texture" of papers, faithful modeling of the papers' 3D microstructure is crucial. Papers are generally composed of multiple layers of globally-oriented, but locally random sparse fiber nets, whose spaces are filled partially with talc for surface smoothness. A fiber net is modeled geometrically by instantiating defaced, napped, and constricted cylinders. On the other hand, a constrained blobby approach is taken to model the distribution of talc. Such a microstructure of papers is then 3D-scan converted into a thin volume model, whose field value indicates the density of a paper component or pigment. The resulting paper volume is volumetrically ray traced to simulate paper semitransparency and subsurface scattering. A volume visualization and graphics software system called VolVis ver. 2.0[2] is used for the purpose of test rendering.

Modeling Pigment Distribution

Pigment distribution is modeled based on the paper microstructure model described above. Many chinks left in the layered structure of papers are the most dominant factor in governing how pigment is distributed. The offset distance accessibility (ODA)[3] is calculated to approximately locate the chinks in the paper volume, where fractions of pigment can be distributed, by accounting for the pencil point's shape, pressure, and stroke as well as pigment fragility. Here again, the geometry of pigment peeled off from a pencil and deposited into the paper volume is modeled by the collision-detected blobby model, and then 3D-scan converted into the paper volume.

Figure 1 shows three perspective views of the microstructure of a square piece of paper: drawing without pigment (top); virtual effect of graphitizer (middle); and drawing with a single color of pigment (bottom) The graphitizer is a well-known tool commonly used in paper science for evaluating the texture of papers by press coating a special kind of pigment uniformly on pieces of paper. It can be seen also from the middle and bottom images respectively that the virtual graphitizer reveals the fiber nets more clearly, while in the regular drawing, most of the pigment is accumulated in the concave regions lying on the fore side of fibers with locally maximal height with respect to the pencil stroke direction. Furthermore, in both cases, it is revealed that pigment is more likely to be attached onto surface areas covered with talc, because these relatively flat areas possess lower ODA values, and talc has a relatively high pigment-adsorption rate. Such pigment distribution patterns qualitatively coincide with physically observed ones. An example of a macroscopic view of the resultant CPD is shown in Figure 2.

Modeling Pigment Redistribution with Water

Currently, our interest is drawn also to yet another principal CPD operation: redistributing pigment with water. Using water-soluble colored pencils, spreading and blending of pigment with water can yield a sense of smooth color fading and blending, and hence play a key role in depicting objects in a precise and natural manner.

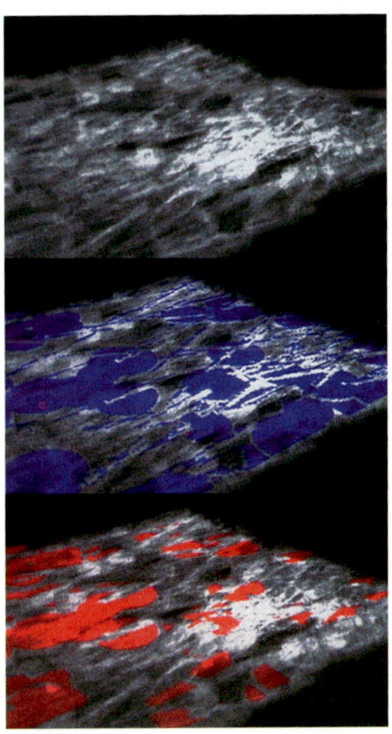

A
Drawing: without pigment

B
Graphitizer

C
Drawing: with single color of pigment

FIGURE 1 Microscopic images of paper microstructure.

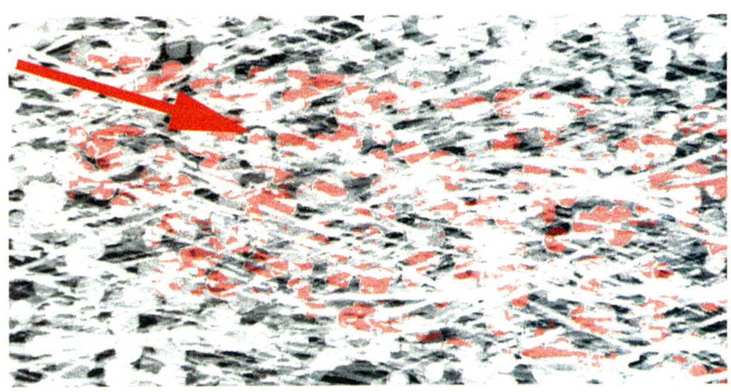

FIGURE 2 Macroscopic image of paper microstructure. Arrow depicts the primary direction of pencil stroke.

Saeko Takagi, Issei Fujishiro
Department of Information Sciences
Ochanomizu University
Bunkyo-ku
Tokyo, JAPAN
{takagi, fuji}@imv.is.ocha.ac.jp

REFERENCES

1 Hutton-Jamieson, I. Colored Pencil Drawing Techniques, North Light Books, 1986.
2 Avila, R., et al. VolVis: A Diversified Volume Visualization System, in Proc. IEEE Vis'94, pp. 31-38, October 1994.
3 Miller, G. Efficient Algorithm for Local and Global Accessibility Shading, Computer Graphics (Proc. SIGGRAPH 94), pp. 319-326, August 1994.

Line drawing provides an excellent medium for communicating ideas. Unfortunately, because line density determines tone and line curvature conveys form, computing lines is simultaneously a two- and three-dimensional problem, making algorithms to create convincing computer-generated drawings difficult to design.

As in previous approaches, we simplify this problem by converting the three-dimensional model into two-dimensional data before calculating hatching. The resulting data include several vector fields generated by projecting the surface hatching direction of each object onto the image plane. In our system, the vector field streamlines are then calculated and converted into hatching by simply distorting them in a sketchy fashion.

Figure 1 depicts the complete process of generating a streamline drawing. Four types of two-dimensional data are extracted from the model. Some or all of the visible lines are sketchily distorted and added to the image.

Several vector fields are calculated for varying surface hatching directions, one or more of which are applied to each object (Figures 2 & 3). A global illumination image is referenced as a tone map to control the hatching density. Any tones captured in the tone map, including soft shadows and specular effects, are reproduced in the drawing. An ID map facilitates assigning custom hatching attributes to objects.

A simple one-pass algorithm was developed to calculate streamline direction and density. The algorithm employs an image mask to track the completed portions of the drawing. When all of the tonal areas are hatched, the algorithm terminates.

Because this technique avoids calculating hatching in three dimensions, it is not plagued by the robustness issues common to three-dimensional modelers and non-photorealistic rendering systems.

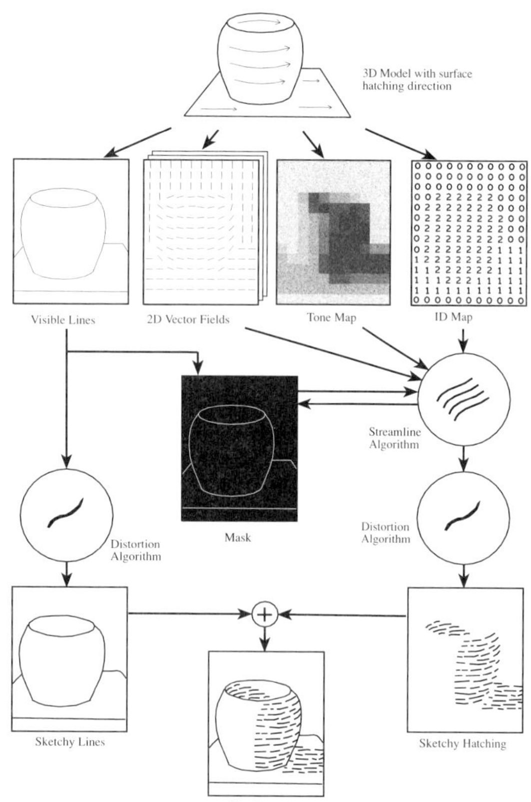

FIGURE 1 Process for creating a streamline drawing from a model.

FIGURE 2 Various hatching orientations. They are, from left to right, (1) oriented with respect to the major axis, (2) oriented with respect to the light source, and (3) oriented along the principal curvature directions. Note that the surface shadow is not depicted for the principle curvature directions because principle curvature is not defined for flat surfaces.

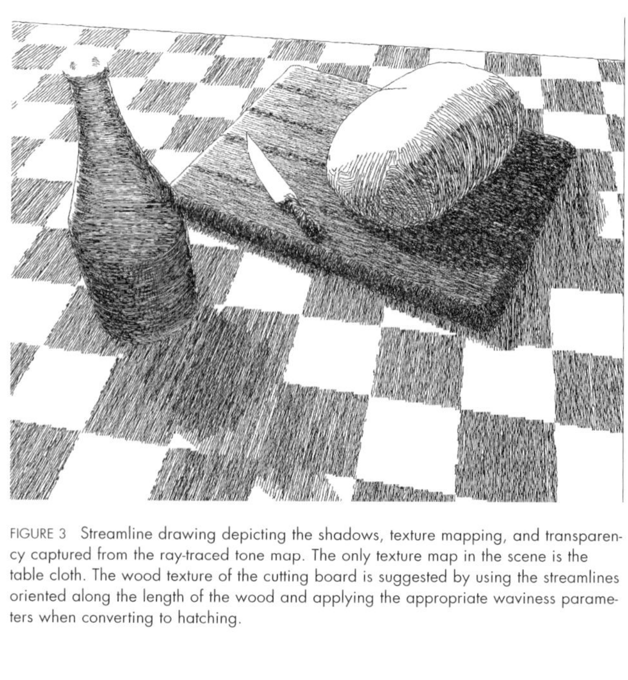

FIGURE 3 Streamline drawing depicting the shadows, texture mapping, and transparency captured from the ray-traced tone map. The only texture map in the scene is the table cloth. The wood texture of the cutting board is suggested by using the streamlines oriented along the length of the wood and applying the appropriate waviness parameters when converting to hatching.

Richard Coutts, Donald P. Greenberg
580 Rhodes Hall
Cornell University
Ithaca, New York 14852 USA
rcoutts@graphics.cornell.edu

REFERENCES

1 G.Winkenbach, D. Salesin. Computer-Generated Pen-and-Ink Illustration, Proceedings of SIGGRAPH 94, August 1994.

2 T. Saito, T. Takahashi. Comprehensible Rendering of 3D Shapes, Proceedings of SIGGRAPH 90, August 1995.

3 D. Dooley, M. Cohen. Automatic Illustration of 3D Geometric Models: Lines, Proceedings of SIGGRAPH, August 1990.

4 P. Haeberli. Paint-by-Numbers. Proceedings of SIGGRAPH 90, August 1990.

Realistic image generation in computer graphics is greatly facilitated by either using texture mapping of real images or writing shaders, programs that procedurally describe textures. Using texture mapping (e.g. scanning a photograph) is rarely adequate, as the photograph may capture information about the lighting direction and may cause aliasing problems. Another problem with a scanned texture image is that it has a finite size and resolution, and tiling the texture across a surface may cause unnatural periodicity. Writing shaders might seem to be a powerful approach, but in practice it is often very difficult to achieve the desired look.

This sketch presents a system that generates procedural textures or shaders using genetic algorithm techniques. The system operates in both artist-directed and automatic texture matching modes. In interactive artist directed mode, aesthetic evaluation and selection are controlled by the user. In automatic mode, the system compares rendered images of generated shaders to images of target textures, using texture matching techniques.

Representation
In our system, a shader is a hierarchical directed acylic graph of nodes, where each node represents a predefined function or texture.

Initial Selection
An initial population of shaders is obtained by searching through a predefined library of shaders, testing these images from the shaders against the target texture and scoring the images. The system selects the initial population from those receiving the best scores. Selection in the interactive mode is similar but based on the users' aesthetic judgment.

Breeding and Ongoing Evaluation
"Parent" shaders are selected and bred to create new children for the ongoing population. When breeding two hierarchies of shaders, the breeding procedure selects a random node in each hierarchy and swaps the subtrees under these nodes. The system evaluates images of generated shaders in automatic mode, while in interactive mode users assign scores to images of shaders based on their aesthetic judgment.

The new population of shaders is determined based on this fitness evaluation. A genetic algorithm procedure is used to determine which shaders will survive and reproduce and which will die, based on this fitness. Shaders are shuffled, and each pair of shaders is selected to breed. After a new population is generated, using the interactive mode users repeat previous steps to generate a new population and so on until they are satisfied with the result. In the automatic mode, the generation continues until a generated shader is sufficiently close to the target texture or a maximum number of generations has been reached.

Mutation
Random mutation is used to introduce diversity into the population. After breeding, the hierarchy is traversed, leaf node input variables are randomly selected, and depending on the mutation rate, changed to other valid values.

User Interface and Operation
The figure shows the system as it appears to the user and a collection of generated shaders. The top row of the interface contains generation parameters, while the middle three rows contain rendered images of the current population of shaders. On the bottom row are images of temporarily stored shaders.

The interactive mode has been used to generate a variety of complex shaders including both surface and displacement shaders, such as those shown in the figure. When running in interactive mode, the user selects two parents for breeding, and the top two images on the interface show the currently selected parents. On the other hand, in automatic mode, the top two images show the target texture, and the middle three rows show images of shaders that are attempts to match the target shader. In this case, parent selection and breeding takes place automatically.

Aladin M. Ibrahim, Donald H. House
Visualization Laboratory
216 Langford Center
Texas A&M University
College Station, Texas 77843 USA
aladin@viz.tamu.edu
house@viz.tamu.edu

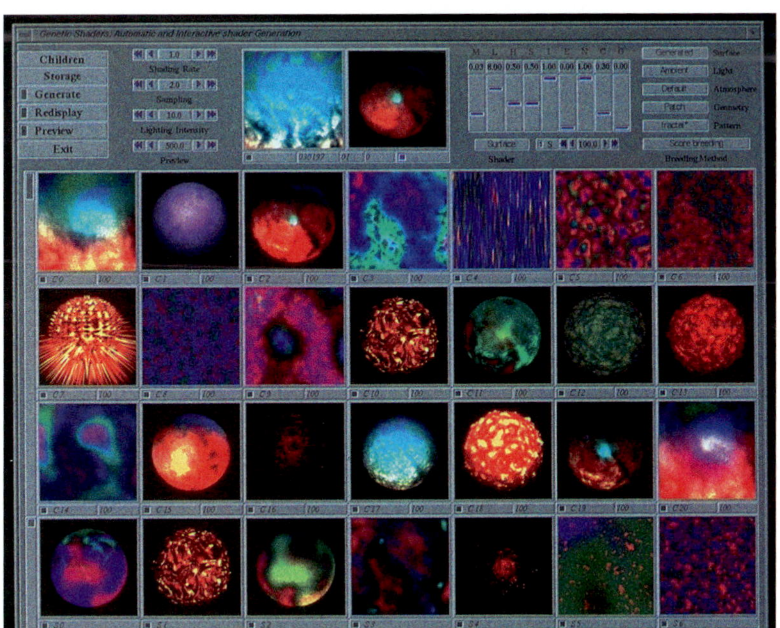

While procedural shaders provide an interface for evaluating the shader function at a single point, it is not easily possible to obtain an average value of the shader together with accurate error bounds over a finite area. Yet the ability to compute such error bounds is crucial for several interesting applications, most notably hierarchical area sampling for global illumination using a finite element approach and for the generation of textures used in interactive computer graphics.

Using affine arithmetic (AA) for evaluating the shader over a finite area yields tight, conservative error bounds for the shader function. Compilers can automatically generate code for utilizing AA from within shaders implemented in a dedicated language, such as the RenderMan shading language.

Affine Arithmetic

Affine arithmetic (AA), first introduced in J. L. D. Comba and J. Stolfi, is an improvement of interval arithmetic. Like interval arithmetic, AA can be used to manipulate imprecise values and to evaluate functions over intervals. In addition to keeping track of the interval, AA also maintains dependencies between sources of error during the computation, and thus manages to generate tighter error bounds. Prior studies[1,2] show that the bounds generated by AA are typically significantly tighter, even for much simpler functions than procedural shaders. The more complicated functions get, and the more dependencies between the sources of error exist, the bigger the advantage of AA.

Application to Procedural Shaders

In order to use AA for obtaining conservative error bounds for area samples of procedural shaders, the shader code simply has to be evaluated using AA instead of normal floating point arithmetic. For this purpose, the complete feature set of the shading language (in our case the RenderMan shading language) has to be implemented in AA. In addition to the functionality found in normal mathematical libraries, shading languages offer a series of domain specific features, most importantly control structures, splines, noise, and derivatives of arbitrary expressions. All these features can be implemented in AA,[3] and yield tight, conservative error bounds when executed.

Results and Future Work

We have implemented a hierarchical subdivision scheme for procedural RenderMan shaders using AA. Given a tolerance value, the algorithm recursively subdivides the parameter domain of the shader, until the area samples for all subdivision cells are within the tolerance, or a maximum recursion level is reached. Experiments show that, using AA, conservative error bounds for an area sample can be computed in roughly the time it takes to compute 7-10 point samples.

Using this subdivision scheme, it is possible to adaptively precompute textures from shaders with an unknown amount of detail information. These textures can then be used, for example in an OpenGL renderer. We are currently working on integrating the subdivision scheme into our rendering system in order to improve finite-element-based global illumination.

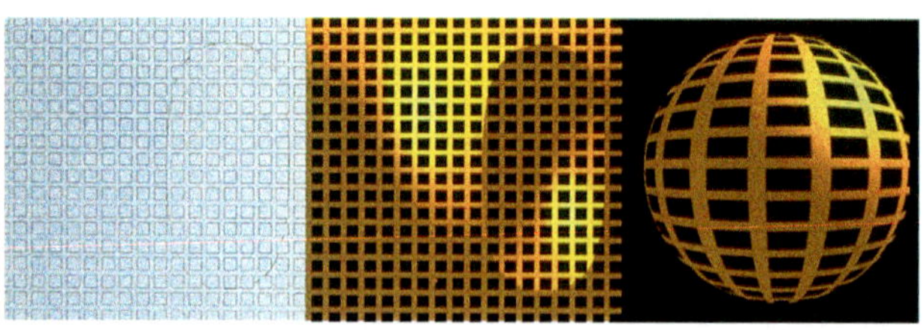

Screen shader sampled using AA, together with color coded error bounds.

Blue marble shader.

Wolfgang Heidrich, Philipp Slusallek, Hans-Peter Seidel
Computer Graphics Group - IMMD IX
University of Erlangen
Am Weichselgarten 9
91058 Erlangen, Germany
heidrich@informatik.uni-erlangen.de

REFERENCES

1 J. L. D. Comba and J. Stolfi. Affine Arithmetic and its Applications to Computer Graphics, In Anais do VII Sibgrapi, pages 9–18, 1993.

2 L. H. Figueiredo and J. Stolfi. Adaptive Enumeration of Implicit Surfaces with Affine Arithmetic, Computer Graphics Forum, 15(5):287–296, 1996.

3 W. Heidrich, Ph. Slusallek, and H.-P. Seidel. Sampling of Procedural Shaders Using Affine Arithmetic, Technical Report TR-11-1996, University of Erlangen Computer Graphics Group, 1996.

Open Inventor is an object-oriented 3D graphics toolkit. Because Open Inventor is written in C++, typical user code development consists of a program/compile/debug iteration cycle. In this sketch, we introduce InvenTcl, an interpretive version of Open Inventor that uses Tcl, (Tool Command Language)[4] and its object oriented extension (incr Tcl)[3] for the conversion. The advantages of InvenTcl include: scriptable and direct manipulation of objects in an Open Inventor scene, easy prototyping of 3D graphics and animation, and low-bandwidth communication of 3D scenes and animations (using scripts).

There are three command types provided by InvenTcl, which correspond to the main functions available in Open Inventor: object creation commands, object interaction commands, and animation commands. For object creation, there are command names for instantiating objects. These commands have the same names as the class names in Open Inventor. For interaction, InvenTcl has binding mechanisms to allow Tcl procedures to be called when objects in the 3D scene are selected. For animation commands, InvenTcl provides access to animation functions found in Open Inventor (i.e. engines and sensors). To illustrate creation commands with an example, the following code shows how a simple scene graph is created interpretively:

```
SoSeparator >root>separator1
SoMaterial >root>separator1>material1
SoCube > >root>separator1>myCube
```

This series of commands adds a SoSeparator node separator1 to the root node, a SoMaterial node to separator1, and a "SoCube" node to separator.1 Notice that we use the '>' notation to specify parent/child relationships. This is consistent with how the most common toolkit used with Tcl, Tk,[4] works.

There are four main technical problems to overcome to make Open Inventor interpretive:

1 Accessing Open Inventor's object functions and the object's public methods and variables from the Tcl interpreter.

2 Open Inventor event management within Tcl/Tk.

3 Binding Open Inventor objects to Tcl procedures and interaction modes.

4 Synchronization of Open Inventor and Tcl processing.

A utility called Itcl++[2] is used to convert Open Inventor objects' methods into [incr Tcl] classes. Event management is done using a handler callback mechanism available in Tcl. Implementation of event management within Tcl does cause some performance penalty. Object binding is accomplished using callback mechanisms and Open Inventor selection utilities. Object binding is an important feature of InvenTcl. By using bindings, it is possible for Tcl procedures to be called as a result of interaction with Open Inventor objects. Not only does this allow for fast prototyping of direct manipulation interfaces with 3D objects, but it also allows designers to easily create novel 3D interfaces for controlling other systems using the "glue-language" properties of Tcl. Synchronization is performed using a semaphore. Implementation for accessing Inventor objects' public variables has not been done in a generalized fashion yet. Further, making Open Inventor interpretive has come as an offshoot of another project;[1] hence, we still have some commands that are tailored to our application.

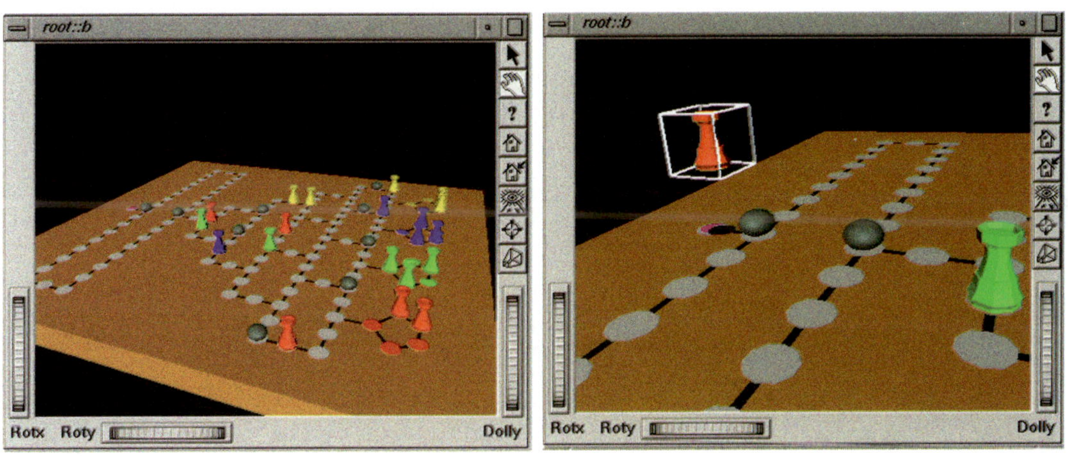

These scenes show some 3D graphics created and being manipulated with InvenTcl

Sidney Fels, Silvio Esser, Armin Bruderlin, Kenji Mase
ATR Media Integration & Communications Research Labs
Seika-cho Soraku-gun
Kyoto 619-02, Japan
fels@mic.atr.co.jp

REFERENCES

1 Bruderlin, A, Fels, S, Esser, S, and Mase, K. Hierarchical Agent Interface for Animation, Accepted in IJCAI Animated Interface Agent Workshop, Workshop Proceedings of the International Joint Conference on Artificial Intelligence (IJCAI'97), August 1997.

2 Heidrich, W., and Slusallek, P. Automatic Generation of Tcl Bindings for C and C++ Libraries, In Proc of the Tcl/Tk Workshop, July 1995.

3 McLennan, M. [incr Tcl]: Object-Oriented Programming in Tcl, In Proc. 1st Tcl/Tk Workshop, University of California at Berkeley, CA, USA, 1993.

4 Ousterhout, J. K. Tcl and the Tk Toolkit, Addison-Wesley, New York, 1994.

In this sketch, we introduce the contour spectrum[1], a user interface component for improving user interaction and quantification in visualization of isocontours.[2] The contour spectrum is a signature consisting of a variety of scalar data and contour attributes computed over the range of function values. Each attribute is presented as a 1D plot, giving the user a quantitative measure of the function to assist in selecting relevant isovalues for informative visualization. For time-varying data, properties can be computed over time and displayed in 2D interface, giving the user a global overview of the time-varying function and allowing interaction in both isovalue and time.

Exploratory visualization is an iterative process, with many visualization parameters to control. Without effective user-interface tools, the user must rely on a-priori knowledge about the data of interest in choosing effective parameters. Informative and effective visualizations often mask the amount of time and effort required to create such a successful visualization. Recent approaches in user interfaces for controlling visualization parameters have aspired to provide the user with the tools to more rapidly choose parameters that result in an effective visualization.

In isocontouring, a common technique is to select a set of isovalues that are evenly spaced throughout the range of the function. It is clear that such a technique is prone to miss features that may be considered important. The ability to manipulate the isovalue in real time allows the user to browse the function for interesting features. However, in the absence of additional guidance, users may only use their prior knowledge of what they expect to see in the data and query for isocontours through a trial-and-error process.

Each attribute of the contour spectrum – such as surface area, volume, and gradient integral – is presented as a 1D plot providing the user a quantitative measure of the corresponding function to assist in selection of relevant isovalues for informative visualization. The computation of each property can be performed exactly, as it corresponds to a spline-shaped function in each cell of the mesh where scalar field is evaluated. The sum over all cells may be expressed as a single spline function for each scalar field attribute. For time-varying data, properties can be computed over time and displayed in a 2D interface, giving the user an overview of the time-varying function, and allowing interaction in both isovalue and time step.

The left of the figure shows a MRI scan of a heart. The maximum of the gradient (yellow function plot of the spectrum on top) corresponds to the isocontour (red contour) bounding the relevant portion of the data.

The right of the figure shows the scalar field obtained from a CT scan of an engine. The main component of the engine can be easily determined by selecting the maximum of the gradient integral. Of course, this remains simply an aid in the interactive querying stage of the dataset, as the concept of "interesting" feature of a scalar field remains highly dependent on the domain of the dataset we are dealing with.

To enhance the understanding of the scalar field structure, a contour tree[3] can be superimposed on the spectrum as displayed in the middle spectrum of the figure. For each edge in the contour tree, there is a connected component of an isocontour in the scalar field. If, while varying the isovalue, two contour components merge together, we have in the contour tree two edges that join. Similarly, if an isocontour splits in two or more components, we will have in the contour tree an edge that splits in two or more edges. Moreover, the comparison between the contour tree and the spectrum may aid in the selection of "interesting" contours. Typically, an isovalue that has a contour tree with many edges but a relatively small overall contour length/area corresponds to a noisy region. Symmetrically, a single component of large length/area corresponds to a well-defined feature of the scalar field.

For time-varying data, we selectively display one function at a time by pseudocoloring of the function values over a 2D grid, as shown in the bottom spectrum of the figure. The value of the selected property is mapped to a colormap, while the vertical direction of the 2D spectrum represents the time evolution of the dataset.

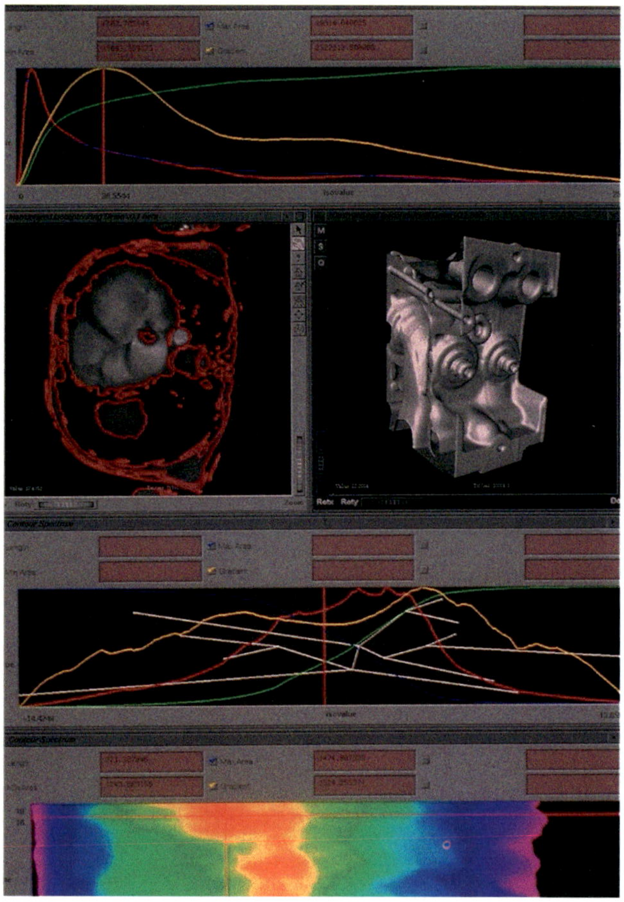

Chandrajit L. Bajaj, Valerio Pascucci, Daniel R. Schikore
Department of Computer Sciences
1398 Computer Sciences Building
Purdue University
West Lafayette, Indiana 47906 USA
{bajaj,pascucci,drs}@cs.purdue.edu

REFERENCES
1 C.L. Bajaj, V. Pascucci, D.R. Schikore. The Contour Spectrum, In Proc. IEEE Visualization 97 (to appear).
2 C.L. Bajaj, V. Pascucci, and D.R. Schikore. Fast Isocontouring for Improved Interactivity, In Proc. 1996 IEEE Symposium on Volume Visualization, pages 39-46, San Francisco, Oct 7-8, 1996.
3 M. van Kreveld, R. van Oostrum, C.L. Bajaj, V. Pascucci and D.R. Schikore. Contour Trees and Small Seed Sets for Isosurface Traversal, In Proc. ACM Symposium on Computational Geometry (Theory Track), 1997, (to appear).

The University of California at San Diego/San Diego Supercomputer Center TeleManufacturing Facility (TMF) project has integrated a solid freeform fabrication (SFF) capability with the Internet to make production of prototype parts easy and convenient. As a result, manufacturing "amateurs," such as biologists, chemists, ecologists, geologists, and mathematicians are able to produce 3D solid models to better visualize their work.

The TMF uses a Laminated Object Manufacturing (LOM) machine from Helisys, Inc. In the LOM process, the 3D object is made from layers of paper or plastic. New paper or plastic is spooled into place and laminated to the layers beneath it with a hot roller. A laser cuts the part outlines at this level. The outlines are essentially the contour lines for this height on the 3D object. The process continues until the 3D part is completed.

The goal of this project is to make the use of physical model-making an everyday aspect of scientific and engineering visualization. Fabrication methods for visualization must not require any manufacturing knowledge, or they will not be used. The use of this type of visualization display must require no previous manufacturing experience in order to be successful.

To make access to this technology familiar to all users, the TMF project is using the World Wide Web as an interface. Users can submit their geometry files from their favorite browser, have those files automatically checked for geometric and topological consistency, have a corrected STL file returned, or have the file queued for fabrication. When the part is being fabricated, the Web page can also be used to get feedback on the manufacturing process, including video images from cameras surrounding the machine.

This sketch discusses how the hardware and software have been integrated with the WWW, and the computational geometry aspects of the project that allow many geometric and topological flaws to be automatically corrected. Finally, we show some examples of the visualizations with which the project has been involved and talk about the perceptual differences between having a real model in your hands versus having a virtual model on a graphics screen. The presentation includes real solid models so that attendees can hold them and experience their perceptual advantages first-hand.

Light Harvesting I Proteins and Photosynthetic Reaction Center.

Michael J. Bailey, Dru Clark
University of California at San Diego and
San Diego Supercomputer Center
P.O. Box 85608
San Diego, California 92186 USA
mjb@sdsc.edu
dru@sdsc.edu
http://www.sdsc.edu/tmf

ACKNOWLEDGMENTS
This work was supported by the National Science Foundation under grant MIP-9420099. The Light Harvesting II complex is from Klaus Schulten, University of Illinois.

Hardware-Assisted Volume Rendering for Oil and Gas Exploration

The search for oil in the earth's subsurface begins with acquisition of terabytes of data, the result of measuring the return of sound waves sent into the earth's crust. These data are processed to form 3D volumes of seismic data, known in the industry as surveys. Very small surveys are in the 60Mbyte range, and typical surveys now approach the 1Gbyte range or higher.

Seismic data are relatively noisy, and determining oil reserves requires the ability to distinguish between subtle features from the noisy data. Because of numerous classification difficulties, interpreters use various color maps and opacity settings, often with very sharp transitions, combined with spatial and color space animation, to highlight different attributes and determine the extent of a given surface. The interpreter will often "roll" the color map, looking for breaks in the data, or interactively change the alpha transfer function to filter noise and determine edges and fades in the surfaces to interpret the connectivity of a given rock boundary.

Fast post-interpolation color lookups are needed to ensure that the application of transfer functions does not become the bottleneck in achieving the desired frame rate. In order to maintain data integrity, color transfer functions cannot be applied directly to the voxel data. They can be used only after all interpolation and compositing has been completed for the rendered scene. If the transfer functions are applied to the voxels using pre-interpolation color lookups, then interpolation essentially happens in color space. Color space interpolation tends to blur the already poorly defined transitions between rock layers. In addition, post-interpolation lookups are necessary to reduce the computational complexity of rendering large data volumes.

Rendering a survey must take into consideration the other data types that an interpreter uses when classifying an unknown survey. Typical data types are either measured geophysical data (well bores, well logs, etc.) or interpreted polygonal surfaces selected from the data (faults, horizons, event markers, etc.). These data items are embedded in the survey as either opaque or partially transparent objects. The interpreter uses multiple data types to tie the interpretations back to the original data and to ensure that the interpretation is valid in all cases. Proper 3D interpolation of data for both volumetric rendering and textured polygonal surfaces is critical to the interpreter.

One approach that can be used to both volume render a survey and map survey data onto embedded surfaces is to use 3D textures. Given the natural mapping of 3D textures to volumetric data, hardware 3D texturing for volume rendering is a natural progression from massively parallel software volume renderers. Volume rendering a seismic survey using 3D texturing starts with creating a 3D texture directly from the survey volume data. The rendering process traverses texture space back-to-front relative to the eye point and intersects the texture with polygon slices that are orthogonal to the eye. Aliasing artifacts are controlled by adjusting the number of slice planes that cut through texture space. Embedded textured opaque geometries can be rendered using a two-pass algorithm with the same 3D texture used for both passes. Rendering transparent geometries can be handled by only rendering the portion of each surface that intersects each pair of polygonal slices during the volume rendering process. When alpha channel transfer functions are used for volume rendering, and surfaces are rendered within the same volume, interpreters are able to, for the first time, view and correlate their interpretations with respect to actual data in 3D.

Over the past two years commercial 3D oil and gas exploration packages have become available for use by the exploration geophysicist. These packages, using hardware 3D texturing and post-interpolation texture lookup tables, have enabled a paradigm shift away from 2D slice-by-slice interpretation to fully 3D interactive interpretation.

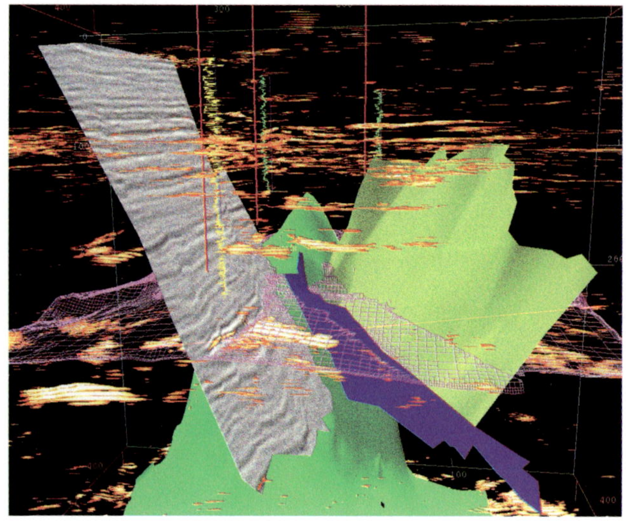

Image courtesy of Landmark Graphics

Alan Y. Commike, Scott Senften
Silicon Graphics, Inc.
11490 Westheimer, Suite 100
Houston, Texas 77077 USA
{senften,commike}@sgi.com

REFERENCES

1 Siliva, Claudio, Arie E. Kaufman, and Constantine Pavlakas. PVR: High-Performance Volume Rendering. Computational Science & Engineering, Vol. 3, No. 4 (Winter 1996), pp 18-28.

2 Fishman, Elliot, et. al. Surgical Planning for Liver Resection. Computer, Vol. 29, No. 1, January 1996, pp. 64-72.

3 Cabral, Brian, Cam, Nancy, and Foran, Jim. Accelerated Volume Rendering and Tomographic Reconstruction Using Texture Mapping Hardware, Proceedings 1994 ACM/IEEE Symposium on Volume Visualization (IEEE CS Press) pp. 91-97 (Order No. PR07067, 1995).

Many scientific experiments result in data that are difficult to visualize using traditional techniques. A typical laboratory experiment, for example, will set up several experimental systems in each of two or more groups (for example, a "control" group and various "treatment" groups). The investigator will then measure various parameters for each system over time (sometimes dozens to hundreds of parameters). The investigator then tries to discern the contrast in evolution of the groups: what is it that is different between the control and treatment groups?

Field monitoring of polluted and unpolluted sites results in the same kinds of data, and the same difficulties in visualization. Plotting multiple lines on a single 2D plot quickly gets confusing, and the dynamic interactions are not readily visible. Graphical 3D scientific visualization can solve some of these problems, by taking advantage of the human visual system to enable qualitative inferences about data that would otherwise be invisible.

We have developed a 3D plotting technique, called "WormPlots," for visualizing these kinds of data. To see how they work, consider first a 2D plot of, say, 24 samples, six from each of four groups, on two axes (measured parameters). We summarize the response of each treatment group (six points) with a 2D shape (for example, a circle centered at their mean and with radius proportional to their variance). This 2D picture represents the groups at a single moment in time. To visualize the evolving dynamics of the systems, we connect these circular time slices with conic sections, giving us "spacetime worms" that can be displayed graphically.

When colorized and displayed on an interactive terminal, the display looks like Figure 1. This figure shows the data from a controlled laboratory toxicology experiment on aquatic microcosms. Over a period of two months, the aquatic populations of some 20 species in 24 microcosms (six microcosms in each of four treatment groups) were sampled on 16 dates. In the figure, time moves out of the page, toward the viewer. The axis pointing to the left shows an algae species (Scenedesmus) combined with a detritivore species (Ostracod), while the vertical axis shows an algae consumer (Daphnia). The four doses of the toxin (low to high) are shown by the coloring of the worms: blue, green, yellow, and red.

Early in the experiment, you can see a classic "predator-prey" situation between Daphnia and Scenedesmus. In the green worm, the Daphnia consume all the algae and their population grows, while Scenedesmus does not. In the red worm, the Daphnia have been depleted by the toxin, and the algae population grows first, with the Daphnia population's growth delayed. Later on, the Daphnia start to recover, and their upswing is matched by a simultaneous downswing in the population of algae. The typical corkscrew shape of the worm illustrates this interaction, and the strength of the effect, from low dose to high dose, is readily apparent in the four worms. By the end of the experiment, both the Daphnia and the algae have diminished to small numbers, and the primary effects of the toxin in the system have disappeared.

Toward the bottom of the figure, however, secondary effects of the toxin can be seen. Ostracods, a species that eats detritus and which is present only in low numbers throughout the early part of the experiment, have now begun to increase. Further, their increase is directly related to the strength of the toxic dose. Evidently, the differing population dynamics of the systems during the early weeks of the experiment have conditioned the detritus (food) for the Ostracods, with the most favorable situation being found in the lowest-dosed systems. This secondary effect in microcosms had not been noticed in previous experiments.

We believe that our visualization prototype solves some particularly thorny problems in visualizing multivariate time series from grouped data and can play an important part in laboratory experiments and field monitoring data analysis.

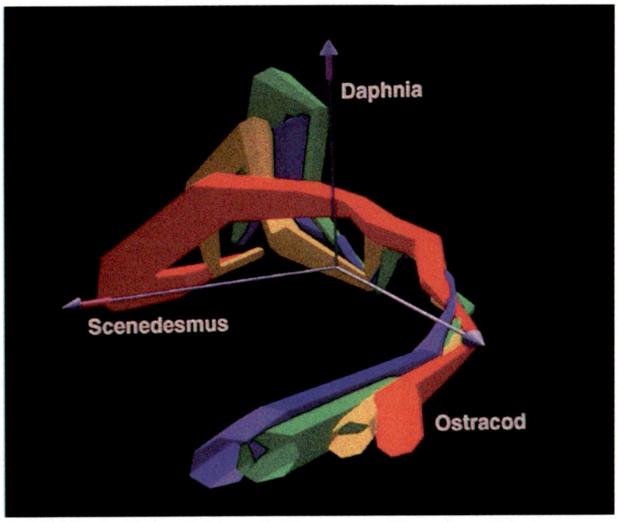

FIGURE 1

Geoffrey Matthews
Computer Science Department
Western Washington University
Bellingham, Washington 98225 USA
matthews@cs.wwu.edu

Mike Roze
Applied Software Technology, Inc.
25 Central Way, STE 333
Kirkland, Washington 98003 USA
roze@astnet.com

A Visualization of Music

The most popular method of visualizing music is music notation. However, most listeners are unfamiliar or uncomfortable with the complex nature of music notation. The goal of this project is to present an alternate method of visualizing music.

In *A Visualization of Music*, music data are mapped into three-dimensional graphical representations. The data, which are captured from input MIDI data files, are transformed with a mapping function. This function maps musical tones to spheres of various size and color within a three-dimensional rectangular volume.

The first step in mapping music data is to map the individual tone data. Each tone can be characterized by its pitch, volume, and timbre. Variations in pitch are mapped to locations along the y-axis. Differences in volume are depicted as spheres of different sizes in the visualization. Tones produced by instruments with similar timbre are represented by spheres of the same color.

The second step of the mapping function involves mapping instrument data. In a musical composition, individual instruments play sequences of tones with specified rhythms. Tones produced by a specific instrument are mapped to locations along the x-axis. Starting times and durations of tones determine spacing along the z-axis.

Information relevant to the music itself is displayed in a legend located on the right-hand side of the visualization. This information includes static data such as title, composer, instrument group color key, and axes color key. Dynamic information such as the current tempo, current time signature, and the current metronome beat is also displayed in the legend.

A record of the tones that have already played is also shown in the visualization. This "note history" is represented by spheres that are smaller in size and lighter in color than the original tones.

In the accompanying video, arrangements of the first movement of Franz Schubert's "Octet in F Major, Op. 166 (D. 803) for Strings and Winds" and Carl Orff's "Tanz, Uf Dem Anger" from "Carmina Burana" are used to demonstrate the results of this method.

Sean M. Smith, Glen N. Williams
Department of Computer Science
Texas A&M University
College Station, Texas 77843 USA
seans@stlnet.com
williams@cs.tamu.edu

Imagine combining the proven entertainment value of professional broadcast television with the enduring appeal of audience chat and participation, and you have a vision of "Inhabited TV." *The Mirror*, an early experiment in Inhabited TV, involved 2,000 viewers of the BBC2 multimedia magazine series "The Net." A research project created by BT, Sony, the BBC and Illuminations, *The Mirror* comprised six multi-user VRML2.0 worlds built on the themes of the broadcast material. The worlds were launched on 13 January 1997 with the broadcast of the first program, and they closed after seven weeks at an "End of the World" party, complete with online dance floor and beer tent.

Goals

The aim of the project was to explore the concepts of fully interactive TV, allowing professional developers to build a content framework within which their audience was free to explore, extend, and script their own program extensions.

Implementation

Use of the Sony Community Place multi-user 3D spaces software allowed the worlds to contain extensive shared state and interaction. Elements of the content were specifically designed to encourage group cooperation and rivalry between visitors. Features included a rocket that required three people to launch, a shuffleboard with a persistent scoreboard to foster competition, and a bouncy castle whose features changed as more people joined.

Scheduled "special events" were also an important aspect of *The Mirror*. These included online debates with a real-time voting facility, game shows with audience participation, and an art exhibition. A debate between science fiction author Douglas Adams and BT's head of research Peter Cochrane attracted an audience of 45, who rejected the idea that "The book is dead."

Results

The Mirror was introduced to the half million viewers of The Net in a three-minute item on 13 January. The program ended at 2355, and there were more than six hundred successful registrations in the first hour. Over the next seven weeks, the number of registered citizens of *The Mirror* rose to 2,250, including 300 from outside the UK. A total of almost 5,000 user hours were recorded, and over 250,000 lines of chat were exchanged. Availability of *The Mirror* worlds was close to 100 percent, and total data transferred from the server was 40 Gbytes.

An online Forum provided an opportunity for citizens to post news and views about *The Mirror*. The Forum was not moderated, and overall the comments were favourable. Several postings applauded the vision of the collaboration in exploring the current technical boundaries of Inhabited TV. There were also calls for a "Mirror anonymous" group for addicts and a threat from one citizen to withhold the BBC license fee if the project really did come to an end!

Conclusions

In addition to the technical hurdles, perhaps the greatest outstanding challenges are in understanding the economics and structure of compelling content. *The Mirror* confirmed the appeal of social chat, and supported the argument that anonymity acts as the alcohol of shared spaces, lubricating creative and open dialogue that challenges the conventions of physical gatherings. Inhabited TV as a commercial service remains a long-term vision, but *The Mirror* is an important early experiment, from which enduring lessons have been learnt.

Graham Walker
BT Laboratories
Admin 2/op6b, BT Laboratories
Martlesham Heath, Ipswich IP5 7RE UNITED KINGDOM
graham.walker@bt-sys.bt.co.uk

Rodger Lea
Sony Distributed Systems Lab
Suite 1140 Regency Plaza
2350 Mission College Boulevard
Santa Clara, California 95054 USA
rodger@csl.sony.co.jp

Peloton: A VRML-Based Bicycling Simulator

Peloton is a distributed simulation system, suitable for athletic training and competition, that creates virtual environments for bicycle rides. Peloton users ride stationary bicycles within computer-generated environments that provide the sights, sounds, and pedaling resistance of actual road courses. The bicycle serves as the rider's primary control device during a simulation session. It is connected to a local computer through sensors and feedback devices. The computer uses input from the sensors to regulate creation of the simulation's virtual environment.

The visual component of this environment is a synthetic, three-dimensional landscape, which combines computer-generated graphics with images of actual road courses. When the rider pedals faster or slower, a corresponding avatar moves along the synthetic course more quickly or slowly. The virtual environment also includes auditory and force feedback. Users' bicycles are connected to devices that regulate pedaling resistance. When the cyclist is climbing a steep hill in the simulated environment, the resistance applied to the bicycle's rear wheel is much greater than it is when the cyclist is traveling on a simulated stretch of level terrain.

People may participate in a common Peloton simulation even while they are geographically separated. When two or more people are interacting through a common simulation, their computers are connected to a Peloton server by the World Wide Web server that coordinates activities on participant computers to create a common virtual environment for the system users.

Peloton is an experiment to discover ways to build virtual reality systems for collaboration over the Web. With Peloton, we connect exercise equipment to the Web, allowing people to share physical activities during group interactions. While it focuses initially on bicycling, Peloton can serve as a prototype for a variety of athletic events over the Web. It is built with standard Web programming tools. Its simulation coordinator, communication session manager, and parts of its input/output modules are programmed with Java. The visual component of its virtual environment is modeled with the Virtual Reality Modeling Language (VRML) and is rendered by a VRML browser. (Java is also used to program behaviors of VRML objects.)

Peloton represents a new class of applications for the Web. This sketch describes the system in more detail and discusses ways that Peloton's implementation has dealt with some of the limits of existing Web technology (especially Java and VRML). It discusses Web browsers and applet security constraints, describing their impact on Peloton's client/server architecture, communication network configuration, and interfaces for unconventional input/output devices. The sketch also highlights significant shortcomings of the VRML specification, including its lack of support for real-time interaction among users in shared environments and its binding of a world's current viewpoint to the current camera to the viewer's avatar.

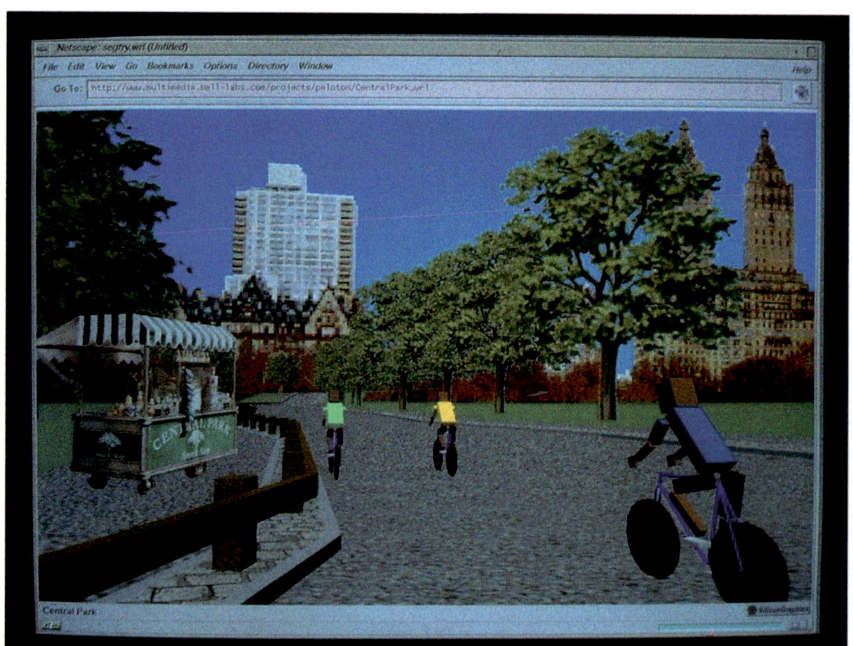

J. Robert Ensor, Gianpaolo U. Carraro
Bell Laboratories
101 Crawfords Corner Road
Holmdel, New Jersey 07733 USA
jre@dnrc.bell-labs.com
paolo@dnrc.bell-labs.com

The Electric Body Project is a software tool for creating choreography using gestural sampling and mapping techniques. Movement is sampled using Ascension Technologies Flock of Birds, a six-degree-of-freedom motion capture system.

The project is a stand-alone software package running on the SGI platform that is designed to work as a plug-in with Life Forms choreographic software and create movement for choreography and animation. What was previously accessible only through synthesized movement phrases in Life Forms can now be accessed and explored with real-time sampled movement phrases input directly from a participant "dancing" within the system.

Movement of the participant is literally sampled, displayed, and metaphorically treated to influence, direct, and determine what is presented and represented visually. The Electric Body uses a series of mapping systems, which originate from the physical mirrored body and result in the transformed mapped body. Mapping strategies include "imprinting," "following," and "tracing," concepts informed by choreographic studio techniques. Movement is sampled and treated using inverse kinematics techniques.

The Electric Body extends the literal, photo-realistic world model of motion capture by introducing the concept of metaphorical mapping used in composing and choreographing movement for dance in the studio. Metaphorical mapping means that a sampled input gesture can be transformed using User Defined Maps that are predefined, or that are created on the fly during the data capture process. Sampled input data can be amplified, filtered, mapped to alternate limbs or limb groups, and distributed to multiple limb groups using the concepts of acceleration (gradual increase of the range of movement over time) or deceleration (gradual decrease of the range of movement over time). In addition, User Maps can be combined over time, to produce additive phasing. These filters can be applied infinitely to sampled movement, enabling movement definition in layers (much in the same way that images can be layered in Photoshop). These techniques provide a mechanism for composing movement that parallels the sound filtering used in music composition and image filtering used in image processing.

Users can work directly with the computer display, or in a performance situation, interact with their own life size projected images. It is possible for performers to replicate and enhance those images, and encounter and respond to imprints of their own projected movements. This enables dancers to use characteristics of their own gestures to compose and influence movement created through the filtering process. Gesture enables participants to compose their own places within a dance, modify timing and placement of visual images, and select and integrate movement phrases.

This real-time movement exploration system can be used in performance by creating virtual dancers whose movement is generated directly from the live performer in such a way as to produce a complex responsive system.

This project has been sponsored by the Media Arts Section of the Canada Council.

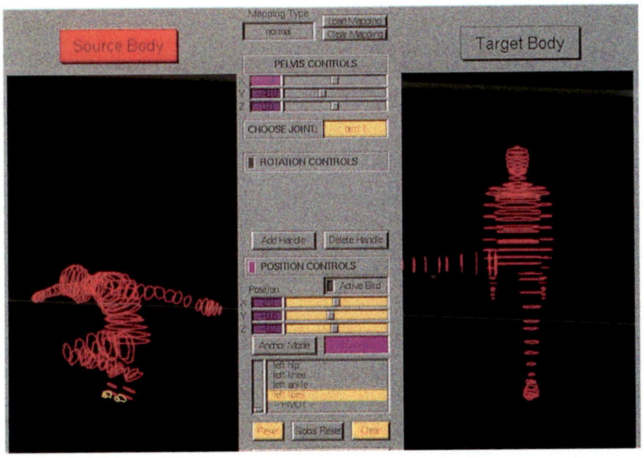

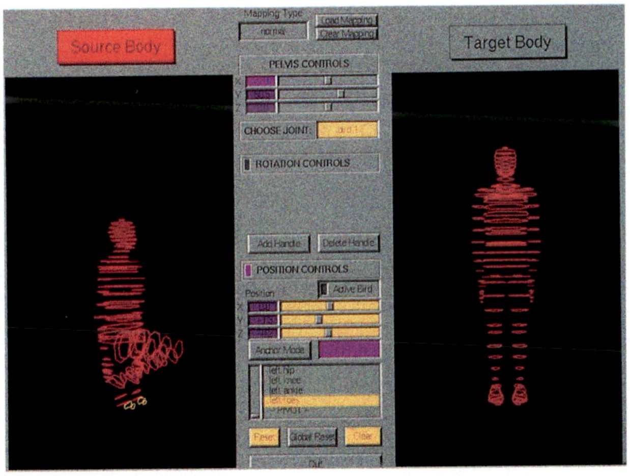

Thecla Schiphorst, Sang Mah
Credo Multimedia Software Inc.
1128 Rose Street
Vancouver, British Columbia V5L 4K8 Canada
thecla@cs.sfu.ca
sang@cs.sfu.ca

Visualization of the Best Approximation

Computer images, animation, and graphical user interfaces have many applications in undergraduate linear algebra teaching. Topics like vector spaces, linear transformation, orthogonality and eigenvalues can be represented by computer graphics, and interactive techniques and visualization of math objects can strengthen understanding of linear algebra theories. On the other hand, linear algebra is an important foundation for a computer graphics class where topics like geometric transformation and viewing are based on linear algebra theories.

Several computer projects are proposed for a linear algebra class: Flying Objects in 3D Space, Shears Transformation, Eigenvalues on a Circle, the Principle of Least Squares, etc. Graphics, animation, and GUI techniques are used to visualize concepts such as subspace spanned by vectors, theories of linear transformation, orthogonality, and eigenspace and develop mathematics games such as least squares competition. Computer graphics are implemented with the Java programming language so that students can learn and play on the Internet.

In this sketch, a computer graphics project is used to demonstrate the concept of orthogonal projection in a least-squares procedure. A way of looking at the least-squares problem geometrically is to minimize the length of the error vector. The error vector is at a minimum when the error vector is an othorgonal projection of the column space of the coefficient matrix. The visualization of the least-squares is designed as the following:

Let A be the coefficient matrix, S=(au + bv) be the column space of A spanned by vector u and v. On the Java applet, the plane S in 3D space is used to represent the column space. One end of a vector w is connected to the plane S. The error vector of the least-squares approximation is represented by e.

To demonstrate the orthogonal projection, the error vector e is connected to the projection p of the vector w in the column space S. A mouse is used to drag the connection point of the vector e and the projection p. Meanwhile, the length of the vector e and the angle between e and the projection p are calculated and displayed on the Java applet. The vector e and the projection p are also painted on the applet following the movement of the mouse.

In this project, students will visualize the relationship among the projection angle, the value of the least-squares cost function, and the length of the error vector. The visualization and the interactive techniques will strengthen the understanding of the principle of least squares.

Li Chao
University of Houston Victoria
2506 East Red River
Victoria, Texas 77901 USA
chaol@cobalt.vic.uh.edu

In the traditional digital video publishing paradigm, video editing and deployment compression tasks require separate applications. Generally an edited videotape, once completed, is sent to an outside compression house to be compressed to the deployment media standard, usually MPEG1 for CD-ROM. In this paradigm, the information about the video editor's manipulation (special effects, transition, cuts) is not used during the compression process. Conversely, there is no method for the compression engine to impact how the video editor creates his title. With this lack of integration, the process of video editing and compression for multimedia projects is a slow and costly process.

Video compression can benefit from information that the compression engine can extract from the video material to aid it in discarding irrelevant and/or redundant video information. In this environment, the video editor can manipulate the video to achieve the desired effect. The combination of editing and deployment compression in a single application has advantages above and beyond increased productivity due to integrated workflow.

RenderComp is the set of processes in which edit rendering and MPEG compression occur as a single real-time process with automatic feed-forward and feedback. This communication is facilitated by the fact that both the edit engine and compression exist locally within the same application. The edit engine is capable of feeding forward information about the video to the compression engine to aid it in its compression of the video. Conversely, the compression engine can feed back information to the edit engine that will aid the editor in creating video that is optimally compressible. This sketch provides a primer on RenderComp and how the combination of editing and deployment compression in a single application improves productivity, creative control, and video quality.

Two examples:

1 Fade to Black is arguably one of the most common transitions used in video today. One of the many video tools used by the compression engine is to select a subset of light intensities that can be used to represent a picture. This subset is chosen at the outset of the compression process to produce the best achievable video quality given the particular type of video material (e.g. natural vs. graphics vs. sports). With RenderComp, the editor can indicate to the compression engine that the following frames will be getting progressively dimmer, and to change the subset of light intensities it uses for compression appropriately.

2 As an example of the converse process, the compression process outputs compressed video in groups of related frames with a particular pre-determined length (this is an oversimplification). If the editor creates a scene that is slightly longer or shorter than this length, extra overhead will be required to represent the video. In this case, the compression engine can inform the editor about how the video can be more optimally compressed.

Marcus Julian
Vibrint Technologies
23 Crosby Drive
Bedford, Massachusetts 01730 USA
mfj@vibrint.com

We are investigating the use of Virtual Reality Modeling Language (VRML) to represent engineering parts of CAD/CAM origin in Internet-accessible supplier catalogs. In its present form, our application can load pre-defined assembly databases and manipulate them in various ways. And it now runs on various UNIX and PC-based VRML browsers (for example, SGI CosmoPlayer, InterVista WorldView). This application is now functional in both the CAVE and ImmersaDesk platforms – VR platforms developed at the University of Illinois at Chicago (UIC) Electronic Visualization Laboratory (EVL). A VRML 2.0 browser for these environments is in the beta stage of development.

As of this writing, user interaction consists of the following: loading and unloading one of three assembly databases; turning on/off animation sequences displaying simple dynamics that would occur as the assembly is functioning; toggle transparency; toggle exploded view of assembly; toggle display specific VRML browser dashboard; sequentially move through pre-defined viewpoints; toggle between manipulation mode of the assembly's orientation; and displaying anchors or links on individual parts of the assembly. When anchors are active, the user can click with the mouse or other pointing device on particular parts and bring up an HTML document that displays the specifications for the part.

Current efforts are focused on three major areas of research and development:

1 Database engine integration/intercommunication, which is still in the conceptual phase. VRML 2.0 is very new and still in the refinement stage. There are a number of ways that a VRML application can be coupled to a commercial database. Which approach is taken may also depend upon a particular VRML browser. For instance, some VRML browsers support a Java External Authoring Interface (EAI), a proposed informative Annex to the VRML specification. This would lead one down the road of using Java Applets to link communication between the HTML browser, the VRML browser, and the database engine. Other options also exist, and are presently being investigated.

2 Collision detection, which will be implemented using a high-level wrapper around I-COLLIDE, which introduces convex masks to reduce the necessity of decomposing non-convex objects. The rationale behind convex masks is the fact that not every object feature is of interest for our collision detection process. A convex mask encapsulates all relevant object features. This then becomes a highly efficient method for collision detection. How best to integrate this into a VRML application is under investigation.

3 A group of controlled experiments involving subjects in a mock training environment. A strict set of criteria will be used to compare level of training progress achieved with respect to various aspects involving industrial assemblies.

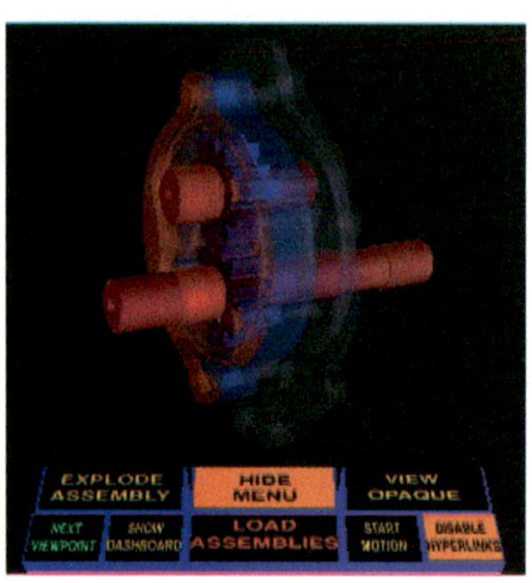

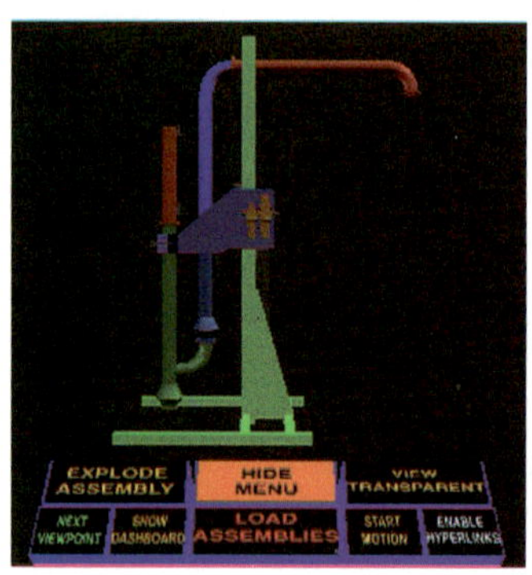

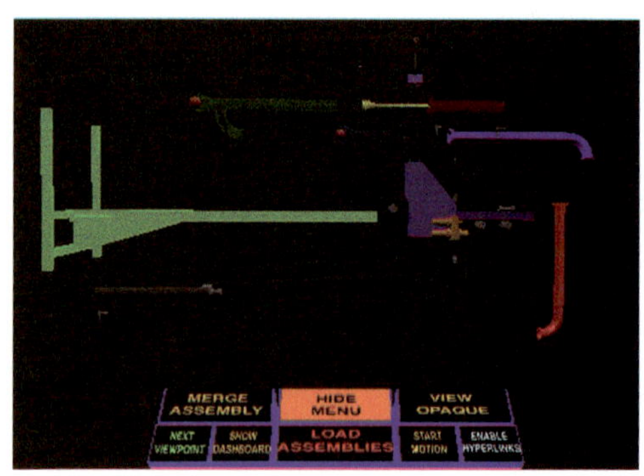

Fred Dech, Swaminathan Narayanan, Rade Tesic, Prashant Banerjee, Sudhir Anantharaman, John Yan
University of Illinois at Chicago
Chicago, Illinois 60607 USA
fdech@uic.edu

1 Structure

We have designed and realized a text-driven deaf-mute sign language synthesis system. Its input is text, and its output is a virtual 3D human body that represents real-time movements of hand posture. The 3D human body is synthesized using computer graphics methods. See Fig. 1.1.

2 Geometric Model of 3-D Human Body

The articulated human body is composed of 44 kinetic units and 42 joints. The kinetic units are represented by an irregular triangle network, and the joints are represented by non-uniform rational B-splines.

3 Kinetic Control Model of Human Hand and Arm

One human hand and one human arm have a total of 18 joints and 27 degrees of freedom. Movements of the human hand and arm can be formally presented by a 54-dimensions state space. Each state of state space represents a posture of human hand and arm. One state sequence presents a sign-language word. The hand posture changes of sign language are presented by the state changing of state space.

4 Construction of the Gesture Base

A sign-language word is presented by continuously changing hand postures (the state number of state sequence is infinite in state space). We can only use infinite state to approximately represent changes in hand posture. Since each sign-language word is composed of many gesture actions, we use the initial and final hand posture state of gesture action to approximately represent the gesture, and then name these state values as sign-language parameters. The result: a visual interactive description language that obtains sign-language parameters. We use description language to interactively obtain state values for hand postures. The state value sequence that presents sign language words is stored in a database (the gesture base).

5 Experiment and Conclusion

With this method we have successfully synthesized a 3D human body that can display changing hand posture sequences according to input text. Experimental results prove that the method is effective. The results basically meet human visual demands. Fig.5.1(a) is the gesture for the letter a, and (b) is the gesture for the number 1. Fig. 5.2(a), (b), and (c) are the first, second, and third gestures of sign language for the word "future."

6 Application

This *Text-Driven Deaf-Mute Sign Language Synthesis* system can be used to teach sign language and create interactions between users and avatars in virtual environments.

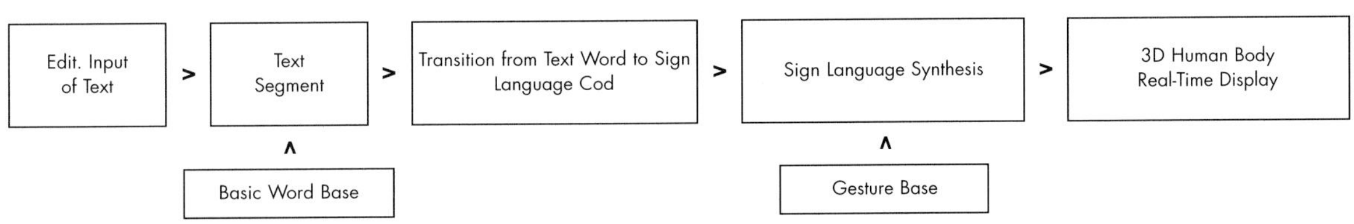

FIGURE 1.1 Text Driven Deaf-mute Sign Language Synthesis System Structure

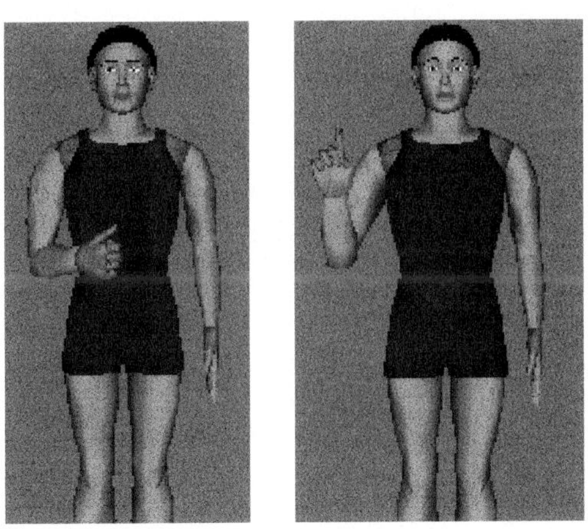

(a) (b)

FIGURE 5.1 Hand postures of letter "a" and number "1".

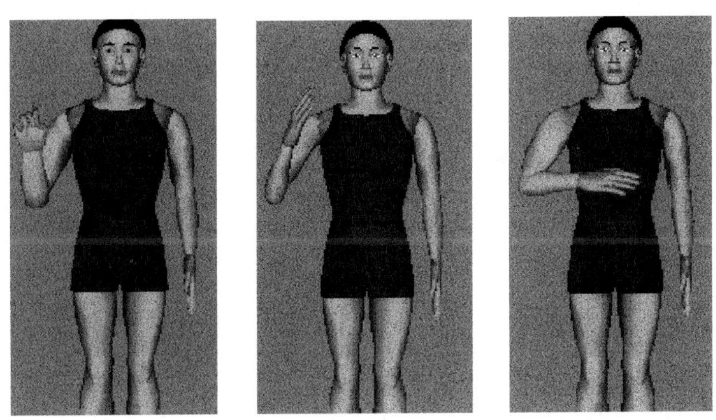

(a) (b) C

FIGURE 5.2 Hand postures of sign language word "future."

Yibo Song, Wen Gao, Baocai Yin, Ying Liu, Lin Xu, Jie Yan, Haito Chen, Jian Zhou
Harbin Institute of Technology
Harbin 150001, China
syb@vilab.hit.edu.cn
wgao@jdl.mcel.mot.com
ybc@jdl.mcel.mot.com

Virtual Arts Therapies

Arts therapies involve the performing and graphics arts (music, dance, movement, drama, painting, photography, and so on) in a systematic, controlled, therapeutic environment, supervised by board-certified arts therapists, often in conjunction with medical practitioners (physicians, psychiatrists, psychologists, nurses, and others). These therapies, which often appear to untrained observers as "play sessions," are actually respected methods of communication – a palette upon which clients and care-givers may reveal expressive, non-verbal ideas with detail and precision, for further analysis.

Virtual Arts Therapies (VAT) combines traditional arts therapy techniques with computer technology to alleviate symptoms, enhance creativity, induce relaxation or other mood states, and promote client well-being. Through VAT, group and individual participation is no longer restricted to local access. It can occur remotely, with patients and therapists separated by great distances. Another advantage of VAT is that immediate self-therapeutization can be provided when and where it is needed. Furthermore, therapy sessions can be recorded for analysis, experimentation, or repetitive administration with a level of precision previously unattainable with traditional methods.

In our research, we have worked closely with the Music Therapy Department of Immaculata College to develop and explore settings for clinical use of computer art tools. Many of these experiments have incorporated both audio and visual components. For example, we created SoundWorld, an interactive setting where musical instruments can be played, using the Jack Human Factors Modeling System from the University of Pennsylvania. 3D graphics and sound have also been used in a comics-style setting in order to elicit thoughts about fears by young teenagers. Work with blind and severe psychiatric inpatient subjects has illustrated the successful use of gestural devices for expressive MIDI instrument control by untrained musicians. Web-based systems and virtual metaphors have been used to examine themes of community art, music performance, and social discourse. Various aspects of the neighborhood – the garage in which music is created, the porch on which conversations take place, the walls on which murals are painted – are presented in an interactive setting to enable communications among diverse populations of participants.

This sketch includes brief video segments depicting the various *Virtual Arts Therapies* applications mentioned above. If time permits, we will review the results of some of our clinical trials, and discuss the limitations and potentials of arts technology in the health care setting.

Rebecca Mercuri
University of Pennsylvania
P.O. Box 1166 - CSMT
Philadelphia, Pennsylvania 19105 USA
mercuri@acm.org

Ranjit Bhatnagar
University of Pennsylvania
P.O. Box 1166 - CSMT
Philadelphia, Pennsylvania 19105 USA
ranjit@best.com

This computer-assisted curriculum to teach Foundation Design 1 (two-dimensional design) in the Ball State University Art Department used short interactive programs written in Macromedia Director, which became the basis for more complex and extensive finished pieces using traditional artist's materials and techniques such as paint and collage. Since the learning time for this software was minutes, many solutions to given problems were required, and students were expected to fully explore many variables in each assignment.[1]

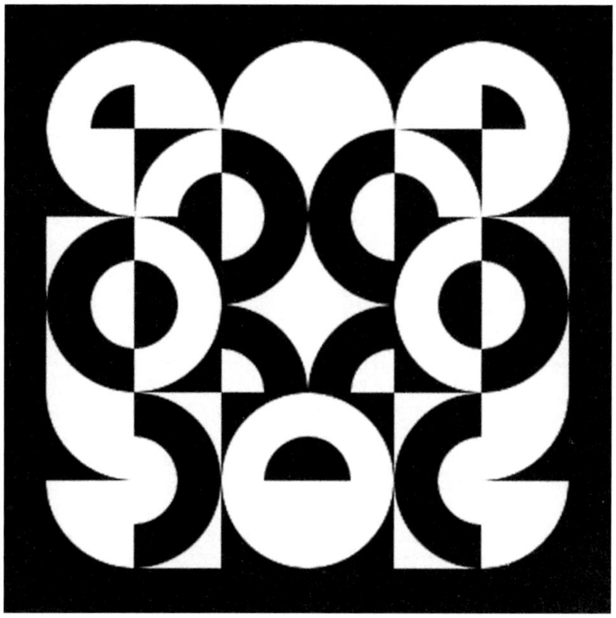

The software is now being modified to solve more and new problems. One of these new problems will be the exploration of grids, both visible and invisible. Grids have long been an organizing device in design. From the Renaissance to the present, graphic designers, painters, and others have explored grids in order to make sense of information and create unity on a surface. Showing a beginning design student the significance and potential of a grid is the basis of the interactive problems and software programs demonstrated in this sketch.

Three approaches are utilized in designing the problems:

1 Grids with units acting as windows with elements trapped inside, but movable within the window. The windows butt to windows that are adjacent to each other. Window outlines can be turned on and off. Elements can be added, subtracted, scaled up or down, colored, moved, and drawn inside each window. If the element edge intersects its windows edge, it disappears underneath it, so the grid structure is always evident in any overall design. Positive/negative and Gestalt relationships are emphasized. The entire grid surface can be randomly reorganized via a "randomize" button, which produces totally unexpected results.

2 Pre-existing grids overlayed with elements. In this version, a pre-existing grid pattern is overlayed and modified with elements chosen from a menu. The grid structure can be "broken" or "violated" by placing these chosen elements in positions not strictly adhering to the underlying grid structure. In this fashion, the grid structure can be obscured, but the underlying sense of order is preserved.

3 Grids with elements that can be changed, but the positions of the elements cannot change. Internal patterns can be developed by changing groups of elements. Each element can undergo up to 15 changes. The resulting surfaces can lead to results very similar to optical art, such as that of Victor Vasarely.

We also plan to introduce variations of the above approaches, utilizing grid structures based on the golden mean, and other irregular grids. Students will also do one exercise on a network, in real time, via Shockwave. They will "improvise" on each oother's solutions to a grid problem, much like jazz musicians improvise on a theme together.

Patricia Nelson, Barbara Giorgio-Booher
Department of Art
Ball State University
Muncie, Indiana 47306 USA
pnelson@wp.bsu.edu
bgiorgio@wp.bsu.edu

Loren Mork
Cool Software Inc.
355 NW 200th
Seattle, Washington 98177 USA
lmork@aol.com

REFERENCES

1 Nelson, P., Giorgio Booher, B., Mork,L. Computer Assisted Foundations-Interactive Design Problems in Proceedings of CHI 97: Human Factors in Computing Systems. 1997 Atlanta, pp 271-272.

WordNozzle

WordNozzle is equal parts digital graffiti and digital concrete poetry, an experiment in "painting" with text. It enables the user to select any text-only file as input to the "nozzle," and then spray the words in a continuous stream while controlling the font, size, style, and color of the text.

WordNozzle was motivated from two directions, one quite practical and the other quite theoretical. On the practical side, *WordNozzle* is an attempt to address the clumsiness with which current page-layout and graphics programs handle text manipulation. First, the user must type in the text, then select it (or portions of it), select a different font from a menu, view the result, select another font from the menu, view the result, go to a different menu to change the size, view the result, go to the menu again to change the size, view the result, and so on. The same steps must occur in order to sample styles and color as well. The entire process requires multiple repetitive steps. *WordNozzle* attempts to circumvent this laborious process by treating the text like a stream, much in the same way the "paint" used in the spraycan of most popular graphics packages treats color. The user chooses a text stream and can then manipulate the visual appearance and location of each word as it comes out of the nozzle in a continuous, free-flowing fashion.

The theoretical motivation stems from a study I undertook of the Concrete Poets of the mid-60's and onward, and their Futurist and Dada ancestors in the early part of this century. These artists treated the visual appearance of text as a principal dimension in the production of meaning. Their interest in such experimentation grew out of – among other things – a deeply held belief that traditional forms of written communication, with its clean spacing, rectilinear layout, and sober letterforms, no longer did justice to the cultural schizophrenia of the modern age. Working within the constraints of traditional letterpress, these artists artists and poets managed to explore text's visual presence in ways that seem fresh even to the MTV- and David Carson-jaded eyes of the 90's. *WordNozzle* represents my attempts to partially answer the question: What would a Futurist/Concrete Poet want in a tool for digitally manipulating text?

Interaction

As *WordNozzle* boots up, a title screen appears while the program loads the fonts particular to the user's computer. The program then fades onto the main screen. As soon as the user clicks anywhere, she is prompted to choose a text source. This text, or more appropriately, text-stream, is loaded, and the first word appears at the nozzle. It is at this point that the writer can change the appearance of the word by using the characteristics palette to the left of the writing surface.

The characteristics palette works via rollovers. By moving the word currently at the nozzle over the area marked font and letting it hover there, the user can cycle through all the fonts available on the system. This action applies each font to the word in turn. The user selects a particular font by simply moving the word out from the font area. Adjusting the size works in a similar manner, and picking a color is simply a matter of dipping the word into the appropriate area of the bar at the top of the screen. When the user has achieved the appearance she wants, she simply locates the word on the canvas where she wants it and clicks. This sprays the word down, and the next word appears, ready to be manipulated. If the user holds the mouse button down, the words come out in a continuous stream.

File input-output is handled in the area below the characteristics palette. Positioning the current word over wipe canvas and then clicking clears the screen. (The current position in the text-stream is maintained in this action.) Doing the same over load text allows the user to select another text document as the text-stream. Clicking on save-image lets the user name and save the canvas as a PICT file.

Next Steps

WordNozzle is currently at the proof-of-concept stage. The interface in particular does not take advantage of an even wider functionality supported by the software engine. For instance, the software engine is capable of allowing the user to choose between having the text-stream advance a character at a time, a word at a time (as it is presently set), a sentence at a time, or a paragraph at at time. It also supports using keys to adjust the size and font parameters anywhere, without having to resort to the characteristics palette. Giving the user access to such functionality is part of the next iteration.

Eventually I would like to rewrite *WordNozzle* from the ground up in C++ in order to attain satisfactory interaction speeds. I see such a version as both a stand alone application and as a plug-in for something like Photoshop or Painter.

Jason Lewis
Interval Research Corporation
1801c Page Mill Road
Palo Alto, California 94103 USA
lewis@interval.com

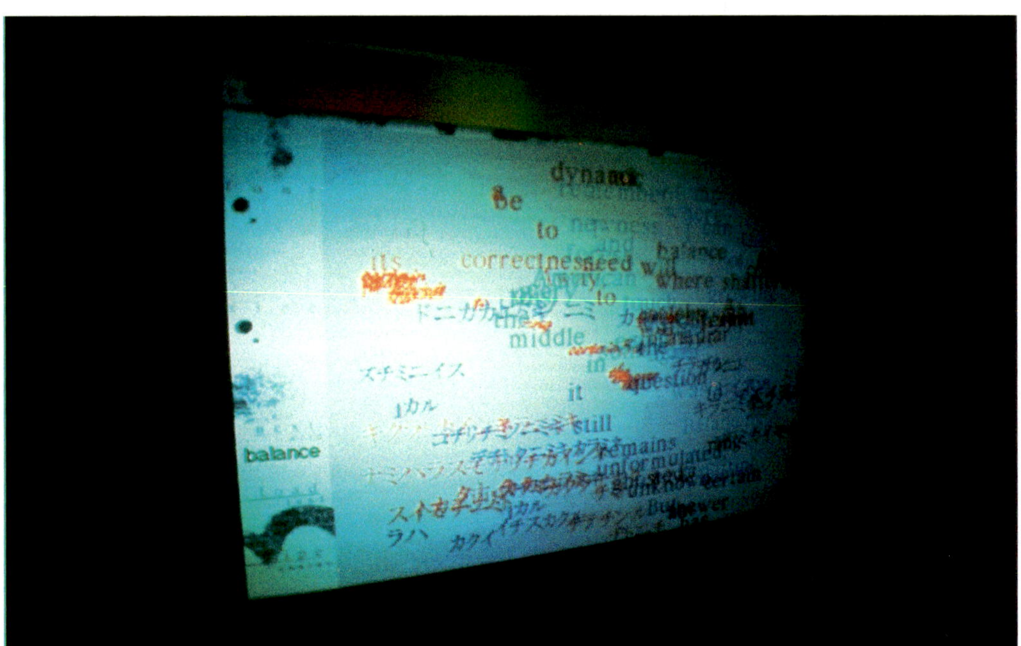

This sketch presents the process used to create a realistic animated walk-through of a portion of the Midway Face region of the Dixie National Forest in southern Utah. The project was part of a study being conducted by environmental psychologists at the University of Arizona to compare computer-generated walk-throughs in two different formats with video and actual walk-throughs of the same forest path. At the Texas A&M Visualization Laboratory, our job was to create a highly realistic prerecorded animation, while landscape architects at the University of Illinois produced an online walk-through at a lower level of realism using interactive technology .

Purpose

The goal of the study is to provide definitive experimental data about the efficacy of computer visualization of a natural site in eliciting human responses similar to responses to the actual site. The study also seeks to establish whether or not high realism is an important factor in refining response. This has important scientific and public policy implications. It is common practice for planners to use predictive simulations to determine the future state of a forest under various management plans. This study will tell planners what level of visualization they need to reliably depict these future states and will lend credibility to their presentations.

Process

The project is among a select few, in the short history of scientific visualization, that has employed the expert skills of an artist from the beginning, as an integral part of the research process. The first step in development of the visualization was to send the artist on a visit of several days to photograph and sketch the site. This radically changed our original perspective. For example, we found that the existence of aged trees – trees almost falling down, dead trees lying on the forest floor, and decaying nursing trees covered with small, new trees – were as significant to the appearance of the forest as were the healthy trees. The imagery and impressions of that early visit were used daily, and the eye of the artist continually played an essential role in ongoing work.

Starting with detailed tree surveys and terrain data, a four-minute animation was created. It contains approximately 1,500 trees and covers 66,000 square meters. The animation simulates a person walking through a forest, stopping at predetermined points, turning around for a 360-degree look at the forest, and then continuing on to the next point. The process involves creating the following elements: a parameter set to grow realistic Engleman Spruce trees, a reformatted survey dataset to be used in later programming, a smooth camera path through the forest, motion tests, rendered texture maps of individual trees, and approximately 1,100 rendered scenes of the complete forest.

Using BOGAS (the Branching Object Generation and Animation System of Kitagawa-DeLeon), a detailed geometric model of the trees was created, down to the needle cluster level. Texture maps and shadowed scenes were formatted as RIB files with custom software and rendered with Pixar's PhotoRealistic RenderMan on an SGI Power Challenge supercomputer. Significant effort was expended to reduce computation time. First, the level of rendered detail was controlled for distant trees by using texture maps on rectangular polygons, and for nearer trees by interpolating between geometry with and without displacement and texture shaders. Second, the quantity of stored geometry was reduced by using multiple instances of the same tree. Depth cuing provides a realistic depth of field.

Donald House, Scott Arvin, Greg Schmidt
Texas A&M University
gschmidt@cs.tamu.edu
http://www-viz.tamu.edu/students/greg/greg.html

Midori Kitagawa DeLeon
The Ohio State University

Over the last 10 years, motion capture has evolved into a powerful animation tool if not a controversial one. If the nature of the character requires extremely realistic or very characteristic motion, then capture tools can be employed to extend the palette of the character animator into uncharted regions of expression for digital characters.

At Digital Domain, we have utilized capture tools and methodology to this end. Performance Capture, as we term it, was used to "digitize" the essence of two very distinct performers: Michael Jackson and André Agassi. The technology allowed them to have a significant hand in the authoring of their respective characters and allowed audiences to enjoy the new artistic expression of these two traditional performers.

In the first example, Michael Jackson was able to author the skeleton character through Performance Capture and cutting edge computer graphic techniques. Under the direction of Stan Winston, Michael danced very specific blocked and timed motion before the capture hardware. Once the motion was processed and edited, we translated the basic kinematic skeleton into Alias PowerAnimator, attached this motion to a Polygonal and NURB model and proceeded to build the overall scene.

Through a set and lighting survey and careful integration, we were able to place the skeleton character anywhere within the virtual set. Because the virtual camera had to match the real camera dynamics exactly for proper compositing, the set survey allowed us to track the real camera against the background plates. This allowed the director and visual effects supervisor to visualize the skeleton character in context for final placement and performance.

Most shots required layering of key-frame animation. Animators helped realize aspects of the performance that we couldn't capture or that the director wanted to see well after the fact. Once the animations were finalized, each shot was rendered with exact lighting placement, to match the on-set lighting for the final integration before compositing. Once all elements were rendered, each was composited, in Flame or Nuke (Digital Domain's in-house compositing system), back into the background plate and tweaked to place the character into the scene as envisioned by the director to help tell the story.

In the second example, André Agassi was captured to bring his performance into a purely virtual world. The nature of the commercial required that virtual André play tennis with a human opponent who wielded a cyber-headset and racket wand. The point of the spot was high energy and fast action.

Unlike the skeleton, we were going to be representing a near photo-real André Agassi. This required us to start with a head Cyberscan and model his body and Nike clothing in NURBS. Once André's motion was captured and processed, we brought the internal skeleton into Alias and proceeded to build the shots. The key to this commercial was moving the virtual camera in ways that would be impossible to do in the real world, all the while featuring the kind of tennis performance only André Agassi could do.

Once the cameras were animated, we rendered the foreground elements in either Alias or Lightwave and then composited them into backgrounds rendered in Lightwave for the final dynamic effect, all within Flame.

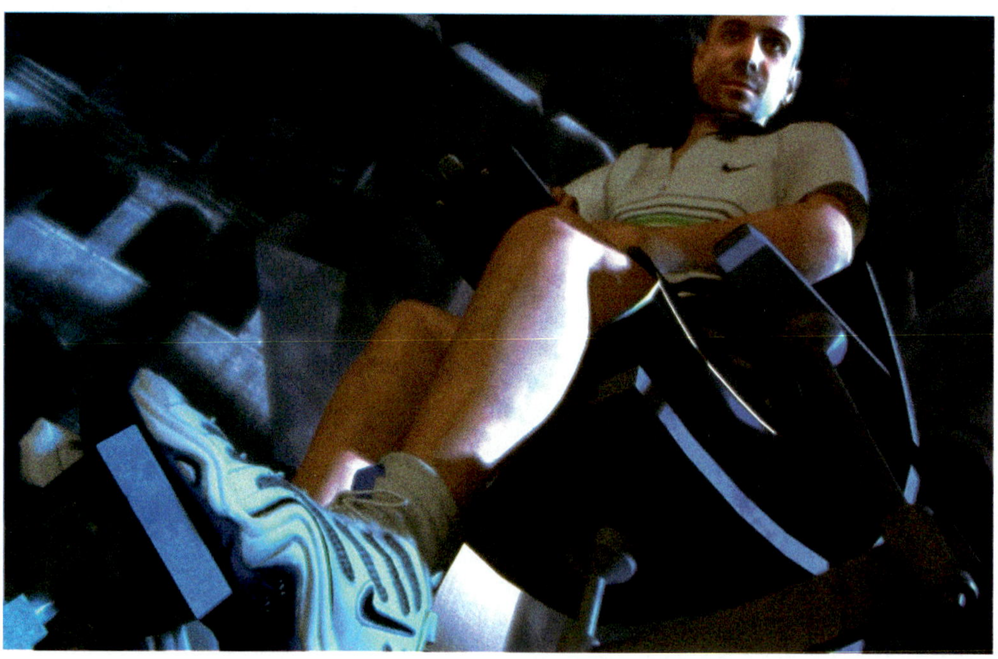

André Bustanoby
Digital Domain
300 Rose Avenue
Venice, California 90291 USA
+1.310.314.2814
apb@d2.com

It is possible to do a wider range of work with motion capture than people usually think – by using it more like puppetry and less like acting.

Floops is an episodic animated cartoon for the Web. So far, we've made 40 25-second episodes. SGI Webcasts these in VRML2.0. Working for this application means working within limitations: few polygons, few textures, no morphing, only one full character. With so many limitations, I wanted to make the character animation as good as possible.

The main issue is that *Floops* is supposed to be a peppy, hyperactive little pet. Motion capture doesn't do this kind of motion easily – it's realistic, and unexaggerated. How could I get the kind of stylized movements I wanted? I devised a me-to-*Floops* mapping that exaggerated his limbs while retaining the overall sense of mass in his body. With this, even when I was walking casually across the stage, *Floops* would bound across it like a five-year-old. These tricks only go so far, and aren't generically usable in all cases. They also have an unfortunate tendency to deaden the original motion a little. So this alone wasn't enough.

Another partial solution was to exaggerate my own movements as I performed. I found it was a big help to think like a puppeteer, to focus on *Floops'* movements and ignore my own entirely. (We use a video visor to watch our characters as we perform.) It was not a matter of being casual or performing movements that felt natural, even though you'd think that would always be best with motion capture. What reads well on a person doesn't necessarily read well on a *Floops*. For that matter, given that I was using an unusual movement mapping, movements wouldn't be 1:1 translated on *Floops* anyhow. Even though I'm sure I looked silly, the moves looked right to me on *Floops*.

Another challenge: stylizing as I performed. I tried to simplify the movement down to its essence, avoiding all inessential movements. This would happen after rehearsing a scene a number of times. It would start to fall into a pattern, and I'd know where and when every major pose was going to be. Settling into poses also made it more likely that people would be able to read the movements even at six fps. I was excited to receive mail from a couple of keyframe animators who'd seen *Floops*, and liked it, but weren't sure whether it was motion capture or keyframe!

You can also do some even stranger mappings. One of our characters is a worm. Your right hand manipulates his head, your left hand his tail, and your feet his mid-segments. This requires real puppeteering skills to do well, but it also takes on a stylization that is fun and interesting, with a very different look than the serious realism of most motion capture. Another example is a series of walking letters that spell out words. To give these a less human, peppier look, I put sensors on a piece of foam rubber, and manipulated that as a puppet, walking it around our stage.

Non-realistic motion can sometimes be a lot more interesting. It has gone through an artistic interpretation. The other reason to do it is that there are some body types you can do with puppetry (such as the worm) that are so different from the human shape that there's no other way to do it live. This is a messy, fuzzy, unscientific process, and not as all-purpose as keyframe animation. Yet, I think this whole grey area has some of the benefits of keyframe animation (exaggerated, stylized movement), while keeping the real-time benefits of motion capture. Maybe it won't be long before we see worms as well as monkeys hosting TV shows.

Emre Yilmaz
Protozoa, Inc.
2727 Mariposa Street, Studio 100
San Francisco, California 94110 USA
+1.415.522.6569
+1.415.522.6522 fax
emre@protozoa.com

This work was done with **Steve Rein, Dan Hanna, Floops, Mike Morasky,** and other characters at Protozoa.

Ubiquitous Animation: An Element-Based Concept to Make 3D Animations Commonplace

So far, 3D animations have not been able to establish themselves as multimedia elements anywhere near as well as graphics, video, and audio. The reason for this is the great amount of time and expense associated with creation of a 3D animation. In order to overcome this obstacle and make animations commonplace, we are developing CASUS.

The system's framework consists of an animation tool (CASUS Anim), the public-domain VRML2.0 browser CASUS Presenter, and additional tools for simple linking of event-oriented simulators and integration of CAD data. The integral part of the concept, however, is the animation elements library CASUS Base.

Animation elements are analogous to Clipart when using graphics. They are the objects prefabricated by designers with object-specific functionalities and possessing an independent intelligence. For example, the animation element "worker" generates animated behaviors, such as walking, carrying, sitting, and discussing, which can be fetched for the creation of animations. This can occur graphic-interactively through the user or through linked simulators. An animation element even possesses knowledge about itself (for example, about its geometric proportions) in order to avoid distortion when scaling, as well as for mapping simulator events on visible behavior. Animation elements can be flexibly tailored to meet certain requirements, as in the sense of derivation in the paradigm of object orientation, in order to realize the demand for cost-effectiveness. Since so much preliminary work is taken care of by the animation elements, animation development becomes less time-consuming.

CASUS Base, however, is more than just a loose collection of animation elements. Because it also includes element classification, multimedia database functionalities, and network capability, CASUS Base offers the possibility of functioning as a distributed marketplace for animation elements and offering them in catalog form. Security mechanisms have been conceived that allow animation elements to be offered commercially. This encourages third-party developers to make these kinds of elements available for a fee.

Our current research is focused on identification of basic functionalities and generation of a standardization proposal for animation elements. First results, applications to date:

- Visualization of simulation results in the area of storage/shipping.
- Internal validation of simulation models in the area of logistics (in both cases, automatic animation generation through simulator linking).
- Presentation film: production planning of an automobile manufacturing plant (the model of protocol layers was filled with animated workers and shipping elements).

Ralf Dörner, Volker Luckas, Ulrike Spierling
Fraunhofer Institute for Computer Graphics
Rundeturmstrasse 6
D-64283 Darmstadt GERMANY
doerner@igd.fhg.de
luckas@igd.fhg.de
ulisp@igd.fhg.de
http://www.igd.fhg.de

REFERENCES

1 V. Luckas, T. Broll "CASUS - An Object-Oriented Three-Dimensional Animation System for Event-Oriented Simulators", Ed. N. Magenat Thalmann, D. Thalmann. Proceedings of Computer Animation '97, University of Geneva and Swiss Federal Institute of Technology, Lausanne, Geneva, 1997

Isaacks is one of the latest choreographic works by Jimmy Gamonet De Los Heros ("Jimmy") of the Miami City Ballet Company. It is the first of five sections for the neoclassical ballet piece entitled "Supermegatroid," which was commissioned by Wolf Trap in Washington, D.C. Three of the five sections composed by Jimmy, including *Isaacks*, were choreographed on the computer using only the Life Forms animation software to direct a company of virtual dancers. Life Forms, originally designed for human movement animation, is now one of the tools being used to refine the *Isaacks* choreographic work into an animated short of the same name.

This sketch shows how the animation evolved from an empty stage to a few sets of shape palettes, a vast vocabulary of locomotor sequences, and multiple versions of the full choreography. In the initial preparatory work with the music and score, Jimmy treats Life Forms as a virtual studio to actualize and explore movement ideas inspired by the music. From the start, he knows how his dancers will move in his mind. He uses Life Forms to physicalize the movement in his mind to movement with virtual bodies; to transform between known middle, beginning, and end points in each movement phrase; and to work out key formations for constantly changing groups of interacting dancers.

Issacks has over 100 associated files, which are used to produce approximately 20 different versions of the full choreography. Most of the files contain short single-figure movement sequences that define the vocabulary of the piece. A new version of the full choreography is created when there is a major change in the order of key formations. Most of Jimmy's one-month animation time for *Isaacks* involved the creation of the vocabulary. After the work on the computer, it required only three hours for the live dancers to learn the piece in the studio. Of course, a two-week training period follows, for perfection of the dance for performance!

Creation of *Isaacks* on film as an animated short will take much longer than two weeks. The current work in progress is focused on fine-tuning the animated movement and starting the design work for storyboarding, modeling, and rendering. Related issues, approaches, and early storyboards and renderings show the next steps in the production of *Isaacks* as a rendered dance animation.

Supermegatroid was inspired by the big band music of the 1940s. In particular, *Isaacks* was choreographed for a full-orchestra arrangement of "When the Saints Go Marching In" created by Keiko Endo of The Miami City Ballet Company. The three-minute *Isaacks* animation builds on Jimmy's maturing style, which has been described as "the true, laughing love-child of an affair between ballet's neoclassic movement vocabulary and the geometric possibilities of cyberspace."

Jimmy Gamonet de Los Heros
The Miami City Ballet Company

Sang Mah
Credo Interactive, Inc.
sang@cs.sfu.ca

The Tapir: Combining Myth and Contemporary Musical Structures to Create a Personal Perspective with 3D Computer Animation

Rather than the typical western way of storytelling, in which the audience expects a moral at the end of a story, *The Tapir* has an unusual narrative. It presents a conflict, develops it into an action-climax situation, and surprises the audience by ending in suspense. Because the narrative in *The Tapir* is a myth, it can contain numerous meanings. There is also an underlying notion that the story was always there, complete.

In my creative process, I intend to search for similarities between ideas that have guided musical composition in the 20th Century and the fundamental elements of storytelling. I intend to extract from stories the essential structure of the narrative, starting with the descriptive outer layer of characters, places, and situations, and ending with the inner layer, where just the structure of a narrative is revealed. My sequential images can be read as a musical score, or vice versa.

There are three main reasons I have chosen contemporary music as a template for my piece: the structural aspect of the musical composition, its close connection with the studies of physics of sound, and its singular understanding of the graphic translation of sound events.

The three ideas that I have chosen to guide the visual construction of the animation are: a traditional harmonic construction ending in suspension instead of repose; simultaneous layering of events; and an atypical beginning that is filled with elements (props, characters, situations) that will all disappear as the story progresses.

Narratively, the story is divided into nine scenes, each one corresponding to a different layer within the same space. The camera moves from the front layer to the last, passing by all the different events. The simultaneity of the events is depicted in the nine layers, which are horizontally superimposed. From the point of view of the first layer, one can see part of each one of the subsequent layers.

The simultaneity of musical events is also introduced in the abstract level, where each character is constructed of a set of polygons layered on top of each other. The design is basically made of bi-dimensional shapes superpositioned in a three-dimensional space. The emphasis in not in the creation of three-dimensional models. Instead, the three dimensionality is explored horizontally, when the camera travels in space from the first scene and makes its way to the ninth. The sound track is based on a musical interpretation of these layers of polygons. The images were read as a musical score, and the simultaneity, the harmonic construction, and the empty ending were musically described.

Later in the creative process, the sound and images were cleaned out and the visual elements stripped away, so the structural matter would not overwhelm the importance of the storytelling. The animation is constructed within a half sphere, which acts as a metaphor for both the sky and the "oca" (a typical Indian dwelling in the Amazon). Here the geometry in the three-dimensional space suggests a reference to the background of the myth and the people and culture from which it comes. Societies create their myths as a way to keep and worship their ancestral knowledge. As an artist, what interests me is deconstruction of the myth by manipulating the visual and musical structures of the narrative. The deconstruction is followed by a new construction as a myth, in an artistic type of game, where the structure does not destroy the myth, but recreates its quality. The 3D space is the medium for a new interpretation of the myth, but it can never overpower the essential and universal nature of its storytelling.

Raquel Coelho
BlueSky Studios
One South Road
Harrison, New York 10528 USA
+1.914.381.8400
+1.914.381.9790 fax
raquel@ns.blueskystudios.com

Starting in the fall of 1994, the directors of "Hercules," John Musker and Ron Clements, whose previous credits include "The Little Mermaid" and "Aladdin," decided they wanted an unprecedented monster. Working from the Greek myths, they envisioned a battle between Hercules and the multi-headed Hydra. But to be really wild, instead of a three- or six-headed beast, they wanted a 30-headed monster.

Contrary to popular misconception, the Disney films are still animated with pencil and paper, just as "Snow White" was made 60 years ago. The difference today is that on each film we look for opportunities to incorporate computer animation to bring something to the screen that was previously unattainable in a traditionally animated film. Bringing the Hydra to life was just such an opportunity.

With a crew of 10 technical directors and eight animators, over the course of two and a half years, we worked to create a computer character that doesn't look like a computer character. Our two main challenges were matching the movement and the visual style of a traditionally animated film. The hand-drawn animation in "Hercules" is especially cartoony, with an amazing looseness and freedom. So we had to create a computer animation skeleton that would allow our animators to achieve the same level of flexibility and elasticity in their acting.

Secondly, the graphic, ink, and paint style of "Hercules" is not what computer animation normally resembles. So we created a rendering technique to produce line "drawings" that matched the hand-drawn pencil line. These were combined with rendered flat paint areas and graphic highlights to seamlessly blend the Hydra with the hand-drawn characters and hand-painted backgrounds.

This tight collaboration between designers, programmers, technical directors, and animators produced the first fully computer-animated character ever to co-star in a traditionally animated film. The final result is a five-minute action sequence that stands as the centerpiece of the movie.

Roger L. Gould
Walt Disney Feature Animation
2100 Riverside Drive
Burbank, California 91521 USA
rogerg@fa.disney.com

Turner Classic Movies: "Hopper"

In 1995, Colossal Pictures was asked to produce three 30-second station IDs for Turner's new channel, Turner Classic Movies. The idea behind the new station was to deliver classic films on a dedicated channel. With this in mind, Colossal was asked to create something unique and memorable that was also able to address the aesthetic tastes of people who are interested in "classic" films. The idea was to bring to life something truly American, something that held in its iconography familiar symbols that spoke of classic America.

Colossal chose to bring to life the American painter Edward Hopper. The first question was how would we tackle the aesthetic and technical challenges presented by such a daunting task. Many other questions followed: How could we create a sense of time and space with only a given set of existing paintings? What are the legal issues surrounding the re-purposing of famous paintings scattered all over the globe? Would the environments be 3D? Parallaxing paintings? Or maybe even traditional cel animation?

With each project, we try to look at what is the most creative way to work with the tools we have, to create the best imagery. In this case, we searched for the most cost-efficient and creative way to make Hopper's art move. Our chosen platform was the Apple computer system, using a combination of 2D and 3D animation packages. In addition, we used traditional art, which was scanned into the computer and digitally manipulated. Boards were drawn up and approved by the client. The next phase was to create the hand-painted traditional artwork.

The director selected several original Hopper paintings to use as reference points for creating new "Hopperesque" images. The line drawings of these paintings were then used as templates to create 3D environments. These would later be used to create the moving shadows contained within the scenes. Stills were taken of the 3D environments and used as (locked-off) camera positions to create the traditional paintings. By doing this, we could make the shadows match the paintings directly. Traditional animators drew the key frames for the human elements, which were then hand painted, scanned, and morphedinto their respective positions. Other elements, such as background plates, poles, and chimneys, were all painted as individual elements. We found that, when looking at them on television, these traditional painted elements gave us the look and feel of a real painting but lacked the punch we wanted. Fortunately, because all of the hand-painted elements had been scanned into the computer, we were free to make creative changes to color, value, and focus.

After the elements were repainted, After Effects was used to not only composite, but give dimensionality to the piece. Multi-plane movement and rack focus techniques were used to achieve this effect. Finally, we rendered the spot to D1. We feel the final product addresses all the issues Turner Broadcasting brought to the table. In addition, Colossal created a dreamy world that blurs the lines between traditional painting and the digital realm.

Tom McClure, Jeffery Roth, Colin Miller, Ingrid Overgard, Jance Allen, Jana Canellos
Colossal Pictures
2800 Third Street
San Francisco, California 94107 USA
jeffery@colossal.com

Up... Down... Up..., like many of the projects we do, is a hybrid production combining traditional cel animation with the best enhancement that digital animation can offer. Our goal in this 30-second commercial, as with every project we undertake, is to push the envelope in existing software, and in our techniques, a little further each time.

On this production we worked closely with a director from a traditional animation background, John Hays, of Wild Brain Inc. On first looking at the boards, it seemed that our task would be to model elements and render and print out digital frame reference for the cel animators to ink and paint. However, we felt strongly that we could also create many of the elements and animate them in 3D, saving time and money, and more importantly pushing the technique of combining cel and digital animation further. Because a 2D woodcut look and fee had to be preserved at all costs, a seamless synthesis had to be forged between the traditional cel animation and the 3D digital animation. This began a series of experiments that led to the dragonesque sea-serpent, along with the sea of mutual funds and all the letters representing the wake and splashes from the sea, being created, animated, and rendered in 3D.

Boards and loose sketches were quickly interpreted, and changes were made almost on a daily basis to create a more cinematic story line. Elements were modeled, and specific black-and-white textures were hand drawn and applied to the polygonal-based models to give them just the right 2D look and feel. Our biggest challenge by far was the 3D sea serpent. Again, for the sea serpent, each texture was hand drawn and applied to the model. There are over 20 different textures on the head alone.

Special code was then written to create a field chart that could ensure the deadly accurate registration for the cel to digital ink and paint transitions essential to hybrid productions such as this. Digital frames were printed as reference to guide the cel animators at Wild Brain who were creating the cel sailboat, cloud god, water effects, droplets and splashes. This digital referencing program is designed to work with the standard Softimage Toonz settings in NTSC or PAL for ease of use in digital ink and paint.

At Little Fluffy Clouds, we are seeing a movement back to the traditional style of animation, almost as a refreshment from the automated special effects look. Through experiment and play, even within the tight confines of the creation of a 30-second commercial, we were able to satisfy our clients' needs and take digital animation one step higher. All of which proves that it is possible to create different kinds of looks that are not generally associated with 3D, and that we can synthesize 3D and 2D in a such a seamless way that no one can tell the cel from the digital. We continue to work in this style, with a very specific look combining cel and digital animation. In this way, we hope to revive a very traditional look and preserve all the benefits of digital animation.

It's worth noting that this entire spot was composited in-house using Softimage's Eddie. The benefits of this are not only felt in the budget, but more in that each scene, as completed, can be composited, shown to the client, and approved during production. This saves time and allows the client to truly be a part of the production. This is especially important for smaller digital animation studios that put their time, effort and energy into focusing specifically on digital animation, but who still have to compete with the ever expanding larger houses and the trend to place 3D "quick fix" departments in post houses.

Betsy de Fries, Jerry van de Beek
Little Fluffy Clouds
Pier 29 Annex
San Francisco, California 94111 USA
+1.415.956.8699
betsy@littlefluffyclouds.com

Dynamically Simulated Characters in Virtual Environments

Virtual environments and games often include animated characters that must respond to the actions of the user. The unpredictable actions of the user require a highly interactive environment that is not amenable to motion-generation techniques based on a library of predefined sequences. In this sketch, we present one approach to populating interactive virtual environments: using dynamic simulation to generate the motion of characters that respond in real time to the actions of the user. Simulation provides an effective way to generate realistic and compelling motion for virtual environment applications in which realism is essential.

To illustrate the use of simulation in virtual environments, we have built two environments with interactive characters. The first is a game in which a herd of one-legged hopping robots moves around the environment. The user navigates by steering and pedaling a stationary Tectrix bicycle and attempts to herd the robots into a corral. Each robot has knowledge of the locations of the other robots and of the user, and uses that knowledge to avoid collisions in a reactive fashion. This environment served as an aggressive testbed for control algorithms for dynamically simulated robot groups[1] and as a driving application for distributed computing.[3]

The second environment is a virtual recreation of the Atlanta Bicycle Road Race of the 1996 Olympics. The goal is to create a virtual environment where an athlete can experience the course both visually and physically in the presence of simulated bicyclists. Such an environment should prove valuable to the avid biker or professional racer who is limited by time, money, bad weather conditions, or insufficient situational training. For example, the racers at the Olympics are allowed only limited time on the course without traffic and might benefit from additional time to tune their racing strategies to a particular course or field of competitors. We plan to explore the use of this system for both physical and strategic training for individuals and teams.

The virtual environment is designed to accurately reflect the terrain of the road race. Using topographic maps of Atlanta, we digitized and modeled the 13 km course, preserving dimensions and height information. The user rides a racing bicycle mounted on a motion platform that pitches fore/aft by +/-12 degrees to allow simulation of hills. The bicycle is instrumented to measure the speed of the rear wheel and the turning angle of the front wheel (+/-20 degrees). The rear wheel is mounted on a generator and flywheel to allow limited freewheeling and to match the wheel load to the terrain angle. The system will eventually model such effects as wind drag and increased efficiency from drafting.

Much of the visual interest of the virtual environment comes from the synthetic bicyclists. Each actor is dynamically simulated and pedals in a realistic fashion around the race course using control algorithms described in Hodgins et al.[2] We have implemented a distributed system that allows us to simulate multiple bikes in nearly real time and to display the graphical environ-ment at 15 frames per second. The dynamic simulations are computationally intensive and are distributed one per processor on an SGI Power Challenge with 12 R8000 processors. A software barrier enforces synchronization between simulations to maintain a consistent world state via shared memory. Graphical information is shipped via sockets to a dedicated graphics server.

Although the presence of the simulated bicyclists in the environment adds greatly to the visual appeal of the scene, we are just beginning to develop algorithms that will allow the synthetic cyclists to mimic the sophisticated racing strategies of human cyclists for drafting, blocking, and breakaways. We expect that the addition of racing strategies will result in a useful training environment by providing the user with virtual opponents and teammates and allowing the exploration of biking and team strategies for a particular race.

David C. Brogan, Ronald A. Metoyer, Jessica K. Hodgins
Graphics, Visualization, and Usability Center and College of Computing
Georgia Institute of Technology
Atlanta, Georgia 30332 USA
jkh@cc.gatech.edu

REFERENCES

1 D. C. Brogan and J. K. Hodgins. Group Behaviors for Systems with Significant Dynamics, Autonomous Robots, 4:137–153, 1997.

2 J. K. Hodgins, W. L. Wooten, D. C. Brogan, and J. F. O'Brien. Animating Human Athletics, In R. Cook, editor, Proceedings of SIGGRAPH 95 (Los Angeles, CA, August 6–11, 1995), Computer Graphics Proceedings, Annual Conference Series, pages 71–78. ACM SIGGRAPH, ACM Press, Aug. 1995.

3 A. Singla, U. Ramachandran, and J. K. Hodgins. Temporal Notions of Synchronization and Consistency in Beehive. In Proceedings of the 9th Annual ACM Symposium on Parallel Algorithms and Architectures (SPAA) (Newport, RI), in press, 1997.

Animating characters for video games is a challenge because a good game requires a wide variety of appealing character motion and realistic responses to unpredictable user input. Video game systems usually generate continuous action by selecting an appropriate motion from a library of data and then smoothly interpolating between the current motion and the newly selected motion. We present an alternative, simulation-based approach that computes the desired motion by making smooth transitions between a set of parameterized basis control systems.

One potential advantage of dynamic simulation is that a basis control system can be parameterized to produce a variety of motions.[1] We use the term basis controller to describe a control system for a specific low-level task such as leaping, tumbling, landing, or balancing. Each basis control system provides a set of parameters for modifying the desired behavior. For example, the basis controller for leaping allows the specification of the height and the distance of the jump. To produce the equivalent range of behavior using a motion library, a number of jumping sequences would have to be interpolated.

By using a sequence of basis controllers, we can create a wider variety of motions for more complex tasks. Control systems can be designed so that the exit state of one control system usually leaves the simulation in a valid initial state for the next control system, making transitions easy to achieve.[2] We demonstrate the basis control systems and transitions between them by generating a diverse set of behaviors for a male and female character, including an inward 2-1/2 somersault pike, standing forward and backward somersaults, a handspring, and various leaping maneuvers.

We have developed a small set of basis controllers to demonstrate the feasibility of this approach. The balance controller prevents the character from falling down by keeping the ground projection of the character's center of mass within the area of support. Two parameters modify the behavior of the balance controller: the height of the hips above the ground and an offset for the desired location of the projected center of mass.

The leaping controller propels the character into the air. The height of the leap can be controlled by modifying the height of the hips at the beginning of the leap. Horizontal distance can be controlled by modifying the location of the projected center of mass with respect to the area of support. Modifying the timing of hip, knee, and ankle extension alters the character's angular velocity at lift-off.

The tumbling controller produces aerial maneuvers from combinations of somersaults and twists in pike, tuck, or layout positions. Although angular momentum is conserved during flight, the angular velocities are modified within the tumbling controller by adjusting the tightness of the tuck or by transferring angular velocity from one axis to another.

The landing controller acts as a transitional controller to take the character from flight to a state suitable for the balance controller. In preparation for touchdown, the legs are positioned such that the velocities of the center of mass are near zero when the projected center of mass approaches the center of the area of support. The kinetic energy attained during the flight phase is absorbed by bending the knees and hips.

Although the system we have developed is not yet complex enough to be a usable alternative to a motion library, we have demonstrated that a small set of parameterized basis controllers can be concatenated to create a set of fundamentally different behaviors. However, more basis controllers would be needed to produce a sufficient variety of motion for a video game. The transitions will likely become more complex as the variety of behaviors increases, and it may be necessary to use several intermediate controllers, like the landing controller, for complex transitions.

Wayne L. Wooten, Jessica K. Hodgins
Graphics, Visualization, and Usability Center and College of Computing
Georgia Institute of Technology
Atlanta, Georgia 30332 USA
wlw@cc.gatech.edu

REFERENCES
1 M. van de Panne. Parameterized Gait Synthesis, IEEE Computer Graphics and Applications, 16(2), pp. 40-49, (1996).
2 R. R. Burridge, A. A. Rizzi, D. E. Koditschek. Toward a Systems Theory for the Composition of Dynamically Dextrous Robot Behaviors, ISRR '95: Seventh International Symposium on Robotics Research, (1995).

All land dwelling animals leave trails of footprints on the ground whenever they walk along an impressionable surface. Our work attempts to do the opposite. Given a four-legged animal, we create the footprints and use these to animate the animal as it might have moved. This allows footprints to be used as a flexible and intuitive means for specifying quadruped motion.

The user interface allows the user to load an animal, set the gait of the animal, and then position the footprints in the environment. Each footprint has several user-controlled parameters, namely a position, direction, time of creation, and duration. Our algorithm then generates movements of the animal that satisfy the footprint constraints.

We use a hybrid physically based/kinematic model to generate the animation. The underlying motion is represented using spline-based trajectories, which are subjected to optimization. A feature of our method is that it uses both physics and *comfort constraints* in the optimization function to ensure that the motion looks physically realistic and visually pleasing. The physical model is a coarse approximation of the real quadruped. Two point masses are used to represent the front half and back half of the animal, and the pairs of virtual legs attach to the body at the spine.

Optimization with respect to physics ensures the feasibility of acceleration in the movement. Note that this is not the same as examining static support, as commonly proposed in dedicated walking algorithms. The comfort constraints are a means of explicitly ensuring that awkward leg positions are avoided. The result of the optimization is a pair of trajectories for the two point masses.

Reconstructing the full motion from the trajectories requires constraining various degrees of freedom until the whole skeleton is constrained. We use the footprints to compute desired bends at the shoulders and hips. For the legs, we incorporate a flexible, parameterized inverse-kinematic model that uses table lookup for accelerated computation. Finally, secondary passive motion is employed to compute the motions of the tail and fur.

The results to date have been encouraging. Walking, running, and jumping motions as well as the associated transitions can be animated over variable terrain with little effort. Animated examples include coordinated jumping motions, bounding over stairs, walking on hind legs, and walking through tires.

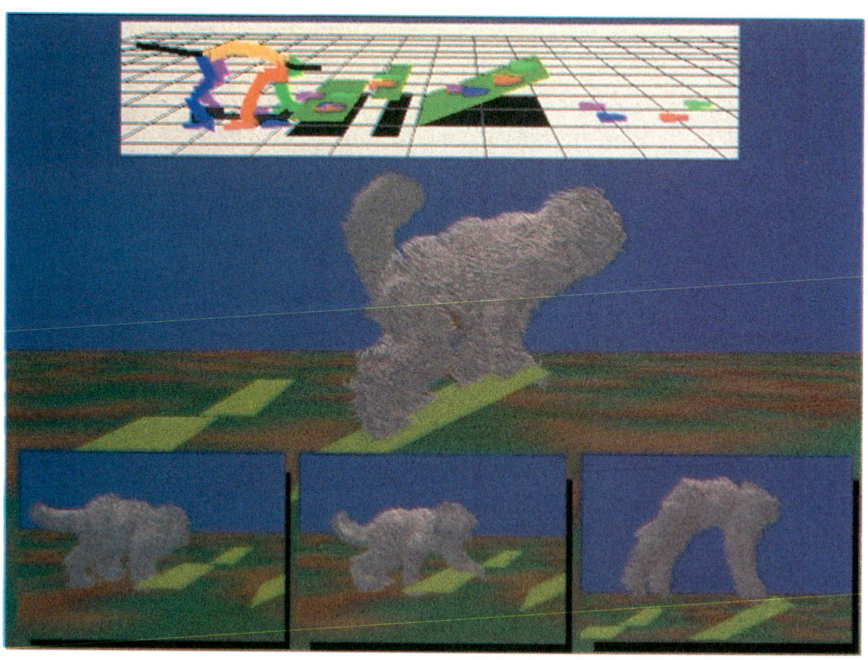

Nick Torkos, Michiel van de Panne
Department of Computer Science
University of Toronto
28 Pritchard Avenue
Toronto, Ontario CANADA M6N 1T3
torkos@dgp.toronto.edu
http://www.dgp.utoronto.ca/people/torkos

REFERENCES

1 M. Girard. Interactive Design of Computer-Animated Legged Animal Motion, IEEE Computer Graphics and Applications, 7(6), 39-51, June 1987.
2 M. F. Cohen. Interactive Spacetime Control for Animation, In Computer Graphics (SIGGRAPH 92 Proceedings), July 1992, 293-302.
3 M. H. Raibert and J. Hodgins. Animation of Dynamic Legged Locomotion, In Computer Graphics (SIGGRAPH '91 Proceedings), volume 25, pages 349-358, July 1991.

On a dark and stormy night, the appliances of a suburban household come to life. They scamper through the house, out to the sidewalk, and join all the other electrical gadgets from the neighborhood to see their cousin who has made the big time: the Electric Car. This scenario was the basis for "Appliances," a commercial for the first car in history designed from the ground up as a mass-production electric vehicle.

Both computer graphics and animatronic models were used to make the spot. Slightly more than half the shots were CG, including the shots of appliances jumping off tables and running down the sidewalk, and the final shot with over 530 characters in it. We used CG whenever complex motion was desired, and when the sheer number of appliances made it impractical to do any other way.

Character design issues were critical in the creative development of the project. Just how would a toaster walk, if it did walk? Who would win if a vacuum cleaner and a blender had a race to the curb? (Answer: vacuum cleaner.) Initial tests used highly exaggerated motion, lots of squash and stretch, and other "cartoony" effects. As we refined the motion, we moved towards a more "realistic" look, while still trying to preserve the character and personality of each appliance. Walk cycles for each character were animated.

This sketch traces the creative and technical development of the project. It includes videotape of the earliest tests, principal photography, character modeling, and animation design.

Alex Seiden
Industrial Light & Magic
P. O. Box 2459
San Rafael, California 94912 USA

KEY CREDITS
Director: **Joe Johnston**
Producer: **Kip Larsen**
Director of Photography: **Allen Daviau**
Visual Effects Supervisor: **Alex Seiden**
Consulting Supervisor: **Sandy Karpman**
Lead Technical Director: **Doug MacMillan**
Lead Animator: **Paul Griffin**
Production Coordinator: **Amy Beresford**

"The Relic"

VIFX created a wide range of visual effects for "The Relic," but the main concern was the construction, animation, rendering, and compositing of the marauding star of the film: Kothoga.

Computer graphics solutions were essential for getting a rampaging performance from a fantastic creature – for the heavy action shots as well as the monster's six-foot tongue, which lovingly licks the heroine. Since the director wanted Kothoga's movement to resemble a big cat, we referenced wildlife footage of lions and tigers. Animators needed to have these ideas firmly planted in their heads.

We then turned our attention to researching animation tools. An armature (digital input device) was built to capture poses, but it was discarded in favor of software controls the R&D group built into the creature. Animators had solid CG backgrounds and, with movement references established, could translate their knowledge into useful techniques for animating Kothoga.

Procedural animation characteristics were also considered and discarded when it became apparent that the director had very shot-specific ideas on Kothoga's movements. Each scene featured some new aspect of the creature, so his animation would be unique from shot to shot. This parameter required that we divide the workflow appropriately, to exploit the strengths of multiple animation packages so animators could build on take after take in an efficient and timely manner.

The problem was broken down in this fashion: We needed a place to track the scene (Prisms); to create reference geometry for scene tracking and character interaction (Prisms); to animate the skeleton many times over (Softimage); to skin the creature and create muscle deformations (Alias); to 3D paint color textures as well as displacement maps (Alias); and finally to render the final creature element (Sage/Prisms/Renderman). The packages were chosen based on their strengths at the time of R&D for this production (fall of 1995). VIFX in-house proprietary compositing software was used to bring the elements together.

Work on "The Relic" consisted of a vast array of CG techniques. A Chicago skyline matte painting was created. Digital skylights were tracked onto a museum rooftop. A stuntman's legs were removed and replaced with CG gore. A CG SWAT cop was decapitated. A CG shadow was added to the clean plate of a frightened dog. Wires and yellow-raincoated puppeteers were digitally removed from shots. Tons of CG debris (glass shards, wood splinters, candelabras) were added to scenes of destruction. CG drool was added to the tongue shots along with a digital "tug" on the heroine's dress and skin. CG rain and rain shaders were used on Kothoga to provide interaction of the water on his skin.

R&D for "The Relic" ran two and a half months, from the end of November 1995 to the end of January 1996. Actual post-production lasted from February through the beginning of May. At the end of this schedule, director Peter Hyams decided it would be extra fun and exciting to see Kothoga chase our heroine while he was on fire. So we quickly developed the look of Barbecued Kothoga.

No one technique seemed to work, so we settled on a combination of real fire elements (patch fire) and CG fire created with noise fields and displacement shaders (shader fire). CG smoke and embers added to the illusion. Construction of the end sequence was made more difficult because the shots into which burning Kothoga needed to be inserted were not designed as effects plates. It all had to be redesigned from scratch.

This last-minute creation demonstrates that CG effects are being used not only as tools of post production. They are also integral tools of the primary production process. The new ending of the film was conceived when the director realized what was available to him to tell his story, and he made production decisions based on possibilities he saw during the process.

John (DJ) DesJardin
Visual Effects Supervisor
VIFX
5333 McConnell Avenue
Los Angeles, California 90066 USA

Most filmmakers choose to use computer-generated visual effects in their projects to go beyond the boundaries of the existing and traditional techniques. Director Roger Donaldson, in our early preproduction meetings, outlined his artistic and technical requirements for creation of synthetic lava and confirmed that "Dante's Peak" would challenge all past attempts to create photo-realistic lava.

The director's wish list included a fast moving river of lava, characterized by the familiar orange-red of molten rock at the edges, with a surface crust that is graphite black for the night shots and generic gray granite for the daylight scenes. The shape, speed, and viscosity of the lava had to be created according to its underlying terrain, interacting with stationary and moving objects in the various scenes, such as cars, furniture, trees, etc. The fast-moving lava nighttime scenes had to cast interactive lighting on the surrounding environment with moving orange light. The energy radiated by the lava surface had to produce a ripple-like heat distortion effect on the background objects. And the majority of the shots had to be photographed using hand-held cameras.

To resolve the complex set of issues involved in creating and integrating CG lava, Digital Domain's team created a production pipeline flexible and generic enough to give the director creative freedom and at the same time applicable to all type of shots.

The first step in creating the digital lava was the scientific approximation of its rough shape, position, and motion according to the production terrain and various locations the lava was moving over. We built a 3D computer model of the terrain for every production location in which lava interacted. The flexibility of this setup allowed artists relative ease in making necessary adjustments, based on creative input from the director, while maintaining the proper physics of the lava flow.

The next step was to make lava interact with objects from the live-action environment. A simulation of interaction between liquid and solid objects is not trivial, so a whole range of techniques including collision detection were developed.

Once the shape and motion of the lava were settled, all the surface details were added when the lava was rendered. Crust, cracks, and molten lava were all generated using a complex series of multifractals. These surface features were altered based on the behavior of the lava and the crust being enveloped by molten lava in areas where the lava geometry was colliding with objects in its path. This procedural method gave the lava a detailed and organic appearance, and was used to help simulate a variety of different lava "looks" for different scenes in the movie.

David Isyomin
Digital Domain
300 Rose Avenue
Venice, California 90291 USA
david@d2.com

"101 Dalmations"

The live-action remake of Disney's classic animated feature, "101 Dalmatians," called for computer-generated dalmatian puppies to seamlessly interact with (and in some cases replace) real dalmatians in a manner that was completely believable. In this project, we developed technical solutions that minimized costs, maximized efficiency, and, in so doing, allowed us to focus our energy primarily on maintaining the highest aesthetic standards. Due to the complexity of the shots in combination with the tight production schedule, we identified opportunities throughout the animation process to leverage reusable models, pre-animated cycles, and motion libraries.

From a creative perspective, animation was always our main concern. We wanted to match the CGI puppies' motion as accurately as possible with the motion of the live puppies. However, animating each individual dog (an average of 90 for every shot) would have been impossible in view of the time and budget constraints. Whatever the approach, we needed to guarantee as much visual consistency as possible in the animation. To address these challenges, we devised an animation pipeline incorporating reusable motion libraries that in turn allowed us to focus on the quality of the animation rather than the quantity.

During preproduction, various walk cycles, run cycles, trot cycles and sitting dogs were animated using Softimage 3.0 and an in-house program called Caricature. Then, using path animation, these cycles were attached to a spline object to recreate the correct amount of forward motion. Thereafter, the cycles were documented and added to a library database. To allow a dog to change its gait or behavior during a scene, various transition cycles (walk to run, run to walk, fast run to slow run, walk to stop) were also created. Together, these new files would offer a wide range of complex behaviors for use by the animators.

The next step in the process involved automatic creation of files with a non-animated figure that we referred to as the "pawn." The pawn was animated on a path that corresponded to the final animated cycle and transitional animation. These were used to choreograph and time the overall animation for each shot to ensure that no dog intersected another at any time. We defined each creature trajectory and projected it onto the "floor geometry," which was match-modeled to the shape of the terrain in the live action plate. A python script was developed so that animators could automatically connect each trajectory to a combination of dog cycle files. The animator would specify the type of gait and relative speed at a number of key frames. The script would insert appropriate motion curves from various gait and transition files, splicing them together and stretching them to fit together seamlessly. The pawn animation file served as an interactive and flexible way of addressing visual shot composition and allowed us to specify the number of dogs required for the shots, accurately reflecting what the final animation was going to be.

Once the overall choreography was approved, the pawn animation file was processed by a second python script to create animation files with complete articulated dogs. Because the motion used in the pawn animation was derived from the actual articulated animation cycle files, the fully animated dogs aligned exactly with their positions and speeds in the pawn animation, including through transitions.

Finally, animation of key dogs created by the script was enhanced by traditional CG animation techniques. In this step of the process, we created unique interactions of the CGI dogs with live dogs or with each other and the environment. The nuances and variations that were incorporated prevented the final animations from appearing cyclical.

"101 Dalmatians" was a landmark project in the development of techniques for addressing the monumental challenges faced when creating photo realistic animation that involves multiple creatures. This technique has been further improved and perfected as illustrated by our recent work on "The Lost World: Jurassic Park."

Daniel Jeanette, Doug Smythe
Industrial Light & Magic
P. O. Box 2459
San Rafael, California 94912 USA

Computer vision techniques are playing an increasingly important role in computer graphics applications requiring enhanced realism.[1,5] This synergy between computer vision and computer graphics is of paramount importance in virtual reality applications, where the use of complex models such as humans or other articulated objects and the modeling of their motions is often necessary.[2,6] A growing number of invasive solutions exist for three-dimensional estimation of the motion parameters of the human body, but these approaches suffer from cumbersome set-ups and alteration of user motion. More importantly, attaching markers makes it impossible for the system to be extended for many other applications such as performance evaluation in real sport competitions.

In this sketch, we describe a system that allows creation of an anthropometrically correct graphical model of a subject and of animations of the subject moving using the vision-based estimated parameters of motion (Figure 1). Our new system has a motion analysis part and a motion playback part. For the analysis part, the input is a sequence of grayscale images taken from multiple views, while the output is the anthropometric dimensions of the subject and the three-dimensional positions and orientations of the subject's body parts at each time instant. The motion playback part animates an anthropometrically correct graphical model of the participant resulting in real-time human motion visualization.

The system is currently passive; that is, the model is driven by the observations. For the current implementation, the background of the scene is static, and the subject is wearing tight-fitting clothes. This new algorithm advances the state of the art in motion capture because:

1 The use of occluding contours obviates the need for markers or special equipment.
2 The accuracy of tracking body parts is comparable to the accuracy achieved using markers.
3 The shape model is obtained from the observations and allows for enhanced realism.
4 The use of multiple cameras mitigates the difficulties arising due to occlusion among body parts since body movements that are ambiguous from one view can be disambiguated from another view.
5 Selection of the subset of cameras that provide the most informative views is accomplished in an active and time-varying fashion.
6 The estimation is based on the whole apparent contour rather than just a few points.

We demonstrate two case studies of possible applications of human body motion tracking, namely performance measurement of people with disabilities and vision-based trajectory input for dynamic simulators.

FIGURE 1

(a-c) Side, front and top views of the subject performing a complex two-arm motion.

(d-f) Recovered three-dimensional pose of the subject's upper and lower arms.

(g-i) The estimated motion parameters for the motion of the subject's arms have been applied to a *customized graphical model of the subject.*

Ioannis A. Kakadiaris, Dimitris Metaxas
GRASP Lab and Center for Human Modeling and Simulation
University of Pennsylvania
Philadelphia, PA 19104
ioannisk@grip.cis.upenn.edu

REFERENCES

1 A. Azarbayejani, T. Starner, B. Horowitz, and A. P. Pentland. Visually Controlled Graphics, IEEE Transactions on Pattern Analysis and Machine Intelligence, 15(6):602–605, June 1993.
2 Norman I. Badler, Cary B. Phillips, and Bonnie L. Webber. Simulating Humans: Computer Graphics Animation and Control, Oxford University Press, New York, NY, 1993.
3 I. A. Kakadiaris and D. Metaxas. 3D Human Body Model Acquisition from Multiple Views, In Proceedings of the Fifth International Conference on Computer Vision, pp. 618–623, Boston, MA, June 20-22 1995.
4 I. A. Kakadiaris and D. Metaxas. Model-Based Estimation of 3D Human Motion with Occlusion Based on Active Multi-Viewpoint Selection, In CVPR '96, pp. 81–87, San Francisco, CA, June 18-20 1996.
5 A. State, G. Hirota, D. T. Chen, W. F. Garrett, and M. A. Livingston. Superior Augmented Reality Registration by Integrating Landmark Tracking and Magnetic Tracking, In SIGGRAPH 96, pp. 429–438, New Orleans, LA, August 4-9 1996.
6 T. K. Capin, I. S. Pandzic, H. Noser, D. Thalmann, and N. Magnenat Thalmann. Virtual Human Representation and Communication in VLNET, IEEE Computer Graphics and Applications, 17(2):42–53, March-April 1997.

Visual Tracking and Pose Recovery for Special Effects

Object outlines are modeled as quadratic B-splines whose control points lie in a linear shape-space of possible configurations.[1] A rigid three-dimensional object can be modeled using a linear shape-space assuming that the outline of the object can be thought of as a wire-frame and that the available object views can be approximated using orthographic projection. The required shape-space is 3D affine and is eight-dimensional; moreover a simple, fast, and robust algorithm exists to compute the 3D pose of the object using the 3D affine coordinates. The pose specifies a coordinate frame for the tracked object, which can be used to render graphics onto the image that appears to be "attached" to the real object.

In order to construct the 3D affine shape-space, two views of the object are needed: one fronto-planar and one rotated through 90 degrees. These are computed using a robust approach that avoids problems with occlusion, using several uncalibrated views, all fairly close to the frontal view and processing them by means of a factorization method.[3] The recovered 3D structure can be used to build a solid model of the object that allows hidden surface removal and therefore rendering of artificial objects that pass behind the real one.

In order to reliably track an object through clutter it is necessary to construct a model of the object's likely motion as well as its shape. We use a standard form of motion model and learn the model from a training sequence.[1] Due to the heavy image clutter, a traditional Kalman filter tracker cannot be used, and we instead rely on the Condensation algorithm,[2] which is slower but more effective in clutter. We filmed two sequences showing the same small bunch of leaves being translated and rotated, first for 26 seconds against a white background, and then against a background of heavy clutter for five seconds. Fifteen views of the leaves were used to construct the 3D affine space, and a motion model was learned using the initial portion of the uncluttered sequence. The leaves were tracked using this model through both full sequences. The pose of the leaves was recovered from each tracked frame and used to superimpose a computer-generated bunch of flowers and flowerpot on the original images as shown in the figure.

Due to the difficulty of the tracking problem, a large number of random samples (N=7500) was used in the Condensation algorithm, and the algorithm ran at approximately two seconds per field on an SGI Indy R4400 200 MHz. Although the background demonstrated is static, no background subtraction was performed, and a moving background could equally well be tolerated. The figure also shows the more traditional matting application of transferring an object from one image sequence to another. Since pose has been recovered, computer graphics can be rendered attached to the foreground object at the same time.

We have demonstrated that state-of-the-art visual motion tracking can be combined with pose recovery to segment complex objects from a complex background and overlay computer-generated models on the original images. We have not, however, exploited all of the potential of the Condensation algorithm. It is clear that motion tracking and pose recovery are now sufficiently powerful and robust that they can usefully be included in the computer graphics toolkit. As graphics researchers begin to use such techniques from computer vision, new problem areas will be isolated and applications will be discovered hat will benefit both fields.

Michael Isard, Andrew Blake
Department of Engineering Science
University of Oxford
Parks Road
Oxford OX1 3PJ, United Kingdom
+44.1865.273919
+44.1865.273908 fax
misard@robots.ox.ac.uk

REFERENCES

1 A. Blake, M. A. Isard, and D. Reynard. Learning to Track the Visual Motion of Contours, Artificial Intelligence, 78:101-134, 1995.

2 M. A. Isard and A. Blake. Visual Tracking by Stochastic Propagation of Conditional Density, In Proc. 4th European Conf. on Computer Vision, pages 343-356, Cambridge, England, Apr 1996.

3 C. Tomasi and T. Kanade. Shape and Motion from Image Streams: A Factorization Method, Int. Journal of Computer Vision, 9(2):137-154, 1991.

We report on research into the lip synchronization of speech that has not been preprocessed into phonetic units. It is based on the notion that given any spoken words as input, a computer can accurately portray the mouth movements made during the pronunciation of those words, and can do so without the necessity of speech recognition or electromechanical devices attached to the jaw.

Our method is based on correlating parameters of lip and jaw movement with parameters drawn from the spectrum of the speech signal. We found a minimum of three parameters – horizontal lip opening, vertical lip opening, and jaw height – sufficient to allow the animation of a model of a generic human mouth. The speech parameters are derived by treating the magnitude of the discrete Fourier Transform as a probability density function and using well known statistical measures called moments to characterize the shape of the distribution.

To establish mouth shape predictor or training functions, which are described mathematically as a surface in multi-dimensional space, we videotape and record a speaker uttering a set of basic training sound transitions that cover the ranges of jaw position, lip rounding, and lip spreading. Using a very accurate glottal pulse estimation technique, the first, second, and third moments; second and third central moments; and various linear and nonlinear combinations of these moments are used to produce a set of independent variables. The mouth measurements obtained from the video are then used as the dependent variable, and a multivariate training surface (a thin plate spline) for each mouth parameter is derived from the training utterances.

When the speaker who was videotaped to train the system is used to test the system, the accuracy of the predictions is extremely high, well above the threshold necessary to animate the mouth in concert with the speech. We are currently working on construction of training surfaces that would provide adequate predicted mouth motion, independent of the speaker. We are also attempting to incorporate vowels that occur in languages other than English. We will then move to include voiced consonants such as /m/, /v/, /r/, and /z/.

We are augmenting this technique to include additional parameters such as tongue position and differentiation between the edges of the lips and the horizontal opening of the lips during speech. These parameters will help introduce more realism into the model. Modeling of actual human faces will be attempted later.

Applications include animation, training in lip reading, speech therapy, video conferencing, man-machine interfaces, voice compression, training and education, linguistic research, and help in speech recognition.

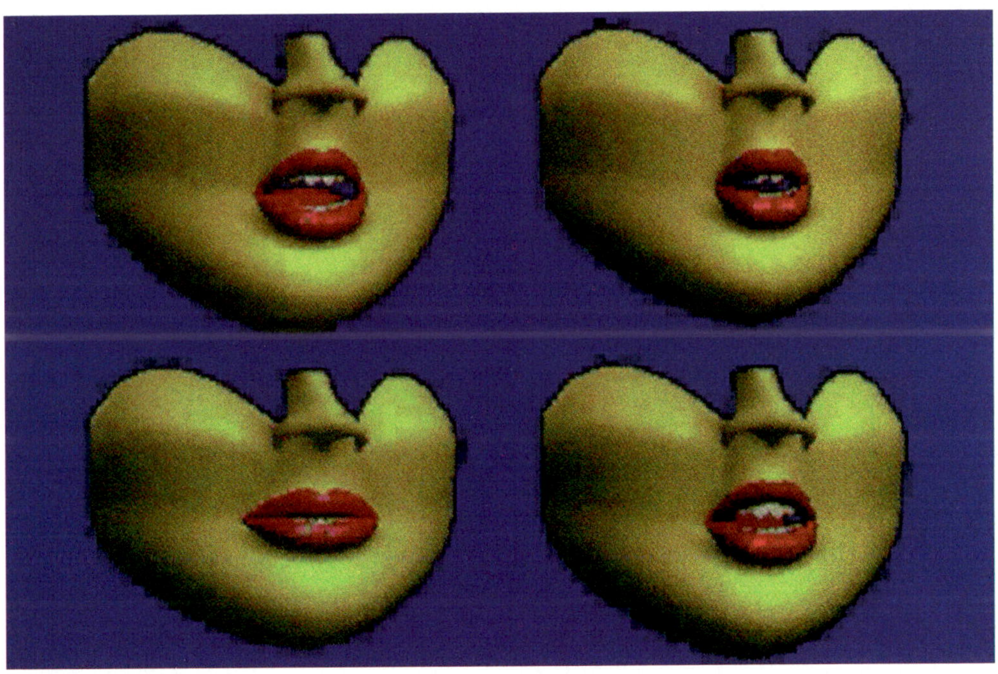

David F. McAllister, Robert D. Rodman, Donald L. Bitzer, Andrew S. Freeman
Department of Computer Science
Box 8206
North Carolina State University
Raleigh, North Carolina 27695-8206 USA
dfm@adm.csc.ncsu.edu

Layered Compositing of Facial Expression

How does one make an embodied agent react with appropriate facial expression, without resorting to repetitive prebuilt animations? How does one mix and transition between facial expressions to visually represent shifting moods and attitudes? How can authors of these agents relate lower-level facial movements to higher-level moods and intentions?

We introduce a computational engine that addresses these questions with a stratified approach. We first define a low-level movement model having a discrete number of degrees of freedom. Animators can combine and layer these degrees of freedom to create elements of autonomous facial motion and then recursively build on this movement model to construct higher-level models. In this way, they can synthesize successively higher levels of autonomous facial expressiveness.

A key feature of our computational approach is that composited movements tend to blend and layer in natural ways in the run-time system. As the animator builds at higher levels, the correct layering priorities are always maintained at lower supporting levels. We have used this approach to create emotionally expressive autonomous facial agents.

Building on our work in improvisational animation (SIGGRAPH 96), we use a parallel layered approach. Our authoring system allows its user to relate lower-level facial movements to higher level moods and intentions by using a model inspired by optical compositing. We first allow the animator to abstract facial motion into a discrete number of degrees of freedom. The system does not impose a particular model at this stage, but rather allows the animator to define the degrees of freedom that he or she finds useful.

Given a set of degrees of freedom, we allow the animator to specify time varying linear combinations and overlays of these degrees of freedom. Each definition becomes a new, derived, degree of freedom. Collectively, these derived degrees of freedom create a new abstraction layer. We allow animators to recursively create successive abstractions, each built upon the degrees of freedom defined by previous ones.

More specifically, we internally represent each of the model's K degrees of freedom by a K dimensional basis vector, which has a value of 1 in some dimension j, and a value of 0 in all other dimensions. The state space for the face consists of all linear combinations of these basis vectors. We allow the animator to create time-varying functions (coherent noise and splined curves) of these linear combinations, to create a simple vocabulary of "basis motions." We then provide a motion compositing engine, which allows the animator to specify a compositing structure for these basis motions. The engine gives motions varying "opacities" and does alpha blending, much as Photoshop composites layers of images. The animator can then encapsulate sets of time-varying weights for each of the basis motions in the above engine and define each such set as a new motion basis. By doing this recursively, the animator can describe successively higher levels of an emotional vocabulary.

We have found that in this way, successively higher semantic levels of facial expressiveness can be effectively synthesized. In particular, we find that movements defined with this method tend to blend together and overlay in natural ways. As the animator works within higher abstractions, the system always maintains correct priorities at all lower supporting abstractions. The result is real-time interactive facial animation that can achieve a convincing degree of emotive expressiveness.

The eventual goal of this work is to give computer/human interfaces the ability to represent the subtleties we take for granted in face-to-face communication, so that they can function as agents for an emotional point of view. By automating the creation of facial expression in the run-time engine of an interactive agent, we enable such an agent to operate without the explicit intervention of a human operator.

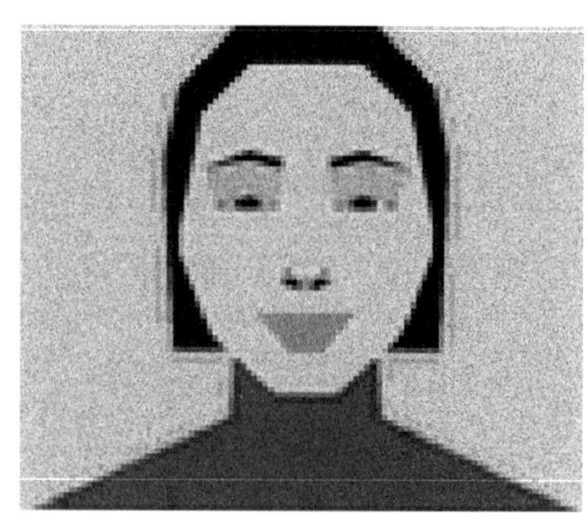

Ken Perlin
Media Research Laboratory
Department of Computer Science
New York University
719 Broadway, 12th Floor
New York, New York 10003 USA
perlin@cat.nyu.edu

Computer Animation Festival Committee

COMPUTER ANIMATION FESTIVAL CHAIR
Judith Crow Digital Domain

ELECTRONIC THEATER CO-DIRECTOR
Jim Hillin Walt Disney Feature Animation

FESTIVAL SCREENING ROOM CO-PRODUCERS
Clunie Holt Sony Pictures Imageworks
Joe Takai Digital Domain

SPECIAL SESSION CO-PRODUCERS
Jini Dayaneni L-Squared
Antoine Durr VIFX

FILM EDITOR
Ladd McPartland Industrial Light & Magic

VIDEO EDITOR
Rob Doolittle Digital Domain

PUBLICATIONS
Michael Vinovich Side Effects Software

INTERNATIONAL LIAISON
Huguette Chesnais

COORDINATOR
Robin Myran

ADMINISTRATOR
Pat Oh

PRE-SHOW ENTERTAINMENT
Jaimes Oh

MUSIC COMPOSITION
Ryan Ulyate Organized Noise

Electronic Theater Jury

Paul Brown Queensland University of Technology
Edwin Catmull Pixar Animation Studios
David Forsey The University of British Columbia
Midori Kitagawa DeLeon ACCAD, The Ohio State University
Chris Landreth Alias|Wavefront

Special Thanks to:

The Center Quickprint Orange, California
Printing Services

Digital Domain Venice, California
Office and Offline Editing Facilities

EFILM Hollywood, California
Laser Film Recording on LUX

Encore Santa Monica Santa Monica, California
Online Editing Facilities

Industrial Light & Magic San Rafael, California
Film Editing Facilities

Intel Corporation Santa Clara, California

Interactive Effects Tustin, California
Amazon 3D Paint Software

The Post Group Los Angeles, California
Online Editing Facilities

Side Effects Software Inc. Toronto, Ontario
Houdini 3D Software

Sony Digital Studios Culver City, California
Digital Sound Editing

Sony Pictures Imageworks Culver City, California
DMD Digital Video Projection System, Rendering, I/O

Spot Welders Venice, California
Offline Editing Facilities

SquareUSA Marina Del Rey, California
Rendering Resources

Walt Disney Feature Animation Burbank, California
Jury Screening Facility

Thanks to:

Tanya Anguita
Frank Bassi
Andrea Bissada
Linda Branagan
Ed Busch
Allen Cappuccilli
Joan Collins
Sara Duran
Frank Foster
Deborah Giarratana
John Giffoni
Andrew Glassner
Maria Gomez-De Lizardo
Ines Hardtke
Kristin King
Joe Lohmar
Tom Moore
Joe Muxie
Adele Newton
Tom Rieke
Ron Rebensdorf
Andrew Saito
Spencer Scott
Paul Yanover

Special Session Support

John "DJ" DesJardin
Andy Kopra
Harish Mandyam
Adele Newton

SIGGRAPH 97 Sketches Overview

Director: Andrew Glassner
Producer: Sue Corcoran
Editor: Drew Kaplan

"Red Green Blues"
Music & Lyrics: Andrew Glassner
Arrangement & Instrumentals: David Thiel
Vocals: Sue Corcoran
Guitar: Will Morgan
Engineer: Rick Senechal

Produced at Microsoft IMP Studios

CONTACT
Andrew Glassner
Microsoft Network
One Microsoft Way
Redmond, Washington 98052-6399 USA
glassner@microsoft.com

SIGGRAPH 97 Electronic Theater Open

Director: Brummbaer
Music Composer: Paul Haslinger
Producer: Frank Foster
Production Coordinator:
Eileen O'Connor
Character Animation: David Schaub, Bill Diaz, John Clark Matthews
Technical Director: Rachel Nicoll
Modelers: Ara Tserunian, Alex Whang
Technical Coordinator:
Anthony Ceccomancini
System Administrator: Bruce Dobrin
Technical Assistant: Steve Rom
Hardware: Integraph Dual & Quad Pentium Pro, NT Workstations
Software: Microsoft Windows NT, Kinetics 3D Studio Max, Character Studio

Editorial Department:
Assistant Effects Editor: John Berri
Negative Assembly: Dee Storm, Willem Barnevel
Video Tape Editor: Ron Vargas
Assistant Video Tape Editors:
Hobart Young, Ray Wong
Digital Production Scheduler:
Kris Matheney

I/O Department:
Input Output Supervisor:
Dennis Webb
Input Output Coordinator:
Geoffory Harjo
Film Recording: Derrick Quarles, Chris Arreola, Robert Davis Oh, Alfredo Barcia
Color Timing: John Nicolard
Color Grading: Paul McGhee

SDDS Sound Mix by Sony Digital Studios Post Production Sound

Michael Kohut
Tom McCarthy
Sound Designer: Steve Ticknov

CONTACT
Eileen O'Connor
Production Coordinator
Sony Pictures Imageworks
9050 West Washington Boulevard
Culver City, California 90232 USA
+1.310.840.8591
eoconnor@spimageworks.com

SIGGRAPH 97 Electronic Theater Close

Annihilation Becomes Creation Through a Stretch of the Imagination

By Kevin Mack and Caleb Howard

Sound: Kevin Mack, Ryan Ulyate
Rendering Resources provided courtesy of SquareUSA
Laser Film Recording provided courtesy of EFILM on LUX
Houdini 3D software provided courtesy of Side Effects Software Inc.
Amazon 3D Paint software provided courtesy of Interactive Effects

Special Thanks to: Steve Gray, Greg Hermanovic, Don Miskowich, Judith Crow, Ryan Ulyate, Mark Elendt, Tom Benoist, Scott Michelson, Ronda Taylor, Martha Mack, Jon Mack, Ray Mack

CONTACT
Kevin Mack
Digital Domain
300 Rose Avenue
Venice, California 90291 USA
+1.310.314.2800
+1.310.314.2888 fax
http://www.d2.com

10,000 Feet

In "10,000 Feet" a teddy bear, skydiving for the first time, is left with one last lesson to learn: that all the hours of learning and theory cannot make up for the actual experience. Unfortunately, the first experience might also be the last, leaving no opportunity for further attempts.

Producer: DJ Cassel/Ringling School of Art and Design
Concept and Animation: DJ Cassel
Audio Mix: DJ Cassel
Faculty Advisor: Ed Cheetham
Video/Audio Support: Phil Chiocchio
Software: Alias PowerAnimator, Composer
Hardware: SGI Indy

CONTACT
DJ Cassel
Computer Animation Department
Ringling School of Art and Design
2700 North Tamiami Trail
Sarasota, Florida 34234 USA
+1.941.359.7536
+1.941.359.7517 fax
mpalazzi@rsad.edu
http://www.rsad.edu

2D Life in a 3D World

This video illustrates an animation process that allows efficient registration of traditional 2D animated characters within 3D computer-generated worlds. Rather than compositing 2D animation on top of 3D backgrounds and overlays, the characters are registered in 3D-space, truly integrating 2D and 3D animation.

Tooned In
Producers: Cindy Ball, Tim Hunkapiller, James Mahoney
Layout and Storyboards: Bill Perez
2D Animation: Kunio Shimamura, Melanie Thomas
2D and 3D Textures: Phil Philipson
2D and 3D Integration Process Designed by: James Mohoney and Cindy Ball
Digital Ink & Paint: Jerry Meyer

Moving Pixels
Producers: Robert Kramer, Tony Smoller
3D Modeling and Animation: Sebastian Bilbao, Brian Wilcox

Rumble
Sound Design: Steve Sauber

Special Thanks to: Alias|Wavefront, Caltech Graphics Group, VIFX

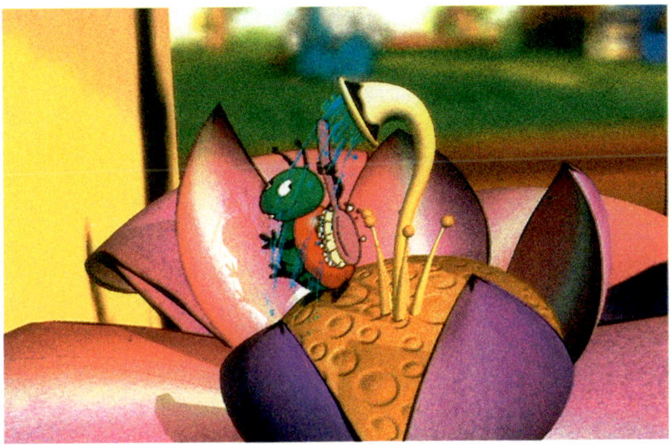

CONTACT
Cindy Ball
Tooned In/Caltech Graphics Group
1127 East Del Mar Boulevard, #321
Pasadena, California 91106 USA
+1.818.405.1960
cindy@toonedin.com
http://www.toonedin.com

The images in this work deal with the making of the CG effects for "ACRI", a Japanese film whose production and post-production were done in Australia. The film was released in Japan last summer and tells the story of present-day mermaids. 'ACRI' is the heroine's name.

Producer: Shinya Kawai
Assistant Producer: Akemi Suyama
Visual Effects Supervisor: Takahiko Akiyama
Visual Effects Producer: Shuji Asano
Associate Visual Effects Supervisor: Dale Duguid
Visual Effects Assistant Supervisor: Kagari 'TEX' Yasuda
3D CGI Animators: Ryuichi Snow, Shoko Kitamura
CGI Animator/Programmer: Tsutomu 'Tommy' Nomoto
3D Titles: Craig Wentworth
3D Video Playback Animator: Diego Guerrero
3D Scanning: Headus PTY.LTD
Executive in charge of Production: Nobuya Okabe
Head Sculptors: Kiya Taishiro, Hiroyuki Nakazawa
Assistant Sculptors: Kyoichi Shimazaki, Tetsuo Suda
Bob McCarron Studio Crew: Lyn McCarron, Elka Wardega, Maria Fowler, Rock Connelly, Grant Boiffin, Belinda Villani
Senior Special Make-up Effects Artists: Wendy Sainsbury, Lesley Vanderwalt
Special Make-up Effects Artist: Karen Robotham
Visual Effects Film Unit Coordinator: Gina Black
1st Assistant Directors: U-ichi Abe, Peter Nathan
Director of Photography: Gene Moller A.C.S.
Underwater Camera Operator: Ross Isaacs
Focus Puller: Aron Leong
Underwater Gaffer: Darryn Fox
Best Boy: Bob Watterson
Grip: CaryVignall

Visual Effects Film Editor: Peter Skarratt
Digital Compositing Supervisor: Peter Webb
Digital Matte Artist: Toshiyuki Kimura
Digital Artists: James Rogers, Dave Morley, Randy Vellacott, Rob O'Neil
System Administrator: Neville Duguid
CGI Coordinator: Rowena Zande
Data Wrangler: Simon Dye
CGI Trainee: Bobbi-lea Dionysius
Software Support: IMAGICA DIGIX Inc., Future Reality, Digital Masters, AVID MEDIA Illusion
Additional Digital Effects: Dfilm Digital Film Services
2nd Grip/Best Boy: Warren Young
Music Operator: Peter Derooy
EDI-Assist Operator: Jacinta Leong
Lighting Rig Engineer: Douglas Vost
Unit Manager: Cameron Wintour
Unit Assistant Location: Garry Brennan
VFX Crew Driver: Darryl Sheen

Life Guard Supervisors: Owen Derek, Andrew Hall, Peter Bofinger
Cast: Tadanobu Asano, Kimika Yoshino, Tomoko Tanaka

CONTACT
Shuji Asano
'ACRI' Project
Overlord Company, Ltd.
#608 3-7-8, Nakarokugo, Ota-ku
Tokyo 144 JAPAN
+81.3.5711.4678
+81.3.5711.4678 fax
CXL00766@niftyserve.or.jp

This piece depicts genetic manipulation and the origin of food.

Producer: Okenite

CONTACT
Marc Thonon and Patrick Chereau
3 rue des Templiers
10350 Le Pavillon
Ste Julie FRANCE
+33.0160662748
okenite@msn.com

Advanced Problem Solving

Digital allegoric manifestation.

Producer: Kevin Souls

Ahoy, The Movie

An old salt, down on his luck and out of money, attempts to nurse a free drink out of a bar room crowd with promises of never-before-heard tales of adventure on the high seas.

Producer: Bruce Pukema

CONTACT
Kevin Souls
USC
181 South Sycamore Street, Apartment 302
Los Angeles, California 90036 USA
+1.213.634.0475
souls@scf.usc.edu

CONTACT
Bruce Pukema
Ronin Animation Inc.
420 North 5th Street, Suite 690
Minneapolis, Minnesota 55401 USA
+1.612.672.0970
+1.612.672.0970 fax
ronininc@primenet.com

American Dream

A suburban metropolis is created over the course of a day, but, in the end, is shown to be nothing more than a two-dimensional representation of itself.

Producer: D. Brian Weber
Contributors: Dan Bailey, Steve Bradley, and Alan Price

CONTACT
D. Brian Weber
University of Maryland, Baltimore County
13012 Triadelphia Road
Ellicott City, Maryland 21042 USA
+1.410.531.6494
dweber2@umbc.edu

Excerpts from "An American Werewolf in Paris"

The werewolves in this work are completely computer generated, as well as the water which is shaken off in the fountain scene.

Digital hair technology was developed in-house at Santa Barbara Studios.
Werewolf animation was done using SoftImage.
Particle animation done in Dynamation.
Werewolf model was done by Viewpoint.
Additional facial modelling was done in-house using Alias.
Skin renders were done in Mental Ray, then motion blurred using in-house utilities.
Dust and other particle rendering done with in-house utility.
Skins were motion blurred using an in-house utility outside of Mental Ray.
Compositing done using Flint, Avid Illusion and Wavefront Composer, and Shake.
Visual Effects by Santa Barbara Studios

Animators: Micheal Parks, Kelly Wilcox, Darren Lurie, Jim Clark
Technical Directors: Scott Liedtka, Matthew P. Welker
Digital Compositors: Dawn Bowery, Robert Scopinich
Additional R&D: Matt Rhodes
3D Camera Match Moves: Steve Galle
3D Matchmove Geometry: Nicholas Waller
Digital Matte Paintings: X.O. Digital Arts
Roto & Paint: Lucy Green Taylor, Lance Wilhoite
Effects Editorial: Yon Van Kline
Technical Assistants: Mark Fattibene, Michael Kaelin, Lila Vesely
Systems Administration: Kathleen Samec, Buckie Claborn, Jason MacLeod
VFX Production Accountant: Sharon Wrinkle
Production Support: Dorothy J. Butler, Mary Cleary, Janet Doran-Veevers, Carla Schwarz
Live Animal Reference: Bear, Roscoe, George, Willy, Cassie, Kadin
Second Unit Cameraman: Wade Childress
Storyboard Artists: Robert Hickson, Phillip Norwood, David Russell

Directed by Anthony Waller
Produced by Richard Claus
Visual Effects Supervisors: John Grower, Bruce Walters
Animation Director: James Satoru Straus
CG Supervisor: Scott Gordon
Werewolf Design/Art Director: Peter Lloyd
Executive Producer: Bruce Jones
Director of R&D: Phil Brock
Compositing Supervisor: John Carey
Eiffel Tower Falling Sequence: Mark Wendell
Visual Effects Producer: Diane Holland
Lead Technical Directors: Ron Moreland, Pete Travers

VFX Legal Support: Ted Baer
Special Thanks to:
Avid Technologies, Inc.
Computer Systems, Inc.
Digital Equipment Corporation
Silicon Graphics, Inc.

Digital Film Scanning & Recording by EFILM
Executive in Charge of Production: Michael Cooper
Producer: Tripp Hudson
Colorist: Alex Zaphiris
Editor: Amy Tomkins
Production Manger: Renzo Soriano

CONTACT
John Grower, Diane Holland
Santa Barbara Studios, Inc.
201 North Salsipuedes Street
Santa Barbara, California 93103 USA
+1.805.568.1902
+1.805.568.3733 fax
john@sbst.com, diane@sbst.com

Anaconda

Sony Pictures Imageworks digitally created two photo-realistic giant Anacondas which would believably attack, coil, eat, and regurgitate their prey. A digital actor is also featured in the waterfall sequence. This vivid CG imagery interacts with live action elements and actors on a level never seen before.

Producer: Sony Pictures Imageworks
FX Supervisor: John Nelson
FX Producer: Robin Griffin
FX Coordinator: Jacquie Barnbrook
Production Assistant: Darcy Fray
CG Supervisor: John Mclaughlin
Animation Director: Eric Armstrong
Animator: Alex Sokoloff
Lead TA: Rob Groome
Lead Digital Artist: Colin Campbell
Animator: David Vallone
Match Mover: Michael Harbour
Digital Artist: Gimo Chanphianamvong
Lead Compositor: Jason Dowdeswell
Technical Director: John Decker

Lead Technical Director: Jim Berney
Painter: Jonn Shourt
Lead Animator: Kelvin Lee
Lead Modeller/Animator: Kevin Hudson
Animator: Manny Wong
Art Director: Marty Kline
Technical Director: Mike Travers
Painter: Raquel Morales
Match Mover: Rodney Iwashina
Lead TD/Production Programmer: Serge Sretschinsky
Animator: David Simmons
Editor: Scott W. Anderson
Negative Wrangler: Dee Storm
Software Coordinator: Audrea Topps-Harjo
Software Developer: Bruce Navsky
Head of Systems: Alberto Velez
Systems Coordinator: Katya Culberg
SA (Resources 3rd Party): Ted Alexandre
SA (Hardware): Dean Miya

CONTACT
Don Levy
Executive Director of Publicity, Promotions and Advertising
Sony Pictures Imageworks
9050 West Washington Boulevard, Suite 3120
Culver City, California 90232 USA
+1.310.840.8234
+1.310.840.8243 fax
don@spimageworks.com
http://www.sonypix.com

The Animation of M.C.Escher's "Belvedere"

M.C.Escher's lithograph entitled "Belvedere" is famous for its impossible objects. Generally, it isn't possible to look at these kinds of objects from different perspectives. Because these impossible objects don't lend themselves to visual illusion, this piece develops a method of rotation and drawing that simulates the expected visual representation of objects.

Producer: Sachiko Tsuruno

CONTACT
Sachiko Tsuruno
Kinki University Faculty of Engineering
Kayanomori 11-6
Iizuka-city
Fukuoka 820 JAPAN
+81.948.22.5655
+81.948.23.0536 fax
sachiko@fuk.kindai.ac.jp

Automated Highways/Excerpts

This work introduces the concept of automated highways, a future system whereby cars will function without the driver having to steer, brake, or accelerate.

Producer: Kleiser-Walczak/ GM-Buick/the Palladian Group
Presented by: Buick Motor Division - General Motors Corporation and The Palladian Group
Produced by: Kleiser-Walczak Construction Company
Designer/Writer/Head Animator: Beau Janzen
Producer: Erika Walczak
Animators: Phearuth Tuy, Greg Juby
Production Coordinator: Santo Ragno
Digital Assistant: Robin Cookis
Production Assistant: Slavica Pandzic
Sound Design & Music: Reel Sound Productions, Chuck Burgess
Narration: Chuck Burgess, Tina Janzen
Post Production Facility: Mist Media Inc., Toluca Lake, CA

CONTACT
Kleiser-Walczak Construction Company
6150 Mulholland Highway
Hollywood, California 90068 USA
+1.213.467.3563
+1.213.467.3583 fax
http://www.kwcc.com

Baby

The challenge was to create a precocious, photo-realistic, two-year-old, opera-singing baby. This was accomplished by photographing an actual opera singer, then tracking and modeling her mouth as a guide to the correct facial deformation of the cyber-scanned head and lip area of the pint-sized actress.

Producer: Digital Domain
Director: David Kellogg
Visual Effects Supervisor: Michael Gibson
Visual Effects Producer: Todd Isroelit
Animator: Andy Jones
Compositor: Lyse Beck
Executive Producer: Ed Ulbrich
Agency: Campbell Ewald

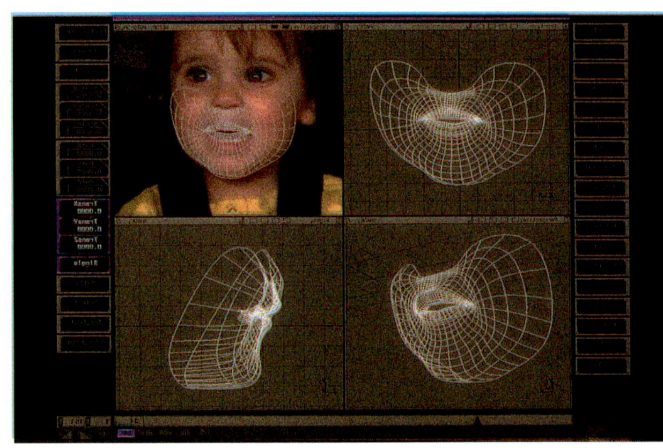

CONTACT
Bob Hoffman
Digital Domain
300 Rose Avenue
Venice, California 90291 USA
+1.310.314.2981
+1.310.664.2701 fax
bhoffman@d2.com
http://www.d2.com

Barbie as Rapunzel

Once upon a time, in the world of computer animation there lived a sphere and a cube. They were unenlightened and were used everywhere. Along came 10 years of experience with many new tools and the cube and sphere were reshaped. They became organic, with movement, hair, and soft textures. This transformation was truly magical and scientific, pretty as a painting with emotion and life. Such is the world of Barbie and Ken.

Producer: Windlight Studios
Client: Mattel Inc.
Director of Creative Advertising Services: Ken Kauffmann
Creative Manager: Aki Umemoto
Computer Animation: Windlight Studios
Creative Director: Don Bajus
Director: Ron Pitts
Technical Direction: Dave Novak and Scott Dyer
Executive Producer: Pam Lehn
Animation: Ron Pitts, Brian Newlin, Joan Staveley
Barbie & Ken Models: Evan Olson, Orie Hegre, Waki Mudi
Set: Dave Novak, Kevin Ochs
Color & Lighting: Dave Novak
Hair: Scott Dyer
Lip & Eye Sync: Don Bajus, Evan Olson
Music: Phil Marshall
Special Thanks to: Alias|Wavefront, Charlie Larson, Toby Timion, Mike Burton, Doug Kingsbury, Nancy Zwiers, Lisa Hodder, Maria Rodriguez, Charles Hubbell, Charity Jones

CONTACT
Pam Lehn
Windlight Studios
702 North First Street
Minneapolis, Minnesota 55401 USA
+1.612.339.9091
+1.612.339.8991 fax
pam@windlight.com
http://www.windlight.com

Batman & Robin

Featuring freeze rays, freezing people, city extensions, and CG vehicles, this piece is comprised of excerpts from the feature film.

Producer: Warner Digital Studios
Visual Effects Supervisor: Wendy Rogers
Visual Effects Producer: Ken Wallace

CONTACT
Suzanne Datz
Warner Digital Studios
1935 Buena Vista Street
Burbank, California 91504 USA
+1.818.977.8452
+1.818.977.0530 fax
sdatz@warnerdigital.com

BBC Autumn On One

All three sequences were created in Alias. Proprietary software, HardImage, was used to create the gentle lantern movement, paper textures, and depth of field. Ray-tracing produced the yoyos' multiple internal refractions, with motion blur enhancing the movement. The complex animation in "Tea Party" created as much action as possible.

Producer: Janice Beale
Contributors: BBC Graphic Design
Designers: Jane Walker, Ahmet Ahmet
Producer: Janice Beale
Post Production: The Moving Picture Company
3D Computer Animation Tea Party: Paul Franklin
3D Computer Animation Lanterns: Eric de Boer
3D Computer Animation Yo Yo: Nigel Hardwidge, Jane O'Callaghan

CONTACT
Amanda Libotte
The Moving Picture Company
25 Noel Street
London W1V 3RD
UNITED KINGDOM
+44.171.434.3100
+44.171.734.9446 fax
amanda-l@moving-picture.co.uk
http://www.moving.picture.co.uk

Bell Atlantic "Big Deal"

In this spot for Bell Atlantic, a computer-generated phone cord bursts with personality and goes through many complex choreographies to illustrate the new calling services being offered by Bell Atlantic.

Producer: Cindy Brolsma
Agency Credits:
Agency: Draft Direct/NY
Client: Bell Atlantic
Product: Bell Atlantic
Producer: Sue Rafter
Art Director: Ted Eyes
Blue Sky Studios Inc. Credits:
Director: Carlos Saldanha
Producer: Cindy Brolsma
Animators: Ed Gavin, Steve Talkowski, Aimee Whiting
Modelors: Ed Gavin
Lighting: Carlos Saldanha
Tech. Directors: Hilmar Koch
Editor: Fritz Archer

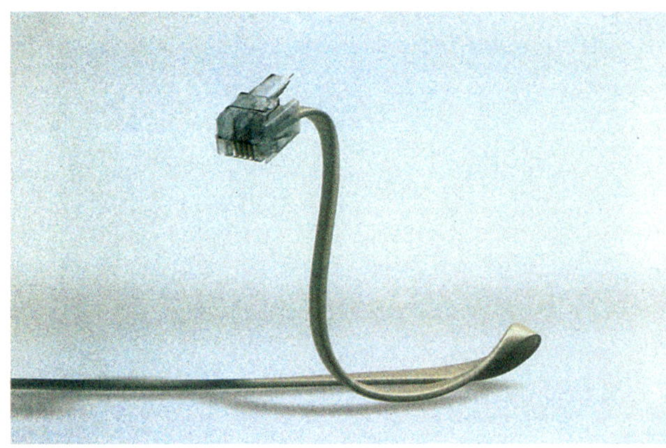

CONTACT
Alison Brown
Blue Sky Studios, Inc.
One South Road
Harrison, New York 10528 USA
+1.914.381.8400
+1.914.381.9790 fax
alison@blueskystudios.com
http://www.blueskystudios.com

Billy Ray Shyster's House of Discount Special Effects & Animation Emporium

"Billy Ray Shyster's House of Discount Special Effects & Animation Emporium" was inspired by locally-made television commercials that were produced in a style similar to this piece. Especially relevant were commercials that were outrageously goofy and obviously very low-budget. "Billy Ray" satirizes the cheap-and-cheesy computer-aided graphics that give this commercial genre such kitschy appeal.

Careful attention was paid to ensure that the quality level of this piece was nothing but the lowest. Colors are video-unsafe, blue-screening is abysmally poor, and craftsmanship in general is intended to represent the nadir of the computer graphics genre.

Producer: Paul Kevin Thomason
Concept, Video, and Animation:
Paul Kevin Thomason
Video Editing: Jeff Griswold

Produced in the Texas A&M University Visualization Laboratory
Master of Science in Visualization Sciences
Course VIZA 643: Video/Photography

CONTACT
Paul Kevin Thomason
Texas A&M University Visualization Laboratory
216-A Langford Center
College Station, Texas 77843-3137 USA
+1.409.845.3465
+1.409.845.4491 fax
kt@viz.tamu.edu
http://www-viz.tamu.edu

BodyVenture

This animation shows the inner workings of the human digestive system, the formation of plaque on artery walls, and the effects of arthritis on bone and cartilage.

Producer: Engineering Animation, Inc.

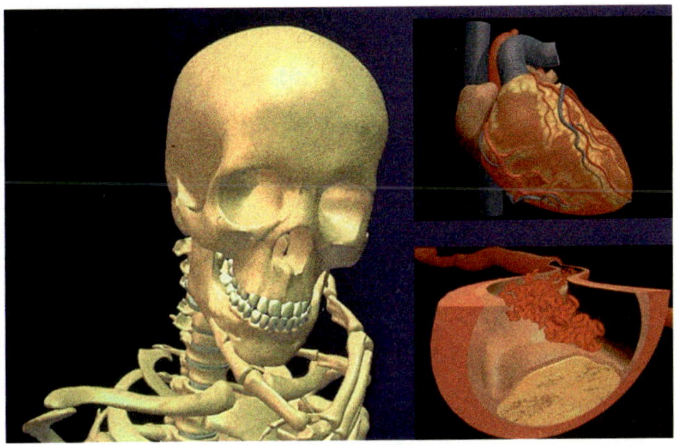

CONTACT
Engineering Animation, Inc.
2321 North Loop Drive
Ames, Iowa 50010 USA
+1.515.296.9908
+1.515.296.9944 fax
http://www.eai.com

The Box

"The Box" is about finding something in life that brings meaning and change to you. Meaning is very important to each of us and can be anything and found anywhere in life.

Producer: Thomas J. Barter Jr./
Ringling School of Art and Design
Concept and Animation:
Thomas J. Barter Jr.
Audio Mix: Thomas J. Barter Jr.
Faculty Advisor: Ed Cheetham
Video/Audio Support: Phil Chiocchio
Software: Alias PowerAnimator 7.5,
Composer 4.0.3, Studio 16
Hardware: Silicon Graphics Indy R4400

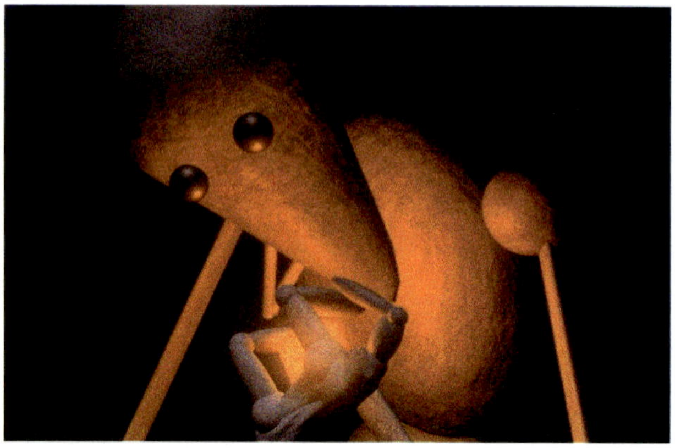

CONTACT
Thomas J. Barter Jr.
Computer Animation Department
Ringling School of Art and Design
2700 North Tamiami Trail
Sarasota, Florida 34234 USA
+1.941.359.7536
+1.941.359.7517 fax
mpalazzi@rsad.edu
http://www.rsad.edu

Butterflies in the Rain

A sunny dance studio comes to life as a butterfly explores a piano which is, mysteriously, being played by water droplets falling from above.

Producer: Mark Fontana
Contributors: Kirk Bowers, Steve May,
Phil Massimi, Brad Winemiller

CONTACT
Mark Fontana
The Ohio State University
Advanced Computing Center for the Arts and Design (ACCAD)
1224 Kinnear Road
Columbus, Ohio 43212 USA
+1.614.292.3416
+1.614.292.7168 fax
fontana@cis.ohio-state.edu
http://www.cis.ohio-state.edu/~fontana

Caltex Starpower

A glowing meteorite changes Caltex forever.

Producer: Brian Kassler
Contributors: David Green, Stuart Smith

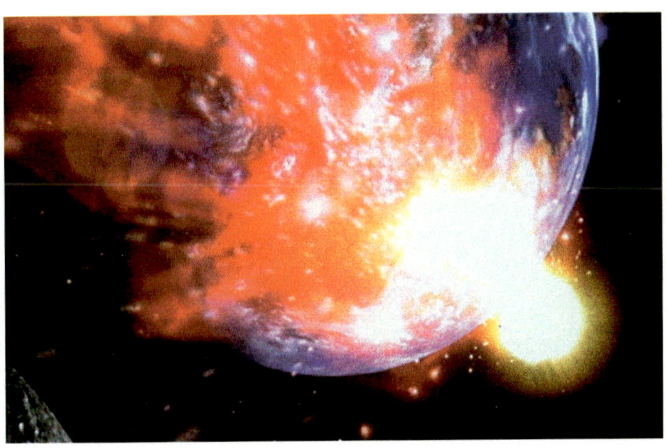

CONTACT
Stuart Smith
Animation Research Ltd.
Level 2, 4-50 Moray Place
Dunedin
NEW ZEALAND
+64.3.477.2995
+64.3.479.9751 fax
stuart@arl.co.nz

Canada Dry "Domino"

How do you train more than two thousand penguins to act as a team in an attempt to garner a can of refreshing soda, only to fall in "domino" fashion all over each other? You create a cast of digital penguins!

Producer: Industrial Light & Magic

Special Visual Effects by Industrial Light & Magic
A Division of Lucas Digital Ltd.
Marin County, California

Director: Steve Beck
Producer: Beth McCombe
Production Manager: Luke Yaryan
Production Coordinator: Jennifer White
Production Assistant: Micheal McCarthy
Post Producer: Paul Hill
Post Production Assistant: Regina Gong
Post Supervisors: Kerie Kimbrell, Lori Muttersbach
Lead Technical Director: Alan Rosenfeld
CGC Visual EFX Supervisor: Guy Hudson
Technical Directors: Brian LaFrance, Will Anielewicz, Melva Young, David Hisanaka
Lead Animator: Izzy Acar
Animators: Ben Hayden, Steve Rawlins
Modeler: Alyson Markell
Enveloper: Aaron Ferguson
Enveloping Consultant: Andy Wang
Matchmovers: Guy Hudson, Keith Johnson, Alia Agha
Viewpainter: Linda Showers
Head of CG Commercials: John Benson
CGC Prod./Operations Manager: Sandra Scott
CGC Prod. Coordinator: Amy Beresford
CGC Prod. Assistant: Eric Schroeder
CG Resource Assistant: Dani Morrow
Video Technical Assistant: Carole Johnson

CONTACT
Vicki Dobbs Beck
Industrial Light & Magic
PO Box 2459
San Rafael, California 94912 USA
+1.415.258.2084
+1.415.721.3551 fax

Certified Public Accountants (CPA) "Pin Heads"

1. Cyberscan head
2. Animate/lip-sync
3. Create grid of nulls
4. Add z-movement
   Render z-depth maps
   Convert to ASCII
   Use python Scripts:
      Read ASCII z-depth
      Make and apply curve
         to corresponding pin
         in grid
      Write animated null file
5. Create RenderMan geometry
6. Bake 200 minutes/frame

Producer: Industrial Light & Magic
Director: Rich Shulze
Producer: Kip Larsen
Production Assistant: Chandra Clark
Post Supervisor: Forest Key
Lead Technical Director:
Doug MacMillan
Technical Directors: Kevin Sprout, Drew DiGenova, Marc Cooper
Animators: Kirk McKinroy, Drew Kausner, Dana O'Connor, Ken King
Modelers: Alyson Markell, Jim Doherty
Head of CG Commercials: John Benson
CGC Prod./Operations Manager: Sandra Scott
CGC Prod. Coordinator: Amy Beresford
CGC Prod. Assistant: Eric Schroeder
CG Resource Assistant: Dani Morrow
Video Technical Assistant: Carole Johnson

CONTACT
Vicki Dobbs Beck
Industrial Light & Magic
PO Box 2459
San Rafael, California 94912 USA
+1.415.258.2084
+1.415.721.3551 fax

Changing Heart - Opening 3D Sequence

This work is from the Imax opener for the Northern Territory's tourist commission.

Producer: Animal Logic
Contributors: Lindsay Fleay, David Dulac, Thomas Kayser, Melanie Ritchie

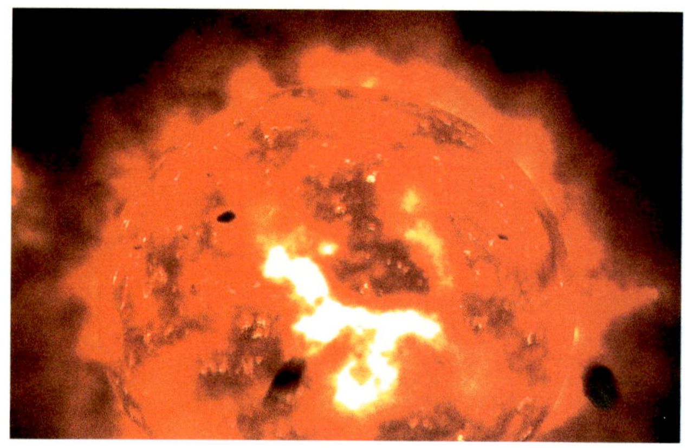

CONTACT
Albert Hastings
Animal Logic
123 Willoughby Road
Crows Nest, NSW 2065
Sydney AUSTRALIA
+61.2.99061232
+61.2.99067433 fax

Cheerful Country

In that cheerful country, tomatoes and mushrooms disturb you.

In that cheerful country, people touch each other and utter joyful cries.

In that cheerful country, I come close to a graceful creature.

Producer: ENSAD/Aii
Author: François Vogel
Music: François Vogel

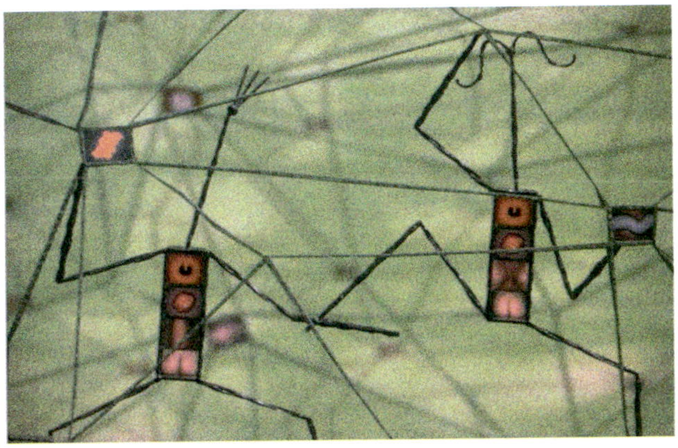

CONTACT
Pierre Henon
ENSAD/Aii
31 rue d'Ulm
75240 Paris Cedex 05 FRANCE
+33.1.53.73.24.80
+33.1.53.73.24.90 fax
pierre@ensad.fr
http://www.ensad.fr

A Cloud is Born

This animation features the formation and fly-through of a volumetric cloud created by combining implicit functions and procedural, turbulence-based, volume density functions. The cloud's geometry and animation are procedurally controlled and its illumination and shadowing are physically-based.

Producer: David S. Ebert
Contributors: David S. Ebert, James Kukla, Ted Bedwell, Susan Wrights

CONTACT
David S. Ebert
University of Maryland Baltimore County
CSEE Department, ECS 210
1000 Hilltop Circle
Baltimore, Maryland 21250 USA
+1.410.455.3541
+1.410.455.3969 fax
ebert@cs.umbc.edu
http://www.cs.umbc.edu/~ebert

Congress Center Messe Frankfurt Visualization

This piece is a photorealistic architectural visualization used for Congress Akquisition before the building was finished.

Producer: ZGDV Computer Graphics Center
Contributors: Uli Spierling, Patricia Lobo Netto

CONTACT
Uli Spierling
ZGDV Computer Graphics Center
Rundeturmstr #6
64283 Darmstadt GERMANY
+49.6151.155.0
ulisp@igd.fhg.de
http://www.igd.fhg.de

Conscience

This piece depicts the deep agony of being confronted by the Lacanian "Other", and the subconscious deconstruction of transpersonal identity that ensues under its scrutiny. The characters are from "Chocolate", a Protozoa short.

Producer: Emre Yilmaz
Direction, Writing, Puppeteering: Emre Yilmaz
Character Concepts: Dan Hanna
Modeling: Dan Hanna, Bay Raitt

CONTACT
Emre Yilmaz
Protozoa, Inc
Protozoa, Studio 100
2727 Mariposa Street
San Francisco, California 94110 USA
+1.415.522.6569
+1.415.522.6522 fax
emre@protozoa.com
http://www.protozoa.com/~emre

Contact

This sequence begins with a NASA-like view of the Earth. The camera then pulls back through our solar system, the Ort cloud and various galaxies and nebulae to the end of the Universe. It continues through a computer-generated eye that blends into the face of our young heroine.

Producer: Sony Pictures Imageworks
Sr. VFX Supervisor: Ken Ralston
VFX Supervisor: Stephen Rosenbaum
Art Director: Marty Kline
Sr. VFX Producer: Debbie Denise
VFX Producer: Julia Rivas
CG Supervisors: Ron Brinkmann, Jerome Chen
Lead Technical Directors: David Jones, Laurence Treweek, Ken Hanh, Jay Redd, Rick Stringfellow, Sam Richards, Mike Perry
Compositors: Bart Giovanetti, Steve Kennedy, Greg Leigy, Scott McKee, Colin Campbell, Michael Harbour, Richard Turner, Kenneth Dackerman, Michael Conte, Colin Drobnis, Betsy Cox, John Rauh
Rotoscope Artists: Maura Alvarez, Lisa Kshatriya, Gimo, Lynn Tigar, Joannie Karnowski, Matthew Capaldo, Mary Nelson, Aaron Smith, Loree Perrett, Krystine Kryttre, Suzy Brown, Megan Brown, John Aretakis
Painters: Kerry Nordquist, John McGee, April Knobbe, Ivo Horvat
Modeler: Marty Havaran
Technical Assistants: Beth Arko, Doug Yoshida, Tim Llewellyn, John Ly, Sean Callan, Jackson Yu, Stephanie Justice, Christian David Juen, Anthony Serenil
Production Assistants: Daniel Kuehn, Jamie Stevenson, Laura Jean McBride
Art Department: Deborah Silverman, Peter Gornstein, Marzette Bonar

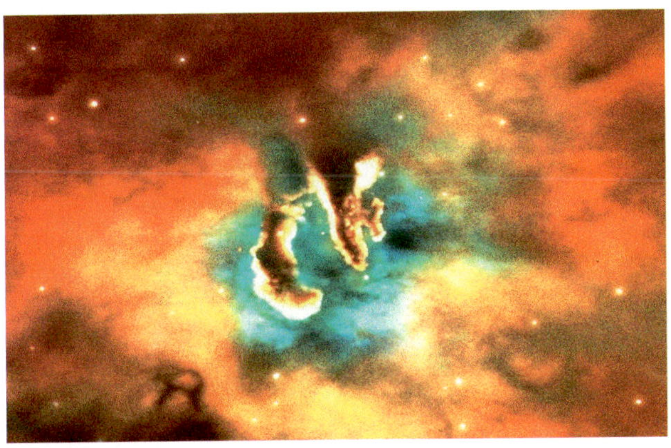

Technical Directors: Clint Hansen, Sho Igarashi, Brian Van't Hul, Dylan Robinson, Matt Farrell, Spender Knapp, Mike McNeil, Jim Berny, Rodney Iwashina, Erik Krumrey, Dean Foster, Daryl Munton, Clunie Holt, Dave Witters
Junior Technical Directors: Kiki Candella, Max Bruce, Lydon Li, Viviana Palacios, John Lee, Geoffory Harvey
Animators: Eric Armstrong, Dave Valone, Kevin Huston, Kelvin Lee, Robin Linn
DPM: Audrea Topps-Harjo
Associate Producers: Megan Jones, Mageara Cameron, Amy Wixson, Ron Vargas, JW Compare, Guy Wiedmann

CONTACT
Ken Ralston, President
Steve Rosenbaum, Supervisor, Special Effects
Sony Pictures Imageworks
9050 West Washington Boulevard, Suite 3120
Culver City, California 90232 USA
+1.310.840.8234
+1.310.840.8243 fax
sir@spimageworks.com
http://www.sonypix.com

'Cowboy' by Noriuki Makihara

This work is a narrative-based CG promo featuring Datacowboy in his debut role.

Producer: Me Company
Contributors: Lost In Space

CONTACT
Alistair Beattie
Me Company
14 Apollo Studios
Charlton Kings Road
London NW5 2SA UNITED KINGDOM
+44.171.482.4262
+44.171.284.0402 fax
meco@meco.demon.c.uk

Critical Depth

"Critical Depth" is an introduction, and part of the ending for a game to be released by Sony and Microsoft this summer. The beginning details the unfortunate fate of the submarine pilot who discovers the alien threshold that forms the basis for the gameplay. The conclusion serves as a generic ending that will lead to a more specific ending, depending on the type of character the player has chosen.

Producer: Benjamin Harrison, Argonaut 3D Graphics
Contributors: Matthew Harrison, Tyler Williams, Bob Lee, Steve Argyle

Deadly Mister Misty

This work tells the story of a little girl, her grandmother, and an icy cold drink.

Producer: Alison Colman
Contributor: Eva Sandor

CONTACT
Benjamin Harrison
Argonaut 3D Graphics
1900 North Canyon Road
Provo, Utah 84604 USA
+1.801.373.7040
+1.801.373.7250 fax
benjamin@argonaut3d.com
http://www.argonaut3d.com

CONTACT
Alison Colman
Advanced Computing Center for the Arts and Design
1224 Kinnear Road
Columbus, Ohio 43212 USA
+1.614.292.3416
arcolman@cgrg.ohio-state.edu
http://www.cgrg.ohio-state.edu/~arcolman/

digital Smoke

"digital Smoke" is an attempt to simulate small-scale smoke plumes. It is based on a direct physical simulation and uses radiosity volume rendering.

Producer: John R. Anderson

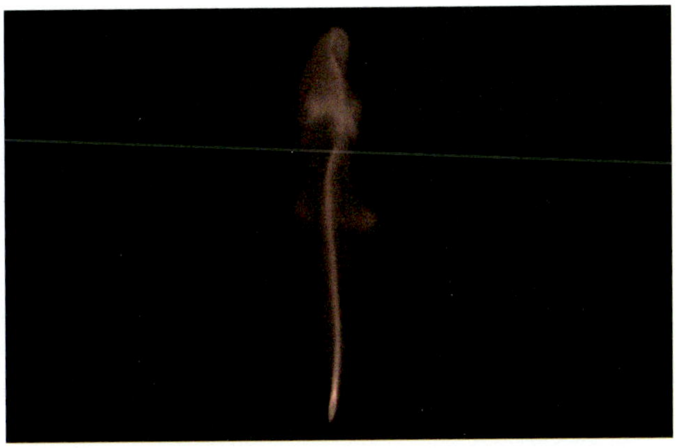

CONTACT
John R. Anderson
U. Wisconsin-Madison SSEC
1225 West Dayton Street
Madison, Wisconsin 53713 USA
+1.608.262.0783
+1.608.262.5974 fax
anderson@ssec.wisc.edu

Digital Truth in Tian An Men

Everybody has seen or heard of the events at Tian An Men. But the demonstration was crushed during the night when no cameras were filming.

Because of this, actual footage was used as the foundation for the continuation of the story using computer images to tell the digital truth.

Manipulation of images is not used by dictators (Hitler, Stalin, Mao), is not used for entertainment (Zelig, Forrest Gump), but for freedom (Amnesty International).

Software: Buf Software, Mental Ray, Softimage, Flint, T_Morph, Eddie, Alias, Wavefront
Producer: Premiere Heure - Buf Compagnie
Contributors: Pasquale Croce, Arnauld Lamorlette

CONTACT
Marianne Barcilon
Buf Compagnie
9, Avenue de Villiers
75 017 Paris FRANCE
+33.1.47660200
+33.1.47660302 fax
ofely@buf.imaginet.fr

"DJ Asylum" - the Orb

This work presents an animated look at the constructivist style based in a ficticious utopian world.

Contributors: Douglas Carney, Adrian Dimond, Robert Bial, Kathleen Judge

CONTACT
Benjamin Stokes
H-Gun Labs
1415 North Dayton Street
Chicago, Illinois 60622 USA
+1.312.787.4486
+1.312.787.6434 fax
HGun@earthlink.net

The DNA Story

This piece depicts a virtual voyage deep inside the cell nucleus to its valuable contents: the DNA, carrier of the coded information necessary for all life. Based on the latest discoveries of the nuclear organization, this work shows DNA transcription, replication and condensation into a mitotic chromosome.

Producer: Digital Studio SA
Director: Andreas Koch
Computer Graphics Supervisor: David Gould
Computer Systems Supervisor: Laurent Larsonneur
Written by: Laurent Larsonneur & Andreas Koch
Computer Graphics Artists: Jerome Boulbes, Laurent-Luc Burtin, Franck Chedozeau, Roberto Daniele, Laurent Larapidie, David Ouanono, Pascal Rouquie
Computer Graphics Software Developers: David Gould, Francis Roux-Serret
Production Assistants: Pascale Mansion, Valerie Lafon, Karine Roulland
Technical Assistant: Jean-Pascal Plettener
Graphic Assistant: Catherine Blanc, David Bonet-Maury, Mathias Ducloux
Scientific Assistant: Didier Casane
Narrator: Dana Westberg
Sound Mixing: Jean-Paul Queste
Music by: Philippe Valembois
Special thanks: Christian Sardet - Centre National de la Recherche Scientifique, Thierry Fouquet - Mobilis Productions

CONTACT
Laurent Larsonneur
Digital Studio SA
12, rue Vivienne
75002 Paris FRANCE
+33.1.42.60.42.60
+33.1.42.60.37.37 fax
llarsonn@digitalstudio.com

"A Drug Against War" KMFDM

This animation's bold, comic-book style speaks out against the ills of war.

Producer: Barbara Schwarz and James Deloye

Contributors: Eric Koziol, Adrian Dimond, Benjamin Stokes, Jon Schnepp, Brute!

CONTACT
H-Gun Labs
1415 North Dayton Street
Chicago, Illinois 60622 USA
+1.312.787.4486
+1.312.787.6434 fax
HGun@earthlink.net

A Dummy Affair

Murphy's Law states that if something can go wrong, it will. Combine this with the dark, romantic mood of Romeo and Juliet and you have the theme of "A Dummy Affair". The situation is a "must adapt" environment which requires a desperate last-minute solution.

Producer: Jason Giddings/Ringling School of Art and Design
Concept and Animation: Jason Giddings
Audio Mix: Jason Giddings
Faculty Advisor: Claudia Cumbie-Jones
Video/Audio Support: Phil Chiocchio
Software: Alias PowerAnimator, Composer
Hardware: SGI Indy

CONTACT
Jason Giddings
Computer Animation Department
Ringling School of Art and Design
2700 North Tamiami Trail
Sarasota, Florida 34234 USA
+1.941.359.7536
+1.941.359.7517 fax
mpalazzi@rsad.edu
http://www.rsad.edu

Dustcity

Producer: Universite de Provence/Lakanal

Emaki

Emaki is a traditional form of Japanese storytelling. This piece is an original story made in that genre.

Producer: Keiji Yamauchi, Hiroshi Abe
Contributors: Keiji Yamauchi, Hiroshi Abe

CONTACT
Drouin Sebastian/Mutin Christophe/Dumont Olivier
Universite de Provence
224-228 rue du Fauboure
Saint Antoine 75012
Paris FRANCE
+33.1.47.66.02.00
seb@buf.fr

CONTACT
Keiji Yamauchi
Dentsu Tec Inc.
Digital Design Dept.
1-8-9, Tsukiji, Chuo-ku
Tokyo 104 JAPAN
+81.3.5551.8828
+81.3.5551.9877 fax

Enhanced Processor Lifetime Through Deuterium Processing

This animation illustrates the recent discovery of enhanced transistor life through deuterium passivation processing.

Producer: Barbara Mason Fossum & Benjamin Grosser
Director: Barbara Mason Fossum
Lead Animator, Modeler, Editor, Composer: Benjamin Grosser
Animation, Modeling: Felix Wong, Joanna Wozniak
First-Generation: Steve Weintz, Derek Storr, Amy Ryan, Joe Lohmar
Model-Conversion Software Development: Chris Trimble, Joe Lohmar, Benjamin Grosser

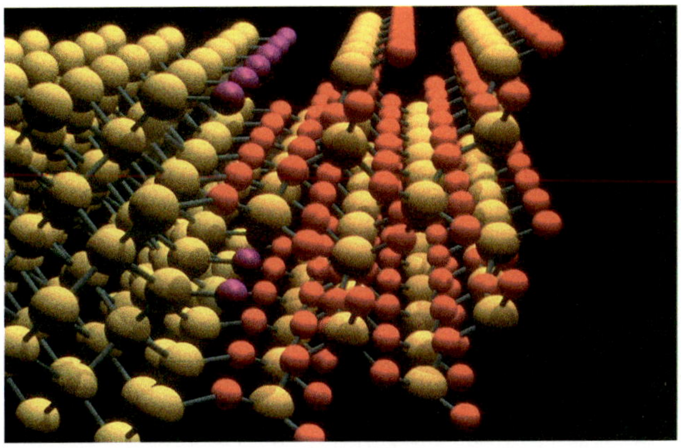

CONTACT
Barbara Mason Fossum & Benjamin Grosser
Beckman Institute Visualization Facility
405 North Matthews
Urbana, Illinois 61801 USA
+1.217.244.4464
+1.217.244.8371 fax
b-fossum@uiuc.edu, grosser@uiuc.edu

"Equus" The Legend of the Unbridled Spirit

"It was then you heard a voice whisper... come with me and you followed... "

The spirit of Equus takes you on an inspiring journey transformed by the elements of fire, earth, air, and water, as it evolves through space and time.

Producer: Alethea Pappas
Contributors: Alethea Pappas and Pat Batrynchuk

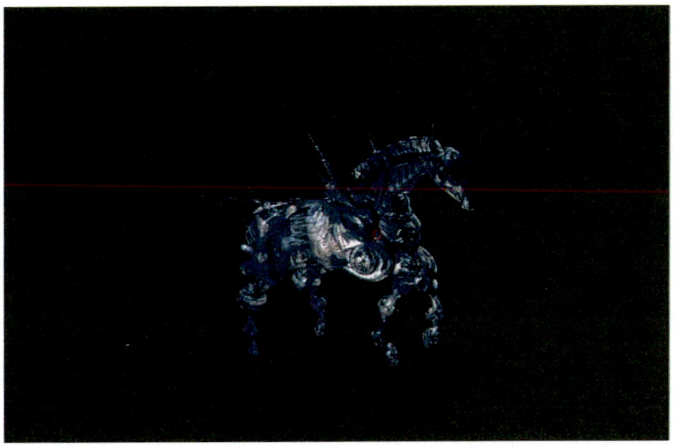

CONTACT
Alethea Renee Pappas
P.O. Box 1673
Pacific Palisades, California 90272 USA
+1.310.473.1041
+1.310.473.1042 fax

F8

F8 is a tragicomedy about the conflict between man and machine. This twisted tale is about a humorous old man's relationship with a vending machine as he pursues a bag of pork rinds.

Producer: Michael J. Clausen/Ringling School of Art and Design
Concept and Animation: Michael Clausen
Music Composer: DJ Cassel, RSAD cd library
Audio Mix: Steve Baker
Faculty Advisor: Jim McCampbell
Video/Audio Support: Phil Chiocchio
Software: Alias PowerAnimator, Composer, Studio 16, Photoshop, 3Design
Hardware: Silicon Graphics Indy

CONTACT
Michael J. Clausen
Computer Animation Department
Ringling School of Art and Design
2700 North Tamiami Trail
Sarasota, Florida 34234 USA
+1.941.359.7536
+1.941.359.7517 fax
mpalazzi@rsad.edu
http://www.rsad.edu

FACADE: Modeling and Rendering Architecture from Photographs and The Campanile Model

The first part of this video describes UC Berkeley's Facade photogrammetric modeling system, emphasizing developments made since it was presented in the SIGGRAPH 96 paper "Modeling and Rendering Architecture from Photographs". Facade allows a user to build photorealistic models of architectural scenes from a small number of still photographs. Recent developments allow for the recovery of arches and surfaces of revolution and can render the recovered models in real time on standard graphics hardware.

The second part of the video is a creative piece entitled "The Campanile Model" which plays on the visual relationship between Berkeley's bell tower, a model miniature of the tower, and a computer model of the tower and surrounding environment. The computer model was created with the Facade system from twenty photographs, including a few photographs taken above the tower from a kite. This model represents the first time a fully immersive and photorealistic model of a real place has been captured. Significantly, this technique allows the director to experiment with and control the path of the camera during post-production, to match virtual camera motion to real camera motion, and to produce camera motion that would be impossible to produce with conventional photographic techniques.

In its principal shot, the film makes four transitions between reality and the virtual environment by matching the virtual camera motion to the real, handheld, camera motion recovered using the Facade system. A custom keyframe animation technique was developed to smoothly bridge the segments of recovered camera motion with arbitrary virtual flight paths.

Producer/Director: Paul Debevec
Modeling: George Borshukov, Jason Luros, Vivian Jiang, Paul Debevec
Visibility and Rendering Algorithms: George Borshukov, Yizhou Yu, Paul Debevec
Matchmove Artists: Jason Luros, Paul Debevec
Flightpath Algorithms: Sami Khoury, Paul Debevec
Flightpath Animation: Chris Wright, Paul Debevec
Camera Work: Chris Wright
Kite Aerial Photography: Charles Benton, Paul Debevec
Campanile Carillonist: Jeff Davis
Model Makers: Dorrice Pyle, Russell Bayba
Video Editing: Chris Wright, Charles Ying

Reconstruction Software and Algorithms: Paul Debevec, Camillo Taylor, George Borshukov, Jitendra Malik
Special Thanks to: Charlie and Thomas Benton, Peter Bosselman, Linda Branagan, John Canny, Magdalene Crowley, Brett Evans, Eva Marie Finney, Tim Hawkins, Carl Korobkin, Lindsay Krisel, Michael Naimark, Eric Paulos, Ellen Perry, Susan Marquez, Al Vera

CONTACT
Paul E. Debevec
387 Soda Hall #1776
Computer Science Division
University of California at Berkeley
Berkeley, California 94720-1776
USA
+1.510.642.9940
debevec@cs.berkeley.edu
http://www.cs.berkeley.edu/~debevec

Forty-two shapes and thirty-nine expressions were employed on three characters to simulate the natural facial expressions used during speech.

Producer: Joji Hayashi
Director: Joji Hayashi
Models and Animation: Joji Hayashi, Kenichi Someya, Naomi Takahashi, Yuichiro Toya

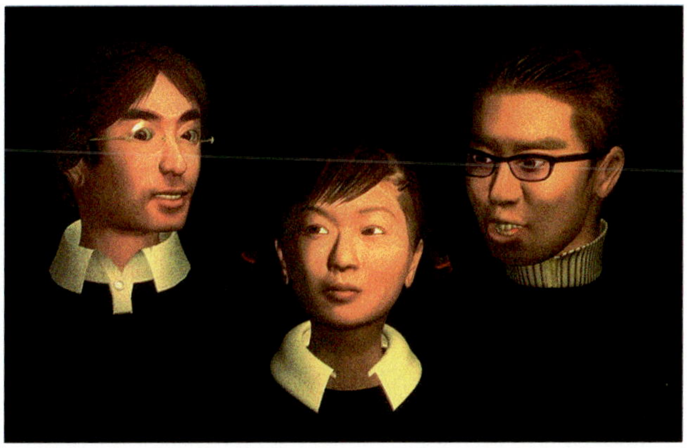

CONTACT
Joji Hayashi
SPICE Inc.
3-6-5 Shibaura, Minato-ku
Toyko 108 JAPAN
+81.3.3452.9821
+81.3.3452.9921 fax
+81.3.3452.9931 alternate fax
joji-h@po.iijnet.or.jp

Director Luc Besson's fantastical New York City of the 23rd century is realized through a combination of richly-layered CG effects and practical photography, at times incorporating over 80 combined elements. The character Leeloo's reconstruction was animated completely via CG, employing data from Alexander Tsiara's Body Voyage project.

Producer: Digital Domain
Special Visual Effects Supervisor:
Mark Stetson
Production Designer: Dan Weil
Digital Effects Supervisor:
Karen E. Goulekas
VFX Producer: Daniel J. Lombardo
Supervising Director of Photography:
Bill Neil
Lead Digital Compositing Supervisor:
Jonathan Egstad
Digital Compositing Supervisor:
Bryan Grill
VFX Editor: Debra Wolff
Art Directors: Ron Gress, Ira Gilford
Digital FX Producer: Tamara L. Watts
Miniature Effects Supervisor: Niels Nielsen
Unit Production Manager:
Crys Forsyth-Smith
Digital Supervisors:
Motion Control Supervisor:
Jeff Baksinski
Tracking Supervisor:
Maurice Bastian
Matte Painting Supervisor:
Rachel Kelley
Animation Supervisor:
Daniel Robichaud
Shader Supervisor:
Simon O'Connor

Sequence Supervisors:
Remo Balcells, Sean C. Cunningham, Sean Dever, Joshua I. Kolden, Christine Lo, Franklin Londin, Rodney J. McFall, Christopher Roda, Scott Stokdyk
Digital Artists:
Eric Barba, Miles Bellas, Dennis M. Blakey, David Bleich, John Michael Courte, Charles Darby, Lori L. Dreischmeier, Rick Dunn, Michael Edland, Michael Fadollone, John Ford, Jr., Brendan Gallagher, Wayne John Haag, Eric Hanson, Thomas Roland Johnson, Paul Kirwan, Carlin Kmetz, Hae-jeon Lee, Daniel Lemmon, Tom Lynnes, Anthony Mabin, Joe Mandia, Gray Marshall, Charles Meredith, Jeff Olm, Rocco Passionino, Darren Michael Poe, David Prescott, Renee Rabache, Scott Rader, Jay Randall, John E. Sasaki, Laura Scholl, Hudson Shock, Liza Sorotzkin, Greg Teegarden, Alfred Urrutia, Paul Van Camp, Christopher Walsh, Vernon R. Wilbert Jr., Tonia Young - Bilderbeck
Production Software Support:
James DiNunzio
Visual Effects Production:
VFX Prod. Coordinator/1st AD:
Kelly L'Estrange
VFX Prod. Coordinator:
Jonathan F. Styrlund
VFX Coordinator: Tracy Takahashi
CG Coordinator: Alissa Randall
CG Coordinator: Allyse Manoff
CG Coordinator: Mikella Kievman
Disk/Image Coordinator: Chris Bayz
Production Office Assistant:
Rebecca Brown

Scan/Record:
Scan/Record Supervisor:
Joseph Goldstone
Color Grader: Margo Bowie

SIGGRAPH Submission Production:
Allen Cappuccilli, Rob Doolittle, Kevin Susman

CONTACT
Bob Hoffman
Digital Domain
300 Rose Avenue
Venice, California 90291 USA
+1.310.314.2981
+1.310.664.2701 fax
bhoffman@d2.com
http://www.d2.com

Filter-Regulator-Lubricator

The task of the visualized pneumatic service unit is to filter, regulate, and lubricate compressed air for pneumatic installations. Filters free the air of dirt particles and water droplets, while regulators maintain the air supply at the desired pressure. Lubricators enrich the filtered air with a precise quantity of oil to protect the pneumatic actuators within the installation from mechanical wear.

Producer: Axel Thallemer
Contributors: Martin Danzer,
Roman Riedmueller,
Thomas Schneider

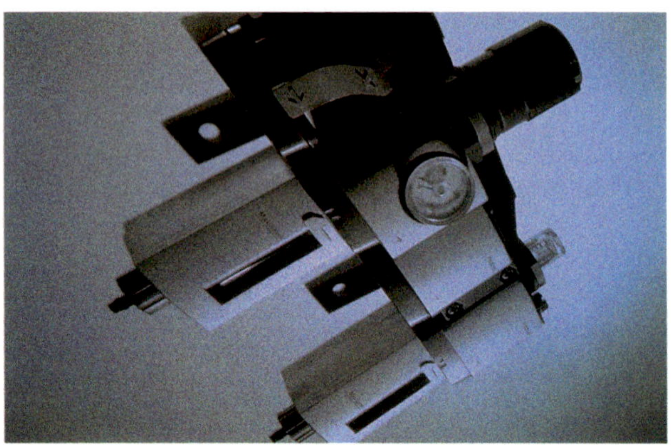

CONTACT
Martin Danzer
Festo KG
Corporate Design
Heugasse 1
D-73728 Esslingen GERMANY
+49.711.347.3850
+49.711.347.3899 fax
dnz@festo.de
http://www.festo.de

Flipbook

This reel is a collection of scenes created over the last year. Presenting these scenes as a flipbook echoes the computer animator's reliance on the flipbook tool essential to reviewing work.

Producer: Satoshi Kitahara

CONTACT
Satoshi Kitahara
Sega Enterprises, Ltd.
AM R&D Dept. #3
1-2-12, Haneda, Ohta-ku
Tokyo 144 JAPAN
+81.3.5736.7237
+81.3.5736.7264 fax
kitahara@mars.dtinet.or.jp

Flux

"Flux" is a composition of rhythm and motion combining the wacky computer animation of strange organic forms, bold cinemagraphic techniques and powerful music. Don't be afraid to get your butt up out of your chair and MOVE!!!

Producer: Jamie DeRuyter/Ringling School of Art and Design
Concept and Animation: Jamie DeRuyter
Music Composer: Eric Diane
Faculty Advisor: Jim McCampbell
Software: Alias PowerAnimator, Composer
Hardware: Silicon Graphics Indy Workstations

CONTACT
Jamie DeRuyter
Computer Animation Department
Ringling School of Art and Design
2700 North Tamiami Trail
Sarasota, Florida 34234 USA
+1.941.359.7536
+1.941.359.7517 fax
mpalazzi@rsad.edu
http://www.rsad.edu

Gabola The Great

"Gabola the Great" is a short work that tells the story of a vaudeville magician whose tricks don't work as planned.

Executive Producer: Carl Rosendahl
Direction, Animation, Story: Tim Cheung
Music: Marco D'Ambrosio
Sound Design: Erich Stratmann
Bloody Mess: Richard Chuang
Special Thanks to: Apurva Shah, Beth Hofer, Drew Olbrich, Gilles Dezeutre, Luca Prasso, Phillipe Gluckman, Scott Singer, Young Joo Paik, PDI Character Group

CONTACT
Judy Conner
Pacific Data Images
3101 Park Boulevard
Palo Alto, California 94306 USA
+1.415.846.8100
+1.415.846.8103 fax
info@pdi.com
http://www.pdi.com

Galaxy Guardian

"Galaxy Guardian" takes a light-hearted look at how rivalry and competition can drive the relationship between siblings. Growing up together can be hard enough without the added presssure of having to share a bedroom!

Producer: Stephen Baker/Ringling School of Art and Design
Concept and Animation: Steve Baker
Audio Mix: Steve Baker
Faculty Advisor: Ed Cheetham
Video/Audio Support: Phil Chiocchio
Software: Alias PowerAnimator, Composer
Hardware: Silicon Graphics Indy Workstations

CONTACT
Stephen Baker
Computer Animation Department
Ringling School of Art and Design
2700 North Tamiami Trail
Sarasota, Florida 34234 USA
+1.941.359.7536
+1.941.359.7517 fax
mpalazzi@rsad.edu
http://www.rsad.edu

General Motors EV-1 "Appliances"

For the EV-1 "Appliances" spot, over 500 animated appliances were required. Most were modeled and rendered with CG and composited side by side with puppets shot in live action. All appliances were animated in the last shot, using a combination of 2D images applied to patches and 3D fully-rendered models.

Producer: Industrial Light & Magic

Special Visual Effects by Industrial Light & Magic
A Division of Lucas Digital Ltd.
Marin County, California

Director: Joe Johnston
Producer: Kip Larsen
Director of Photography: Allen Daviau
Visual Effects Supervisor: Alex Seiden
Consulting Supervisor: Sandy Karpman
Lead Technical Director: Doug MacMillan
Lead Animator: Paul Griffin
Head of CG Commercials: John Benson
CGC Prod./Operations Manager: Sandra Scott
CGC Prod. Coordinator: Amy Beresford
Interns: Katrina Stovold, Andre Vitale
CG Resource Assistant: Dani Morrow
Video Technical Assistant: Carole Johnson
Assistant Technical Director: Tom Fejes
Production Designer: Chris Farmer
Production Manager: Laura Schifrin
Asst. Coordinator: Adrienne Anderson
Concept Art: Jonathan Harb
Post Supervisor: Lori Muttersbach

Technical Directors: Drew DiGenova, Eran Barnea, Brian LaFrance, Simon Cheung, Indira Guerrieri
TD Wrangler: Kevin Sprout
Animators: Marc Chu, Tim Stevenson, Izzy Acar, Steve Rawlins
Modelling Consultant: Wade Howie
Modelers: Brian LaFrance, Tim Stevenson, Izzy Acar, Steve Rawlins, Frank Gravatt
Matchmovers: Guy Hudson, Keith Johnson, Luke Longin, Corey Rosen
Rotoscoper/Viewpainters: Drew Klausner, Pat Jarvis
Viewpainters: Linda Showers, Derek Gillingham, Scott Bonnenfant

CONTACT
Vicki Dobbs Beck
Industrial Light & Magic
PO Box 2459
San Rafael, California 94912 USA
+1.415.258.2084
+1.415.721.3551 fax

(Genererik) L'Oeil du Cyclone

Funny and rhythmical, the generik of L'Oeil du Cyclone presents to you its boosted humanoid creatures which make you travel across fantastic universes.

Uncover your new friends of L'Oeil du Cyclone

EMITTEYE: Sattelite-spinningtop straight out of a mad professor's lab

COSMONEYE: Inflatable man magnetized with pilot eyes

CANONEYE: The most playful of the band members with his toy cannon arms

TELEYE: You're watching him while he's watching you

THE UNNAMED DANCER: Give her a name.

TELEVISEYES: He's become big-headed with a TV-shaped head

OCTOPUSEYE: His multi-ball eyes don't miss anything

Producer: CANAL+
Contributors: Mikros Image
Director: Eric Coignoux
Music: Lefdup & Lefdup, Jose Barinaga

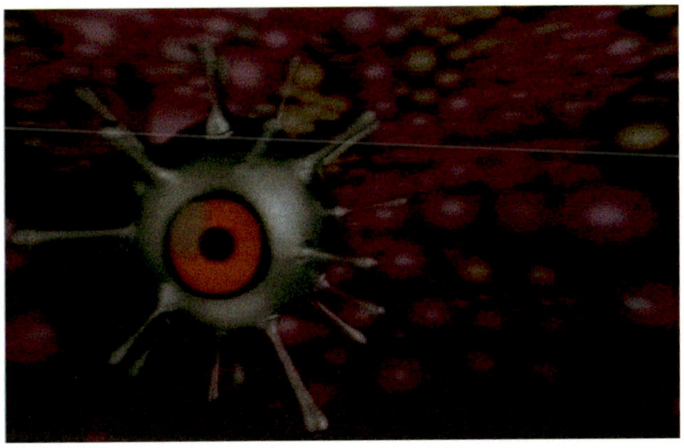

CONTACT
Marie-Laure Tardy
CANAL+
85/89 Quai Andre Citroen
75711 Paris CEDEX 15
FRANCE
+33.1.44257332
+33.1.44257374 fax

Geodesics and Waves

This video introduces geodesic lines as the straightest curves on arbitrary surfaces and studies point waves as a case in point. Geodesics are a suitable tool in the intrinsic definition of numerical algorithms on surfaces. The visualization of interfering waves on arbitrary surfaces uses a branched texture map technique.

Producer: Konrad Polthier
Director: Konrad Polthier
Numerics and Visualization:
Markus Schmies, Konrad Polthier
Modeling: Christian Teitzel
Animation: Martin Steffens
Music: Christoph März
Voice: Eric Hansen
Software: Orange, Grape, Softimage

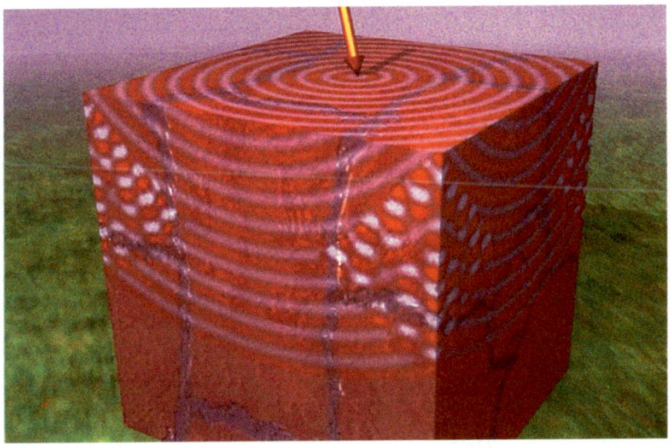

CONTACT
Konrad Polthier
Technische Universitat Berlin
Strasse des 17. Juni 136, FB Mathematic, MA 8-3
10623 Berlin GERMANY
+49.30.314.25782
+49.30.314.21577 fax
polthier@math.tu-berlin.de
http://www-sfb288.math.tu-berlin.de/~konrad/

The Ghost And The Darkness

Digital artists seamlessly integrated live-action lions with computer-generated elements to add intensity and suspense to the film. The lighting was digitally altered to allow left/right mirroring to correct lion eyelines. The lions' color and manes were also digitally altered.

Visual Effects by Sony Pictures Imageworks
Culver City, Californina

Visual Effects Supervisor: Tim McGovern
Visual Effects Supervisor/Producer: Stuart Robertson
Visual Effects Executive Producer: George Merkert
Visual Effects Producer: Joan Collins
Computer Graphic Supervisor: Ron Brinkmann
Visual Effects Art Director: Marty Kline
Senior Technical Designer: Jerome Chen
Visual Effects Editor: J.W. Kompare
Compositors: Scott McKee, Bob Peitzman, Colin Campbell, Randy Brown, Kiki Candela, Andrea Sholer, Megan Omi, Steve Kennedy, Isa AbdulBari Alsup
Digital Effects Animator: Mike Perry
Lead Rotoscope Artist: Nancy Oppenheim
Digital Painter/Rotoscope Artist: Suzy Brown
Rotoscope Artists: Maura Alvarez, Nancy Evans, John Shourt, Sue Kornfeld, Art David
High Speed Compositors: Mark Holmes, Sheena Duggal, Kristen Trattner, Ann Monn, Kelly Pappas
Assistant Visual Effects Editor: Guy Wiedmann
Visual Effects Coordinator: Chris Bailey
Visual Effects Coordinator: Ryan Berg
Computer Graphics Coordinator: Amy Hollywood Wixson
Visual Effects Assistant Coordinator: Yolie Moreno
Assistant Visual Effects Editor: Guy Wiedmann
Software Designers: Amit Agrawal, Chu Tang
Visual Effects Illustrator/Matte Artist: Ivo Horvat
Visual Effects Storyboard Artist: Peter Gornstein
Digital Production Manager: Gayle Reznik
High Speed Compositing Production Manager: Dawn Guinta
Lead Technical Assistant: John Decker
Technical Assistants: Doug Yoshida, John Clark
High Speed Compositing Technical Assistants: Tom Ford, Steve Dobbs
Head of Digital Production and Engineering: Bill Schultz
I/O Supervisor: Dennis Webb
Film Recording Software: John Strauss
Lead Film Recordist: Chris Leone
Film Recordist: Ken Kurras
Location Photography Visual Effects Producer: Mark Oppenheimer
Visual Effects Director of Photography: Chuck Schuman S.O.C.
Motion Control Programmer: Kevin Fitzgerald
Visual Effects Assistant Cameraperson: Ned Martin
Electronics Engineer: David Cornelius
Head of Camera Department: Marcus Kraus
Chief Mechanical Design Engineer: Barry Walton
Camera Equipment Coordinator: Allen Mansour
Mechanical Engineer: Chris Barker
Director of Systems Engineering: Alberto Velez
Senior Systems Engineer: Dean Miya, Todd Outten
Systems Administrators: Steve Kowalski, Rusty Case, David Takayama
Systems Coordinator: Katya Culberg
Software Coordinator: Audrea Topps Harjo
Production Assistants: Joy Kennelly, Lloyd Moss, Melissa Barber

CONTACT
Tim McGovern
Senior Visual Effects Supervisor
Sony Pictures Imageworks
9050 West Washington Boulevard, Suite 3120
Culver City, California
90232 USA
+1.310.840.8234
+1.310.840.8243 fax
tim@spimageworks.com
http://www.sonypix.com

"Ghosts" Motion Capture How-To

One goal of director Stan Winston's collaboration with Michael Jackson was to create an animated skeleton that could magically dance just like the master. This was accomplished through the performance capture of Michael's dancing on stage as the basis of the animated CG character. The skeleton was then comped into the live action plate photography.

Producer: Digital Domain
Director: Stan Winston
Visual Effects Supervisor: Ray Giarratana
CG Supervisor/Lead Animator: Randall Rosa
Performance Capture Supervisor: Andre Bustanoby
Digital Compositing Supervisor: Jammie Friday
Visual Effects Producer: John Kilkenny

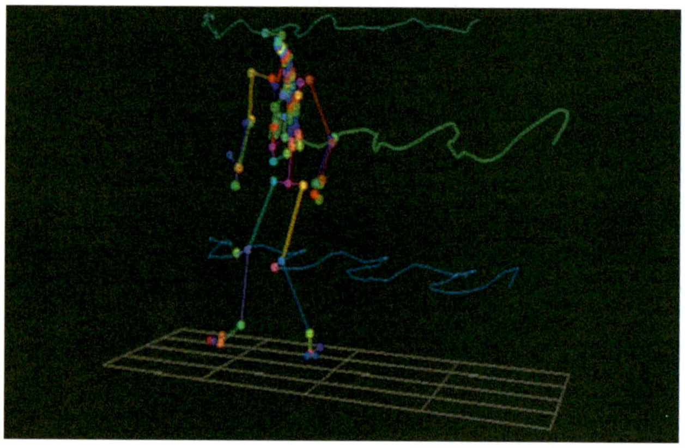

CONTACT
Bob Hoffman
Digital Domain
300 Rose Avenue
Venice, California 90291 USA
+1.310.314.2981
+1.310.664.2701 fax
bhoffman@d2.com
http://www.d2.com

The Giraffes of Mordillo

"The Giraffes" shows us smart and funny Giraffes, created by cartoonist Mordillo. Mordillo's characters and backgrounds create a world of volumes. 3D computer animation allows one to magnify it by adding the relief and depth which the author dreamed of in his comics.

Based on the character created by Mordillo

Producer: Fantome Animation, Dotin BV
Direction: Jose Xavier
Studio: Fantome
Hardware: Silicon Graphics
Software: Softimage

CONTACT
Georges Lacroix
Fantome
51, Rue Pierre
92110 Clichy FRANCE
+33.1.47372727
+33.1.47375596 fax
fantom@fantome.worldnet.fr
http://www.fantome.com

Good Vibrations

Voxels of two tomographic volumes were randomly placed on four walls of a box. The movement to their original location was influenced by two vibrations, which were overlaid using a weighting function. At every sampling time a new volume was created considering the current voxel positions and subsequently rendered.

Producer: Harald Evers
Contributors: Gerald Glombitza, Oliver Werner

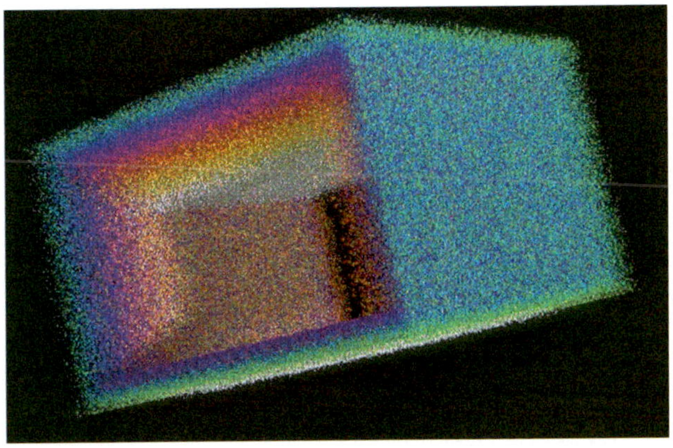

CONTACT
Harald Evers
German Cancer Research Center
Div. Medical and Biological Informatics / 0805
Im Neuenheimer Feld 280
69120 Heidelberg GERMANY
+49.6221.422325
+49.6221.422345 fax
H.Evers@dkfz-heidelberg.de
http://mbi.dkfz-heidelberg.de/mbi/mbi.html

Guten Appetit / good meal

The fridge represents the land of milk and honey for the little bugs. But the cook is coming. The conflict is similar to the battle between David and Goliath.

Producer: HFF-Potsdam-Babelsberg
Directing/Animation: B. Beyreuther, D. Binder, R. Zwirner
Sound: R. Pohle

CONTACT
Robert Zwirner
HFF
Muehsamstr. 35/37
10249 Berlin GERMANY
+49.0331.7215525
+49.0331.7215511 fax

Halls Penguins Airport

Pacific Data Images created ice-skating digital penguins and provided seamless live-action integration for this commercial. As the live-action footage was shot at night, there were significant amounts of shadow casting and ambient lighting to match.

Producer: Martin Oppus
Executive Producer: Denise Minter
Producer: Martin Oppus
Director: Eric Strand
Technical Director: Cassidy Curtis
Asst. Technical Director: Kristi Higgins
On-location TD: Noel McGinn
On-location Producer: Les Hunter
Lighting Director: Jeanie Cunningham
Lighting Specialist: Jin Liou, Sherry Hsieh
Character Motion: Fred Nilsson, Collin Hennen
Asst. Producer: Jennifer Dahlman
Rendering: Chanda Cummings
Agency: J. Walter Thompson, NY
Agency Producer: Gary Bass
Creative Director: Frank Constantini
Production Company: Morton Jankel Zander, Hollywood, CA
Producer: Lisa Rich
Live Action Director: Rocky Morton
Post Production House: Razor Boy, Los Angeles, CA
Editor: Louis Lyne

CONTACT
Judy Conner
Pacific Data Images
3101 Park Boulevard
Palo Alto, California 94306 USA
+1.415.846.8100
+1.415.846.8103 fax
info@pdi.com
http://www.pdi.com

Harvest

This work explores a figure's interaction with particle systems.

Producer: Xaos, Inc.
Creative Director: Mark Malmberg
Concept and Animation: Lisa Slates
Software Development and Sound Design: Sumit Das
Producer: Christina Schmidlin

CONTACT
Christina Schmidlin
XAOS, Inc.
444 DeHaro Street, #211
San Francisco, California 94107 USA
+1.415.558.9267
+1.415.558.9160 fax
@xaos.com

Heartbeat for "Where We Work"

Travel through the inner workings of the human heart, an architecture of pulsating ventricles and valves. This work seeks to portray an accurate 3D model softened by a more illustrative style.

Producer: Home Run Pictures
Animators: Dawn Lohmeyer, Wendy Jobe, Tom Casey
For RedHouse Communications: Pat Klug

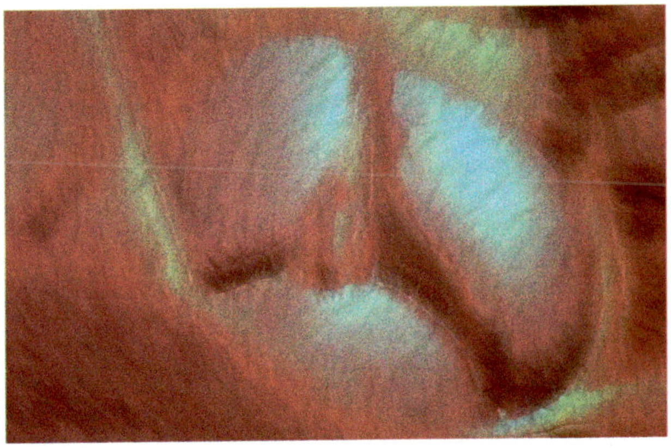

CONTACT
Tom Casey
Home Run Pictures
One Market Street
Pittsburgh, Pennyslvania 15222 USA
+1.412.391.8200
+1.412.391.0185 fax
tom@hrpictures.com
http://www.hrpictures.com

The Hologlobe

The Hologlobe displays Earth-science data in a unique educational and entertaining display at the Smithsonian National Museum of Natural History. The Hologlobe was unveiled by Vice President Al Gore last August as part of the Smithsonian's 150th birthday celebration. The Hologlobe images are moving images from atmospheric, oceanic, biologic, and geologic data that have been collected from satellite observations. The series of animations include a perspective of Earth as seen from the Galileo spacecraft as well as observations revealing water vapor, cloud cover, vegetation, sea surface temperature, El Nino, plate boundaries, earthquakes, and volcanoes. The Hologlobe project supports NASA's mission of communicating science to the general public.

Producer: Smithsonian Hologlobe
Director: Tom Watters
Institutional Contributors:
The Smithsonian Institution
National Science Foundation (NSF)
Defense Advanced Research Projects Agency (DARPA)
Global Change Research Program (GCRP)
National Aeronautics and Space Administration (NASA)
National Oceanic and Atmospheric Administration (NOAA)
Private Contributors:
Dynamic Media Associates (DMA)
New York Film and Animation Co.
Silicon Graphics Inc. (SGI)
Hughes STX Corp.

CONTACT
Barbara Summey
NASA Goddard Space Flight Center, Scientific Visualization Studio
NASA GSFC Code 935
Building 28, Room S121
Greenbelt, Maryland 20771 USA
+1.301.286.5797
+1.301.286.1634 fax
bsummey@okeeffe.gsfc.nasa.gov

Holograph

To create the effect of a man walking through a car, both were digitised, built in 3D, and animated to match motion control passes. There was also a pass of a cube, which was replicated in 3D to match the exact position of the man. Reflection, shadow and intersection mattes were composited in Flame.

Agency: DDB Needham, Dusseldorf
Producer: Annette Berkenbusch
Creative Director: John Meszaros
Production Company: Paul Weiland Film Company
Director: David Garfath
Producer: Mary Frances
Post Production: The Moving Picture Company
Flame Artists: Harry Jarman, Perri Wainwright
3D Computer Animation: Martin Costello, Andy Hall, Jane O'Callaghan

CONTACT
Amanda Libotte
The Moving Picture Company
25 Noel Street
London W1V 3RD
UNITED KINGDOM
+44.171.434.3100
+44.171.734.9446 fax
amanda-l@moving-picture.co.uk
http://www.moving.picture.co.uk

Home

For director Samuel Bayer, "Home" presents an audacious blend of miniature-model photographic elements with still photographs, digital matte paintings, and live action, creating a bleak urban landscape of the near future juxtaposed with a colorful rural setting.

Producer: Digital Domain
Director: Sam Bayer
Digital Effects Supervisor: Gray Marshall
Visual Effects Producer: Margaux Mackay
Animators: Lyse Beck, Craig Mullins, Alan Sonnemon
Executive Producer: Ed Ulbrich
Agency: M & C Saatchi

CONTACT
Bob Hoffman
Digital Domain
300 Rose Avenue
Venice, California 90291 USA
+1.310.314.2981
+1.310.664.2701 fax
bhoffman@d2.com
http://www.d2.com

human nature

"human nature" is about mankind's relationship with nature, one man's personal transformation, and a discovery of our relationship with nature.

Producer: Scott Carroll/Ringling School of Art and Design
Concept and Animation: Scott Carroll
Music Composer: Cremers/Jelmers
Audio Mix: Scott Carroll
Faculty Advisor: Ed Cheetham
Video/Audio Support: Phil Chiocchio
Software: Alias PowerAnimator, Composer
Hardware: SGI Indy

CONTACT
Scott Carroll
Computer Animation Department
Ringling School of Art and Design
2700 North Tamiami Trail
Sarasota, Florida 34234 USA
+1.941.359.7536
+1.941.359.7517 fax
mpalazzi@rsad.edu
http://www.rsad.edu

Hydra of Hercules

The mythological Hydra in Disney's "Hercules" is a fully computer-animated character within a traditionally animated film. As Hercules battles the Hydra, it grows from a single-headed beast into a 30-headed monster. The challenges were for the computer animation to match both the flexibility of movement of hand-drawn animation, and the graphic style of ink and paint characters.

Producer: Walt Disney Feature Animation
Contributors: The Hercules Crew of Walt Disney Feature Animation

I Want to Believe

A humourous look at the real story behind crop circles.

Contributors: Peter Ashford, Jayson Mackie, Geoff Martin, Kylie Robinson, Stephen Stedman

CONTACT
Edward Kummer
Walt Disney Feature Animation
500 South Buena Vista Street
Burbank, California 91521-4870 USA
+1.818.560.8210
+1.818.560.8194 fax
edwardk@fa.disney.com

CONTACT
Geoff Wyvill
University of Otago
Department of Computer Science
Box 56, Dunedin NEW ZEALAND
+64.3.479.8449
+64.3.479.8529 fax
geoff@cs.otago.ac.nz
http://atlas.otago.ac.nz:800/graphics/Geoff.html

Illumination

"Illumination" is a story about the relationships between desire, fear, and conflict. Fears are born out of desire, giving rise to what we experience as opposites. Conflict avoidance buries these already elusive relationships, intensifying our fears and desires. Facing fear is one approach to gaining understanding.

Producer: Vision International, A Division of Autometric
Gwenn Afton Bird: human modeling and animation, environment modeling
Kim Wallace: visual speech, environment modeling, color and light
Mike Darweesh: speech software, tool programming, rendering scripts
Mike Walsh: texture maps, modeling, color and light, story
Gregory Dismond: Creative/Technical Director, story, music
Interface Video: audio/video editing and sound effects
Naval Research Laboratory: Origin 2000 rendering
DARPA: Onyx rendering
Special Thanks: Mikee, Melissa Durley, Kirk Kern, Paul Leevy, Dushy Dismond, Mercedes Michelena, Andrew Wallace, Danny Bird

CONTACT
Gregory A. Dismond
Vision International, A Division of Autometric, Inc.
5301 Shawnee Road
Alexandria, Virginia 22315-2333 USA
+1.703.658.4081
+1.703.658.4021 fax
gregd@autometric.com

(IMC) The Dolphin

All the images in this piece were created by computer graphics. Each detailed movement of the fish was recreated by an original CG program, made possible through a careful study of living fish.

Produced by: Akio Kobayashi/Taiyo Kikaku Co., Ltd.
CG Producers: Masahiro Katsuta, Hitoshi Suenaga
Client: UNISYS
Agency: Asatsu
Directors: Katsuya Kaminuma, Kazuma Morino
Production Managers: Hitoshi Hasegawa, Ryo Uno
Editor: Hideto Kano

CONTACT
Kazuma Morino
Taiyo Kikaku Co., Ltd.
2-26-3 Nishishimbashi Minato-ku
Tokyo 105 JAPAN
+81.3.3436.4540
+81.3.3436.0175 fax
kazuma@t3.rom.or.jp

Impressions of San Francisco

This film was made entirely on Macintosh computers. Video was shot using a hand-held Hi-8 camera, then digitized and automatically processed to produce an animation with an Impressionist look.

Producer: Apple Computer, Inc.
Videographer, Animator and Director: Peter Litwinowicz,
Thanks to: Apple Computer, Inc., Gavin Miller, Sharon Pon, 71 St. Peter, Luis Rodriguez

CONTACT
Peter Litwinowicz
Apple Computer, Inc.
1059 Noe Street
San Francisco, California 94114 USA
litwinow@best.com

Inherited Memories

"Inherited Memories" explores the intertwining and transformation of photographic 2D compositing extended into animation. Based on photographs from Prague, Warsaw, and Krakow, it is a documentation of an imagined cultural past, built from layers of memories of times beyond personal experience.

Producer: Cynthia Beth Rubin
Contributors: Cynthia Beth Rubin, Bob Gluck

CONTACT
Cynthia Beth Rubin
Box 100
306 Thayer Street
Providence, Rhode Island 02906 USA
+1.401.274.7764
+1.401.351.2740 fax
cynthia.rubin@uvm.edu
http://www.uvm.edu/~crubin

Inside the Cell

A virtual trip based entirely on computer-generated 3D images showing the complexity of life inside the human cell, the basic living units of the body. We discover its beauty and complexity, the process of cell division (mitosis), and the process of transmitting genetic information.

Producer: Digital Studio SA
Director: Andreas Koch
Computer Graphics Supervisor:
Laurent Larsonneur
Original Story & Scientific Advisor:
Christian Sardet - Centre National de la Recherche Scientifique
Computer Graphics Artists:
David Ouanono, Jérome Boulbes, Laurent-Luc Burtin, Franck Chedozeau, Roberto Daniele, David Gould, Laurent Larapidie

Computer Graphics Software
Developer: Francis Roux-Serret
Production Assistants: Valerie Lafon, Karine Roulland
Technical Assistant: Jean-Pascal Plettener
Graphic Assistant: David Bonet-Maury
Text: Dana & Christian Sardet
Narrator: Dana Westberg
Music by: Philippe Valembois
Special thanks:
Jeff Halnon - Stereographics, Corp.

Interactive Learning and Teaching Environment

Using high-end animation, this piece presents an interactive learning and teaching environment. The animation focuses on an emergency situation making necessary the rapid identification of knowledge recources and the deployment of sophisticated simulation processes before the actual repair of a pipeline disrupted by an earthquake can take place.

Producers: Stefan Lehmann/
Thomas Overberg

Animation carried through within the research project SOPHIA-Digital Dissemination of Knowledge in the program in Computational Design, University of Wuppertal.

Project coordinator:
Prof. Dr. Mihai Nadin
Audio/Visual Media Center:
Wilfried Wilken, Uli Christmann,
Hardline Music Wuppertal:
Thomas and Chris
Technical Assistance: Thomas Goecke, Stefan Maehler

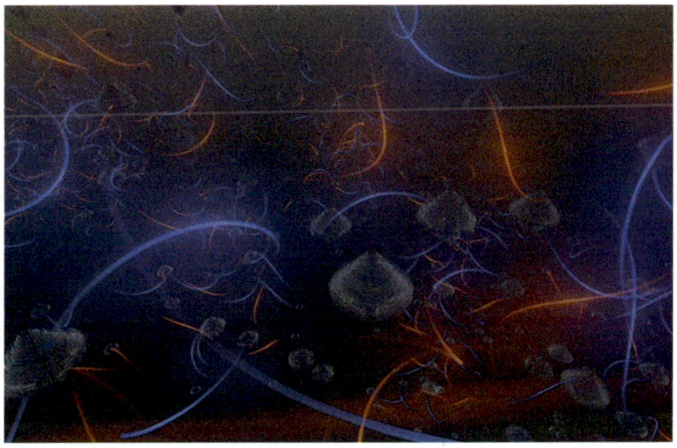

CONTACT
Laurent Larsonneur
Digital Studio SA
12, rue Vivienne
75002 Paris FRANCE
+33.1.42.60.42.60
+33.1.42.60.37.37 fax
llarsonn@digitalstudio.com

CONTACT
Stefan Lehmann
University of Wuppertal
Computational Design
Hofaue 35-39
42103 Wuppertal GERMANY
http://www.uni-wuppertal.de./code

CONTACT
Thomas Overberg
@computational design, Inc.
Robertstr. 5a
42107 Wuppertal GERMANY
+49.202.2442986
+49.202.2442987 fax
co-de@co-de.de
http://www.co-de.de

Interactive Virtual Environment Walkthrough

This work depicts a real-time, interactive, virtual walkthrough of Nanyang Polytechnic's new campus. It is a large-scale VR walkthrough application in which, starting from the blueprints, the entire campus is captured into a system where users can interactively walk through the campus.

Producer: Nanyang Polytechnic
Contributors: Kian Bee Ng and his students from Nanyang Polytechnic Singapore

CONTACT
Kian Bee Ng
Nanyang Polytechnic
20 Yishun Avenue 9
Singapore 768892 SINGAPORE
+65.750.3661
+65.755.5571 fax
nkb@pacific.net.sg
http://home.pacific.net.sg/~nkb

JACK

Some of life's greatest sorrows snap at the heels of what should be life's greatest triumphs. So it is with Jack, a jester who gets his legs and finds that all good things must come to an end. No motion capture was used in this animation.

Producer: Doug Pfeifer
Contributors: Doug Pfeifer, Brian Poer, Eric Speier, Mike Bundlie, Greg Anderson, Paul Churchill, David Couet, Todd O'Leary, Gary Bradt

CONTACT
Doug Pfeifer
IVI Publishing
7500 Fyling Cloud Drive
Minneapolis, Minnesota 55344-3739 USA
+1.612.996.6271
+1.612.996.6001 fax
dougp@ivi.com

Keizan Musouzu (A Reverie in the Mountains)

An excerpt from a ten-minute HDTV program, this piece uses a newly-developed algorithm, HD-CG. A 3D world of ink painting is created in which the viewer can vicariously experience the deep and expansive spiritual wealth of the East.

Producer/Director: Hideo Nakazawa
Executive Producer: Takao Kuroki
CGI Supervisor: Yoshikazu Taoda
CGI Animator: Takashi Fukaya
Software Development: Hiroyuki Sato
CGI Assistant: Koji Sato
Visual Effects: Shinji Nakamura
Animation Supervisor: Kazuto Kawazoe
Illustration: Susumu Mochizuka
CGI Designer: Masayuki Iida
Music: Appassionata

CONTACT
Hideo Nakazawa
NHK HDTV Division
2-2-1 Jinnan
Shibuya-ku
Tokyo 150-01 JAPAN
+81.3.3481.4971
+81.3.3481.1874 fax
nakazawa@hi-vision.nhk.or.jp

Kuru Kuru

Producer: Hiroshi Matsumoto
Composer: Yoshiyuki Usui

CONTACT
Hiroshi Matsumoto
NHK Enterprises 21, Inc.
CG Room
4-14. Daisan Kyodo, Building 4F
Kamiyama-cho, Shibuya-ku
Tokyo 150 JAPAN
+81.3.3481.9412
+81.3.3481.9413 fax

Kutchae!

This is one of the station identifications for MTV Japan. This work has been invited to the first International Animation Expo '97 in Seoul, Korea and has been airing on MTV Japan since Summer 1996.

Producer: Hironori Terai
Director: Isao Nishigori
Sound: Y. Miura / H. Takashima

CONTACT
Hironori Terai
MTV Japan: On-Air Promos
4-2-11 Shirokanedai
Minato-Ku
Tokyo 108 JAPAN
+81.3.5448.1108
+81.3.5448.1408 fax
oap-01@ar.aix.or.jp
http://www.mtv.co.jp/

The Landing Party

This animation, created at the University of Central Florida, is about an alien tour group that comes to earth and spends an evening at the Disney/MGM Studios. It depicts their arrival at the park, and some of their escapades while there. It ends with the arrival of daybreak and the realization that they must leave the park before they are discovered.

Producer: The University of Central Florida
Director: David Haxton
Assistant Director: Candace Skena
Second Assistant Directors:
Geoff Palmer, Betsy Walton
Head Technical Directors for:
Character Animation:
Victor Davila
Animation: Mike Victa
Modeling: Jon Erickson
Lighting: Geoff Palmer
Kinematics: Scott McGuirk
Special Effects: Edward Gross
Disney i.d.e.a.s. Participants:
Bob Allen, Jamie Foehner, Beth Fraikorn, Mark Kyle, Calvin Jobe, Mark Witherspoon, Calvin Kesterson
Animators: Jon Erickson, Geoff Palmer, Edward Gross, Chris Strecker, Victor Davila, Robert Baduini, Betsy Walton, Dave Magno, Jessica Dietrich, Kerri Gilpin, Kirk Nelson, Candace Skena, Mike Victa, Scott McGuirk, Ryan Broley, Tony Martino, Terry Parker
Modelers: Candace Skena, Jon Erickson, Geoff Palmer, Edward Gross, Chris Strecker, Victor Davila, Robert Baduini, Betsy Walton, Dave Magno, Jessica Dietrich, Kerri Gilpin, Kirk Nelson, Mike Victa, Scott McGuirk, Ryan Broley,

CONTACT
David Haxton
University of Central Florida, CREAT, Art Department
Orlando, Florida 32817 USA
+1.407.823.3110
+1.407.823.6470 fax
haxtond@aol.com
http://www.creat.cas.ucf.edu

Las Campanas Redshift Survey in 3D

The Las Campanas Redshift Survey contains data of the position and redshift of galaxies in six slices of the galactic universe. Each slice is 1.5 x 80 degrees. This 3D visualization clearly shows the textural quality of galactic space.

Producer: Home Run Pictures for WQED Pittsburgh
Animator: Tom Casey
For WQED Pittsburgh: Joe Seamans
Special thanks to: Bob Kirshner, Pete Challis (LCRS)

CONTACT
Tom Casey
Home Run Pictures
One Market Street
Pittsburgh, Pennyslvania 15222 USA
+1.412.391.8200
+1.412.391.0185 fax
tom@hrpictures.com
http://www.hrpictures.com

Levi's

This piece depicts mermaids taking a sailor into the depths of the ocean.

Producer: Partizan Midi Minuit
Director: Michel Gondry
Contributors: Pierre Buffin, Marie-Laure Laffitte, Olivier Luffin, Jérome Bacquet, Olivier Gilbert, Yves le Peillet, Christophe Dupuis, Eric Deltour, Stephane Naze, Pasquaale Croce, Geoffrey Niquet, Guillaume Niquet, David Verbeke, Bernard Stulzaft, Martin Fugerole, Sabine Castay
Software: Buf Software, Softimage, T_Morph, Elastic Reality

CONTACT
Marianne Barcilon
Buf Compagnie
9, Avenue de Villiers
75 017 Paris FRANCE
+33.1.47660200
+33.1.47660302 fax
ofely@buf.imaginet.fr

Lindbergh, ∞ and the Trans-Rational Boy

A young boy has constructed a perpetual motion machine powered by mice. The mice who power the machine monopolize the boy's attention as they make their passage across the sea. Simultaneously, Charles Lindbergh moves through time towards Paris. No miraculous transformations occur.

Producer: Joshua Mosley
Contributions of Technical Assistance From: Julie Goldstein, Donghyun Park, Jang Wook Lee, Jamie Raap

CONTACT
Joshua Mosley
The School of the Art Institute of Chicago
1319 West Estes, Apartment 16
Chicago, Illinois 60626 USA
+1.773.338.1572
jmosle@artic.edu

The Lost World: Jurassic Park

The CG imaging for "The Lost World" far surpasses the benchmark set in "Jurassic Park," further integrating CG dinosaurs into live-action environments. Five new dinosaur models were created, and the models from the first film were completely updated to permit naturalistic muscle and skin flexion, bone motion and breathing action.

Producer: Industrial Light & Magic

Dinosaur Visual Effects and Animation by Industrial Light & Magic
A Division of Lucas Digital Ltd.
Marin County, California

Full Motion Dinosaurs: Dennis Muren, A.S.C.
Dinosaur Animation Director: Randal M. Dutra
Visual Effects & Animation Producer: Ned Gorman
Computer Graphics Supervisor: Kevin Rafferty
CG Sequence Supervisors: Erik Mattson, Ben Snow
CG Development Supervisor: Euan MacDonald
Lead Digital Character Animators: Danny Gordon Taylor, Doug E. Smith, Miguel A. Fuertes, Daniel Jeanette
Associate Effects Supervisor: Rick Schultze
Digital Character Animators: George Aleco-Sima, Chris Armstrong, Linda M. Bel, Patrick Bonneau, David Byers Brown, Ken Bryan, Sue Campbell, Bruce Dahl, Pete Daulton, Lou Dellarosa, Michael Eames, Hal T. Hickel, Jason Ivimey, Paul Kavanaugh, Heather Knight, Victoria Livingstone, Julie Nelson, Dana O'Connor, Mark Powers, Magali Rigaudias, Chi Chung Tse, Tim Waddy, Brad Woods, William R. Wright
Digital Effects Artists: Kevin Barnhill, Michael Bauer, Michael DiComo, Christina Hills, Samir Hoon, Ed Kramer, Tom Martinek, Min, Curt I. Miyashiro, Patrick Neary, Kenneth J. Nielsen, Khatsho John Orfali, David Parrish, Bruce Powell, Amanda Ronai-Dahle, Corey Rosen, Frederic Schmidt, B. Durant Schoon, Jeff Shank, Doug Sutton, Christopher Townsend, John Walker, Andy Wang, Howie Weed, R. Christopher White
Digital Model Supervisor: Paul Giacoppo
Compositing Supervisors: Pablo Helman, Jon Alexander
Visual Effects Art Director: George Hull
Lead Viewpainter: Susan Ross
Lead Matchmover: Terry Chostner
Lead Roto Artist: Jack Mongovan
Location Matchmover: Jack "Edsel" Haye
Sabre Artists: Caitlin Content, Grant McGlashan
Digital Compositors: Tim Alexander, Jeff Doran, Mary McCulloch
Viewpainters: Donna Ashley Beard, Catherine Craig
Visual Effects Editor: Michael Gleason
Senior Effects Coordinator: Vicki L. Engel
Visual Effects Coordinators: Christine M. Owens, Megan I. Carlson

CONTACT
Vicki Dobbs Beck
Industrial Light & Magic
PO Box 2459
San Rafael, California 94912 USA
+1.415.258.2084
+1.415.721.3551 fax

Stage Effects Coordinator: David S. Dranitzke
Stage Manager: Edward T. Hirsh
Effects Director of Photography: Patrick Turner
Model Shop Project Supervisor: Lorne Peterson
Matchmove Artists: Selwyn Eddy III, David Hanks, Randy Jonsson, Jodie Maier, David Manos Morris
Rotoscope Artists: Christine Cram, Kate Elsen, Debbie L. Fought, Susan Goldsmith, Scott Charles Stewart, Michael Van Epps, Susan M. Weeks
Digital Timing Supervisor: Kenneth Smith
Digital Matte Artist: Paul Huston
Senior Scanning Operator: Randall K. Bean
Scanning Operator: Michael Ellis
CG Resource Assistant: Kimberly Lashbrook
Negative Line-up: Andrea Bilkian
Digital Plate Restoration: Melissa Monterossa
Assistant Visual Effects Editor: Greg Hyman
Projectionist: Kenn Moynihan
Software Development Supervisor: Christian Rouet
Software Development: Cary Phillips, Jim Hourihan, Rod G. Bogart
Video Engineering: Dana Barks
Computer Systems Engineering: Ken Beyer, Greg Dunn
Mechanical Effects: Geoff Heron
Stage Technicians: Billy Barr, Dick Dova, Bob Finley III, Mathew Heron, Tim Morgan
Visual Effects Camera Assistant: Vance Piper
Model Makers - Miniatures Unit: Giovanni Donovan, Michael Lynch, Robert Edwards, Rodney Morgan, Eben Stromquist, Grant Imahara, Ira Keeler, Barbara Affonso, Wendy Morton, Randy Ottenberg, Chris Reed, Steve Walton, Keith London, Ben Nichols, Phil Brotherton
CG Technical Assistants: Jennifer Nona, Michael Corcoran, Paul Vega
Production Assistants: Monique Gougeon, Alicia Magnant
Computer Graphics Staff: Barry Armour, Cliff Plumer, Ken Maruyama
ILM Senior Staff: Patricia Blau, Gail Currey, Chrissie England, Jeff Mann, Jim Morris

Lup 1 or, Natural Born Collector

Alone aboard his space yacht, the hero returns to earth to commit one last outrage. While admiring his collection of stolen articles, he dreams aloud about becoming a legend.

Producer: Pascal Chappuis, Laurent Fauchere and Nicolas Imhof
Contributors: Music of Antoine Coppey and Mike
Cast: Bernard Theler - 3 paintings of Yves Felley

CONTACT
Stephane Jeandrevin
ECAL - USINE (Art School of Lausanne, Unit of Computer Graphics)
Rue de l'Industrie 46
CH-1030 Bussigny - pres - Lausanne
SWITZERLAND
+41.21.702.95.55
+41.21.702.95.04 fax
stephane.jeandrevin@ecal.vd.ch

Mainstay Mutual Funds' Up... Down... Up...

Utilizing an elegant black and white wood-cut style, "Up... Down... Up...", combines traditional cel animation with new and unique techniques in 3D digital animation to create the overall "woodcut" 2D effect. More than 20 texture maps were hand drawn and applied to the 3DCG sea-serpent to give it just the right traditional effect. There are 17 texture maps applied to the head alone.

Producer: Betsy De Fries
Technique: Combined Traditional Cel and Digital Animation
Production: Wild Brain, Inc.
Director: John Hays
Executive Producer: Paul Golden
Production Manager: Leslie Arvio
Assistant Production Manager: Marc Galvan
Animators: J.T. O'Neal, Ralph Fernan
Assistants: Chris Carter, Lance Hughes, Dick Hill, Joe Sloan, Anna Blomfield, Amanda Tsoukanelis
Digital Animation: Little Fluffy Clouds
Animation Director: Jerry van de Beek
CG Producer: Betsy de Fries
Digital Compositing: Jerry van de Beek
Digital Ink & Paint: Keun Hicks
Sound Design/Music: Michael Boyd Music

CONTACT
Betsy De Fries
Little Fluffy Clouds
Pier 29 Annex
San Francisco, California 94111 USA
+1.415.956.8699
+1.415.956.8599 fax
betsy@littlefluffyclouds.com
http://www.littlefluffyclouds.com

Mandelbloom

Mandelbloom is an aesthetic piece which explores the relationship between fractals, flowers, and form. The film demonstrates the evolution of the Mandelbrot set as it evolves through its first several iterations. A new type of rendering technique utilizes texture-mapped roses to display the set at fractional iterations in order to reveal the connections between the Mandelbrot and its closely related Julia sets.

Producer: Lewis N. Siegel
Contributors: Dr. Benoit B. Mandelbrot
Derek Zimmerman

CONTACT
Lewis N. Siegel
USC MFA Animation Program
6538 1/2 West Olympic Boulevard
Los Angeles, California 90048 USA
+1.310.201.6597
lewis@cvfx.com

Mars Attacks!

This work is comprised of excerpts from the Tim Burton film "Mars Attacks!" featuring flying saucers and robot footage.

Producer: Warner Digital Studios
VFX Supervisor: Michael Fink
Production Supervisor: Ellen Somers
VFX Producer: Lauren Alexandra Ritchie
Digital FX Supervisor: Guy Williams
Art Dept. Supervisor/Matte Artist: Jesse Silver
CGI Lead - Robot: Brian Steiner
CGI Lead - Saucers: Chris Waegner
Technical Director/CG Landing Sequence: Bill Konersman
CG Artists: Rhett Bennett, Jeffrey Benoit, Heather Bushman, Vince DeQuattro, Adam Dotson, Jamie Engel, Mark Farquhar, Vincent M. Giordano, Kelly Hartigan, Christian Hatfield, Matthew Head, Roger Huynh, Todd Jahnke, Arthur Jeppe, Carolyn Ippisch, Hiroki Itokazu, Alice V. Kaiserian, James Kuo, David C. Lawson, Janice Lew, Shanna Lim, Aaron Linton, Mary E. Manning, Rob Ostir, Robert Shrider, David A. Smith, Evelyn Spencer, Kathi Spencer, Kenji Sweeney, Marc Toscano, Kelly Wilcox, Lindy Wilson, Genevieve Yee, Ingrid Yegros
Inferno Supervisor: Victor Jimenez
Inferno Artists: Fortunato Frattasio, John Kohn
2D Artists: Jillian Backus, Katie A. Tucker, Bonjin Byun, Craig Simms
2D Roto Artists: Michael Adkisson, Michael Hemschoot, Nicole Graham
2D Texture Artists: Darren Bedwell, Phil Carlig, Linda Shepard, Christine Serino
Matte Painters: Tim Clark, Michelle Moen
VFX Production Manager: Mimi Medel
2D VFX Production Manager: Lynn M. Gephart
VXF Assistant Coordinator: Lindsay Burnett
Model Prod. Coordinator: Casey Steele
On-Set Plate Manager: Bill Maher
Film Assembly Technician: Diane Caliva
Asst. Film Assembly Technician: Heather J. Morrison
Color Imaging Supervisor: Dave Gregory
Digital Camera Supervisor: Megan Bryant
Digital Color Lead: Jason Piccioni
Digital Camera Operator: Christopher Savides, Robert White
Tape Operations Lead: Michael Wilhelmi
Tape Operator: Walt Cameron
St. Lead/Systems Administration: Chris Steinke
Software Lead/Systems Administration: Kevin Smith
Hardware Lead/Systems Administration: Andy Chua
Systems Administration: Robert Gorichanez
Software Project Managers: Yun Chen Sung, Hiroyuki Miyoshi
Software Engineers: Cesar Velazquez, Phil Graham, Sosh Mirsepassi, Francesco Chiarini
Acme Models:
Acme Model Shop Supervisor: Michael Joyce
Modelmaker: Mark Ross-Sullivan, Ken Swenson

CONTACT
Suzanne Datz
Warner Digital Studios
1935 Buena Vista Street
Burbank, California 91504 USA
+1.818.977.8452
+1.818.977.0530 fax
sdatz@warnerdigital.com

Mass Manipulator

The idea presented in this piece is the representation of the abuse of power through the manipulation of people.

Producer: MTV Latino
Contributors: Nacho Mazzini, Leandro Panetta, Daniel Perez Llebot, Leopoldo Lovera, Swan Glacer, Carlos Pulido, Victor Wolansky, Victor Melton, Begoña Lopez Ñañez, Profilms, Simphony, Mosaico

CONTACT
Pablo Mederico Faivre and Florencia Faivre
Campos Salles 2213
Capital Federal C.P. (1429) ARGENTINA
+54.1.701.1949
+54.1.701.8251 fax
faivre@interactive.com.ar

the NICE project

The NICE project is a virtual reality learning environment in which children can explore and construct virtual ecosystems, collaborate with other remotely located participants, and create stories from their shared experiences.

Producer: the NICE project
Contributors: Craig Barnes, Jim Costigan, Andrew Johnson, Jason Leigh, Thomas Moher, Maria Roussos, Christina Vasilakis

CONTACT
Andrew Johnson
Electronic Visualization Laboratory
University of Illinois at Chicago
M/C 154
851 South Morgan Street, Room 1120 SEO
Chicago, Illinois 60607-7053 USA
+1.312.996.3002
+1.312.413.7585 fax
nice@ice.eecs.uic.edu
http://www.ice.eecs.uic.edu/~nice

NPSNET-IV: Inserting the Human into the Networked Synthetic Environment

The piece shows fully-articulated humans in the NPSNET-IV networked synthetic environment. NPSNET-IV runs on a Silicon Graphics, Inc. Onyx RE-2 in real-time. The humans in NPSNET-IV are animated using the Boston Dynamics, Inc. DI-GUY software. The omni-directional treadmill was designed and constructed by Virtual Space Devices.

Producer: Michael Zyda
Video Editing & Postproduction: Michael Zyda
Omni Directional Treadmill (ODT): Fred Zyda
Cameramen: Paul Barham, Randy Barker
NPSNET ODT Software: David Carmein
Virtual Space Devices: Marc Raibert
3D Modeling: John Locke

CONTACT
Michael Zyda
Naval Postgraduate School
Department of Computer Science, Code CS/Zk
Spanagel Hall 252
Monterey, California 93943-5118 USA
+1.408.656.2305
+1.408.656.4083 fax
zyda@siggraph.org
http://www.cs.nps.navy.mil/people/faculty/zyda

Nurturing Self

"Nurturing Self" is about overcoming fear in order to reach a goal. It shows the transformation that occurs in a girl's life when she leaves her mother's nurturing place and becomes independent. By nurturing herself, she overcomes the comfort of the womb and ventures into the outside world.

Producer: Amanda Hoeltke/Ringling School of Art and Design
Concept and Animation: Amanda Hoeltke
Music Composer: Amanda Hoeltke
Audio Mix: Amanda Hoeltke
Faculty Advisor: Claudia Cumbie-Jones
Video/Audio Support: Phil Chiocchio
Software: Alias PowerAnimator 7.5, Composer 4.0.3, Studio 16
Hardware: Silicon Graphics Indy R4400

CONTACT
Amanda Hoeltke
Computer Animation Department
Ringling School of Art and Design
2700 North Tamiami Trail
Sarasota, Florida 34234 USA
+1.941.359.7536
+1.941.359.7517 fax
mpalazzi@rsad.edu
http://www.rsad.edu

Once

A young man must learn to cope with emotions he's never felt, lessons that are hard to learn, and the love that he has lost.

Producer: Joshua Cordes
Contributors: Bruce Wands, Chairman BFA Computer Art Department School of Visual Arts, NYC
Jason Struogo, Thesis Advisor

CONTACT
Joshua Cordes
School Of Visual Arts
6 Leland Court
Centereach, New York 11720-1204 USA
+1.516.736.3239
+1.516.736.3188 fax
jishjosh@hotmail.com
http://bfaca.schoolofvisualarts.edu/students/students.html

One Fine Evening In Istanbul

A sneak preview of a live show aired on a Turkish TV channel. The belly-dancer depicted in the piece is a one-piece geometric model, whose dancing motions were generated in real-time on a single-processor SGI.

Producer: Telesine Istanbul (Cemil Turun)
Contributors: Everybody working at Telesine Computer Graphics House.

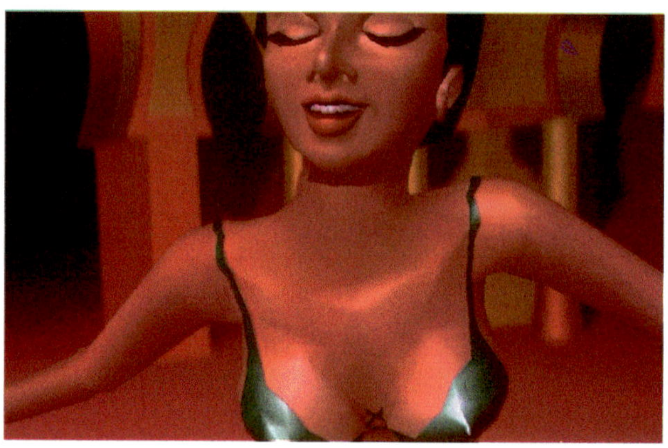

CONTACT
Cemil Turun
Telesine Computer Graphics House
Tepebasi Cad. 28, Beyoglu
Istanbul TURKEY
+90.212.238.0708
+90.212.238.0608 fax
cturun@escortnet.com
http://www.telesine.com

Open-Mike Night

In this excert, a character reads a poem to an unseen audience. Each of the five segments comprising the whole piece opens with a pan in on the "Red Ridge Hotel". The five characters are The Farmer, The Hipster, The Old Woman, The Nerd, and the Bellboy.

Producer: Jonah Hall
Contributors: Janice Earlbaum, Chris Lee, Anne Elliott, Peter HolbenWehr, Cathleen O'Grady, Steve Hoppe, Ray St. Denis, Dean Winkler, Ralph Scaglione, Jonathon Smith, Rahul Thakkar, Tom Allen, Mark Shultz

CONTACT
Jonah Hall
Post Perfect
220 East 42nd Street
New York, New York 10017 USA
+1.212.972.3400 x 5393
jonahh@interport.net

Parasite Eve

This piece is comprised of excerpts from a Japanese horror movie. "Mitochondolian Eve" was visualized by lighting liquid which deforms and becomes a character. It also depicts the ignition of a human body by compositing flame with a character.

Producer: Mikitaka Kurasawa
VFX Producer: Mikitaka Kurasawa
VFX Supervisor: Yoichi Ogawa
Dip Supervisor/Visual Architect: Zin Sago
CGI Technical Supervisor: Yoshihisa Hirano
Dip Technical Coordinator: Toshio Kaneko
VFX Designer: Takashi Yamazaki
VFX Production Manager: Kazyuyuki Haneda
CGI Chief Animator: Shotaro Kusama
CGI Animators: Ken Otani, Natsuyo Kobayashi Kaori Saito, Takahiro Takenaka, Sanae Nakanishi
Flame Technical Manager: Takuro Taketani
Motion Capture Technical Director: Tetue Kawano
Motion Capture Coordinator: Shogo Yabuuchi
Choreography: Miyoko Tuta
Dancer: Keiko Ozeki
Motion Actress: Rie Yasuda
Digital 2D Animation: Yumi Makino
Illustration: Makiko Kato
VFX Cameraman: Jun Suganami
VFX Assistant Cameramen: Masayuki Hosoyama, Sadanobu Ida, Hitoshi Kikuchi
SFX Producer: Shuichi Kishiura
Motion Control Operators: Osamu, Hiroshi Fujishiro, Yoshitaka Makigi
Model Making & Special Effects: Shingi Ienobe, Tadarugu Shimajiri, Mamiko Nakada, Kazuya Shimizu, Fumiya Yoshizaki
Digital Film I/O: Hideo Tuji, Yoshinori Watanabe
Digital 3D Scanning: Imagica Digix

CGI Assistant Animators: Hiroshi Kamohara, Tuyoshi Kobori, Makiko Mizushima, Yuichiro Mouri, Kunihiko Mohara, Terushige Watanabe
CGI Engineers: Kazuhiro Imamura, Kenji Umezawa
CGI Model Maker: Funie Katayama
CGI System Manager: Atsushi Funabashi
CGI Production Assistant: Masabumi Tanaka
Flame Artists: Koji Busaka, Yayoi Sasaki
Flint Artist: Nobuya Ishida
Digital Compositor: Kiyoko Shibuya
Flame System Engineer: Takanori Aoki

CONTACT
Noriko Kurachi
LINKS Corporation
2-14-1 Higashi-Gotanda,
Shinagawa-ku
Tokyo JAPAN
+81.3.5420.5310
+81.3.5420.5330 fax
noriko@links.imagica.co.jp

Pellucid Spaces

This work represents one segment from the video "Turbulence".

Producer: Jon McCormack

CONTACT
Steven Churchill
Odyssey Productions
4413 Ocean Valley Lane
San Diego, California 92130 USA
+1.619.793.1900
+1.619.793.1942 fax
odyssey@odyssey3d.com
http://www.odyssey3d.com

Pepsiman "Montage"

An aluminum superhero dedicates himself to wiping out thirst! "Pepsiman" is a highly-detailed human character, performing a wide range of athletic activities, from surfing to boxing. His "action-figure" antics push the boundaries of the CG model, while his "chrome" body reflects his constantly changing environment in each scene.

Producer: Industrial Light & Magic

Special Visual Effects by Industrial Light & Magic
A Division of Lucas Digital Ltd.
Marin County, California

Directors: Steve Beck, Wade Howie
Producer: Paul Hill
Production Manager: Laura Schifrin
Production Coordinator: Jon Forst

Production Assistants: Adrienne Anderson, Regina Gong, Kay Rough
Post Supervisors: Diane Caliva, Yukiko Ishawata, Lori Muttersbach
Effects Supervisor: Wade Howie
Lead Technical Director: Wade Howie
Technical Directors: Eran Barnea, Aron Bonar, Billy Brooks, Simon Cheung, Leandro Estebecorena, Doug MacMillan, Kirk McInroy, Kim Thompson, Alan Rosenfeld
Lead Animators: Paul Griffin, Kirk McInroy
Animators: Ismail Acar, Marc Chu, Tim Harrington, Tori Livingstone, Neil Michka, Steve Rawlins, Trish Schutz, Tim Stevenson, Marjolaine Tremblay, Jamy Wheless
Viewpainter: Drew Klausner
Rotoscoper/Viewpainters: Derek Gillingham, Drew Klausner, Rebecca Petrulli-Heskes
Enveloper: Rick Grandy
Sock/Enveloping: Kevin Reuter
Modeler/Enveloper: Simon Cheung
Additional Model Chaining: James Tooley
Additional Modeling: Paul Theren
Model Hands: Dan Taylor
Lead Matchmover: Guy Hudson
Matchmovers: Keith Johnson, Alia Agha
Bump Mattes: Doug MacMillan
CG Resource Assistants: Dan Brimer, Dani Morrow, Matt Wallin, Erin West, Michael Keating
Video Technical Assistants: Jennifer Gonzalez, Carole Johnson, Heidi Schmidt
Head of CG Commercials: John Benson
CG Commercials Manager: Paul Nightingale
CGC Production Manager: Sandra Scott
CGC Production Coordinators: Amy Beresford, Kay Rough

CONTACT
Vicki Dobbs Beck
Industrial Light & Magic
PO Box 2459
San Rafael, California 94912
USA
+1.415.258.2084
+1.415.721.3551 fax

Pets

"Pets" is a 3-minute, computer-assisted, animation that is based around a soundtrack of live interviews and other found sources. In this piece, eight different pets discuss their hopes, fears, interests, and anxieties while answering the question: "What do you do when your owner's not home?"

Producers: John Lally and Valerie Mih
Story, Direction, and Animation: John Lally and Valerie Mih
Sound Designers: Matt Butler, John Hoffhines
Faculty Advisors: Corny Cole, Mar Elepano, Vibeke Sorensen, Richard Weinberg, Tom Sito
Industry Mentors: Bob Kurtz, Keith Hunter, Tex Kandonaga, Dan Quarnstrom, Nicholas Titmarsh, Steve Ziolkowski, Brad Reinke, Henry Anderson
Systems Administrators: Eric Furie, Sean Laverty, Anthony Riazzi
Softimage and Eddie Software: Microsoft, Inc.
Hardware: Silicon Graphics, Inc.
On-Line Editing: Alan Starbuck, Bill Wright, Steven Schmitt

CONTACT
John Lally
321 Calle Miramar #1
Redondo Beach, California
90277 USA
+1.310.378.7409
jlally@sqla.com

CONTACT
Valerie Mih
1724 Arlington Boulevard
El Cerrito, California 94530 USA
+1.510.231.2460
valmih@pixar.com

Phantom

This work expresses one's unconscious mind as collages of segmented memories. Both graphics and sound were produced by the artist. A 3D sound system was employed, and an infinite reflection technique was used to create the surrealistic scene. Image processing techniques were added to create the abstract effects.

Producer: Masa Inakage

CONTACT

Masa Inakage

The Media Studio, Inc.

2-24-7 Shichirigahama-Higashi

Kamakura Kanagawa 248

JAPAN

+81.467.32.7941

+81.467.32.7943 fax

inakage@cyberagen8.com

Plug

A man is thrust into the real world after spending his entire life in an electronic incubator, and he struggles to "plug" back into his electronic dreamland.

Producers: Meher Gourjian,
Jamie Waese

CONTACT

Meher Gourjian

University of Southern California Cinema/TV School

1228 North Cedar Street

Glendale, California 91207 USA

+1.818.740.3985

gourjiam@usc.edu

http://www-scf.usc.edu/~gourjian

Protein Lattice

Protein Lattice is an experimental video piece dealing with "tissue engineering", the technology that allowed a human ear to be grown on the back of a laboratory rat.

Producer: Peter Hennessey
Contributors: Patricia Piccinini, Peter Hennessey, Dennis Daniel

CONTACT
Peter Hennessey
Drome Pty Ltd
Level 1, 184 Brunswick St Fitzroy
Victoria 3065 AUSTRALIA
+613.9416.3844
+613.9415.1708 fax
drome@c031.aone.net.au
http://www.artoz.com/drome/

Protozoa's VRML Skits

These skits are an attempt to make entertaining linear content for the Web within the demanding constraints of VRML. They feature Protozoa's simple, yet expressive, characters brought to life with the Alive! performance animation system. They represent a glimpse of things to come in the emerging world of VRML.

Producer: Steve Rein
Contributors: Emre Yilmaz, Dan Hanna, Mike Morasky, Steve Rein, Bay Raitt, Tracey Roberts, Tennessee Reid Norton, Terry Franguiadakis, Michael Stein, David Spivack, Eric Gregory, Marc Scaparro, Jan Mallis, Eric Goldberg, Stephen Kearin, Gerri Lawlor, Erik Bergmann, Brad deGraf

CONTACT
Bryan Kelly
Protozoa, Inc.
2727 Mariposa Street, Studio 100
San Francisco, California 94110 USA
+1.415.522.6500
+1.415.522.6522 fax
bryan@protozoa.com
http://www.protozoa.com

RANKAI

The objects in this film are a metaphor for people who live and work in the Tokyo area. These people are extremely busy, performing repetitive, tedious, and exhausting tasks. A sudden explosion sets them free for a while, but the succeeding days are as oppressive as ever.

Producer: Nobuo Takahashi

CONTACT
Nobuo Takahashi
VS Development Department
NAMCO Limited
1-1-32 Shin-Urashima-Cho
Kanagawa-ku, Yokohama
Kanagawa 221 JAPAN
+81.45.461.8074
+81.45.461.8077 fax
nobuo@vs.namco.co.jp

Rave Art

A phantomorgasmic journey through the archetypical unconsciousness of man.
This is a non-linear hypnogogic dream state filled with rich symbolic icons set to a heart-wrenching techno soundrack for the GenerationX who evolved from the rave culture.

Producer: Emiko Miki
Contributor: Glenn Grillo

CONTACT
Glenn Grillo
Nighttribe, Inc.
42 Brooks
Venice, California 90291 USA
+1.310.396.3738
+1.310.396.0636 fax
mrnazty@aol.com
http://members.aol.com/mrnazty/index.html

Revenge Doesn't Pay

An annoyed tenant attempts to take care of a car alarm once and for all.

Producer: Geoffrey Richardson
Contributors: Neil Greening, Chris Horvath
Special Thanks to: Peter Mataichuck, Alan Harrison, Graeme Gish, Jeff Burt, Judy Shane, Mom and Dad, Vancouver Film School

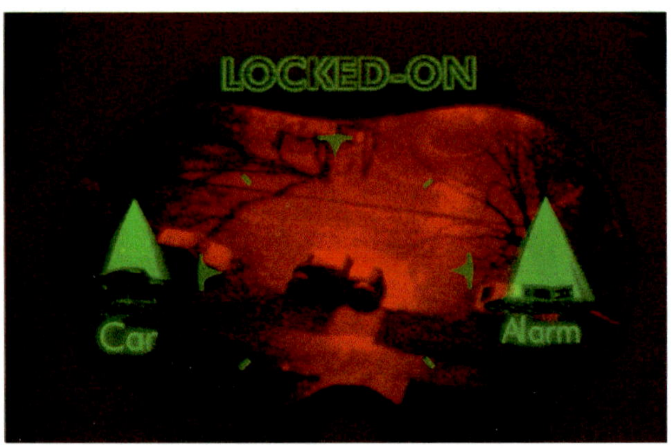

CONTACT
Geoffrey Richardson
Box II, Suite 14, R.R. #4
Edmonton, Alberta T5E 5S7 CANADA
403.973.5368
geoffr@griffin.multimedia.edu

ROBIT

Introducing ROBIT, a ball of energy who has a "thing" for things that are round. Anything is better than nothing and that counts for something, at least for ROBIT.

Producer: Dewey Reid
Created by: Tom McClure
Animation/Modeling: Scott Benza
Sound Design: Sanford Ponder
Voice: Gregory Burns
Special Thanks: Jaime Clifton, Chris Needy, Rick Senechal, Ted Witus
Music: Scott Selfon

CONTACT
Jaime Clifton
Microsoft
One Microsoft Way
Redwest E
Redmond, Washington 98052 USA
+1.206.882.8080
+1.206.936.7329 fax
a-jclift@microsoft.com

Robotic Faculty (Williams College Winter Studies Program 1997)

Produced, directed, and animated by 12 Williams College undergrads during a four-week winter studies program, "Robotic Faculty" solves the problem of skyrocketing college tuition costs.

Producer: Kleiser-Walczak Construction Co.
Contributor: Williams College Winter Studies Program 1997
Sponsored by: Kleiser-Walczak Construction Co., Digital Visual Effects
Directed by: Anthony Barnes, Jade Van Doren, Laird Dornin, Samuel French, Charles Hagenbuch, Udai Haraguchi, Derek Hays, Jeffrey Kaye, Aleksandar Maricic, Sarah Paliulis, Derek Sasaki-Scanlon, Jon Zeppieri
Production Assistants: Wendy Gipp, Joe Hall, Greg Juby, Jeff Kleiser, Scott Lord, Patrick Mooney, Lee Mylks, Slavica Pandzic, Fabio Tovar, Phearuth Tuy, Frank Vitz, Diana Walczak

CONTACT
Kleiser-Walczak Construction Co.
6150 Mulholland Highway
Hollywood, California 90068 USA
+1.213.467.3563
+1.213.467.3583 fax
http://www.kwcc.com

The Rock

For "The Rock", Dream Quest Images was responsible for the creation of computer-generated F18 fighter jets and missiles along with their particle system exhaust trails, all of which required the creation of virtual worlds for motion tracking. A blue screen explosion was composited over Alcatraz Island with animated interactive light and shadows. Digital bubbles and wakes were added to motion-controlled puppet Navy SEAL divers and model submersible vehicles.

Producer: Rae Griffith, Dream Quest Images
Visual Effects Producer: Rae Griffith
Dream Quest Executive Producer: Dennis Hoffman
Digital Effects Supervisor: Dan DeLeeuw
3D Technical Supervisor: Darin Hollings
3D Artists: John Murrah, Megan McBurney, Matt Hightower
2D Technical Supervisor: Baine Kennison
Compositing Art Director: Marlo Pabon
2D Compositors: Amy Pfaffinger, Jen Howard, Michael Miller, Deborah Wiltman
Data Management: Rory Hinnen
Scanning/Recording Technicians: Rick Lopez
Head of Digital Technology: Rob Burton
Digital Department Supervisor: Mitch Dobrowner

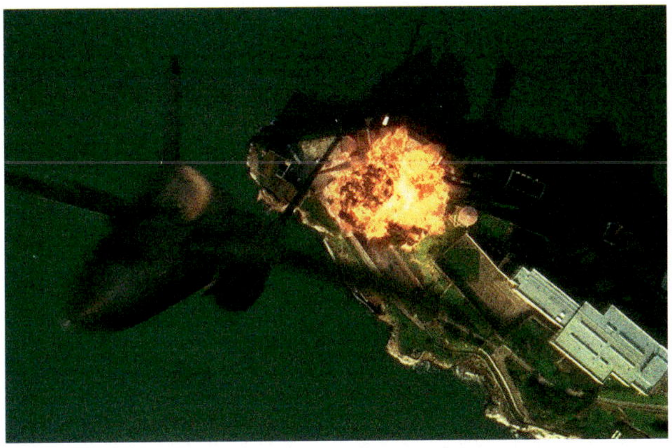

CONTACT
Mary Reardon
Dream Quest Images
2635 Park Center Drive
Simi Valley, California 93065 USA
+1.805.578.3155
+1.805.583.4673 fax
mary_reardon@studio.disney.com

Rolie Polie Olie

Rolie Polie Olie pulls his wagon along the sidewalk delivering newspapers. Unbeknownst to Rolie, his dog, Spot, thinks it's a game of fetch. The "game" continues, until Spot jumps innocently onto a baby carriage, inducing a barrage of finger wagging from the mother and neighbor. Author and creator, William Joyce, is a children's book writer and illustrator living in Shreveport, Louisiana.

Producer: Windlight Studios
Concept/Character Design: William Joyce
Client: Nelvana Entertainment
Computer Animation: Windlight Studios
Animation Director: Dave Novak
Technical Direction: Dave Novak and Matt Durante
Producer: Kelly McManus
Animation: Ron Pitts, Brian Newlin, Peter Hudecki
Models: Orie Hegre, David Nelson, Kevin Ochs
Color & Lighting: Dave Novak
Sound Design: Nelvana Entertainment
Sound Bed Excerpts: Beau Hunks/ Roy Shields Music Company
Special Thanks to: William Joyce, Jennifer Stephenson, Glenn Barna, Fred Luchetti, Toper Taylor, Joan Staveley, Don Bajus
Based on characters by William Joyce
Copyright 1997 Nelvana Limited

CONTACT
Kelly McManus
Windlight Studios
702 North First Street
Minneapolis, Minnesota 55401 USA
+1.612.339.9091
+1.612.339.8991 fax
kelly@windlight.com
http://www.windlight.com

The Roulette

Making love without a condom is like playing Russian Roulette.

Producer: ENSAD/Aii
Author: Nicolas Kalbache
Assistants: Nicolas Gautier, Paul Lepreux, Mark Jouveneau
Music: Hervé Lecoz

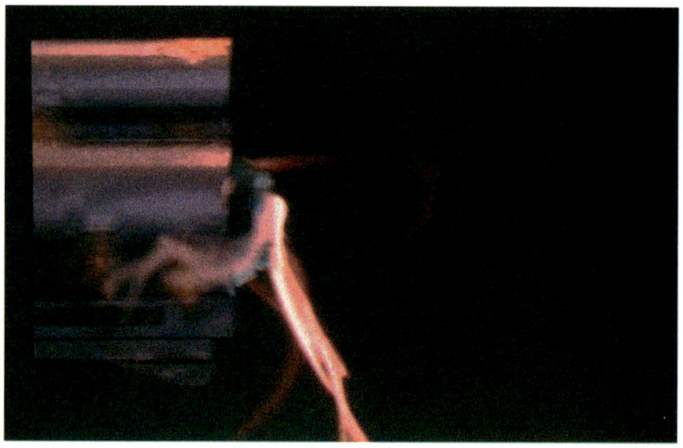

CONTACT
Pierre Henon
ENSAD/Aii
31 rue d'Ulm
75240 Paris Cedex 05
FRANCE
+33.1.53.73.24.80
+33.1.53.73.24.90 fax
pierre@ensad.fr
http://www.ensad.fr

Runners

Figures (dolls) made up of geometric shapes rush around, intertwining themselves with other objects. The work expresses the beauty of interacting objects over time.

Artist: Kazuma Morino
Music Composer: Yoshiyuki Usui
Special thanks to: Satoshi Tsukamoto, Hideto Kana
Produced by: Kazauma Morino, Taiyo Kikaku Co., Ltd.

CONTACT
Kazuma Morino
Taiyo Kikaku Co., Ltd.
2-26-3 Nishishimbashi Minato-ku
Tokyo 105 JAPAN
+81.3.3436.4540
+81.3.3436.0175 fax
kazuma@t3.rim.or.jp

Scientific Visualization of Space-Based Debris

For the "Eyes in the Sky" documentary on the history of satellites, Stony Brook Films and Discovery Communications requested an animation of currently tracked space debris and working satellites. Vision International created this animation using the EDGE Product Family software.

Producer: Stony Brook Films
Scientist: Tom Kacena
Animator: Tim Cotter
Special Thanks to: Dan Gordon, Tony Moraco, Dewey Houck, Melissa Durley, Inga Clark, Carlson Bull
and the CV team: Gwen Afton-Bird, Mike Darweesh, Greg Dismond, Mike Kirby, Michael Lopez, Mike Walsh, Kim Wallace and the entire Edge Development Team.
Post production provided by DC Post

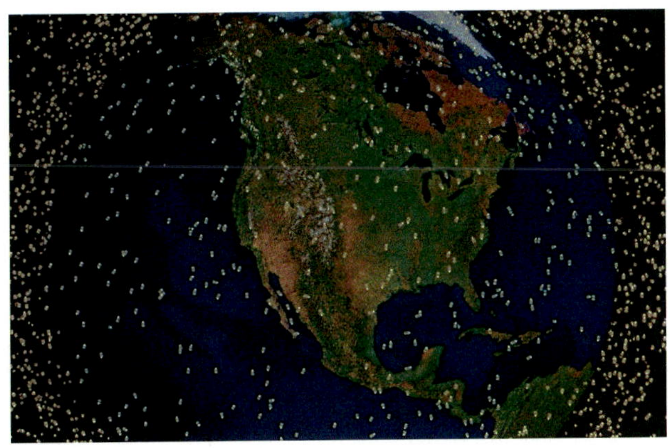

CONTACT
Tim Cotter
Vision International
5301 Shawnee Road
Alexandria, Virginia 22312 USA
+1.703.658.4179
+1.703.658.4401 fax
tcotter@autometric.com
http://www.autometric.com

The Shapemaker Prelude

"The Shapemaker Prelude" is a short digital movie which promotes an unmade feature film entitled "The Shapemaker". Using a desktop Macintosh computer, Mark Allen created a fantasy world where a street artist bending shapes from aluminum foil constructs one shape that begins a revolution.

Producer: Mark Allen
Contributors: Brad Rushing, Lisa Hannan, Mark Setrakian, Sarah Campos, Craig Barnes, Rick Morris, California Communications, Inc., Electric Image Animation System, Opcode, Ultimatte, autodessys, Radius, Random Creations, Necromat, Kristin Calkins, Ernest Hardy, Wendi Granthem, Eiji Inoue, Stuart Weiss, Richard Frank Adams, Wyatt Weed, Dorsay Alavi, Ynot Navillus, Christiane Masterson, Jeremiah Carafano, James Adam Patterson, Matt Ullman, Carey Hollis, Deborah Velarde, Hiroko Imai, Michael Wang, Corey D. Leamon, Dustin McGinnis, Susie Johnson, John Leamon, Kim Snyder, Eric Ford, Vic Randolph, Ziggy, Michael Melamed, Hector Rivera, Karen Rall, Sean Allen, Michael Anastasio, Paul Debenedictus, Alexandra Yessios, Lynn Sauve, Susan Correl, Paul Babb, Sandra Barrera

CONTACT
Mark Allen
XANTHER
mark.allen@shapemaker.com
http://www.shapemaker.com

Sharing

"Sharing" is a short story about siblings. The animation focuses on two boys and how they handle the concept of sharing.

Producers: Michael McCarthy and Jason Zirpolo/Ringling School of Art and Design
Concept and Animation: Michael McCarthy and Jason Zirpolo
Audio Mix: Michael McCarthy and Jason Zirpolo
Faculty Advisor: Ed Cheetham
Video/Audio Support: Phil Chiocchio
Software: Alias PowerAnimator, Adobe Premiere
Hardware: SGI Indy, Intergraph TD-400

CONTACT
Michael McCarthy and Jason Zirpolo
Computer Animation Department
Ringling School of Art and Design
2700 North Tamiami Trail
Sarasota, Florida 34234 USA
+1.941.359.7536
+1.941.359.7517 fax
mpalazzi@rsad.edu
http://www.rsad.edu

Simulation of 1994 Northridge Earthquake Aftershock

"Simulation of 1994 Northridge Earthquake Aftershock" is an educational video illustrating, through data visualization, earthquake research at Carnegie Mellon University. This video shows computer simulation data of how an alluvial basin's structure and composition modifies the horizontal displacement effects caused by a Northridge Earthquake aftershock.

Producer: Gregory Foss
Graphics and Animation: Gregory Foss
Research: Jacobo Bielak (PI) and The Quake Group at CMU
Video and Hardware Support: Anjana Kar
Narration: Joel Welling
Software Support: Grace Giras

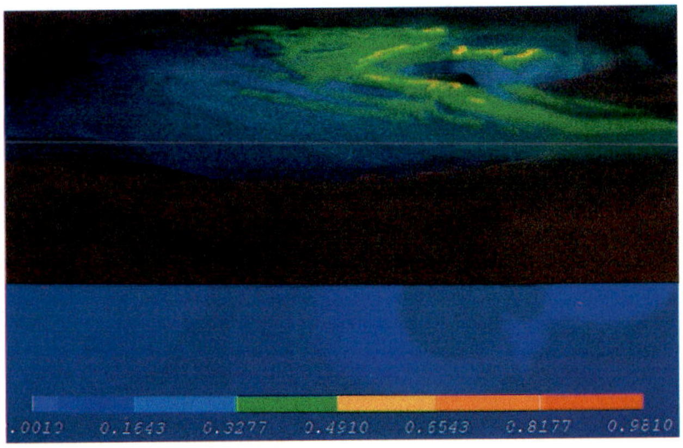

CONTACT
Gregory Foss / Anjana Kar
Pittsburgh Supercomputing Center
4400 Fifth Avenue
Pittsburgh, Pennsylvania 15213 USA
+1.412.268.4960
+1.412.268.5832 fax
foss@psc.edu

Smirnoff

Crazy pursuit in Michel Gondry's world.

Producer: Partizan Midi Minuit
Director: Michel Gondry
Contributors: Pierre Buffin, Yves le Peillet, Geoffrey Niquet, Jérome Bacquet, Claude Chabot, Olivier Gondry, Christophe Dupuis, Eric Deltour, Stephane Naze, Pasquale Croce, David Verbeke, Marie-Laure Laffitte, Laurent Gilet, Marianne Barcilon
Software: Buf Software, Softimage, T_Morph, Elastic Reality, Flint

CONTACT
Marianne Barcilon
Buf Compagnie
9, Avenue de Villiers
75 017 Paris FRANCE
+33.1.47660200
+33.1.47660302 fax
ofely@buf.imaginet.fr

Smithsonian Cinder Cone

The Engineering Animation, Inc. (EAI) Smithsonian Cinder Cone animation depicts the formation of a Cinder Cone volcano, and will be on permanent exhibit in the Gems and Mineralogy Hall of the National Museum of Natural History at the Smithsonian Institute in Washington DC, when the hall opens later this year.

Producer: Engineering Animation, Inc.

CONTACT
Engineering Animation, Inc.
2321 North Loop Drive
Ames, Iowa 50010 USA
+1.515.296.9908
+1.515.296.9944 fax
http://www.eai.com

Some Leaves

While describing what was found on a nature walk, a girl can sometimes get interrupted by a little sister and fragments of songs.

Producer: Stuart Sharpe
Words: Samantha Sharpe, Natasha Sharpe

CONTACT
Stuart Sharpe
42 Sunset Way
San Rafael, California 94901 USA
+1.415.256.9872
+1.415.256.9759 fax
leaves@ssharpe.com
http://www.ssharpe.com

SOULBLADE

Producer: NAMCO VS R&D Division
Contributors: SOULBLADE project team

CONTACT
VS R&D Division
NAMCO Limited
1-1-32 Shinurashimacho
Kanagawaku Yokohama 221 JAPAN
+81.45.461.8074
+81.45.461.8074 fax
satoru@vs.namco.co.jp

Star Trek - The Experience

"Star Trek - The Experience" is a 65mm film created for a motion-based ride. The film was distorted to project onto a 60-foot dome.

Producer: Kristina Reed - Rhythm & Hues Studios
Director/Production Designer: Mario Kamberg
Executive Producer: Ellen Coss
Producer: Kristina Reed
Art Directors: Tim Prentice, William "Bud" Myrick
Computer Graphics Supervisors: Suponwich "Juck" Somsaman, Georgia Cano
Choreography: Steve Ziolkowski

DIGITAL CINEMATOGRAPHY
Birds of Prey: Georgia Cano
Enterprise: Lisa Clarity, John Goodman, Olivier Barbeau
Creatures: Raymond Chen
Creature Animation: John Goodman
Effects Animation: Suponwich "Juck" Somsaman, Chris Sjoholm, Chris Olivia
Eugene Vendrovsky, Perry Kass, Tim Milne, Charles Knowlton
Editorial: Josh Margolies, James Bluma, Brent Young, Antonio Barraza
Systems Administrator: Jay Miya
Film/Technical Support: David Keller, Will McCown, Jeffrey Castel De Oro, Mary Mattern, Daniel Fazel, Ana Burdsall, Greg Hanigan
I/O Coordinators: Chris Haussler, Sheri Cruz
Tape Operators: Apple Vega-Peterson, Jonah Michaud, Michael Erlinger Jr., Homer Linao Cruz, Kevin Tengan, Moamer Qazafi, Farouk Al-Shorafa, Ted Endow, Carmela Mendoza, Colleen Tuffy
Production Coordinators: Robert Schajer, Stephanie Taylor
Las Vegas Photography/Producer: Alex Abramowicz
Las Vegas Photography/DP: Alex Funke
Pyro Photography/Producer: Marlon Staffs
Pyro Photography/DP: Robbie Kanouse
Composer: Jay Chattaway
Sound EFX: Modern Sound
Large Format Mixer: Michael Stearns

Environments: Mary Lynn Machado, Keith Roberts, Sandra Voelker, Didier Levy, Alessandro Jacomini, Rod Paul, Felix Mendoza, Mark Hamilton, Cleveland Mitchell
Production Managers: David Weinberg, Lisa Atkinson, Prashant Buyyala, Barbara McCullough
Modeling Managers: Keith Hunter, Nancy Klimley
Modelers: Ian Hulbert, Yeen-Shi Chen, Karl Herbst, Scott Peterson, Mark Cheng, Brad Sick, Viviana Alonso, Max Okazaki, John Butiu
Programmers: Linda Martino, Keith Goldfarb, Toshi Kato, Paul Allen Newell, Bob Powell,

CONTACT
Suzanne Datz
Rhythm & Hues Studios
5404 Jandy Place
Los Angeles, California 90066 USA
+1.310.448.7531
+1.310.448.7600 fax
suze@rhythm.com
http://www.rhythm.com

Star Wars Trilogy Special Edition

Using the latest advances in digital image creation, George Lucas revisited the Star Wars Trilogy to bring his original vision for the three films to the screen. New images include a computer-generated Jabba the Hutt, and revamped Cloud City and Jedi Rocks synthetic environments.

Producer: Industrial Light & Magic

Special Visual Effects by Industrial Light & Magic
A Division of Lucas Digital Ltd.
Marin County, California

Visual Effects Supervisors: Dave Carson, John Knoll, Joseph Letteri, Dennis Muren, Bruce Nicholson, Alex Seiden, Stephen Williams
Ending Celebration Supervisor: Yusei Uesugi
Visual Effects Producers: Ned Gorman, Tom Kennedy
Michael Ludlam, Jodie Maier, Greg Maloney, Tia Marshall, Tom Martinek, Stuart Mashwitz, Terrence Masson, Neil Michka, Julie Neary, Ken Nielsen, Kerry Nordquist, David Parrish, Scott Pasko, Eddie Pasquarello, Ricardo Ramos, Tom Rosseter, Damian Steel, Lawrence Tan, Danny Taylor, Paul Theren, James Tooley, Chris Townsend, Hans Uhlig, Timothy Waddy, Matt Wallin, Li-Hsien Wei, Colie Wertz, Ken Wesley, Ron Woodall, Heidi Zabit
Digital Matte Artists: Ronn Brown, Eric Chauvin, Brian Flora, Paul Huston, William Mather, Yusei Uesugi
Chief Creature Maker: Howie Weed
Model and Creature Makers: Carol Bauman, Don Bies, Giovanni Donovan, Wendy Morton, Anne Polland, Mark Siegel, Steven Walton
Visual Effects Cameraman: Patrick Turner
Visual Effects Gaffer: Robert Finley III
Software Development: Christian Rouet, David Benson, Rod Bogart, Eric Enderton, John Horn, Jim Hourihan, Zoran Kacic-Alesic, Florian Kainz, Brian Knep, Cary Phillips, Jeff Yost
Visual Effects Layout and Storyboard Artists: Alex Jaeger, Derek Thompson
Digital Scanning Supervisor: Joshua Pines
Digital Scanning Operators: Earl Beyer, Randall Bean, Michael Ellis, George Gambetta, Todd Mitchell, John Whisnant
Digital Plate Restoration Artists: Alan Bailey, Sxott Bonnenfant, Wendy Hendrickson, Melissa Monterossa, Mike Van Eps, Corey Rosen
Negative Supervisor: Doug Jones
Negative Line-up: Andrea Biklian, Tim Geideman
Projectionist: Tim Greenwood
Assistant Visual Effects Art Director: Alex Laurant

Second Unit Director & Cameraman: Joe Murray
Visual Effects Art Directors: Ty Ruben Ellingson, George Hull, Mark Moore
Computer Graphics Supervisors: John Berton, Tom Hutchinson, James Tooley
Visual Effects Editor: Michael McGovern, David H. Tanaka
Digital Color Timing Supervisor: Bruce Vecchitto
Sabre Group Supervisor: Daniel McNamara
Digital Scanning Supervisor: Joshua Pines
Visual Effects Coordinators: Margaret Lynch, Lisa Todd
Computer Graphics Artists: Karen Ansel, Mark Austin, Scott Bonnenfant, Don Butler, John Campanaro, Amelia Chenoweth, Terry Chostner, Michael Conte, Lou Dellarosa, David Deuber, Natasha Devaud, James Doherty, Lisa Drostova, Selwyn Eddy III, Tom Fejes, Howard Gersh, Paul Giacoppo, Jeremy Goldman, Joanne Hafner, James Hagedorn, Andrew Hardaway, Carol Hayden, Matt Hendershot, Guy Hudson, Keith Johnson, Ken King, Marshall Krasser, Stewart Lew,
Visual Effects Project Manager: Edward T. Hirsh
Visual Effects Video Assistant: Clark Higgins
Visual Effects Camera Assistant: Vance Piper
Stage Technicians: Carl Assmus, Dick Dova-Spah, Richard Demolski, Ronald Diggory, Robert Doherty, Robert Johnson, Brad Jerrell, Nicolas Meeks
Props and Costumes: Barbara Affonso, Anne Polland
Sabre Artists: Caitlin Content, Grant Guenin, Mary McCulloch, Chad Taylor, Rita Zimmerman
Assistant Visual Effects Editors: Angela Leaper, Scott Balcerek, John Bartle, Forest Key
Video Editor: Angela Leaper
Animatics Artists: David Dozoretz, Jonathan Rothbart
Digital Effects Technical Assistants: Okan Ataman, Noel Brevick, Peter Chesloff, Carole Johnson, Joshua Levine, Dawn Matheson, Daniel Shumaker
Digital Effects Resource Assistant: Daniel Brimer
Digital Production Assistants: Ronn Brown, Megan Carlson, Julie Creighton, Kela Hicks, Joshua Marks
Video Assistants: Wendy Bell, Dawn Martin
Production Engineering: Fred Meyers, Ken Beyer, Ken Corvino, Dan Large, Gary Meyer, Marty Miramontez, Arnold Yee
Computer Graphics Resource Managers: Nancy Jill Luckoff, Lam Van To
Computer Graphics Production Manager: Suzie Vissotzky Tooley

CONTACT
Vicki Dobbs Beck
Industrial Light & Magic
PO Box 2459
San Rafael, California 94912
USA
+1.415.258.2084
+1.415.721.3551 fax

The Steadfast Tin Soldier

This portion of "The Steadfast Tin Soldier" is from a segment of Disney Feature Animation's sequel to "Fantasia". The three main characters of the segment – the Ballerina, Tin Soldier, and Jack-in-the-box – are 3D CG animated elements. In-house physical dynamics were used to animate some of the "reactive" elements of the Ballerina, such as her cloth skirt and hair curls.

Producer: Walt Disney Feature Animation
Contributors: The Steadfast Tin Soldier Crew of Walt Disney Feature Animation

CONTACT
Edward Kummer
Walt Disney Feature Animation
500 South Buena Vista Street
Burbank, California 91521-4870
USA
+1.818.560.8210
+1.818.560.8194 fax
edwardk@fa.disney.com

Submarine Garden

This piece is excerpted from the video "Turbulence".

Producer: Jon McCormack

CONTACT
Steven Churchill
Odyssey Productions
4413 Ocean Valley Lane
San Diego, California 92130 USA
+1.619.793.1900
+1.619.793.1942 fax
odyssey@odyssey3d.com
www.odyssey3d.com

The Taj Mahal

Producer: VR Real Technologies (P) Ltd.
Contributors: Anuj Rawla,
Sanjit Daniels, Prem Kumar,
Praveen, Madhu

CONTACT
Anuj Rawla
VR Real Technologies (P) Ltd.
777 X, 13th Main, HAL II Stage
Indira Nagar, Bangalore INDIA
+91.80.5262967
rawla@giasbg01.vsnl.net.in
http://www.vrrt.com

Tanabata

Tanabata is the traditional Japanese Star Festival held around the seventh night of July. The central motif used in this work is the imagery of Tanabata's bright, colorful ornaments. The many and complicated colorful objects presented in this work will help the viewer imagine the Tanabata festival.

Producer: Yasuo Ohba
Animator/Technical Director: Yasuo Ohba
Hardware: SGI INDIGO2 Maximum IMPACT, SGI Indy, Apple Power Macintosh 8100/80AV, SONY BVW75, Accom RTD4224
Software: Original, ENERGE, Adobe Photoshop
Music: Shinji Hosoe, Hiroto Sasaki

CONTACT
Yasuo Ohba
Namco Ltd.
1-1-32 Shin-Urashima-Cho, Kanagawa-ku
Yokohama, Kanagawa 221 JAPAN
+81.45.461.8013
+81.45.461.8014 fax
ohba@rd.namco.co.jp

The Tapir

The animation "The Tapir" is based on a story told by Konkuat, from the Tupari Tribe in the Rondonia State (Amazonian Forest). This story was collected by the anthropologist Betty Mindlin and published in the book "Tuparis and Tarupas" (University of Sao Paulo press - EDUSP). The story is part of the Brazilian Indian's mythology, and explains the origin of the Amazons, the warrior women supposedly living in the heart of the rain forest. The work was created as part of Raquel Coelho's thesis at the School of Visual Arts in New York City in 1996, using a Silicon Graphics Indy and Indigo 2, and Softimage. The design is based on puppet theatre and cut-outs, as an extension of Raquel Coelho's work as children's books illustrator. The visual concept is based on the idea of superposition of layers, where nine scenes are layered in 3D space and the camera travels from scene 1 to scene 9 revealing the story as their 9 layers come to life. The models are constructed following the same idea of superposition, layering different polygons to create figures, characters, and props. The sound track follows the same idea of layers and superposition, and was constructed by Arthur Kampela from pieces of electronic sounds, Indian songs, and the sounds of water, wood, and wind.

Producer: Raquel Coelho
Sound Track: Arthur Kampela and Raquel Coelho
Additional music by Marlui Miranda

CONTACT
Raquel Coelho
School of Visual Arts
30 Maple Tree Avenue, Apartment E2
Stamford, Connecticut 06906 USA
+1.914.381.8400
+1.914.381.9790 fax
raquel@blueskystudios.com
http://www2.sva.edu/thesis/raquel/thesis/htmls/front.html

In 1985, the wreck of the Titanic was discovered as two separate pieces almost one half-mile apart. In 1996, a scientific research team dove to the site looking for evidence to answer the question: "What really happened?" This animation, created for The Discovery Channel, is a dramatic depiction of the events that transpired on the night of her sinking.

Produced by Home Run Pictures for Stardust Visual and The Discovery Channel
Animation Director: Tom Casey
Animators: Dawn Lohmeyer, Patricia Whittington, Wendy Jobe
Editing: Thad Christian
Audio: Sue Hartford, Jeff Pitman

For Stardust Visual: Greg Andorfer, David Elisco, Charlene Haislip, David Cohen, Gary Hines, Brandon Plonka
For The Discovery Channel: Maureen Lemire, Steve Burns, Bob Wise, Linda Guisset
Special Thanks to: D'elia Wittkofski Productions, Kaleidoscope Animations, IFREMER, Silicon Graphics, Alias|Wavefront, Sense 8 Software

CONTACT
Tom Casey
Home Run Pictures
One Market Street
Pittsburgh, Pennsylvania 15222 USA
+1.412.391.8200
+1.412.391.0185 fax
tom@hrpictures.com
http://www.hrpictures.com

One series of views of director James Cameron's "Titanic," digitally created and presented in full daylight, brings together such fully digital elements as water, wake, sky, birds, clouds, smoke, and most importantly CG passengers composited with complex miniature photography to create the photo-real illusion of the Titanic at full sail.

Visual Effects Supervisor: Rob Legato
Visual Effects Producer: Crystal Dowd
Visual Effects Line Producer: Cari Thomas
Visual Effects D.P.: Eric Nash
Digital Effects Supervisor: Mark Lasoff
Digital Compositing Supervisor: Michael Kanfer
Digital Effects Supervisor: Judith Crow
Digital Compositing Supervisor: Mark Forker
Night Compositing Supervisor: Carey Villegas
Compositing Creative Consultant: Price Pethel
Digital Effects Producer: Karen Murphy
Lead Character Animators: Mark Brown, Andy Jones, Bernd Angerer
Deck Animation Sequence Supervisor: Keiji Yamaguchi
Character Animators: Robin Finn, Gonzalo Garramuno, Stephane Couture, Martine Delage, Clunie Holt, Gregory Ecklund, Sunny Lee, Fumihiko Sori, Hae-jeon Lee, Giancarlo Lari, Keith Smith, Miles Bellas
Character Integration Software: Daryll Strauss
Character Integration Software Support : Marcus Mitchell, Patrick Dalton
Character Lighting Lead: Scott Stokdyk
Character Texture Lead: Frederic Soumagnas
Character Texture Painters: John Hart, Chris Cortese
Stunt Integration Lead: Rocco Passionino
Dock Integration Lead: Jeff Basinski
Character Integration Digital Artists: Mike Edland, Jon Aghassian, Dan Lemmon, Alfred Urrutia, Grant Anderson
Digital Matte Painters: Martha Mack,

Peter Baustaedter
Visual Effects Editor: Michael Backauskas
Visual Effects Production Coordinator: Susan Thurmond
CG Technical Supervisor: Bill Spitzak
Data Integration Supervisor: Matthew Butler
Digital Ocean Supervisor: Richard Kidd
Digital Paraphernalia Supervisor: Kelly Port
Character Supervisor: Daniel Loeb
Character Integration Supervisor: Umesh Shukla
Animation Supervisor: Daniel Robichaud
Motion Capture Supervisor: André Bustanoby
Data Integration Leads: Mike O'Neal, Chris Springfield, David Santiago
Data Integration Digital Artists: Candida Nunez, Sean Faden, Ed Svetlik, Franco Pietrantonio
Digital Ocean Software: Jerry Tessendorf, Jim Rothrock, Lucio Flores, Ken Musgrave
Ocean Digital Artists: Aaron Pfau, David Isyomin, John Gibson, Sandor Rabb, Zsolt Krajcsik, Nikos Kalaitzidis, Laura Di Biagio
Paraphernalia Digital Artists: Matthew T. Hackett, Franklin Londin, Marcus Kurtz, David Bleich
Digital Smoke Lead: Francisco DeJesus
Motion Editing Software: Doug Roble
Motion Capture Animation: Dan Ma, Michael Sanders
Character Modeler: Shawna Olwen
Supporting Digital Compositors: Andrea Scholar, Rick Dunn, Donovan Scott
Lead Rotoscope Artist: Howie Muzika
Rotoscope Artists: Mike Frick, Byron Werner, Tonia Young, David Lockwood, Paolo De Guzman
Digital Effects Coordinators: Lisa Harriman Scott, Lisa Spence Lissak
Compositing Coordinators: Laura McDermott, Mikella Kievman
Image Data Coordinators: Allyse Manoff, Brian Peyatt
Digital Production Coordinator: Melissa Darby
SIGGRAPH Submission Production: Allen Cappuccilli, Rob Doolittle, Kevin Susman

CONTACT
Bob Hoffman
Digital Domain
300 Rose Avenue
Venice, California 90291 USA
+1.310.314.2981
+1.310.664.2701 fax
bhoffman@d2.com
http://www.d2.com

Top Ramen - Space Search

The astronauts were off to space to search for the most delicious ramen. They drive a specially-crafted, bowl-shaped spaceship to aid in their quest.

Producer: Victor Wong
Contributors: Eddy Wong, Thalia Tau

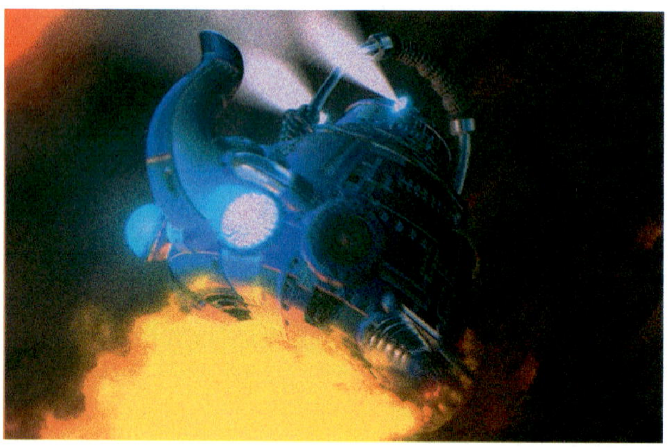

CONTACT
Victor Wong
Menfond Electronic Art & Computer Design Co. Ltd.
30/F Sunshine Plaza, 353 Lockhard Road
Wanchai HONG KONG
+852.2802.3382
+852.2802.3386 fax
menfond@hk.super.net
http://www.menfond.com.hk

TotaPet

This animation is a story about a caged pet who runs amok in its absent owner's one-room apartment. It is a cautionary statement about taking exotic pets out of their natural, and deserved, environment.

Producer: Alan Price
Created at the Imaging Research Center, University of Maryland Baltimore County

CONTACT
Alan Price
Imaging Research Center
1000 Hilltop Circle
Baltimore, Maryland 21250 USA
+1.410.455.3373
+1.410.455.1035 fax
alan@irc.umbc.edu
http://imda.umbc.edu/~alan

Tour Into the Picture

This piece demonstrates how our software TIP (Tour Into the Picture) works when you wish to tour through a picture or photograph.

Producer: Ken Anjyo
Animation and Music: Youichi Horry
Software: Youichi Horry, Kiyoshi Arai

CONTACT
Ken Anjyo
Hitachi, Ltd.
Visualware Planning Dept.
4-6 Kanda-Surugadai
Chiyoda, Tokyo 101 JAPAN
+81.3.5295.5410
+81.3.3258.5082 fax
anjyo@cm.head.hitachi.co.jp

Toy Racer

"Toy Racer" is a simulator ride from the point of view of a toy race car on a toy race track in a zany room.

Producer & Director: Lee Ford Parker
Art Director: Tim Eilers
Animator: Tim Claycomb
Sound & Music: Cary Carloff
Production Company: McFadden Systems

CONTACT
Lee Ford Parker
McFadden Systems
1212 North Berkeley Avenue
Turlock, California 95380 USA
+1.209.668.2955
+1.209.668.4010 fax
xldaedalus@aol.com

Toy Story Treats

The "Toy Story Treats" have been airing this season on ABC. They are used as little bits of entertainment in between regular Saturday morning programs and commercials and are thus referred to as "interstitials". Each piece is either ten or thirty seconds in length and features the popular Toy Story characters.

Producers: Pixar Animation Studios & Walt Disney Television Animation
Contributors:
Michael Berenstein, Dave Devan, Cynthia Dueltgen, Keith Gordon, Les Major, Glenn McQueen, Jeff Pratt, Doug Sheppeck, Warren Trezevant, Bill Wise, Steve Upstill, Lauren Alpert, Sonoko Konishi, Keith Olenick, Don Schreiter, Allison Smith Murphy, Kori Rae

CONTACT
Allison Smith Murphy
Pixar Animation Studios
1001 West Cutting Boulevard
Richmond, California 94804 USA
+1.510.215.3541
+1.510.236.0388 fax
allison@pixar.com

Tug Wilson

This piece relates the story of a bulldog named Tug Wilson who is head of the streets in Southbank – a small dockside town. Tug teams up with others like himself to solve a problem with a nasty property developer named Barington Sloane who is building apartment blocks all over town, each of which have signs saying: NO PETS/NO DOGS ALLOWED.

Producer: John Francis
Animation/modeling/compositing (everything visual): John Francis
Music: Greg Ham
Voices: Tom Bywater

CONTACT
John Francis
Surreal World
8/178 Toorak Road West
South Yarra, Melbourne 3141
AUSTRALIA
+613.9818.5033
+613.9818.4252 fax

Usonia: Frank Lloyd Wright's Vision for America

The term Usonia was often invoked by Frank Lloyd Wright to describe his vision for the American landscape. For the first time, through the utilization of computer animation, Wrightian spaces are now presented in an engaging three-dimensional format with animated elements suggesting spatial use.

Producer: Columbia University Graduate School of Architecture - Digital Design Lab
Contributors: Urs Britschgi, Mike Hsu, Ashley Schafer, Max Strang

CONTACT
Max Strang
Columbia University
Graduate School of Architecture
Planning, and Preservation
Digital Design Lab
400 Avery Hall
New York, New York 10027-6699 USA
+1.212.769.0447
max@strang.net
http://www.arch.columbia.edu

Virtual Andre

Employing proprietary software along with the Lightwave and Alias | Wavefront animation packages, the "virtual" Andre Agassi spot was aided with cyber-scanning and performance capture techniques blended into a fully CG-rendered virtual tennis cathedral.

Producer: Digital Domain
Director: Allan Van Rijn
Visual Effects Supervisor: Fred Raimondi
Visual Effects Producer: Eileen Moran
Animators: Mark Glaser, Derek Spears
Executive Producer: Ed Ulbrich
Agency: Wieden & Kennedy

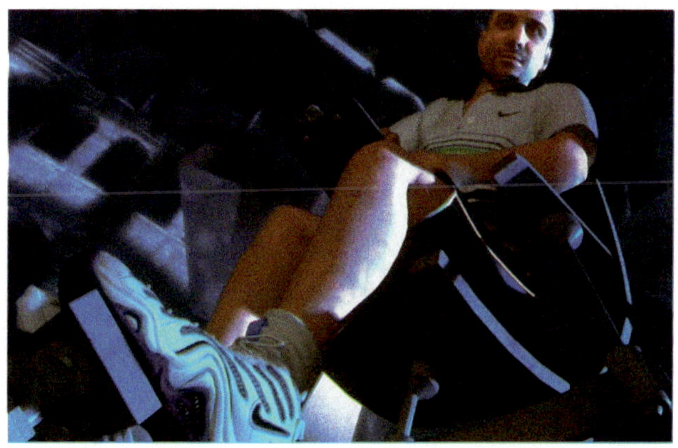

CONTACT
Bob Hoffman
Digital Domain
300 Rose Avenue
Venice, California 90291 USA
+1.310.314.2981
+1.310.664.2701 fax
bhoffman@d2.com
http://www.d2.com

Waterman

The human body is 70% water. Polluted water in the environment is analogous to polluted water inside our body. This piece stresses the necessity of keeping our water clean.

Producer: Victor Wong
Contributors: Eddy Wong, Thalia Tau

CONTACT
Victor Wong
Menfond Electronic Art & Computer Design Co. Ltd.
30/F Sunshine Plaza, 353 Lockhard Road, Wanchai
HONG KONG
+852.2802.3382
+852.2802.3386 fax
menfond@hk.super.net
http://www.menfond.com.hk

The Wishing Dream

"The Wishing Dream" is a story about hope and the fulfillment of dreams. It symbolizes the wonder of faith and the innocence of childhood. No matter how old you are, amazing and wonderful things can happen when we least expect them to. All it takes is a wish and a dream.

Producer: Christopher Roos/Ringling School of Art and Design
Concept and Animation: Christopher Roos
Music Composer: Christopher Roos
Audio Mix: Christopher Roos
Faculty Advisor: Jim McCampbell
Video/Audio Support: Phil Chiocchio
Software: Alias PowerAnimator 7.5, Composer 4.0.3, Studio 16, 3Design
Hardware: Silicon Graphics Indy R4400

CONTACT
Christopher Roos
Computer Animation Department
Ringling School of Art and Design
2700 North Tamiami Trail
Sarasota, Florida 34234 USA
+1.941.359.7536
+1.941.359.7517 fax
mpalazzi@rsad.edu
http://www.rsad.edu